August 8–9, 2011
Providence, RI, USA

Association for Computing Machinery

Advancing Computing as a Science & Profession

ICER'11

Proceedings of the ACM SIGCSE 2011 Workshop on
International Computing Education Research

Sponsored by:
ACM SIGCSE

Supported by:
Rhode Island College

Association for Computing Machinery

Advancing Computing as a Science & Profession

The Association for Computing Machinery
2 Penn Plaza, Suite 701
New York, New York 10121-0701

Copyright © 2011 by the Association for Computing Machinery, Inc. (ACM). Permission to make digital or hard copies of portions of this work for personal or classroom use is granted without fee provided that copies are not made or distributed for profit or commercial advantage and that copies bear this notice and the full citation on the first page. Copyright for components of this work owned by others than ACM must be honored. Abstracting with credit is permitted. To copy otherwise, to republish, to post on servers or to redistribute to lists, requires prior specific permission and/or a fee. Request permission to republish from: permissions@acm.org or Fax +1 (212) 869-0481.

For other copying of articles that carry a code at the bottom of the first or last page, copying is permitted provided that the per-copy fee indicated in the code is paid through www.copyright.com.

Notice to Past Authors of ACM-Published Articles
ACM intends to create a complete electronic archive of all articles and/or other material previously published by ACM. If you have written a work that has been previously published by ACM in any journal or conference proceedings prior to 1978, or any SIG Newsletter at any time, and you do NOT want this work to appear in the ACM Digital Library, please inform permissions@acm.org, stating the title of the work, the author(s), and where and when published.

ISBN: 978-1-4503-0829-8 (Digital)

ISBN: 978-1-4503-1395-7 (Print)

Additional copies may be ordered prepaid from:

ACM Order Department
PO Box 30777
New York, NY 10087-0777, USA

Phone: 1-800-342-6626 (USA and Canada)
+1-212-626-0500 (Global)
Fax: +1-212-944-1318
E-mail: acmhelp@acm.org
Hours of Operation: 8:30 am – 4:30 pm ET

Printed in the USA

Foreword

It is our great pleasure to welcome you to Providence and to the Seventh International Computing Education Research Workshop, ICER 2011, sponsored by the ACM Special Interest Group in Computer Science Education (SIGCSE). This year's workshop continues its tradition of being the premier forum for computing education research, from discussions of preliminary ideas to presentation of research results.

The call for papers attracted 47 submissions. All papers were double-blind peer-reviewed by members of the international program committee. After reviewing, 18 papers (38%) were accepted for inclusion in the conference, written by authors from eight countries: Australia, Finland, Germany, New Zealand, the Philippines, Sweden, the United Kingdom, and the United States. The papers span a wide variety of topics, including collaborative learning, informal learning, CS1, research design, general-education computing, tools to support learning, and the ways in which students choose to study computing and specialize within computing. The program also includes a keynote address by Eric Mazur of Harvard University discussing his work on peer instruction in physics education.

Putting together ICER 2011 was a team effort. First of all, we would like to thank the authors for providing the content of the program. We would also like to express our gratitude to the program committee, who worked very hard in reviewing papers and providing insightful feedback. Special thanks go to Brian Dorn for initiating the new Lightning Talks, to Robert McCartney for his work as Speakers Chair, to Jan Erik Moström for maintaining the website (and porting it to a new location), to Simon for his invaluable and efficient efforts as Submission Chair, and to Beth Simon for organizing the post workshop. Finally, we would like to thank our sponsor, ACM SIGCSE, for its continued support of these successful meetings and our supporter, Rhode Island College, for assistance with local arrangements.

We hope that you will find this program interesting and thought-provoking and that the workshop will provide you with a valuable opportunity to share ideas with other researchers from around the world.

Michael E. Caspersen, *Aarhus University, Denmark*
Alison Clear, *Christchurch Polytechnic Institute of Technology, New Zealand*
Kate Sanders, *Rhode Island College, Providence, Rhode Island, USA*

Table of Contents

ICER 2011 Workshop Organization vii

ICER 2011 Sponsor & Supporter viii

Keynote Address

- **The Scientific Approach to Teaching: Research as a Basis for Course Design** 1
  Eric Mazur *(Harvard University)*

Session 1: Choosing Computing

- **Deciding to Major in Computer Science: A Grounded Theory of Students' Self-Assessment of Ability** 3
  Colleen M. Lewis *(University of California, Berkeley)*,
  Ken Yasuhara, Ruth E. Anderson *(University of Washington, Seattle)*

- **How CS Majors Select a Specialization** 11
  Michael Hewner, Mark Guzdial *(Georgia Institute of Technology)*

- **CS Majors' Self-Efficacy Perceptions in CS1: Results in Light of Social Cognitive Theory** 19
  Päivi Kinnunen *(University of Eastern Finland)*, Beth Simon *(University of California, San Diego)*

Session 2: Food for Discussion

- **Research Design: Necessary Bricolage** 27
  Sally Fincher *(University of Kent)*, Josh Tenenberg *(University of Washington, Tacoma)*,
  Anthony Robins *(University of Otago)*

- **Exploring Programming Assessment Instruments: A Classification Scheme for Examination Questions** 33
  Judy Sheard *(Monash University)*, Simon *(University of Newcastle)*, Angela Carbone *(Monash University)*,
  Donald Chinn *(University of Washington)*, Mikko-Jussi Laakso *(University of Turku)*,
  Tony Clear *(Auckland University of Technology)*, Michael de Raadt *(University of Southern Queensland)*,
  Daryl D'Souza, James Harland *(RMIT University)*, Raymond Lister *(University of Technology, Sydney)*,
  Anne Philpott *(Auckland University of Technology)*, Geoff Warburton *(RMIT University)*

- **Do Values Grow on Trees? Expression Integrity in Functional Programming** 39
  Guillaume Marceau, Kathi Fisler *(Worcester Polytechnic Institute)*, Shriram Krishnamurthi *(Brown University)*

Session 3: Collaborative Learning

- **Peer Instruction: Do Students Really Learn from Peer Discussion in Computing?** 45
  Leo Porter, Cynthia Bailey Lee, Beth Simon *(University of California, San Diego)*,
  Daniel Zingaro *(University of Toronto)*

- **PeerWise: Exploring Conflicting Efficacy Studies** 53
  Paul Denny *(The University of Auckland)*, Brian Hanks *(BFH Educational Consulting)*,
  Beth Simon *(University of California, San Diego)*, Spencer Bagley *(UCSD/SDSU)*

Session 4: Informal Learning

- **Students' Perceptions of the Differences Between Formal and Informal Learning** 61
  Jonas Boustedt *(University of Gävle)*, Anna Eckerdal *(Uppsala University)*,
  Robert McCartney *(University of Connecticut)*, Kate Sanders *(Rhode Island College)*,
  Lynda Thomas *(Aberystwyth University)*, Carol Zander *(University of Washington, Bothell)*

- **ScriptABLE: Supporting Informal Learning with Cases** 69
  Brian Dorn *(University of Hartford)*

Session 5: CS1

- **What Students (should) Know About Object Oriented Programming** 77
  Peter Hubwieser, Andreas Mühling *(Technische Universität München)*

- **Predicting At-Risk Novice Java Programmers Through the Analysis of Online Protocols** 85
  Emily S. Tabanao *(MSU-Iligan Institute of Technology)*, Ma. Mercedes T. Rodrigo *(Ateneo de Manila University)*, Matthew C. Jadud *(Allegheny College)*

- **Explaining Program Code: Giving Students the Answer Helps – But Only Just** 93
  Simon, Susan Snowdon *(University of Newcastle)*

Session 6: Tools and Techniques

- **CAL Programming Tutors That Guide Students in Solving Problems and Help Students Building Skills** 101
  Wei Jin *(Shaw University)*, Albert Corbett *(Carnegie Mellon University)*

- **Personifying Programming Tool Feedback Improves Novice Programmers' Learning** 109
  Michael J. Lee, Andrew J. Ko *(University of Washington)*

- **The "Prototype Walkthrough": A Studio-Based Learning Activity for Human-Computer Interaction Courses** 117
  Christopher D. Hundhausen, Dana Fairbrother *(Washington State University)*, Marian Petre *(The Open University)*

Session 7: Before CS1

- **Learning Web Development: Challenges at an Earlier Stage of Computing Education** 125
  Thomas H. Park, Susan Wiedenbeck *(Drexel University)*

- **Computing as the 4th "R": A General Education Approach to Computing Education** 133
  Quintin Cutts *(University of Glasgow)*, Sarah Esper, Beth Simon *(University of California, San Diego)*

Doctoral Consortium Abstracts

- **Integrating Students' Prior Knowledge into Pedagogy** 139
  Colleen M. Lewis *(University of California, Berkeley)*

- **Student Views on Learning Concurrency** 141
  Jan Erik Erik Moström *(Umeå University)*

- **Building Professional Identity as Computer Science Teachers: Supporting Secondary Computer Science Teachers Through Reflection and Community Building** 143
  Lijun Ni *(Georgia Institute of Technology)*

- **Pedagogical Content Knowledge in Programming Education for Secondary School** 145
  Mara Saeli *(Eindhoven University of Technology)*

- **Encouraging Students to Think of Code as an Algorithmic Symphony: The Effect of Feedback Regarding Algorithmic Abstraction During Code Production** 147
  Leigh Ann Sudol-DeLyser *(Carnegie Mellon University)*

Author Index 148

ICER 2011 Workshop Organization

General Chair: Kate Sanders *(Rhode Island College, Providence, Rhode Island, USA)*

Program Co-Chairs: Michael E. Caspersen *(University of Aarhus, Denmark)*
Alison Clear *(Christchurch Polytechnic Institute of Technology, Christchurch, New Zealand)*
Kate Sanders *(Rhode Island College, Providence, Rhode Island, USA)*

Submission Chair: Simon *(University of Newcastle, Australia)*

Pre and Post Workshops Chair: Beth Simon *(University of California, San Diego, California, USA)*

Publicity Chair/Webmaster: Jan Erik Moström *(Umeå University, Sweden)*

Speakers Chair: Robert McCartney *(University of Connecticut, Storrs, Connecticut, USA)*

Lightning Talks Chair: Brian Dorn *(University of Hartford, West Hartford, Connecticut, USA)*

Program Committee: Mordechai Ben-Ari *(Weizmann Institute of Science, Rehovot, Israel)*
Yifat Ben-David Kolikant *(Hebrew University, Jerusalem, Israel)*
Tzu-Yi Chen *(Pomona College, Claremont, California, USA)*
Donald Chinn *(University of Washington, Tacoma, Washington, USA)*
Michael Clancy *(University of California, Berkeley, California, USA)*
Sally Fincher *(University of Kent at Canterbury, UK)*
Sue Fitzgerald *(Metropolitan State University, St. Paul, Minnesota, USA)*
David Ginat *(Tel Aviv University, Tel Aviv, Israel)*
Mark Guzdial *(Georgia Institute of Technology, Atlanta, Georgia, USA)*
Orit Hazzan *(Technion-Israel Institute of Technology, Haifa, Israel)*
Chris Hundhausen *(Washington State University, Pullman, USA)*
Lisa Kaczmarczyk *(Educational Consultant, San Diego, California, USA)*
Paivi Kinnunen *(University of Eastern Finland, Joensuu, Finland)*
Raymond Lister *(University of Technology, Sydney, Australia)*
Lauri Malmi *(Aalto University, Helsinki, Finland)*
Robert McCartney *(University of Connecticut, Storrs, Connecticut, USA)*
Renee McCauley *(College of Charleston, South Carolina, USA)*
Laurie Murphy *(Pacific Lutheran University, Tacoma, Washington, USA)*
Arnold Pears *(Uppsala University, Uppsala, Sweden)*
Marian Petre *(Open University, Milton Keynes, UK)*
Anthony Robins *(University of Otago, Dunedin, New Zealand)*
Jorma Sajaniemi *(University of Eastern Finland, Joensuu, Finland)*
Carsten Shulte *(Freie Universität Berlin, Germany)*
Judy Sheard *(Monash University, Melbourne, Australia)*
Beth Simon *(University of California, San Diego, California, USA)*
Josh Tenenberg *(University of Washington, Tacoma, Washington, USA)*

ICER 2011 Sponsor & Supporter

Sponsor:

Supporter:

Keynote Talk

The Scientific Approach to Teaching: Research as a Basis for Course Design

Eric Mazur
School of Engineering and Applied Sciences
Harvard University
Cambridge, MA 02138
mazur@physics.harvard.edu

ABSTRACT

Discussions of teaching – even some publications – abound with anecdotal evidence. Our intuition often supplants a systematic, scientific approach to finding out what works and what doesn't work. Yet, research is increasingly demonstrating that our gut feelings about teaching are often wrong. In this talk I will discuss some research my group has done on gender issues in science courses and on the effectiveness of classroom demonstrations.

Categories and Subject Descriptors

K.3.2 [**Computer and Information Science Education**]: Computer Science Education

General Terms

Design, Experimentation, Verification

Bio

Eric Mazur is the Balkanski Professor of Physics and Applied Physics at Harvard University and Area Dean of Applied Physics. An internationally recognized scientist and researcher, he leads a vigorous research program in optical physics and supervises one of the the largest research groups in the Physics Department at Harvard University.

After obtaining a Ph.D. degree in experimental physics at the University of Leiden in the Netherlands in 1981, Dr. Mazur came to Harvard University in 1982. In 1984 he joined the faculty and obtained tenure six years later. Dr. Mazur has made important contributions to spectroscopy, light scattering, the interaction of ultrashort laser pulses with materials, and nanophotonics.

In 1988 he was awarded a Presidential Young Investigator Award. He is Fellow of the Optical Society of America and Fellow of the American Physical Society, and has been named APS Centennial Lecturer during the Society's centennial year. In 2007 Mazur was appointed Phi Beta Kappa Visiting Scholar. In 2008 Mazur received the Esther Hoffman Beller award from the Optical Society of America and the Millikan Medal from the American Association of Physics Teachers. In 2010 he was elected Director at Large for the Optical Society of America. Dr. Mazur has held appointments as Visiting Professor or Distinguished Lecturer at Princeton University, Vanderbilt University, the University of Leuven in Belgium, National Taiwan University in Taiwan, Carnegie Mellon University, and Hong Kong University.

In addition to his work in optical physics, Dr. Mazur is interested in education, science policy, outreach, and the public perception of science. He believes that better science education for all – not just science majors – is vital for continued scientific progress. To this end, Dr. Mazur devotes part of his research group's effort to education research and finding verifiable ways to improve science education. In 1990 he began developing Peer Instruction a method for teaching large lecture classes interactively. Dr. Mazur's teaching method has developed a large following, both nationally and internationally, and has been adopted across many science disciplines.

Dr. Mazur has served on numerous committees and councils, including advisory and visiting committees for the National Science Foundation, has chaired and organized national and international scientific conferences, and presented for the Presidential Committee of Advisors on Science and Technology. He serves as consultant to industry in the electronics and telecommunications industry. In 2006 he founded SiOnyx, a company that is commercializing black silicon, a new form of silicon developed in Mazur's laboratory. Mazur is currently Chairman of the Scientific Advisory Board for SiOnyx. Mazur is Chairman of the Instructional Strategy Advisory Group for Turning Technologies, a company developing interactive response systems for the education market. He also serves on the Scientific Advisory Panel for Allied Minds, a pre-seed investment company creating partnerships with key universities to fund corporate spin-outs in early stage technology companies, and on the Scientific Advisory Board for the Lifeboat Foundation, a nonprofit nongovernmental organization dedicated to encouraging scientific advancements.

Dr. Mazur is author or co-author of 237 scientific publications and 12 patents. He has also written on education and is the author of *Peer Instruction: A User's Manual* (Prentice Hall, 1997), a book that explains how to teach large lecture classes interactively. In 2006 he helped produce the award-winning DVD Interactive Teaching.

Deciding to Major in Computer Science: A Grounded Theory of Students' Self-Assessment of Ability

Colleen M. Lewis
Graduate School of
Education
University of California, Berkeley
Berkeley, CA, USA 94720

colleenl@berkeley.edu

Ken Yasuhara
Center for
Engineering Learning & Teaching
University of Washington, Seattle
Seattle, WA, USA 98195-2183

yasuhara@uw.edu

Ruth E. Anderson
Department of
Computer Science & Engineering
University of Washington, Seattle
Seattle, WA, USA 98195-2350

rea@cs.washington.edu

ABSTRACT
There is great interest in understanding and influencing students' attraction to computing-related majors. This qualitative study is based on interviews with 31 students enrolled in introductory programming courses at two public universities in the United States. This paper presents a model of five factors that influence student decisions to major in CS and elaborates on our grounded theory analysis of one of these factors: how students assess their CS-related ability. We describe how students measure their ability in terms of speed, grades, and previous experience and how students make interpretations and decisions based upon these measurements. We found that students' interpretations were influenced by experiences in their environments and beliefs about ability as being fixed or malleable.

Categories and Subject Descriptors
K.3.2 [**Computers and Education**]: Computer and Information Science Education – *computer science education, self-assessment*

General Terms
Human Factors

Keywords
Ability, major choice, grounded theory

1. INTRODUCTION
Although there are signs of a possible turnaround in the sharp drop in undergraduate computer science (CS) enrollment in the U.S., levels are still very low and unlikely to be sufficient to meet projected demand [15, 29]. Accordingly, there is great interest in understanding student experiences and perceptions of CS, as well as how they shape student decisions to major. For example, Margolis and Fisher documented undergraduates' experiences of CS and reasons for leaving the major [19]. Barker and colleagues identified aspects of CS classrooms that create a hostile and defensive environment [3, 4]. Other work that examines students' interest in CS and how they select CS as a major has been primarily quantitative [5, 6, 7, 12]. This quantitative work bears the risk of missing subtle, unanticipated ways in which students' experiences and perceptions influence their decisions about majoring. To remain sensitive to these subtleties in students' decision making, we selected a grounded theory methodology [8, 27], which is an inductive and iterative research approach that explores the variety of responses that emerge from the data for the purpose of developing an explanatory theory for a phenomenon.

We conducted a qualitative analysis of interviews with students at two large, public universities in the U.S. From the data, we identified five factors that students assessed in deciding whether to major in CS. These factors were ability, enjoyment, fit, utility, and opportunity cost. For this paper, we have selected a single factor, *ability*, and will present our theory, developed using grounded theory. Our theory details the types of measurements of ability made by students, their interpretations of those measurements, and their decisions based upon those interpretations. An integral part of the theory describes how students' experiences of their academic and institutional context, as well as their beliefs about CS ability as being fixed or malleable, influence interest in the CS major.

Related work has documented that there is a common assumption of the existence of an innate aptitude that determines students' success learning to program [18, 23], which education research has found can lead students to pursue less effective learning strategies [10]. The belief that some students cannot succeed in CS also has the potential to disenfranchise populations and exacerbate the lack of diversity in computing [10, 25]. As educators, we hope to provide all motivated students with environments in which they can become competent at programming, and we seek to understand students' processes of self-assessment, as well as the myriad influences that shape them.

This paper contributes a theory for students' self-assessment of ability in deciding whether to major in CS. It describes how both internal and external influences, particularly student beliefs about CS ability and a competitive context, affect how students measure ability and how they interpret and act on those measurements. Grounded in interview data, the details of how these influences interact with self-assessment to impact interest in CS offer educators new insights on ways they can dramatically shape students' experiences, learning, and motivation.

2. PREVIOUS RESEARCH
Previous research on high school and college students' interest/disinterest in CS provides valuable but fragmented insights on the topic. Based on surveying high school students, Carter found that expectations of having to sit at a computer all day, prior interest in another major, and interest in a more "people-oriented" field were common reasons for disinterest in CS [7]. From interviews with 18 CS minors who dropped CS1,

---

Permission to make digital or hard copies of all or part of this work for personal or classroom use is granted without fee provided that copies are not made or distributed for profit or commercial advantage and that copies bear this notice and the full citation on the first page. To copy otherwise, or republish, to post on servers or to redistribute to lists, requires prior specific permission and/or a fee.
ICER'11, August 8–9, 2011, Providence, Rhode Island, USA.
Copyright 2011 ACM 978-1-4503-0829-8/11/08...$10.00.

Kinnunen and Malmi identified lack of time and motivation, low comfort level in class, and prior commitment to a non-CS field as commonly cited reasons [14]. In a quantitative survey of 113 students who had taken introductory CS, Barker and colleagues found that student-student interaction was the most powerful predictor of students' intention to continue studying CS [3, 4]. Higher education research has identified similar influences and predictors for major choice, including social supports and barriers [17], personality and values [1, 22], and demographics such as gender, race, and socioeconomic status [13]. Given these disparate findings, it is productive to develop theories, such as the one presented in this paper, which can synthesize findings and provide rich qualitative details to aid practitioners in interpreting the theory within their local context.

3. METHODOLOGY

3.1 Interview Sites

Interview data was collected in the U.S. at two large, public, research-focused universities. University A has a two-course introductory programming sequence (UA-CS1 and UA-CS2) taught in Java using an "objects late" approach. UA-CS1 is taught with a weekly format of three 50-minute lectures with over 200 students and one 50-minute quiz section, typically led by an undergraduate teaching assistant, with 15–25 students. The format of UA-CS2 is identical except it has two 50-minute quiz sections per week. There are two majors at University A that enable students to pursue CS. For the purposes of this paper, the differences are unimportant, and we use "CS" to refer to both. Admission to the CS major is competitive at University A. Less than 25% of majors are accepted directly out of high school. Most prospective majors apply after two years of prerequisite coursework, and approximately 40% are accepted.

University B has a course sequence that begins with an optional course (UB-CS1). Advanced Placement CS or UB-CS1 serve as preparation for the first official course for majors (UB-CS1.5). UB-CS1 is taught in Scheme with six hours of closed lab and a single hour of lecture a week. Each lab section has approximately 30 students and a single graduate or undergraduate teaching assistant. Students interested in pursuing CS at University B can do so in the College of Engineering (EngCS) or in the College of Letters and Sciences (CS). For EngCS, students indicate their intention to major on their university application and are selected through a competitive admissions process, with less than 15% admitted and the rest denied admission to the university. For CS, students apply for the major after enrolling at the university and completing several prerequisites. At times this process has been competitive, but in recent years this has not been the case.

3.2 Data Collection

At University A, nine participants were recruited from UA-CS1 and eleven participants were recruited from UA-CS2. At University B, eleven participants were recruited from UB-CS1. All participants responded to a recruitment e-mail and were compensated $15. Of these 31 students, about one third intended to major in CS, and an additional third were unsure or intended to minor, with the rest not intending to major or minor. Just over half of the students in the sample were women. At UA, women were oversampled and at UB no screening was done. While the two universities are similar, we relied on the differences in these populations to provide variation in experiences and attitudes.

The interviews used a semi-structured interview protocol, which affords the interviewer the flexibility to pursue unanticipated, relevant topics but does not guarantee that all participants are asked the same questions [8]. The interviews proceeded in a conversation-like pattern, with the interviewer asking follow-up questions. Topics included students' experiences in the current CS course, academic interests, and interest in and preconceptions of CS. Interviews lasted 30–60 minutes and were audio recorded and transcribed. Quotes in this paper are associated with anonymous identifiers including university and course level.

3.3 Data Analysis: Grounded Theory

We developed a *grounded theory* [8, 27] of students' assessments of their CS ability in shaping their decisions to major in CS. We selected grounded theory to identify the range of factors that shape student decisions to major and the context in which they operate and interact. This inductive and iterative research approach is commonly used to collect and analyze qualitative data to form and substantiate explanatory theories. The grounded theory approach differs from research approaches that test *a priori* hypotheses and is a particularly appropriate method to highlight and value participants' individual experiences.

Our analysis began with the coding of noteworthy patterns in the data, referred to as open coding within grounded theory. Based upon this initial open coding, we identified dozens of codes related to an emergent high-level theme of what students think it takes to succeed in CS. Codes were clustered into categories that represented the higher-level patterns and connections between the codes, referred to as axial coding within grounded theory. Throughout this coding process, we negotiated definitions for approximately 75 codes and 25 categories, and continually developed or refined codes and categories to represent the variation and themes within the categories.

In an attempt to narrow our analysis, we focused on students' responses to interview questions about what makes majoring in CS interesting and appealing or uninteresting and unappealing. Returning to open coding on this subset of the data, we developed 39 new codes for students' responses to these questions. During axial coding, these codes were then clustered into five categories that students linked to their decisions to major in CS or not: ability, enjoyment, fit, utility, and opportunity cost.

We found that the factors that students listed as interesting and appealing or uninteresting and unappealing appeared throughout the interview. For example, one student considering a CS major mentioned his perception that CS becomes increasingly competitive as something that makes CS less appealing. He described it as *"a little bit more competitive...that there is less that spirit of collaboration" (UA_CS1_007)*. His response tells us that some students consider the competitive environment when deciding upon a major but does not give a rich sense of students' experiences of competition. For each of the 39 codes, we returned to the entire data corpus and initial 75 codes to elaborate on the variation amongst students' experiences and beliefs. In the sections below, we do not distinguish between students that have decided to major or not. Instead, we focus on the variation in students' experiences and beliefs related to one of the five factors that students cited as affecting CS interest or appeal.

In developing a grounded theory of the factor of self-assessment of ability, we gathered codes that were relevant to understanding the process of measurement and interpretation of CS ability. From our data, we noticed that students' interpretations of assessments were shaped by their perceptions of context, their beliefs about ability, and their specific methods of measurement. These connections in the data formed the wire frame of the initial drafts of our grounded theory. Throughout our analysis, we returned to the transcripts, codes, and categories in an attempt to refine our theory. We schematized the process of students' assessment of ability in parallel to comparing our model to a diagram template used in some grounded theory work [26]. Our resulting model, discussed in detail in the Results section, is a modified version of a traditional diagram, customized to match the specifics of our process of interest.

4. THEORETICAL FRAMEWORK

During analysis, research by Dweck and colleagues [10, 20] shed light on the emerging codes and categories and was subsequently incorporated into our theory. Dweck and colleagues have found that the belief that intelligence or ability is fixed (*e.g.*, innate) is associated with avoiding challenges, giving up in the face of difficulty, and other "maladaptive" learning behaviors. In contrast to students with this "fixed mindset," students with a "growth mindset" believe that intelligence or ability is malleable (*e.g.*, extensible through effort), which is associated with challenge seeking, persistence, and, ultimately, attainment of learning goals. Particularly relevant to our grounded theory of self-assessment of CS ability are the ways in which mindset can affect interpretations of achievement and failure. A student with a fixed mindset concerning CS ability might take a low exam grade as a sign that they are ill-suited for CS study, while one with a growth mindset might, from the exact same grade, conclude that they need to study harder and prepare differently for future exams. This example illustrates how the belief that CS ability is innate can impact learning behaviors and motivation, potentially stifling academic growth [10, 24]. A survey of faculty and students suggests that the belief that CS ability is fixed is not uncommon in the field [18].

5. RESULTS

5.1 Five Factors that Shape Decision to Major

Our interviews suggest that students consider some combination of five interrelated factors in deciding whether to major in CS:

- Their **ability** as related to CS: experiences and expectations of success as CS majors
- Their **enjoyment** of CS: how much they would enjoy majoring in CS
- The **fit** between their identity and CS: the extent to which their own values and identity align with values and cultural expectations they associate with CS
- The **utility** of CS: the extent to which CS would provide potential value to society or to them as individuals
- The **opportunity cost** associated with majoring in CS: practical constraints, as well as ways in which majoring in CS might restrict other plans

5.2 A Grounded Theory of Students' Assessment of Ability

This paper describes a grounded theory for the first of the five factors, with the central focus on students' self-assessment of their ability as related to CS. Below we present an overview of the theory as diagrammed in Figure 1 and in the paper elaborate on the variation and themes within each node and the influences between nodes. In parentheses below, we indicate the traditional labels used in similar grounded theory diagrams [26].

To characterize students' process of self-assessment, we separated it into two sequential stages: *measurement* and *interpretation*. In our theory, *measurement* of ability (Central Phenomenon) refers to uninterpreted measurements of ability, such as course grades and speed completing assignments. The process of *interpreting* these measurements of ability (Strategies) is distinct from the uninterpreted measurement. Sometimes measurements were explicit, and sometimes measurements were visible only through students' interpretations. For example, the following quote includes multiple interpretations and implies a measurement: *"In sixth grade, I tried to learn some HTML, but I don't think that counts"* (UB_CS1_04). An element of interpretation from the quote is the attitude that her experience with HTML does not count as previous experience with CS, and she explicitly devalued this measurement. Her qualifier that she *"tried to learn"* suggests an additional interpretation, potentially that she considered herself not fully successful in learning HTML. From this quote we can infer that this student considered her sixth-grade experience with HTML, which we classify as a measurement. Frequently, only from these interpretations can we infer specific measurements that inform the interpretation.

We identified the need to select a major and the belief that ability is relevant to major selection (Causal Conditions) as conditions that caused students to measure their ability (Central Phenomenon). Interpretations of measurements (Strategies) were shaped by students' experience of their external context (Context) and students' beliefs regarding whether CS ability is innate (Intervening Conditions). These interpretations informed students' major decisions (Consequences).

For the purposes of this study, we customized a common grounded theory diagram by distinguishing between *intervening conditions* and *context* as follows:

- *Intervening conditions* are internal to the student and refer to beliefs held by the student. In the analysis of the central phenomenon of measurement of ability, the key beliefs pertain to the fixed or malleable nature of CS-related ability.
- *Context* includes aspects of the external environment as experienced by the student. Key elements of the external environment are the student's institutional and departmental context, peers and instructional staff, and educational experiences. In particular, perceptions of a culture of competition among students were a significant aspect of the external context at one of the studied institutions.

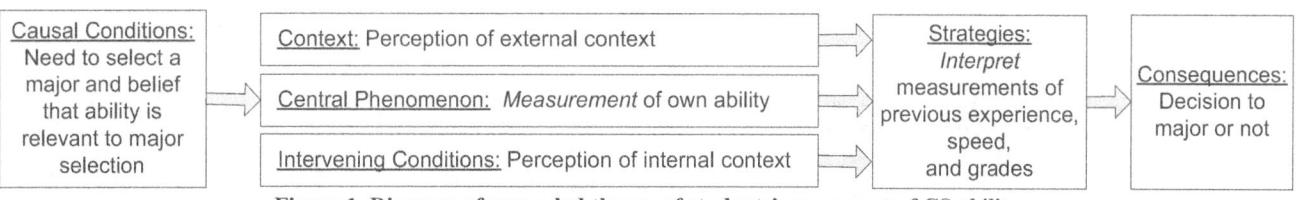

Figure 1. Diagram of grounded theory of students' assessment of CS ability

We begin by describing students' perceptions of intervening conditions, external context, and three ways students described measuring their ability: previous experience, speed, and grades. Later we discuss how intervening conditions, external context, and self-measurements were interpreted by students and influenced their decisions to pursue a CS major.

5.3 Intervening Conditions

In this study, we define intervening conditions to be the key beliefs of students relevant to assessment of ability. We focus on the spectrum of students' beliefs about the fixed or malleable nature of CS ability, which informed our selection of the theoretical framework based upon research by Dweck and colleagues [10, 20]. From our data and the work of Dweck and colleagues, we have evidence that these beliefs influence the ways in which students interpret measurements of their ability. There were instances where participants identified CS ability as shaped by effort, while other times, students discussed assumptions about CS ability or CS ways of thinking as something *"you are just born with"* (UA_CS2_104). To characterize the intervening conditions, we elaborate on the variation within students' beliefs regarding CS ability, the potential sources of this information, and the potential consequences for student learning and motivation.

There is a sense among many students that it is necessary to have a natural inclination toward CS, from which students appear to derive both negative and positive motivation. One student explicitly linked a decision to become a CS major to the presence or absence of a natural inclination: *"You know it's not your thing because you know, you're not learning it. It like doesn't come naturally to you... If programming comes naturally to you, then being a CS major would be like a good choice I guess"* (UB_CS1_07). In listing reasons to not major, another student included in the list that they *"don't have any natural ability"* (UA_CS2_111). In contrast, one student explained their enjoyment of UB-CS1: *"I guess 'cause programming comes to me pretty naturally"* (UB_CS1_10).

On the other hand, some students identified effort as crucial to their success: *"I'm sure if I try hard enough I can learn"* (UB_CS1_09). Many students identified *"hard working"* (UB_CS1_01) as an important trait for a successful computer scientist. Some students emphasized the role of effort in achieving success in CS: *"Success in [UA-CS2] is basically all up to you, as far as how much you want to put into it and learn"* (UA_CS2_105). Another student attributed a bad grade to his lack of effort, not an aspect of innate ability: *"If I had committed myself, I would have gotten a better grade"* (UA_CS2_110).

We hypothesize that sometimes information about whether CS ability is innate or malleable comes from faculty. One student reported that their instructor directly tied students' success or failure to a *"mental outlook"* (UA_CS2_101) that you are born with, which can be either compatible or incompatible with CS: *"Even my [UA-CS2 professor] told us that some people are just born that way, with that mental outlook that is compatible with CS... They feel it's so easy for them... Yeah, and he told the rest of the people that some of you will try but some of you won't get it, and it's just that your mental outlook isn't made that way. It's something you're born with. You can't help it"* (UA_CS2_101). This student said she now believed this but had not heard or believed this idea before hearing it from her professor.

One reason that expectations of ability being innate are problematic is that they provide the opportunity to disenfranchise an entire community. One student expressed that male students' inclination to CS is innate: *"I think like the girls and guys have different kind of system of thinking, just like, I just think guys are more used to thinking the way that the programming language is thinking... I think that's an inherited thing, like you are born with those characteristics"* (UA_CS2_104). She generalized about men's and women's performance at UA, saying, *"I have to admit that guys do perform better than girls in the [CS] courses"* (UA_CS2_104), and drew further evidence from the fact that there were more male than female teaching assistants.

The range of attitudes toward CS ability can be expected to exaggerate or temper interpretations of assessments of ability, negative or positive. Whereas one student above (UA_CS2_110) tied his bad grades to a lack of effort, it is likely that another student may associate a bad grade or even difficulty on an assignment with a lack of innate ability.

5.4 Context

Context is the external environment as experienced by the student. Key elements of the external environment are conversations with and observations of peers. Perceptions of a culture of competition among students were also a significant aspect of students' experience of the external environment at UA.

5.4.1 Conversations with and Observations of Peers

In our interview data, students often described information they learned both from talking to or observing their peers that influenced their interpretation of their own ability.

Students formed opinions about their peers from first- or second-hand accounts of other students' experiences. One participant reported that *"they told me that even though they have done something similar to [UA-CS2], they are still taking this class"* (UA_CS2_101). Students also heard stories of other students, often those with previous experience, who purportedly received good grades with ease. One UA-CS2 student reported that her friend skipped UA-CS1 and *"found [UA-CS2] really easy and got a 4.0"* (UA_CS2_101).

Some students mentioned that they observed the behavior of others during class in gathering information about the ability and experience of their peers. At UA, one student discussed her observations of students pretending not to listen: *"When I look around the room, I notice how students will pretend they're not listening to the lecture at all... They will play chess on laptops, just to show that like, 'Oh yeah, this is a piece of cake for me.' ...You see a lot of people playing games"* (UA_CS2_103). Another student noted that some students finish labs quickly: *"There are people that leave so early! It's like, 'Whoa you're done already?'"* (UB_CS1_03).

5.4.2 Competition at UA

In UA interviews, competition among students was a common theme related to assessment of CS-related ability. UA students perceived competition as part of both the process of gaining admission to the CS major and their experience of the introductory CS courses. Such discussion was largely absent in the UB interview sample; however, at both institutions, some students discussed a perception of CS courses lacking collaboration and collegiality.

Many UA students described the CS admissions process as being competitive in general, saying that the admissions rate was low, and that it was *"really competitive"* or, worse, *"nearly impossible."* Knowing about students who were denied admission reinforced these perceptions. Many UA students believed that exceptionally high grades, particularly those in the introductory CS courses, were critical to admission and were told this directly by non-CS-specific university advisors. Students drew similar conclusions concerning the importance of grades from what they observed in and heard from their peers. There were also accounts of students strategically retaking CS1 or CS2 to get higher grades and boost their chances of admission.

Some UA students described their introductory CS courses as having a competitive atmosphere. This was especially true of UA-CS2, which multiple students described as having a reputation of being a *"weed-out"* course that the department used to select out higher-achieving, *"super-smart"* students. In such an environment, students reported feeling *"discouraged,"* *"like an outsider,"* and *"lonesome."* A few students saw competition among students as a direct consequence of course grading, which they incorrectly believed to be curved. Concerns about competition in the introductory courses were heightened by recognition that students with a wide range of prior programming experience enroll in the same introductory course sequence.

UA students and a few UB students described their experiences in introductory CS as lacking collaboration and collegiality. While not necessarily symptomatic of competition, one student believed that the *"antisocial"* nature of CS gave rise to a feeling of *"you against the rest of the class" (UA_CS2_103)*. Other students' observations concerning the lack of collaboration used words like *"isolation,"* *"snobby,"* *"separated,"* and *"individual."* At UA, students were *"scared"* of talking about assignments at a conceptual level, for fear of being accused of academic misconduct.

It seems likely that if students perceive themselves as competing with other students, they will be more likely to assess their ability, and it will shape their interpretations and decisions based upon these assessments.

5.5 Central Phenomenon: Measurements of Ability

From students' statements, we can infer that they gathered information that informed their interpretations of their CS ability. We refer to students' methods of gathering information as measurements, and we identified three primary ways that students measured their ability: the amount and type of their previous experience, the speed with which they accomplished various tasks, and the grades they received.

5.5.1 Previous Experience

Students considered specific personal experiences, both formal and informal, in assessing their previous experience. Some students made factual statements about their experience during the interview, and the following interview prompt, used near the end of the interview, asked students about their experience: "In total, how many years of computer programming experience would you say you have, including both in-course and extracurricular experience?" For example, one student responded, *"I took a Visual Basic class in high school" (UA_CS1_007)*.

5.5.2 Speed

Students considered their speed completing tasks such as exams or programming assignments as a way of assessing their CS ability. It was rare for students to provide concrete information about the time taken on CS assignments. In one exception, a student quantified time spent on CS assignments: *"a couple of them did take a couple days" (UA_CS2_103)*. Instead, students evaluated the time spent with interpretive descriptions such as *"forever,"* *"a lot,"* and *"really long."* This kind of interpretation was common, and we have little information about the actual measurements students made of their own experience of time to inform these interpretations.

5.5.3 Grades

Students used their course grades, as well as grades on exams and homework, to assess their CS ability. Students at UB had relatively fewer opportunities for measurement, given the timing of the interviews. Students interviewed at UA had nearly completed their first or second university-level CS course, whereas most of the UB students were interviewed before their first exam in their first university-level CS course. This might partly account for the greater amount of discussion about grades in the UA interviews.

5.6 Strategies: Interpretations of Measurements of Ability

To elaborate on our theory, schematized in Figure 1, we detail students' interpretations of their measurements of previous experience, speed, and grades, as influenced by intervening conditions and external context.

5.6.1 Previous Experience

We identified four patterns of interpretation of previous experience measurements. Students evaluated their level of experience, the relevance of their experiences, and their experience relative to their peers, and they made inferences about the climate of the class. These interpretations were shaped by students' measurements, their internal beliefs, and their context, such as the experiences of their peers.

Some students provided interpretations of their measurements of previous experience, irrespective of their peers. One student responded regarding his previous experience and described it as *"probably one year of dedicated work" (UA_CS2_106)*, and he later interpreted this experience as *"still very, very novice" (UA_CS2_106)*. Another student reported on his experience as being *"three-quarters of a year"* and characterized it as *"not a whole lot" (UA_CS1_003)*.

Students had both positive and negative evaluations of whether their prior experience was relevant. One student deemed her experience to be relevant: *"But it was familiar and kind of easy because I understood the concepts because I had programmed before" (UA_CS1_009)*. Another student reported, *"Freshman year of high school, first semester, I took a computer programming class which was Visual Basic... I guess that kind of helped me with some concepts, I think" (UA_CS1_002)*. In contrast, another student interpreted a required Visual Basic course in high school as not relevant and explained, *"I don't really count that, because I don't think that's computer science... It was all memorizing... It didn't teach you how to write your own code" (UA_CS2_104)*.

Some students used measurements of their previous experience and information from their context to come to conclusions about their level of experience relative to their peers. Many students appeared to believe that their peers had more programming experience. One UA student likened his introductory course experience to being in a foreign language class with classmates who were already native speakers. He described how they impacted the course: *"Everyone else already knows what's going on, so you'd think that would help you more, but the teachers* start to adjust to the natives, so the people that are completely new to the idea are getting left behind in the dust, unless they work their asses off" (UA_CS2_109).

In drawing implications for classroom climate, one student expressed being intimidated to ask questions in her classroom that she identified as having many people with prior experience: *"It's intimidating to ask questions, 'cause you feel like people are going to scoff at you, like, 'How do you not know that?' And you're like, 'Because I didn't take AP computer science. Because I haven't been programming since I was four'"* (UB_CS1_02).

5.6.2 Speed

Students interpreted their measurements of speed to inform their opinion of their personal speed as well as to inform their opinion of CS. Students' interpretations can be divided into two groups. Some students identified external factors that shaped their experience of speed within the course, while other students focused on their personal experiences without attribution, making it unclear whether they interpreted these experiences as within or beyond their control.

Students sometimes attributed their speed to external factors such as exam pressure, the course's pace, peers' experience level, and the time-consuming nature of programming. Taking a long time to complete an exam was often attributed to the nature of the exam: *"I feel like we were tested more on how fast we could do it, as opposed to how well we knew the material"* (UA_CS1_008). However, one student interpreted a similar experience from an apparent mindset that ability is malleable: *"On my midterm, we had time limits and pressure and stuff, so... I mean I guess I did not study enough"* (UA_CS1_005). Some students perceived a mismatch between the amount of material being taught and the number of weeks in the course: *"Too much information was given to us, and we were given too little time to master it"* (UA_CS2_101). Finally, some students attributed their assessment of slowness in learning material to the fact that other students had more experience: *"It takes a little bit longer to grasp concepts... I just need more time to read and understand and practice... Maybe the majority of them have more experience"* (UA_CS2_103).

Some students stated that being *"a fast learner"* (UA_CS1_003) was a trait of a successful computer scientist, and this kind of speed could be interpreted as either within or beyond students' control. One student (UA_CS2_105) reported that, due to the time pressure on exams, he specifically practiced solving problems quickly. Many examples were not explicit in attributing speed to innate ability. However, consistent with fixed mindset, these also did not include attribution to an external cause or draw implications for their effort. For example, one student reported that the amount of time needed to complete the assignments was *"kind of discouraging"* (UA_CS2_103). Students described interpretations that they were slower than their peers and general interpretations that their time spent programming was *"longer,"* *"forever,"* or *"lots"*: *"I think I take a longer time [coding] than most people"* (UB_CS1_06), and *"I know it takes me forever to think through a problem and finally come up with the code that'll work"* (UA_CS2_108).

Students also came to conclusions about speed and the nature of CS work. For one student, this was based in part on her experiences in UA-CS1: *"I think it like takes a few hours or a few days to like think and actually program stuff"* (UA_CS1_005). Without referencing ability measurements, other students made general statements about CS work being *"really time-consuming"* (UA_CS2_101) or that *"it takes a long time"* (UB_CS1_02).

5.6.3 Grades

Students interpreted their grades as both reflective of their ability and unfair in the context of a class where many students have prior experience.

One student interpreted her grades as information about her ability to handle the workload in the course and thus the field: *"I would realize, if I had gotten a higher grade, I would think that, okay, the amount of hard work I put in was sufficient enough. Right now I feel like, even though I worked hard, I'm not getting a good enough grade"* (UA_CS2_101). Another student interpreted an exam grade as a positive reflection of his ability: *"When I first got my score, I was like, 'Yes!', you know? 'I rock at this!'"* (UA_CS2_110). We saw evidence that some students felt that grades were unfair or otherwise provided inaccurate information about their learning: *"I feel like I understand, like I learn a whole lot, but my grade's not going to show it"* (UA_CS2_108).

Students at both universities referenced the existence of competition in the form of a grading curve, where students with previous experience had an inherent advantage: *"They mess up the curve. You're always thinking about that"* (UB_CS1_07) and *"It's hard to make the curve, because a lot of people in there are already like, 'Man, I'm already good at programming. I don't have to study. Watch me get a 4.0'"* (UA_CS2_109). One student felt that first-time programmers did not have a reasonable shot at getting a good grade in UA-CS1 and UA-CS2 (UA_CS2_101). At UA, university-level advisors were even reported to suggest to a student that they take a CS course during a particular term based on how many people with previous experience were expected to enroll (UA_CS2_108). Having a "good enough" grade was so important for admissions at UA that taking the course over again was a strategy used for getting a better grade and increasing chances to get into the major (UA_CS2_104).

5.7 Consequences: Decision to Major or Not

5.7.1 Previous Experience

Students drew both positive and negative conclusions about majoring in CS from their interpretations of their previous experience measurements. One student discussed his two reactions: *"Part of me was kind of like, 'Major in it! Fight the power!' and stuff like that, but the other part of me was like, 'Do I really want to be in a major like that, where you know a lot of these people were experts in their field before they even started college?'"* (UA_CS2_109). One student contrasted her frustration with others having more experience with her enjoyment of the course: *"And people have programmed like since they were eight, so it is impossible to start learning a new language in college and catch up with them. So I was not sure if I should take [UA-CS1] or not, but, it is fun"* (UA_CS1_005). A student with high school programming background linked his ability as motivation to continue pursuing CS: *"Also that I'm good at it. That is encouraging. I mean, if it is something that I enjoy and I'm good at it, that is a lot of encouragement to continue forward"* (UA_CS1_007).

5.7.2 Speed

Students explicitly connected their speed and the amount of time that CS work requires to decisions to pursue CS. One student, based upon their interpretation that some people overcame difficulties faster, said that this *"makes you feel like, 'I might not be best fit in this field'"* (UA_CS2_110). In contrast, one student felt well-suited for CS on account of his speed: *"I feel I can learn things quickly"* (UA_CS1_003). Another student connected programming speed with prior experience and expectations of admission to the major: *"This is my first time, and I take really long to program something. So like, I don't think I have enough experience I think. So, I'm not sure if I can get into the major"* (UA_CS1_005). Other students concluded that majoring in CS would take too much time: *"Like if I chose CS, I know that I'll have to put in like so much time in the lab... I knew it'd be time consuming"* (UB_CS1_07).

5.7.3 Grades
Students drew both positive and negative conclusions from their interpretation of their grade measurements. Sometimes bad grades were enough to discourage students from pursuing the major, as one student noted: *"I enjoyed the homeworks... The hard work was worth it, but once you see the grades, and I guess the way I analyzed was, once I go into the 300-level classes, it's going to get tougher, and if I'm not good enough in the 100-level courses, then I should back out right now. It's not going to get any easier"* (UA_CS2_101). Another student mapped their assessment of grades, interrelated with the issue of previous experience, to the decision to major: *"It kind of sucks, because like, when you try to apply for a competitive major, you're basically competing against someone that's had five or six years on you"* (UA_CS2_109). Good grades could encourage students to pursue the major: *"My own performance in these two courses, so, like spur some of my intention to get into the major"* (UA_CS2_104).

6. DISCUSSION
The fact that students consider their CS-related ability when deciding whether to major in CS is consistent with a variety of long-standing theories concerning motivation and achievement-related choices [2, 11, 16]. The grounded theory presented above details the specifics of how students went about measuring their ability, how these measurements were influenced by internal and external context, and how they were linked to interest in the CS major. Our analysis indicates that students employed information in three categories as the basis for their measurement and interpretation of CS-related ability: previous experience, speed, and grades. Students often deemed previous experience with programming as relevant, but not other computing experiences (*e.g.*, Microsoft Office or HTML). Measurements of ability related to speed mostly considered the time required to complete exams, programming assignments, and labs. Finally, grade-based measurements were based primarily on exam and homework scores, as well as grades in previous CS courses.

Partly based on the information described above, students interpreted measurements of their CS-related ability. Students at both institutions also considered information about external context, such as conversations with and observations of peers. Internal context, specifically beliefs about the fixed or malleable nature of CS ability, also influenced assessments of ability. In turn, these interpretations led students to various decisions regarding whether to major in CS and a variety of conclusions about themselves, their peers, and the field and culture of CS. Particularly at UA, competition and perceptions of peers engendered comparisons with peers. These comparisons of ability led students to different conclusions about their prospects of success as CS majors.

7. VALIDITY AND LIMITATIONS
In interpretive qualitative research, subjectivity is inherent in the process, but we attempted to address related validity concerns in our study's analysis and presentation. All three researchers have experience teaching introductory CS courses and background in education research in CS and engineering. This meant that we were familiar with the language of CS, as well as the pedagogical context, which guided follow-up questions during interviews and aided data interpretation. In addition, interpretations and conclusions presented here were the result of negotiations by at least two researchers who examined transcript data. Finally, in keeping with qualitative traditions, we offer the reader context and numerous quotes for our claims, allowing them to make judgments of validity.

As is common with grounded theory work, our goal was not universal theory, so we make limited claims about the generalizability of our findings and the prevalence of observed phenomena. We do, however, expect that many of the complex relationships our theory describes apply to other settings. We described the interview sites to help readers determine the transferability of findings to other contexts.

A potential limitation was the fact that participants were self-selected volunteers. However, the sample included roughly equal numbers of students intending to major, considering majoring or minoring, and not intending to major in CS, suggesting limited relevance of self-selection bias. A clearer limitation stems from our sole focus on the perceptions of students. Important as they are, we expect there are other influences on interest in majoring in CS that students are not conscious of or do not self-report for some other reason.

8. CONCLUSION
This paper presents a grounded theory for one of five factors that we found students considered when deciding whether to major in CS: ability, enjoyment, fit, utility, and opportunity cost. Based on interview analyses, our theory details the different kinds of information that serve as bases for measurement of CS-related ability. It also describes how students interpret and respond to these measurements, subject to a variety of contextual influences. Some of these influences represent external context, such as peers' behavior or speech and admission policies that induce competition, as at UA. We also observed the influence of internal context, particularly in the form of beliefs about the nature of CS-related ability—*i.e.*, whether it is innate or extensible through effort.

Assuming that one role of introductory CS courses is to help students make informed decisions about majoring in CS, CS educators can reflect on ways in which they can influence the self-assessment process as modeled above. Are speed, prior programming experience, and grades in introductory courses appropriate metrics, given mixed empirical evidence of the latter two's value in predicting longer-term success in undergraduate CS [19, 28]? How can educators affect these measurements and interpretations through decisions about curriculum, courses, and classroom environment? Our theory identifies multiple points of influence in the process linking self-assessment of ability to interest in majoring.

Despite efforts at UA to make CS more accessible, competition significantly influenced how students interpreted their measurements of ability. Comparisons with peers with respect to prior programming experience and speed caused some students to question whether they should pursue their interest in CS.

Competition also led students to characterize introductory courses as weed-out courses and associate CS with a culture of isolation. Faculty and advisors have some control over competition and its effects on students by addressing misconceptions about grading policies and admissions criteria. Given heightened concern among novice programmers at UA about competing with more experienced students, educators might consider entry paths tailored for students with no prior programming experience. Regardless of admissions process, integration of cooperative and collaborative learning might challenge cultural stereotypes and set more accurate expectations of CS professions.

Our theory provides CS-specific examples of how a student's mindset can affect self-assessment of ability and, ultimately, motivation to major in CS. Given this and the extensive research of Dweck and colleagues on the negative learning behaviors associated with fixed mindset [10], CS educators should consider the risks of endorsing unsubstantiated assumptions that CS ability is fixed. Further research is needed to examine potential connections between mindset and the persistent gender gap in CS, as suggested by Murphy & Thomas [21], as well as CS-specific interventions to influence mindset [9, 24].

Our future work includes developing theories for the remaining four factors related to interest in majoring in CS, as well as interactions among them. This body of work might inform a quantitative study to further validate causal relationships and document the prevalence of various beliefs and experiences. We hope these investigations will directly inform the design and validation of interventions to help potential CS students make informed major choices.

9. REFERENCES

[1] Astin, A. W. (1993). *What matters in college?* San Francisco, CA: Jossey-Bass.

[2] Bandura, A. (1977). Self-efficacy. *Psychological Review, 84*(2).

[3] Barker, L. J., Garvin-Doxas, K., & Jackson, M. H. (2002). Defensive climate in the computer science classroom. In *Proc. SIGCSE*.

[4] Barker, L. J., McDowell, C., & Kalahar, K. (2009). Exploring factors that influence computer science introductory course students to persist in the major. In *Proc. SIGCSE*.

[5] Beyer, S., Rynes, K., & Haller, S. (2004). Deterrents to women taking computer science courses. *IEEE Technology and Society Magazine, 23*(1).

[6] Boyle, R., Carter, J., & Clark, M. (2002). What makes them succeed? Entry, progression and graduation in Computer Science. *J. Further & Higher Education, 26*(1).

[7] Carter, L. (2006). Why students with an apparent aptitude for computer science don't choose to major in computer science. In *Proc. SIGCSE*.

[8] Corbin, J. M., & Strauss, A. C. (2008). *Basics of Qualitative Research*. Thousand Oaks, CA: SAGE Publications.

[9] Cutts, Q., Cutts, E., Draper, S., O'Donnell, P., & Saffrey, P. (2010). Manipulating mindset to positively influence introductory programming performance. In *Proc. SIGCSE*.

[10] Dweck, C. S., & Leggett, E. L. (1988). A social-cognitive approach to motivation and personality. *Psychological Review, 95*(2).

[11] Eccles, J. S. (2007). Where are all the women? In S. J. Ceci & W. M. Williams (Eds.), *Why aren't more women in science?* Washington, DC: American Psychological Association.

[12] Gal-Ezer, J., Shahak, D., & Zur, E. (2009). Computer science issues in high school. In *Proc. ITICSE*.

[13] Goyette, K. A., & Mullen, A. L. (2006). Who studies the arts and sciences? *J. Higher Education, 77*(3).

[14] Kinnunen, P., & Malmi, L. (2006). Why students drop out CS1 course? In *Proc. ICER*.

[15] Lacey, A. T., & Wright, B. (2009). Employment outlook 2009–18. *Monthly Labor Review, 132*(11).

[16] Lent, R. W., Brown, S. D., & Hackett, G. (1995). Toward a unifying social cognitive theory of career and academic interest, choice, and performance. *J. Vocational Behavior, 45*(1).

[17] Lent, R. W., Lopez, Jr., A. M., Lopez, F. G., & Sheu, H. (2008). Social cognitive career theory and the prediction of interests and choice goals in the computing disciplines. *J. Vocational Behavior, 73*(1).

[18] Lewis, C. (2007). Attitudes and beliefs about computer science among students and faculty. *SIGCSE Bulletin, 39*(2).

[19] Margolis, J., & Fisher, A. (2003). *Unlocking the Clubhouse*. Cambridge, MA: MIT Press.

[20] Molden, D. C., & Dweck, C. S. (2006). Finding "meaning" in psychology. *American Psychologist, 61*(3).

[21] Murphy, L., & Thomas, L. (2008). Dangers of a fixed mindset. In *Proc. ITICSE*.

[22] Porter, S., & Umbach, P. (2006). College major choice. *Research in Higher Education, 47*.

[23] Robins, A. (2010). Learning edge momentum. *Computer Science Education, 20*(1).

[24] Simon, B., Hanks, B., Murphy, L., Fitzgerald, S., McCauley, R., Thomas, L., & Zander, C. (2008). Saying isn't necessarily believing. In *Proc. ICER*.

[25] Steele, C. M. (1997). A threat in the air. *American Psychologist, 52*(6), 613–629.

[26] Strauss, A. C., & Corbin, J. M. (1990). *Basics of Qualitative Research*. Thousand Oaks, CA: SAGE Publications.

[27] Suddaby, R. (2006). From the editors: What grounded theory is not. *Academy of Management J., 49*(4).

[28] Wilson, B. C. (2002). A study of factors promoting success in computer science including gender differences. *Computer Science Education, 12*(1–2).

[29] Zweben, S. (2010). Undergraduate CS enrollment continues rising. *Computing Research News, 22*(3).

How CS Majors Select a Specialization

Michael Hewner, Mark Guzdial
Georgia Institute of Technology
School of Interactive Computing
85 5th St. NW
Atlanta, Georgia
hewner@gatech.edu, guzdial@cc.gatech.edu

ABSTRACT

As CS becomes a larger field, many undergraduate programs are giving students greater freedom in the classes that make up their degree. This study looks at the process by which students within the CS major choose to specialize in some area. In this study we interviewed student advisors, graduated CS students, and students currently in the undergraduate process about their view of CS and how they make decisions. The interviews were analyzed with grounded theory approach. The analysis presents four forces that affect student decision making. One, students often use the amount they enjoy individual classes as a sign of how well they fit with a particular specialization. Two, students often do not research, so they select specializations based on misconceptions. Three, students often rely on the curriculum to protect against poor educational choices. Four, students usually do not have a personal vision for what they hope to do with a Computer Science degree.

Categories and Subject Descriptors

K.3.2 [**Computers and Education**]: Computer and Information Science Education—*Curriculum*

General Terms

Experimentation, Human Factors

Keywords

Curriculum, Concentrations, Tracks, Multi-disciplinary

1. INTRODUCTION

Recent trends in Computer Science education have given students more choices about their computing degree program. Schools such as Georgia Tech [7] and Stanford [14] have developed CS curricula that require students to select from specialized sequences of courses. Some of these specialized sequences highlight traditional areas of Computer Science (e.g., artificial intelligence, theory) and some highlight areas that combine CS with other fields (e.g., biocomputation). Students in these specialization–oriented curricula must select one or more specialization; each specialization contains both required courses and a constrained set of electives students select between. In general, colleges that have implemented these programs have reported that students are excited about the opportunity to specialize their coursework and that this excitement has improved CS enrollment [14, 7].

As CS Educators, the idea of students using specializations to design a course of study specific to their goals is appealing. Designers of specialization–oriented curricula are motivated by the idea that specializations allow students to pursue multidisciplinary options [14] and gain skills outside CS that make them more attractive to potential employers [7]. There are also potential problems. Students do not always make decisions based on the best educational reasons [11]. Previous work in Computer Science education suggests that students may not really understand what CS is [5]. Given that many CS programs are offering students more choices, it is important to understand how students choose the classes that make up their CS degree.

In this paper, we call a decision about which courses to take during a degree program a *curricular decision*. A curricular decision can be as small as choosing a particular elective course from a list or as large as choosing to switch to a major with different course requirements. Even in programs without specializations, students have to make many decisions about their curricula. In this paper, we will focus on how students select a specialization.

This paper presents a study of CS undergraduates at Georgia Tech. Georgia Tech has a CS degree program that allows students a great deal of freedom to customize their course plans. Students must select two of eight specializations or "threads": Devices, Information Internetworks, Intelligence, Media, Modeling and Simulation, People, Platforms, and Theory. By selecting two of these specializations, a CS major chooses about two thirds of the CS courses they take. Although this particular program is unique to Georgia Tech, we think that it is similar to curricular decisions students make at other schools. At other schools, students take a set of elective classes without ever officially stating they are pursuing one area of CS or another. Some schools also offer several CS–related degree programs (e.g., Software Engineering, Bioinformatics) that students select between. All of these curricular choices are similar because they require students to make real tradeoffs in their education and they require knowledge of the subfields of CS that ordinary col-

Permission to make digital or hard copies of all or part of this work for personal or classroom use is granted without fee provided that copies are not made or distributed for profit or commercial advantage and that copies bear this notice and the full citation on the first page. To copy otherwise, to republish, to post on servers or to redistribute to lists, requires prior specific permission and/or a fee.
ICER'11, August 8–9, 2011, Providence, Rhode Island, USA.
Copyright 2011 ACM 978-1-4503-0829-8/11/08 ...$10.00.

lege students would not have (e.g., the difference between CS and Software Engineering). Because many schools offer a great deal of freedom, it is worthwhile to look at what influences CS majors' choice at a more detailed level.

This study analyzes interviews of undergraduate students, graduated CS majors, and student advisors to understand:

1. Do students have an accurate view of the courses they are selecting when they make curricular decisions?

2. How do students make important curricular decisions such as which specialization to select?

2. RELATED WORK

In this selection, we look at two areas of related research. The first area is about student understanding of the field of Computer Science at the college level. Based on the related research, we argue that there may be some reason to suspect that students may still have some misconceptions about areas of CS when they have to make curricular decisions. The second area is about student college experiences and decision making beyond the CS field. Based on that research, we argue that student curricular decision making is likely to be complex (and, in some cases potentially problematic).

2.1 Student Understanding of the Field of CS

Much of the research in conceptions of the field of CS has focused on the perspective of precollege students, generally middle school and high school students. The large–scale WGBH study [16] of students age 13-17 indicates that careers in Computing interest students. That said, precollege students do not generally have a ready definition for "Computer Science"; both Greening [9] and Carter [3] asked high school students to define CS and found that students would generally indicate they did not know.

At the introductory college level, McGuffee [12] describes student responses to the question "What is Computer Science?" He reports that at the beginning of CS1, student conceptions are too broad, while at the beginning of CS2, students definitions are too narrowly focused on programming. In their work to develop a breadth–first CS1 course, Dodds et al. [5] find student views of CS to initially be mostly vague or naïve (though significantly improved after experiencing the breadth–first curriculum).

Biggers et al. [2] compares conceptions of CS in seniors: some of whom left the CS major and some of whom stayed in the major to completion. The CS seniors surveyed were likely to define CS broadly. This result was similar to a study by Hewner and Guzdial [10] in which CS seniors frequently emphasized the breadth of the field of CS in their essays about computing.

To sum up this work, what seems to be clear is that many students begin their study of Computer Science with an incomplete understanding of the field. By the end of their careers in Computer Science, their view definitely changes. But little is known about when students begin to gain a strong understanding of the field of CS; this suggests that students may be making educational decisions about what courses to pursue with a problematic understanding of the field of Computer Science.

2.2 Research on Student Educational Decisions

A great deal of research has been done on student choice. Large educational decisions like choice of college major have been shown to be influenced by a wide variety of both internal and external factors. Students differ in the amount of value they attach to different goals, self–efficacy, and how valued particular life goals are in their social groups [6, 17]. Students often change major in college, and the major change is often to a related field [1] which may suggest that they refine the partly uninformed choice they made when they arrived.

Once student have chosen a particular major, there is less research about how students come to understand the subfields and make major–specific choices like specializations. In longitudinal study of engineering students, Stevens [15] emphasizes that students experience the process of selecting a major and fulfilling degree requirements in very different ways. College requirements and factors outside the curriculum cause students to question whether they fit within their major. This "fit" with a major is often evaluated without really understanding what skills the major is trying to develop.

Even when students stay within a major, they can make their own decisions about what content is important if they feel the curriculum is not meeting their needs. Nespor's [13] observational study of management major culture at one school revealed that the student body felt the material learned in class was not valuable. As a result, the students collaborated to subvert their classes while at the same time practicing the interview skills and other interpersonal skills they believed were actually valued in the management community.

The main thing to take away from this research is that, in all majors, students struggle to understand and integrate themselves into their chosen major's curriculum. At least in some cases, students do make decisions about whether to persist in a major or focus on class material for different reasons than their instructors might expect. This suggests that understanding how students make decisions about their CS courses is likely to find some interesting results.

3. DATA SOURCES

This study is based on interviews with three different groups, for a total of fifteen interviews.

1. *Advisors.* At Georgia Tech, the Computer Science department has staff members to help undergraduate students succeed. All of the advisors worked with CS students for several years and answered student questions about what classes to take and academic problems. None of the advisors have degrees in Computer Science, although several have backgrounds in student advisement. We wanted to include undergraduate advisors because they deal with a broad range of students. We interviewed four advisors.

2. *CS Graduates.* We interviewed three participants who had graduated with degrees in Computer Science. We wanted to include graduated students because they could reflect on how the decisions they made as an undergraduate affected them afterward. Two of these students were in the Georgia Tech Ph.D. program, and one had a Computer Science masters degree who was working in industry. All of them did their undergraduate degrees at CS programs outside of Georgia Tech.

3. *CS Students.* We interviewed five students currently

taking the introductory Computer Architecture course. This course generally follows after courses on introductory programming, data structures, and discrete math. These students were all in the first or second year of their CS degree.

The introductory architecture course has an important place in the curriculum because it is the last course that every CS major, regardless of specialization, needs to take. Students are not required to have declared their specialization when they take this course but they will need to make a decision when they register for classes in the following semester.

Care was taken to select students that were having different levels of academic success in the architecture course. From our discussion with advisors, we knew that this course was often considered a "weed out" course for students, and from the literature [15], we knew that grade feedback has a strong influence on students' perception of themselves in the major. We also chose to interview two women, which was far greater than their representation in the actual class.

We also interviewed three students at later points in their undergraduate CS curriculum. We wanted to see how CS majors reflected on their decisions now that they had experienced specialization specific courses. These students were recruited from both traditional and interdisciplinary CS specializations.

The interviews themselves were semi–structured and took about an hour. Students were asked about their experiences in the CS major, how they viewed the field of Computer Science, and about the curricular choices they had made or were about to make. Students were also asked to reflect on how their views about CS had changed over time, and if they felt that misunderstandings of CS had caused them problems in the past. In situations where it seemed like students might have incomplete understanding of aspects of CS they were considering exploring, the interviewer would probe the student on details of what the student expected to learn and why they felt this area would be interesting or useful to them. We asked the advisors similar questions about their students: how the students viewed CS, how the students' views changed over time, and if students made choices that caused them problems.

4. METHOD

We chose a qualitative approach because very little is known about how students make educational decisions. Grounded theory was selected as the method for analyzing the interviews for several reasons:

1. *Emphasis on developing a theory grounded in the participants.* Because not much is known about how CS students make decisions about CS courses, we liked the explicit goal of developing a theory that could then be tested with other methods.

2. *Emphasis on integrating multiple data sources.* The interviews integrate the views of CS advisors, current CS students, and students whose undergraduate CS experience is long past. All of these participants are going to have a very different perspective; grounded theory encourages the integration of very different viewpoints as an important part of the theory development process.

3. *Theoretical Sampling.* Given the wide range of students, there is no hope of interviewing every combination of even a few factors that might influence student decision making. Instead, grounded theory suggests that the researcher should select later participants based on what emerges in the earlier interviews. This allows great flexibility, which is preferable in an exploratory study across a diverse population.

In our research, we chose grounded theory data analysis method outlined by Charmaz [4]. Our interview analysis started with line–by–line analysis of the relevant sections of interview transcriptions. We developed initial codes that describe what is being expressed in each line of the data. After developing initial codes, we went back through the body of research accumulated and selected 'focused' codes that explain larger segments of the data. Finally, we considered how each of the students fell on various dimensions (axial codes) that seemed to explain how curricular decisions were made. These axial codes formed the basis of the "forces" that we describe as our theory in the later sections.

To illustrate this process, here is an example quote that eventually became part of the "abdicating responsibility to the curriculum" force:

> Software engineering, it looked like it was more offered by lower tier colleges...I figured, even though I don't really like theory, there's probably some stuff in it that's useful and probably would make me a better programmer overall. So I figured I'll stick with Computer Science but try to take more practical side of classes.

One of the things we coded about this quote was the student's decision to rely on the reputation of the CS curriculum, despite negative experiences with CS theory in high school. The initial coding was abstracted into the focused code "trust in the curriculum", which included several other students who specifically mentioned they chose particular specializations because the specializations were considered "traditional" CS. When comparing looking at all our student choices, we noted the similarity between the code "trust in the curriculum" code and different students who argued that specializations were unimportant because they would all cover any really essential CS topics. From that, we created a superordinate axial code about how students negotiate with the perceived prestige of CS, even when they often don't know what parts of CS will be useful to them. Eventually, this code became called "abdicating responsibility to the curriculum".

4.1 Limitations

The larger study that these interviews are a part of is being expanded to incorporate students from different schools and in different stages of their degree program. As a result, the theories described here are still tentative; the data has still not fully reached saturation. That said, the particular part of the theory about student curricular decision making is one of the best elaborated portions of the developing theory.

Though this study attempted to get a variety of perspectives from current undergraduates, student advisors, and graduated CS students, there are always limitations on interview–based studies. Because the size of the group was small, we cannot make claims about how prevalent the various viewpoints are in the student body. Other very different perspectives may exist in the CS student body. This study was based at a single school; every CS department's culture is in some ways unique. These limitations are part of any interview–based study: interviews allow us to deeply understand the situations of only a few students. Because not much work has been done about how CS students make curricular decisions, we feel that getting an accurate view of a few students is preferable to attempting to interpret the short responses in a survey or other larger–scale approach.

5. RESULTS

5.1 Enjoyment of CS Classes

In all the interviews, students made decisions based on how much they enjoyed particular classes. One student was hesitant to consider CS because of unenjoyable experiences in high school CS ("bad teacher") but was convinced to pursue the CS major because he/she enjoyed programming robots in the college–level CS introductory course. This sort of decision is common according to advisors – one might expect students who had initially incorrect views (e.g., CS as configuring computers and using applications) about CS to want to leave the major. According to advisors, whether students initially understood CS was less important than whether they liked programming. Students who enjoyed programming stayed in the major, even if it was not what they anticipated when they chose to major in CS.

Although grades and enjoyment seemed to be very strongly related, what students and advisors spoke about was generally enjoyment and not grades. In two cases in our interviews, students did not enjoy a class they did academically well in (although the reverse was never true – students never enjoyed a class they did poorly in). Despite the relationship between grades and enjoyment, the emotional experience of enjoyment (rather than pragmatic goals about maximizing their grade) was what students seemed to retain and use to think about future specializations.

Enjoyment of a particular class experience seemed to be a 'test' in students' minds as to whether they were a good fit within the major. Sometimes this led to students considering decisions that seemed counterintuitive. One student describes experiences in introductory architecture that caused him/her to seriously consider switching majors:

> Student: Well, I just wanna explore more aspects of where I could go and what I could do in the future, and so maybe having a more people-oriented major, more literature basically, which might involve the major computational media, so maybe I could explore that, but I just - I know that I'm interested in languages, and I've become more interested in history, so instead of just technology.
>
> Interviewer: So did you - would you say that it had anything to do with what you were learning about in [computer architecture] that made you reconsider this?
>
> Student: Yeah, I found it boring, and I didn't grasp it so quickly, so that generally discouraged me and what was good about that AP computer science class was that it was really slow and everyone was at your same level or below you.

What is interesting is that this student acknowledged that the architecture course was unusual—that the rest of the CS curriculum would probably be more like algorithms courses (which the student had enjoyed). Despite this, the student seriously reconsidered his/her major (although at the time of the interview he/she had decided to tentatively persist in CS).

Student enjoyment of a particular course seemed to trump specific life plans. The student who enjoyed robots in their introductory course planned to pursue robotics as a specialization. When we asked this student about future goals, the student was thinking about a career managing software developers, perhaps eventually returning for an MBA and starting his/her own business. None of the student's plans involved robotics. Not to say necessarily that robotics was a bad thing for this student; the point is that simply enjoying a particular course can exert a strong influence on a student's curricular decisions.

A student advisor who worked with students in choosing their elective sequences identified student enjoyment as a primary determinant of completion in a particular specializations sequence. The advisor argued that students would often choose a specialization such as Intelligence, based on an abstract intellectual interest (e.g., philosophical interest about the nature of human and computer intelligence). This caused problems when students were surprised by the large amounts of programming in the Intelligence specialization. By making the activities explicit in each of the specializations, the advisor hoped that students would have better success and not have to switch specializations later in their degree programs.

It's not news to say that students choose classes they think they will enjoy, or that students generally enjoy getting good grades in their classes. But a student enjoying (or disliking) a particular class may have a greater effect than their teacher realizes. Enjoying or not enjoying a particular course can significantly impact a student's curricular decisions and that change can happen without the student switching out of the major or failing the course itself. Oftentimes it is taken for granted that certain courses in any curriculum are going to be unpleasant; students experiencing these courses nonetheless attach meaning to what the bad experience means about them and about how they will pursue their degree going forward.

5.2 Confusion about Specializations

The students we interviewed were very close to the point when they would have to choose what specializations to pursue in Computer Science. They had all given some thought to the issue of what specializations they would choose, and some had taken an introductory 1–credit departmental course that introduced the specializations (among subjects relevant to freshman orientation). However, students often had incorrect ideas about the specializations they were considering.

Each specialization tended to have its on set of misconceptions. The Media specialization, for example, was often confused with with using commercial graphics applications such as Photoshop and Maya 3D. This specialization requires a computer graphics course which is then followed up with courses in video game design, computer animation, or computer audio. The Media specialization was also often thought to include GUI design, even though HCI–oriented courses are in a different specialization. One student who was seriously considering the media specialization described it this way:

> Media? Well, that deals with media. So it could be anything in maybe the news, in broadcasting, certain media outlets like YouTube or Flash and basically design, I'd say. If you were designing a video game you might choose media as one of your [specializations] if you wanted to design one... [You would learn] Flash, different ways of representing just colors and to admit, that whole unit user interface.

Even when students did correctly identify the specializations associated with their interests, they often had only a preliminary idea of what content was associated with their specializations. One student was interested in robotics and correctly identified the two specializations of Intelligence, which is basically AI, and Devices, which is a mix of hardware–focused CS courses and ECE (Electrical and Computer Engineering) classes, as the two closest specializations. The student was trying to choose between these two specializations. However, the student could not identify any difference between what sort of robotics would be learned in the two specializations except that Intelligence likely had more theory (and was therefore a less attractive choice) while Devices had more to do with hardware.

Some students had an approximate idea of what would be covered in the various specializations; no student we talked to had a detailed knowledge of what specific topics would be covered in their specialization. Here is a student describing the Platforms specialization (which includes languages, compilers, OSes, etc.) in a way that is as specific as students were able to explain:

> Student: I think you really need a fundamental knowledge in platforms, how to create your own languages, operating system stuff, memory and all that. I think no matter where you go, whether you're working on a desktop or for mobile phones, you'll need a fundamental knowledge in platforms.
>
> Interviewer: So is there anything else? You mentioned creating your own languages and understanding operating systems and memory. Is there anything else that you think this is definitely important knowledge that you anticipate will be in platforms?
>
> Student: Yeah. Not really. I mean, I'm not really— I haven't set my plans in stone yet, so but this is like my general idea.

Based on this interview, this student seemed capable of making an informed choice of specializations. But it is worth noting that even students with strong interest in CS make curricular decisions based on approximate ideas about what they will learn.

In terms of selecting their specializations, students generally referred to the CS departmental website as their primary source for selecting specializations. The CS website does not get deeply into the specifics. For example, the website describes the Media specialization like this: "The media [specialization] prepares students by helping them to understand the technical and computational capabilities of systems in order to exploit their abilities to provide creative outlets." [8] While this is not how the student described Media in the quote above, it is also not specific about the serious programming requirements in Computer Graphics and other courses. The courses are listed specifically, but the student would have to do additional searching to find course syllabi or other materials. No students mentioned doing detailed internet searches, talking to advisors, or discussing things with professors. Several students mentioned talking with other students, but that discussion seemed to focus on which specializations were harder or easier.

Having a misconception about a specilization may seem like a small problem: if students have bad experiences in a specialization course, they can easily switch specializations (perhaps with the added benefit knowing a little more about a subject they might have avoided if they were better informed). Advisors noted that switching was a problem for some students because too many specialization switches could delay graduation. Students who wanted to switch out of one specialization often had to make a choice: either select a specialization that would guarantee them high grades (and on–schedule graduation) or choose another specialization based on interest (and risk delaying graduation if the new specialization had problems and they needed to switch again).

Even for students and advisors who fully understand the choices involved, selecting something like a specialization is rarely clear. Our interviews made it clear that students often do not take the time to fully understand the tradeoffs they are making when they select specializations. Instead, students are choosing specializations with vague ideas or sometimes clear misconceptions.

5.3 Abdicating Responsibility to the Curriculum

> Interviewer: Would you say there's any difference in sort of what your area of specialty would be if you take devices versus artificial intelligence?
>
> Student: Actually I really don't think so. I don't think, because when you graduate from Georgia Tech you just have like a computer science, you're a computer science major. It doesn't specify anything about [specializations] but I feel like once you take classes here you just focus on different aspects but you have some similar classes as well... While we're talking about it I'd rather take a devices [specialization] just because there's a lot more ECE classes and I think once I graduate the jobs, I think I would have the same number of jobs available if I took either of them. I don't think it'd make a difference.

This quote exemplifies the attitude of many of the students we interviewed: they generally believed that no matter what specializations they choose, it would not make a significant difference post–graduation. Although this student is probably right that both specializations have good career prospects, this student does not seem to understand the big differences in jobs between someone focused on device design and AI work. At another point in the interview, we asked the student to talk about potential robotics projects in the various specialties: again the student suggested that the two specializations were pretty similar. By assuming that the curriculum ensures that all students are prepared for careers and just focuses on "different aspects" of the same thing, the student makes the choice of specialization more about personal interests than long–term goals.

One of the advisors stated that student ambivalence to specializations comes from CS industry recruiters. Because the employers student speak to at recruiting events, such as career fairs, do not understand Georgia Tech's specialization system and do not ask for particular specializations, students view their choice as essentially unimportant. It also may be that because students are not ready to commit to a particular long–term goal, they have no choice but to assume that there will be no long–term repercussions of a poor choice of specialization. However, looking at the curriculum, it is definitely true that the choice of specialization has a huge impact on what the student learns in CS. The specialization system at Georgia Tech gives students a great deal of control, including the control to avoid classes that employers in certain careers assume CS majors will have.

Students also left the responsibility for choosing courses to the curriculum in other ways. Several students, when explaining their choice of particular specializations, made it clear that they selected the choices they did because they wanted the "traditional" computer science experience. When we pressed them, they made it clear that although they were unclear on some of the courses in these specializations, they were confident that the courses would give them the best possible background to pursue CS. Their commitment to CS was interesting insofar as they frequently did not have a detailed idea of what they wanted to *do* in Computer Science.

One graduate student we interviewed had a story about their experience in CS that emphasized relying on the curriculum can sometimes make students unaware of parts of their education that may be missing. The student entered the Computer Science of a small liberal–arts school with an explicit goal to program video games. In the spring of his junior year, he applied to internships at a variety of video game companies (and no where else). In the interviews, he was surprised by the questions on computer graphics: his small school did not have computer graphics courses and he didn't realize that that would be important to a video game career. Interestingly, his school had paired him with a professor in the CS program as an academic advisor, who he met with to discuss course requirements but he never brought up the issue of video games. This student was positive about his experience in CS overall — perhaps because he was enjoying his CS coursework and making good progress, he did not stop and reflect about whether all the skills he needed were being taught in class.

Students were also quite willing to believe that the materials covered in their courses were good for them, even if they couldn't explain why. We asked students to comment on courses they disliked, then asked them to explain why they felt the material was in the curriculum. The most common answer was that the course taught ways about thinking about things that would change their perspective.

Students definitely seem to trust that the courses offered to them contain what they need to achieve their goals. Advisors mentioned that students frequently complain when courses listed in their specialization are not offered. Students do not, in general, request that the university offer courses about topics currently not in the course catalog. Students in interviews frequently said that they liked the control the specializations gave them over their curriculum, however before the specialization system was implemented advisors said that students did not in general complain that they had insufficient control. This suggests that students are willing to take their cues from the curriculum about what is "possible" in Computer Science. On one hand, this explains why students are attracted to curricula that explicitly include some of the broader possibilities of CS. On the other hand, when students simply assume that everything the curriculum allows is different aspects of the same content then they may be setting themselves up for surprises after graduation.

5.4 No "Big Picture" CS

Giving students freedom in their curricular choices allows them to engage with CS in new ways and potentially pursue multidisciplinary goals outside the framework of "traditional" CS. The CS departmental website deemphasizes programming and emphasizes that Computing "enables progress in nearly any field imaginable and drives social and scientific advancement in the world" [8]. Based on our interviews with students however, students are often vague:

> Interviewer: Okay. So what would you say your goal is post-graduation?
>
> Student: To get a job. That was basically my reason for going to Georgia Tech and technology is of the future, and we always need computer scientists if we're gonna have computers dealing with every part of our lives.
>
> Interviewer: Do you have any particulars as to sort of what kind of job would be particularly exciting?
>
> Student: Maybe in a bioinformatics field. I was considering that earlier, but anything's up for grabs, anything that would be involving design maybe or biology.

Other students expressed similar uncertainty. One student was considering either continuing in CS to get a Masters or Ph.D., perhaps joining the Navy, perhaps web programming. Discussion with advisors indicated that this sort of confusion is common, that students often are unsure what they want to do with their CS knowledge after they finish their introductory coursework. Even students who are focused on programming and know which specializations they are interested in do not seem to have a particular vision beyond "working as a game programmer" or "working at Google" (because they've heard it's a fun job).

Students as a whole seem to view CS as a set of technical skills that employers will find valuable. Although students generally thought of CS as something bigger than simply programming, they could not think of careers for someone with a CS degree that were not programming–related. At the time they selected their specializations, students did not think about themselves as innovating or their specializations as representing exciting multidisciplinary approaches.

One of the graduate students we interviewed expressed a similar feeling, that as an undergraduate he felt initially very excited about CS and programming, but that he viewed it simply as techniques for implementing different kinds of computer programs. Near the end of his undergraduate curriculum, he decided that CS was boring and switched majors. Although he eventually returned to CS, he expressed regret that his undergraduate courses did not give him the "bigger picture" view of CS that he later developed in graduate school.

Some students we interviewed had approximate plans for after graduation and some students had no concrete plan. None of the students we interviewed were motivated by a view of CS as multidisciplinary or CS as a source for societal change or even had a particular area of CS that they had explored on their own. It is not unreasonable for students to be motivated by more practical concerns, but this does suggest that students do not treat the ability to customize their curriculum as a way to realize an innovative personal vision of the field of CS. This suggests that there may be a disconnect between the way flexible curricula are marketed and the way students within those curricula really make their decisions.

6. A TENTATIVE THEORY

Although the student interviews have not achieved saturation, based on the interview data described above we have developed a tentative theory that describes two unexpected influences that seem to be unexpected parts of student curricular decision making:

- *Abdicating Responsibility to the Curriculum*. Students are willing to assume that the curriculum is designed to put them in a good position to achieve their goals. For some students, this causes them to make the assumption that every specialization is essentially the same. For others, it encourages them to take what they view as the most "traditional" CS topics even if they do not fully understand the intentions of these courses. For both groups, trusting the curriculum allowed students to avoid making a commitment about what their long term goals are.

  The idea that students might be undecided about their long–term goals is not surprising. What is interesting is that when they are undecided, rather than explicitly choosing a set of specializations that are flexible, or choosing a set of specializations that let them explore a set of possible interests, students will assume that the curriculum itself will ensure they make good choices. Even more, it seems that students are willing to make this assumption without conferring with an advisor.

  This is also interesting because, based on previous research, there was reason to think that students in CS might explicitly reject their curriculum. The management students Nespor [13] interviewed exhibited the opposite behavior – building their own curriculum to match their view of the management world. There are also anecdotal stories about students rejecting the CS curriculum – for example students who refuse to learn languages not used in industry, or who question the utility of CS theory. At least at Georgia Tech students blindly accepting the curriculum seems to be a bigger problem than students rejecting it.

- *Enjoying Classes*. Although it is not surprising that students consider going further in classes they enjoy, it seems that for many students the extent to which they enjoy particular classes is an extremely strong motivator. Students pursue classes they enjoy, even when their personal goals are in other areas. When students do not enjoy classes, they can interpret that lack of enjoyment as a sign they are poorly suited for some area of CS, rather than as a problem with a particular teacher or class.

There are two things that we might have suspected would influence student behaviors but did not seem to, at least in the students we interviewed:

- *Detailed Understanding of the Specializations*. None of the students we interviewed had detailed knowledge of the courses they were considering. None the students referred to speaking to either faculty in the various specialization areas or trusted experts (e.g., other faculty, contacts from internships, etc.). None of them mentioned doing research for this decision beyond examining the CS department webpages. Sometimes, students even had very significant misconceptions about specializations they were considering. Overall, the impression the students gave was that they did not consider the selection of specialization areas to be a major decision.

- *A "Big Picture" Vision of CS*. Part of the argument for allowing students choices in their curriculum is that students' have individual opinions about what is exciting in Computer Science and want the freedom to design a multidisciplinary curriculum for themselves. Despite the language present in sources students used (such as the CS department website) students did not talk about things like computing's potential for innovation. Given the misconceptions students had about the content of the specializations, we are not sure that most of the students really had a clear enough understanding of what computation could do, to have a clear vision of computational innovation.

All the students we talked to were influenced by other normal forces that you might expect. Students were concerned about specializations that they had heard were academically difficult. Sometimes they preferred one specialization over another because it just "sounded more interesting". Advisors mentioned that students often selected specializations based on which could get them a degree most efficiently and by what specializations were thought to command the best salaries.

7. DISCUSSION

This theory suggests that students may not attach as much importance to curricular decisions as instructors and curriculum designers might hope. If we want to ensure students make well–informed curricular decisions, we need to treat the information about curriculum like any topic we teach. Students at Georgia Tech had taken a class that supposedly covered this material; perhaps more careful testing needs to be done to ensure students really understand what is being presented. Students may also be taking a cue from the fact that they never need to apply or officially 'declare' a specialization; by making the choice more explicit it might be possible to encourage students to evaluate their options more carefully.

Students were tentative about their goals in Computer Science; they were motivated by short term factors such as class enjoyment and were hesitant to commit to specific things they hoped to learn or do with CS. One of the rationales given for specialization–oriented curricula is such curricula allow students to pursue unique approaches that go beyond traditional CS degrees [7]. It seems that this sort of "big picture" goal does not come naturally to students. Students seem to like the idea of choice but that is not because they have a strong particular vision for themselves or the field of CS. With encouragement, students might be able to articulate a personal vision for CS. This kind of "big picture" view of CS might let students choose specializations without giving so much weight to classes they enjoyed or what specializations are easiest.

The extent to which bad experiences in classes were part of student curricular decisions is concerning. Obviously, no instructor designs a course to frustrate students. That said, a bad class seems to be able to exert long term effects on what courses students pursue in the future and how confident students feel as Computer Scientists. Even if some courses have to be difficult, there are plenty of ways to try and prevent student frustration from getting too high.

8. CONCLUSION

Although this study focused on the students at one particular CS department, we believe the results of this work can be useful in any CS program where students have to make significant decisions about what courses they should take. Students who feel strongly connected to the CS major are likely to take courses they view as "traditional", even if perhaps the longer term goals might benefit from exploration outside the major. Students who have had unenjoyable experiences in their CS classes are likely to try and select paths that let them avoid classes they feel ill–suited for. All students are likely to make curricular decisions based on a cursory understanding of what topics are covered and some students can have misconceptions about their courses that may cause real problems.

Although this paper has pointed out some significant issues with student curricular choice, it is worth emphasizing that the authors do not think the idea of student choice is necessarily a bad thing. In our interviews, students often remarked that they liked the idea of having choice. Beyond that, after graduation all CS major have to learn on their own if they intend to maintain their skills; graduates have to make educational choices. By understanding the difficulties students have with curricular decisions, we can help support students to make good choices in school as well as after graduation.

9. ACKNOWLEDGMENTS

This research supported in part by a grant from the National Science Foundation BPC Program #0634629.

10. REFERENCES

[1] A. W. Astin. *What Matters in College: Four Critical Years Revisited*. Jossey-Bass, Jan. 1997.

[2] M. Biggers, A. Brauer, and T. Yilmaz. Student perceptions of computer science. In *Proceedings of SIGCSE 2008*, pages 402–406, Portland, OR, USA, 2008. ACM.

[3] L. Carter. Why students with an apparent aptitude for computer science don't choose to major in computer science. In *Proceedings of SIGCSE 2006*, pages 27–31, Houston, Texas, USA, 2006. ACM.

[4] K. Charmaz. *Constructing Grounded Theory: A Practical Guide through Qualitative Analysis*. Sage Publications Ltd, 1 edition, Jan. 2006.

[5] Z. Dodds, R. Libeskind-Hadas, C. Alvarado, and G. Kuenning. Evaluating a breadth-first cs 1 for scientists. In *Proceedings of the 39th SIGCSE technical symposium on Computer science education*, pages 266–270, Portland, OR, USA, 2008. ACM.

[6] J. S. Eccles. Understanding women's educational and occupational choices. *Psychology of Women Quarterly*, 18(4):585–609, Dec. 1994.

[7] M. Furst, C. Isbell, and M. Guzdial. Threads: how to restructure a computer science curriculum for a flat world. In *Proceedings of SIGCSE 2007*, pages 420–424, Covington, Kentucky, USA, 2007. ACM.

[8] Geogia Tech CS Dept. BS computer science. http://www.cc.gatech.edu/future/undergraduates/bscs. Accessed 19-April-2011.

[9] T. Greening. Computer science: through the eyes of potential students. In *Proceedings of the 3rd Australasian conference on Computer science education*, pages 145–154, The University of Queensland, Australia, 1998. ACM.

[10] M. Hewner and M. Guzdial. Attitudes about computing in postsecondary graduates. In *Proceeding of the ICER 2008*, pages 71–78, Sydney, Australia, 2008. ACM.

[11] R. James. How school-leavers chose a preferred university course and possible effects on the quality of the school-university transition. *Journal of Institutional Research*, 9(1):78–88, 2000.

[12] J. W. McGuffee. Defining computer science. *SIGCSE Bull.*, 32(2):74–76, 2000.

[13] J. Nespor. *Knowledge in motion: Space, time, and curriculum in undergraduate physics and management*. Routledge, 1994.

[14] M. Sahami, A. Aiken, and J. Zelenski. Expanding the frontiers of computer science: designing a curriculum to reflect a diverse field. In *Proceedings of SIGCSE 2010*, pages 47–51, New York, NY, USA, 2010. ACM.

[15] R. Stevens, K. O'Connor, L. Garrison, A. Jocuns, and D. M. Amos. Becoming an engineer. *Journal of Engineering Education*, 97(3):355–368, 2008.

[16] WGBH Educational Foundation and ACM. New image for computing: Report on market research. http://www.acm.org/membership/NIC.pdf, 2009.

[17] A. Wigfield, J. S. Eccles, and D. Rodriguez. The development of children's motivation in school contexts. *Review of Research in Education*, 23:73–118, Jan. 1998.

CS Majors' Self-Efficacy Perceptions in CS1: Results in Light of Social Cognitive Theory

Päivi Kinnunen
University of Eastern Finland
Philosophical Faculty
School of Educational Sciences and Psychology
+358 13 251 4085

paivi.kinnunen@uef.fi

Beth Simon
Computer Science and Engineering Dept.
University of California, San Diego
La Jolla, CA 92093-0404
+01 858 534 5419

bsimon@cs.ucsd.edu

ABSTRACT

This paper discusses the results of a Grounded Theory study on students experience with introductory programming assignments in the light of social cognitive theory. In previous studies we have found CS majors experienced the process of doing CS1 programming assignments in different ways; but they universally made programming-related self-efficacy assessments along the way. Notably, students may reflect negatively on their self-efficacy after successfully completing an assignment, or positively after struggling with an assignment. CS majors tended to use their comparisons with self and classmates as a base for their self-efficacy perceptions. This paper takes a deeper look at these results from the lens of Bandura's self-efficacy theory with the goal of detailing viable pedagogical interventions to support students' introductory programming course experiences.

Categories and Subject Descriptors

K.3.2 [**Computer Science Education**]: Introductory Programming

General Terms

Human Factors.

Keywords

CS1, programming assignments, self-efficacy, Grounded Theory

1. INTRODUCTION

Although CS1 is a much-researched topic, there are not many studies on students' remembered experiences of programming assignments. However, since students often spend a lot of time doing the assignments we argue that assignment related experiences are important to study in more detail.

To name but a few CS1-related research topics, there are studies on how students understand (or misunderstand) some of the concepts and constructs introduced in CS1 [8, 28, 29], which content students find difficult to learn in CS1 courses [e.g. 14, 22, 23], and why students drop out of CS1 [11]. Others have also looked at students' experiences related to programming assignments. These studies can be placed roughly into three categories. First, there are studies that focus on students' behavior while doing programming assignments. For instance, Isohanni and Knoberstdorf [10] looked at how students use programming visualization tools when doing programming assignments in CS1. On the other hand, Murphy et al. [18] analyzed students' interactions during pair debugging. McCartney et al. studied [17] the help-seeking strategies of successful students. The studies by Robins, Haden &Garner [22] and Hanks [9] examined what kinds of problems students asked for help with in lab.

There are studies that focus on affective issues related to programming assignments. Ebel and Ben-Ari [7] characterized the affective effects of using programming visualization tools. Rodrigo and Baker [24] were also interested in students' affective reactions. They sought to automatically detect students' frustration while doing programming assignments in CS1 by looking at pairs of consecutive compilations. Simon and Hanks [27] looked qualitatively at students' experiences of pair programming in CS1.

Previously discussed studies do not bring forward how students remember the whole experience of doing the assignment after the fact. It is likely that when students are thinking about whether to persist with the CS major or not, they reflect, in hindsight, on their many experiences with the course. Thus we argue that remembered experiences are worthwhile to consider (not just their actions or questions). Since students' remembered experiences are mostly unknown in the field, we used a Grounded Theory approach, which is an appropriate research method for situations where prior knowledge does not exist in which to base hypotheses [31].

In this paper we further explore the results of a Grounded Theory (GT) study on how nine CS majors reflect on the experience of doing programming assignments in a CS1 course [12, 13]. One of the strongest themes that emerged from the study was the ways students constructed their programming related self-efficacy perceptions. Self-efficacy perception is defined here as "beliefs in one's capabilities to organize and execute the courses of action required to produce given attainments" [3, p. 3]. Previous studies have shown the importance of self-efficacy perceptions on performance outcome (for a meta-analytic review on domain-specific self-conceptions' role as a predictor of later academic achievement see [34]; for programming-specific self-efficacy see [35]). In this paper, we further explore our findings; seeking to define pedagogical interventions grounded in the literature of self-efficacy theories.

Previous studies on programming self-efficacy have demonstrated (by using quantitative measures) students' self-efficacy perceptions' predictive force for learning outcomes [21, 35]. Hence, we know that self-efficacy perceptions play a focal role in success in CS1 courses. However, we do not know exactly how students form self-efficacy perceptions in the context of first programming courses. Our Grounded Theory research differs from other research on programming-related self-efficacy perceptions in that it takes "a magnifying glass" and offers a deep, richly described look at episodes during which students construct their programming self-efficacy perceptions in CS1 courses.

In this paper we concentrate on interpreting our results through the lens of Bandura's self-efficacy theory (combined with a hint of goal orientation theory). We are aware that there are other theoretical frameworks through which we could analyze our results, such as Pintrich's theory of self-regulation [20]. However, here, we choose to concentrate on Bandura's theory because it helps us to analyze our results further. Additionally, this theoretical framework supports construction of actionable pedagogical interventions. Bandura's theory helps us to rise above the concrete level to see our results in the larger context of human behavior. It provides us greater depth in considering our results – beyond the definition of key characteristics of the student experience. We also believe that, by discussing our results in light of self-efficacy theory, we are able to reinforce the importance of viable pedagogical interventions that are anchored in theory rather than just anecdote or experience reports.

For clarity, the order of the representation deviates somewhat from the chronological order of our study (according to the tenets of Grounded Theory we first collected and analyzed the data and then draw the connections to existing theories). The paper is organized as follows. First, we shortly describe some focal aspects of social cognitive theory. Then we move on to our research procedure and the results. Both the procedure and the results have been reported previously elsewhere [12, 13] and are therefore only shortly summarized here. Next, we highlight a key finding of the results and discuss it in the light of social cognitive theory. The key finding is that students can develop self-efficacy beliefs that lie in contrast to their immediately preceding programming experience.

2. SOCIAL COGNITIVE THEORY

The core construct of social cognitive theory is self-efficacy. Bandura [3, 2] summarizes several focal factors of self-efficacy that are relevant for understanding our results. In this paper we limit our discussion mainly to the sources of self-efficacy and its influence on students' study-related behavior. Bandura's theory discusses people's actions in more general settings, but in the following sections we place his basic tenets into the context of learning when possible.

2.1 Roots of self-efficacy perceptions

Judgments of self-efficacy are mainly based on four sources [2]:

- Enactive attainments: Previously materialized attainments provide the strongest and highest increase in coping efficacy. On the other hand, repeated failures lower self-efficacy. This is especially true if repeated failures occur early in the course of events (in our context, studying programming).
- Vicarious experiences: Seeing similar others (peers) succeed in the task may raise efficacy expectations. This effect is based on the idea that modeling displays provide people with information on the nature of the event and thus people perceive they have more control over the event. However, vicarious experiences are not always positive. If a person with low self-efficacy perception sees a similar other (classmate) succeeding in a task, s/he might experience severe self-criticism.
- Verbal persuasion: Telling people they are able to complete a task may have a positive effect on self-efficacy if people consider the task to be realistic.
- Physiological state: Physiological cues (such as being tense or agitated in stressful situations) are interpreted as a sign of the possibility of not being able to complete the task.

There is no straightforward way of knowing how much each of the previously listed sources weighs when individuals judge their self-efficacy. Judgments are based on the learned strategy; which cues to use, how much each cue weighs in the decision, and how the information is interpreted. In addition, it is worthwhile remembering that self-efficacy perceptions vary across situations and activities. Thus, one experience of a high self-efficacy perception in one domain does not necessarily lead to high self-efficacy perceptions in later situations or other domains [2].

2.2 Changing self-efficacy beliefs

Since self-efficacy perceptions have such a profound influence on students, the question arises how instructors might help students enhance their self-efficacy perceptions. Previous work on sources of self-efficacy perceptions suggests that successful experiences would be the most powerful way to enhance students' perceptions [2]. However, it seems that enhancing perception is not straightforward when it comes to students with low self-efficacy perceptions. According to [2], low self-efficacy perceptions are not usually changed by a single successful performance (Bandura says self-efficacy perceptions are held in "provisional status"). If students (with low self-efficacy perception) encounter cues that suggest some deficiencies in their ability while successfully completing a task, the result is not enhanced, but rather lowered self-efficacy judgment.

Study by [1] provides evidence that setting proximal goals helps students to enhance their self-efficacy perception. Gaining mastery over several smaller subgoals (vs. one distant large goal) provides students with incentives and guidance for performance as well as indication of mastery of the skill. These small gains enhance self-efficacy perceptions.

2.3 Influence of self-efficacy perceptions

Self-efficacy perceptions affect several aspects of a person's choices and behavior. Theory by Bandura [3] discusses the influences of self-efficacy perceptions in a general context. In the following section we highlight the aspects of activities that we find are especially important in the context of studying programming.

Self-efficacy theories [3, 2] suggest that students' self-efficacy perceptions influence the course of action they choose to pursue. Students undertake activities that they believe they can succeed in and avoid activities they believe will exceed their abilities. Therefore, in order to encourage students to study, the study activities should be attainable (as judged by students). Second, self-efficacy perceptions influence how much effort students put forth when studying and how long they will persist when encountering difficulties and failures. In addition, students with strong self-efficacy beliefs are likely to persist with the task until they succeed. This aspect is especially interesting since learning to program often involves dealing with many different kinds of difficulties such as compiler and run-time errors. Third, self-efficacy perceptions influence students' thought patterns – whether the thought patterns are self-hindering or self-aiding (cf. fixed or growth mindset). Fourth, self-efficacy perceptions affect the level of stress students experience in taxing or tiresome situations. Finally, self-efficacy judgments also influence how students perceive their accomplishments.

Bandura [2] also emphasizes that self-efficacy perceptions alone do not predict behaviors well. Instead, self-efficacy perceptions combined with **outcome beliefs** (e.g., what people assume will be the outcome of their actions in the future), predict behaviors best. Bandura suggests four combinations of perceptions and outcome beliefs and their effect on behavior. Even though Bandura's examples reflect a broader context of people's life trajectories it is easy to see the parallels with narrower studying contexts as we discuss below.

First, there are people with high self-efficacy judgments who may judge a specific outcome as either positive or negative. If their outcome judgment is positive then these people feel reassured. If their outcome judgment is negative then people with high self-efficacy judgment still take actions (e.g., social activism, protest, grievance, and milieu change). Second, people with low self-efficacy judgment give up any action if they believe their actions do not produce the expected outcome. This may lead people to resignation and apathy. The negative emotions are highlighted further if relative-others are able to succeed in the same context. On the other hand, even in the cases where their outcome is judged as positive or expected, people with low self-efficacy judgment may devalue themselves and feel despondency. These four scenarios can be visualized as Figure 1.

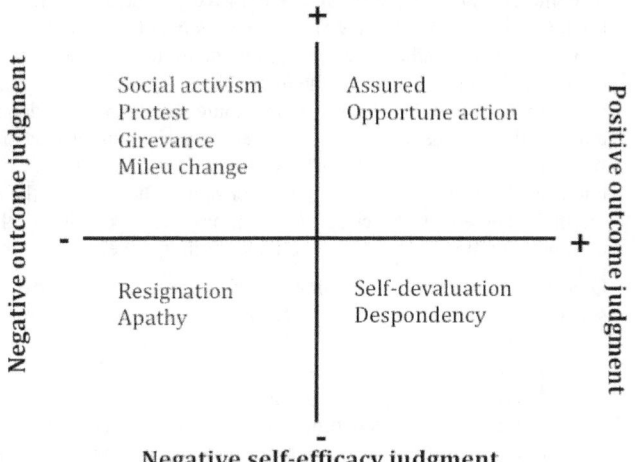

Figure 1 Effects of self-efficacy perceptions and outcome expectations on behavior and affective reactions [2, p. 140].

2.4 Moderators to self-efficacy

The study by O'Sullivan and Strauser [19] summarizes yet additional moderators to self-efficacy: motivation (internal vs. external motivators), worldview (individualistic vs. collectivistic cultures), socioeconomic status (low status affects efficacy perceptions negatively, high status positively), task difficulty (too-easy tasks do not enhance efficacy perceptions, too-hard tasks diminish efficacy perception), racial identity (People go through stages to establish the sense of racial identity. Here authors refer to how far a person is in the process of establishing his/her racial identity), and achievement goals (e.g. performance-oriented vs. mastery-oriented). These additional factors add dimensions to Figure 1 and complicate the model considerably.

From a pedagogical point of view, motivation, task difficulty, and achievement goals are interesting moderators since instructors can try to affect them. For instance, the learning environment affects students' orientations as demonstrated by Church, Elliot, and Gable [5]. Lecture engagement and the absence of focus on harsh evaluation fosters mastery orientation (intrinsic motivation, learning itself and self-improvement are important). A strong focus on evaluation in the class fosters performance-approach goals (it is important to demonstrate higher competence than peers in the class). Performance-oriented students score lower on self-efficacy than students with mastery orientation. [4.]

3. GROUNDED THEORY STUDY OF STUDENTS' EXPERIENCES

We started our research on computing majors in a CS1 course with a general research goal in mind: We wanted to know how students *remembered* the experience of doing the programming assignment shortly after the assignment was due. We believed that remembered experiences (versus observed, actual experiences) were of interest since they are the ones students walk away with from the lab. Remembered experiences seem likely to influence students' opinions regarding the study of computing and, later, perhaps their thoughts about whether CS is the right major for them. We chose to study programming assignment-related experiences because students report spending significant time doing the assignments in this course (compared to lectures, reading the text book, or labs). Thus, this work assumes programming assignment-related experiences are a focal part of students' general CS1 experience.

3.1 Procedure

The full description of our research procedure including a discussion of how to evaluate its quality is described in [12, 13]. Therefore, we only summarize the procedure here. In fall 2009 we collected the data from nine computing freshmen in the U.S. using repeated interviews. The nine interviewees were selected through a multi-phase selection procedure which sought to capture variation in previous programming experience and to over-represent women and minority students (to ensure maximum variation in the data). All interviews were voluntary.

Each of the nine students was interviewed five times during the fall term (every two weeks one or two days after the programming assignments were due). In total we conducted 45 interviews (20 – 55 minutes/interview) of which we used 36 for this study (the first interviews involved development of the study topic). Our interview protocol evolved during the course of four interviews covering topics including encountered difficulties and episodes leading to affective reactions (positive or negative) during the process of doing programming assignments. The same themes were always discussed with each of the interviewees. The interviewer was not part of the teaching team in the course and the preliminary discussions of the interviews did not affect how the course was delivered. The non-interviewing researcher was the course instructor, which led depth and explanatory power to the analysis of the interview data.

The course was taught using Java with a media-computation approach following the textbook by Guzdial and Ericson. The 10-week long course included lectures, weekly labs, and nine programming assignments (done using pair programming with fixed partners for the term). An example of the programming assignment is as follows: Make a song (a collage of sounds) using at least 4 methods (reverse, changePitch, one of a set we provided, and one of the student's own design).

The data was analyzed using open, axial, and selective coding as described in [31]. During selective coding we developed and reviewed the results of open and axial coding further and as a result we chose self-efficacy assessments as our core category. In our previous publications [12, 13] we have presented our results but have not discussed them deeply from the lens of existing theories, which is the contribution of this paper.

3.2 Validity discussion

We took measures both before and during the data collection and analysis phases to enhance the quality of our study. Before data collection we used prolonged engagement as suggested by Lincoln and Guba [16] to make sure we would be able to understand our interviewees. For instance, both researchers have first-hand experience of CS1 course from the student perspective and both have experience in studying students in CS1. Additionally, one researcher (not the interviewer) has taught CS1 for several years. During the partly overlapping data collection and analysis periods we used peer debriefing, field notes, and memos to enhance validity [16, 31]. In addition, our choice to use multiple interviews with the same students made it possible to get richer data: We were able to adjust the interview protocol from one interview round to the next based on the preliminary results (as suggested by [31]). In addition, over time, students became more comfortable talking to the interviewer, which resulted in richer and more personal information from students.

A weakness of our study lies in the lack of data triangulation. We only used students' interviews for this analysis. Additional observations of actual programming experiences would have provided an interesting comparison to students' remembered experiences. This would be an interesting subject for future work.

Since our interviewees were in a CS1 course that uses a media computation approach with pair programming, readers will have to make their own judgments as to how far our results are transferable to other types of CS1 courses. However, despite some of the unique characteristics of the course studied, we believe that our results provide useful insights to students' self-efficacy related experiences in CS1 courses of various flavors.

4. RESULTS

Through the analysis process we were able to distinguish several different levels of results. As a result of open and axial coding we were able to construct a six-phase process (getting started, encountering difficulty, dealing with difficulties, succeeding, submitting, and stopping) (Figure 2) [12]. Each of the phases of the process included emotion-induced mini-phenomena that described students' experiences during that phase. For instance, during the encountering difficulty phase some students had 'Hit by lightning' experiences that illustrate the total surprise of encountering a difficulty (such as compiler errors). Since self-efficacy assessments were clearly an overarching theme that was present in one form or another in all previously found mini-phenomena we selected it as our core category. In the following sections we summarize students' self-efficacy assessments in four varying contexts that emerged from our data.

As demonstrated in Figure 3, the following four stories (quarters in Figure 3) can be organized in a similar way to Bandura's model (Figure 1). However, there is one notable difference. Our results combine students' self-efficacy perceptions and **realized study episodes as interpreted by students** (vs. assumed or expected outcomes as in Bandura's model). Next we discuss each quarter (Figure 3) but emphasize the theoretical parallels with Bandura's self-efficacy theory, which might help us find ways to help more students succeed in their studies.

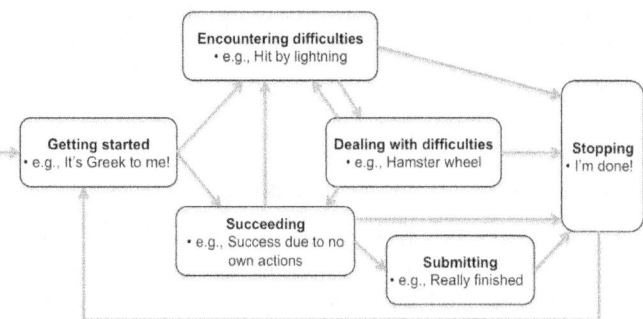

Figure 2 Six stages and an example of a student experience associated with each phase. The stages and the phenomena are reported in more detail in [12, 13].

1) Quarter 1: I will succeed eventually (negative experience, positive self-efficacy assessment).

This describes the situation where students had been struggling and had not got the assignment done yet. This often happened in the 'dealing with difficulties' -stage. Despite the negative programming episode, students felt positively about their ability to complete the task eventually. Cognitively, students were off-track (not knowing what to do). However, students did not despair and give up, but rather interpreted the situation in the context of being in the course; surely the instructor wouldn't have given them an impossible assignment, it should be doable. Students' emotional reactions to the situation were negative (annoyance and frustration) but not overly negative. In addition, students did not compare their own accomplishments (or rather, their lack of them) or their perceived "fluency with the process" of doing the assignment with the abilities or actions of other students.

Quarter 1 represents the combination of programming episode and self-efficacy judgment that is preferable, especially in the context of learning programming. It is likely that all students face some kind of difficulties while studying programming and have to learn to deal with negative programming episodes (such as having to deal with compiler or run time errors). One difference between quarter one and four is that students who think they will overcome difficulties eventually seem to be able to place the current problem in the context of the course ("*I wasn't really that stressed 'cause I knew she wouldn't hand us an impossible assignment*" [I5-J]) Alternately, they express confidence in their own problem solving abilities in general. Another discriminating feature seems to be that, in these cases, students did not seem to compare their situation with that of other students. One possible explanation for the lack of comparisons is that these students may have adopted a mastery-orientation towards learning (intrinsic motivation, self-improvement is important).

2) Quarter 2: I am good at this (positive experience, positive self-efficacy assessment).

This describes the situation where students had experienced a positive programming episode (e.g., had been able to fix a bug) and therefore felt positively about their ability to program. These experiences often emerged during the 'getting started' ("I know how to do this assignment"), 'succeeding', 'submitting', and 'stopping' -phases. Cognitively, students were on-track (knew what to do/understood why something worked). Students' emotional reactions included feelings of accomplishment and happiness. Physiological sensations of being relaxed and having low levels of stress corroborated students' positive self-efficacy assessment. Students used comparisons with themselves (e.g., how long did it take to complete the assignment compared to previous assignments) and other students (e.g., how did I do compared with my peers in the class) as a cue when constructing their self-efficacy assessment.

Quarter 2 represents the unsurprising combination of a positive programming episode and high self-efficacy judgment. From a pedagogical point of view, this combination is not problematic. In our data, students used several "comparison points" to come up with this judgment. Students interpreted the episodes in the light of how they did in their own previous programming experiences, how others in the course did, and their fluency with the process of doing the assignment. Especially if the code worked on the first try, students interpreted it as a sign of "really understanding" the topic (cf. from the professional point of view getting something right on the first try is not always realistic). Therefore, even though this is a non-problematic combination of high self-efficacy and positive programming episode, it is good to keep in mind that not all students' judgments are based on valid notions, which might cause problems later on.

3) Quarter 3: Severe hindsight (positive experience, negative self-efficacy assessment).

Positive programming episodes did not always lead students to assess their self-efficacy positively. Sometimes students reflected on the programming episode (that had a positive outcome) with severe hindsight. They thought that they should have been able to complete assignment sooner or with less effort. Severe hindsight often occurred in the 'encountering difficulties', 'succeeding', and 'stopping' -phases. Cognitively, students were on-track. Emotional reactions included feelings of being pathetic, stupid, or dumb. A low self-efficacy assessment was reached by comparing their "fluency" with the programming process and their own cognitive processes to previous episodes.

Quarter 3 represents a somewhat surprising combination of positive programming episode and negative self-efficacy judgment. According to Bandura's theory these students could be the ones that hold their low self-efficacy perceptions in "provisional status" even in the face of positive experiences. Maybe the positive programming episode (such as being able to submit the assignment) was a result of a process during which students got many negative cues (e.g. needed a lot of help, it took a long time get the assignment done), but eventually succeeded.

4) Quarter 4: I am not good at this (negative experience, negative self-efficacy assessment).

Negative programming episodes often led to negative self-efficacy assessments. This combination frequently happened during the 'getting started', 'encountering difficulties', and 'dealing with difficulties' phases. Cognitively, students were off-track and disoriented. Emotional reactions were negative including feelings of apprehensiveness, frustration, and feeling stupid. Physiological sensations of being tired corroborated the negative experience. Students used comparison with self (fluency with the programming process, cognitive abilities) and other students in the course (their fluency with the process and outcome of the process) as a cue to form their self-efficacy assessments.

Quarter 4 represents the unsurprising combination of negative programming event and low self-efficacy judgment. According to Bandura, people with low self-efficacy judgment and negative outcome expectancy may experience resignation and apathy. Our data corroborated the experience of resignation. The following quote illustrates an interpretation of an episode by a student who had recently been struggling with a programming assignment (side note: This student got the assignment done eventually and he

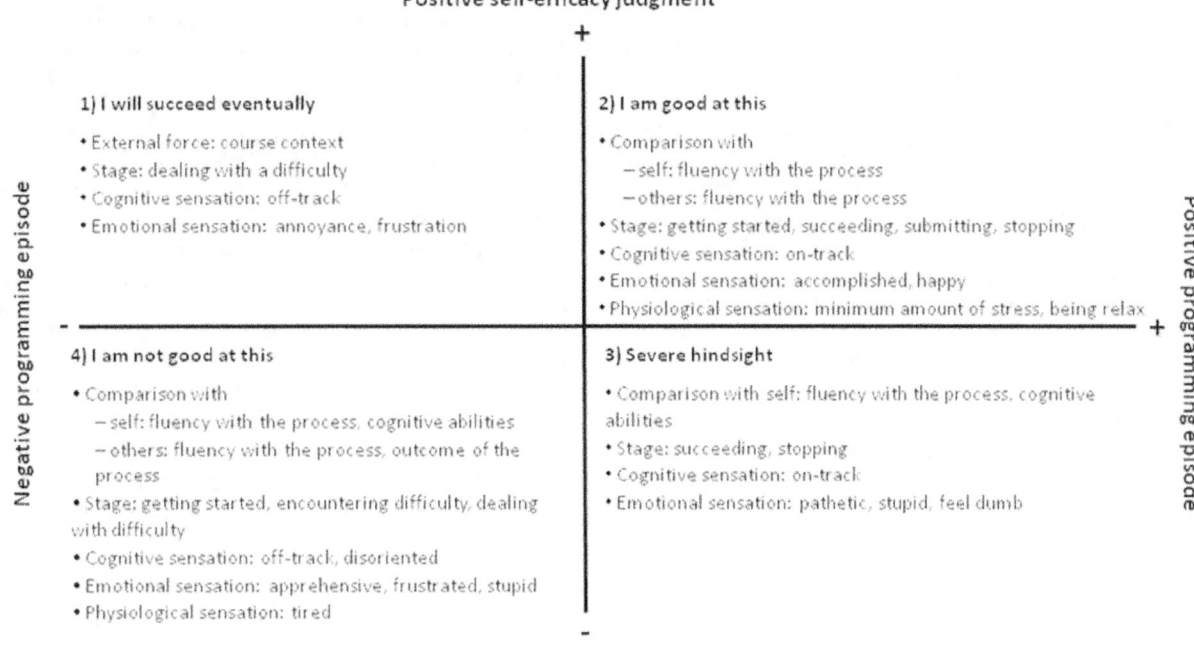

Figure 3 Results of Grounded Theory study as seen through self-efficacy theory

also finished the course with an average grade (B). Nevertheless, he had already decided during the course to change his major; which he did).

> *I felt stupid I guess you could say because I've seen other people be like alright, da, da, da, da, da. They do stuff that's like way beyond what I could do at my current level, even though we're in the same class.... Like there are people that really get it and it takes them like less than three hours to finish and they create something that looks outstanding and they did something that goes above and beyond what's called for in the PSA. So it makes you feel a little inferior, like okay. [12-F]*

What is striking about this example is how much weight this student puts on how he is doing compared with others. This could be an indication of performance-orientation towards studying (it is important to demonstrate higher competence than peers in the class). This example also illustrates some of the possible factors behind the cases where good or average students (as judged by course grade) decide to leave the CS major.

The common theme to all four combinations of self-efficacy assessment and the remembered programming episode was students' tendency to compare the programming episode (and the outcome from it) with their own previous experiences and the perceived experiences of their classmates. When comparing with their own experiences, students took notice of the time it took to complete the assignment (or fix a bug), how much help they needed while doing the assignment, how happy they were with the outcome of the assignment (the edited picture or sound), and how much they struggled cognitively while doing the assignment.

When comparing their own episode with classmates' episodes students looked at the time it took for classmates to complete the task, what their outcome looked like, and whether classmates asked for help from the student (and were they able to help with the problem). All these comparisons had the possibility to lead the student either to positive or negative self-efficacy assessment depending on other factors impacting the situation.

5. DISCUSSION

Several aspects of self-efficacy theory considered in conjunction with the results of our Grounded Theory study provide suggestions to instructors who wish to enhance students' self-efficacy perceptions and, hence, also **academic performance.** Our analysis in light of Bandura's theory suggests the following:

Avoid repeated failures at the beginning of learning process: repeated failures (especially) at the early stage of the learning process lowers self-efficacy. There are instructional approaches and tools in CS that have been designed to reduce students' experiences with syntactic-related difficulties, for example, Alice and Scratch, Greenfoot, and novice IDEs like Dr. Java.

Attainable, concrete subgoals and/or benchmarks along the way may help students to monitor how far they have got and what else they still need to do to complete an assignment. One approach in this vein was that of Spacco, where students are engaged in early and frequent submission to a set of instructor tests [30].

Learning tasks should be at optimal difficulty level; not too easy or too hard. Studies of the habits of highly effective tutors indicate that tutors work hard to engage students with a next problem that best matches and slightly extends their current learning state [15]. Providing different difficulty-level options for the same assignment would give students an option to choose the one that they find challenging enough for their current ability level. This might be accomplished within the format of lab-centric computing [32] where learning material, and the opportunity to test ones' self on that material is provided in a gated format, allowing the student to test their understanding before moving on.

Take care with the learning environment and especially the classroom climate. Standard "science" classroom models which focus on information transmission and where "one answer" appears to exist for any problem often leads students to feel they don't belong to a community, and can encourage students to leave majors where such classrooms predominate [33]. In contrast, *classroom situations which engage students in peer discussion* [6] *and active learning may help students foster a mastery orientation* – focused around understanding what they know (mastery students score higher in self-efficacy).

In conclusion, we would like to highlight two aspects of our own results, as seen through self-efficacy theory, and discuss how instructors could use them in the classroom. We will highlight two somewhat surprising combinations of self-efficacy judgment and positive/negative programming episode; "I will succeed eventually" (quarter one) and "Severe hindsight" (quarter three). While some students struggle but still feel they are able to succeed eventually others do not allow themselves to feel good about success. From a pedagogical point of view it is important to know what makes some students keep a positive mindset about their abilities even when struggling and not sink into quarter four ("I am not good at this"). On the other hand, how could we help more students to climb up from "severe hindsight" to "I am good at this" experience? One obvious place to look for answers is to compare the quarter one and four with each other and quarter two and three each other.

One striking difference between "I will succeed eventually" and "I am not good at this" experiences is that in those cases where students had confidence in their abilities they placed the experience of difficulty in the context of being in a course – the assignment should be doable. Second, at the times students were confident when struggling they did not seem to compare the current situation to the success of others. In a sense, students isolated the negative experience (interpreted it as part of their own learning process vs. comparing it with others' processes) and interpreted it as contextualized in the course. Based on these notions, our suggestion is to *share this story with students and encourage them to see their negative experiences in the context of a course* – in a way encourage students to "have faith" that the instructor knows what s/he is doing and would not overburden students.

In addition, when discussing with students in the classroom about how to deal with the difficulties in the course, it would be important *to bring up the risk of misinterpretation when seeing other students succeeding with apparent easiness*. What you see is not always the whole truth. Maybe the student who completes the assignment quickly and efficiently in the lab has been studying at home before coming to the lab or s/he might have previous programming experience.

To counter the perceived view that others are "getting it" more easily, accurate information on the experiences of others could be helpful. *Near peer mentors (e.g., students from the previous cohort) may be able to share their experiences and keep students' assessments realistic*. Another option might be to develop tutoring videos [25] or debugging videos [26] which can not only show off what challenges others are (also) facing, but also model desired cognitive processes. These measures may also give students a sense of control over the learning process – a better idea of what is going to need to happen to get them from the problem specification to a "working" program. This is especially important since according to [2] the sense of control (as gained through vicarious experiences) is an important factor in self-efficacy judgments. Near peer tutoring might also help students with severe hindsight (quarter three). Even though students in quarter three do not compare themselves to other students they still could benefit from shared experiences of how others have had to struggle before completing assignments but have still been successful students in their CS studies. Another option to help students not get stuck in a low self-efficacy assessment-mode is to *provide students several clear benchmarks and sub-goals within the programming assignment* that students can use to make reasonable and realistic judgments concerning their skills. Making progress visible and concrete should help students to grow their self-efficacy perceptions [1].

6. CONCLUSION

In this study we have discussed the results of a Grounded Theory study on how CS majors experience the process of doing programming assignments in a CS1 course. Specifically, we have looked at our results through the theoretical framework of social cognitive theory in order to place our results into a larger context. In our presentation we did not follow the chronological order of our study. Instead we introduced the theoretical framework first and then discussed our results. This decision, which might sound weird for those familiar with Grounded Theory approach, was done for the clarity of the presentation.

The social cognitive theory guided our suggestions for practical pedagogical interventions to improve students' self-efficacy, and hopefully academic performance and persistence. We specifically highlight lessons to be learned from the surprising combinations of positive experience and negative self-efficacy assessment (severe hindsight) and negative experience and positive self-efficacy assessment (I will succeed eventually). In many CS1 courses, students spend a lot of their study time doing programming assignments. Therefore, it is also likely that students' programming assignment related experiences affect their overall experience with the course (and maybe also with the CS major in general). Thus, we recommend that more studies should be done on the role of programming assignments, and how students experience them. Additional studies on students' experiences with other parts of the course (such as lectures) would provide a more comprehensive picture of how students experience the course as a whole and how that experience affects students' orientation towards studying and ultimately, potentially, their decision to persist in CS.

7. AKNOWLEDGEMENTS

This work is supported by the National Science Foundation under NSF CNS-0933635. We thank the students who so generously talked to us and to Dov Zazkis for his help on this project.

8. REFERENCES

[1] Bandura, A. 1981. Cultivating Competence, Self-Efficacy, and Intrinsic Interest Through Proximal Self-Motivation. *Journal of Personality and Social Psychology*, 41(3), 586–598.

[2] Bandura, A. 1982. Self-Efficacy Mechanism in Human Agency. *American Psychologist*, 37(2), 122–147.

[3] Bandura, A. 1997. Self-Efficacy. *The Exercise of Control*. New York: W.H. Freeman.

[4] Bråten, I., Samuelstuen, M. S., and Strømsø, *H. I. 2004*. Do Students' Self-efficacy Beliefs Moderate the Effects of Performance Goals on self –Regulatory Strategy Use? *Educational Psychology*, 24(2), 231–247.

[5] Church, M. A., Elliot, A. J., and Gable, *S. L. 2001*. Perceptions of Classroom Environment, Achievement Goals, and Achievement Outcomes. *Journal of Educational Psychology*, 93(1), 43–54.

[6] Crouch, C. H. and Mazur, E. 2001. Peer instruction: Ten years of experience and results. *American Journal of Physics*, 69, 970–977.

[7] Ebel, G. and Ben-Ari, M. 2006. Affective Effects of Program Visualization. *Proceedings of the second international workshop on Computing education research (ICER'06)*. Canterbury, UK, 1–5.

[8] Eckerdahl, A. and Thuné, M. 2005. Novice Java Programmers' Conceptions of "Object" and "Class", and Variation Theory. *ACM SIGCSE Bull.*, 37(3), 89–93.

[9] Hanks, B. 2008. Problems Encountered by Novice Pair Programmers. *ACM J. Educ. Resour. Comput.* 7, 4, Article 2.

[10] Isohanni, E. and Knoberstdorf, M. 2010. Behind the Curtain: Students' Use of VIP after Class. *Proceedings of the sixth international workshop on Computing education research (ICER'10)*, August 9–10, 2008, Aarhus, Denmark, 87–96.

[11] Kinnunen, P. and Malmi, L. 2008. CS Minors in a CS1 Course. *Proceedings of the fourth international workshop on Computing education research (ICER'08)*, September 6–7, 2008, Sydney, Australia, 79–90.

[12] Kinnunen, P. and Simon, B. 2010. Experiencing Programming Assignments in CS1: The Emotional Toll. *Proceedings of the sixth international workshop on Computing education research (ICER '10)*, August 9–10, 2010, Aarhus, Denmark, 77–86.

[13] Kinnunen, P. & Simon, B. My program is ok - Am I? - Computing freshmen's experiences of doing programming assignments. Manuscript submitted for publication.

[14] Lahtinen, E., Ala-Mutka, K., and Järvinen, H.-M. 2005. A study of the difficulties of novice programmers. *ACM SIGCSE Bull.*, 37(3), 14–18.

[15] Lepper, M., Woolverton, M., 2002. *The Wisdom Of Practice: Lessons Learned from the Habits of Highly Effective Tutors. In Improving Academic Achievement.* Elsevier Science. 135-158.

[16] Lincoln, Y. & Guba, E. 1985. *Naturalistic Inquiry*. Newbury Park: Sage Publications.

[17] McCartney, R., Eckerdal, A., Moström, J. E., Sanders, K., Zander, C. 2007. Successful students' strategies for getting unstuck. *ACM SIGCSE Bull.*, 39(3), 156–160.

[18] Murphy, L., Fitzgerald, S., Hanks, B., and McCauley, R. 2010. Pair Debugging: A Transactive Discourse Analysis. *Proceedings of the sixth international workshop on Computing education research (ICER'10)*, August 9–10, 2008, Aarhus, Denmark, 51–58.

[19] O'Sullivan, D. and Strauser, D. 2009. Operationalizing Self-Efficacy, Related Social Cognitive Variables, and Moderating Effects. *Rehabilitation Counseling Bulletin*, 52(4), 251–258.

[20] Pintrich, P. R. 2000. *The Role of Goal Orientation in Self-Regulated learning* in Boakaerts, M., Pintrich, P. R., and

Zeidner, M. (Eds.) Handbook of Self-Regulation. Academic press: San Diego.

[21] Ramalingam, V., LaBelle, D. and Wiedenbeck, A. 2004. Self-Efficacy and Mental Models in Learning to Program. *ACM SIGCSE Bull.*, 36(3), 17–175.

[22] Robins, A., Haden, P., and Garner, S. 2006. Problem distributions in a CS1 course. In *Proceedings of the 8th Australian Conference on Computing Education (ACE'06)*. 165–173.

[23] Robins, A., Rountree, J., and Rountree, N. 2003. Learning and Teaching Programming: A Review and Discussion." *Computer Science Education*, 13(2), 137–172.

[24] Rodrigo, M., Baker, R. 2009. Coarse-Grained Detection of Student Frustration in an introductory Programming Course. *Proceedings of the third international workshop on computing education research (ICER'07)*. September 15–16, 2007, Atlanta, Georgia, USA, 75–80.

[25] Scotty D., Michelene, C, Chi, T. H., and VanLehn, K. 2009. Improving Classroom Learning by Collaboratively Observing Human Tutoring Videos While Problem Solving. *Journal of Educational Psychology*. 101(4), 779–78.

[26] Simon, B., Fitzgerald, S., McCauley, R., Haller, S., Hamer, J., Hanks, B., Helmick, M. T., Moström, J-E., Sheard, J., Thomas, L. 2007. Debugging assistance for novices: a video repository. *ACM SIGCSE Bull.* 39, 4 (December 2007), 137–151.

[27] Simon, B., Hanks, B. 2008. First-Year Students' Impressions of Pair Programming in CS1. *ACM J. Educ. Resour. Comput.* 7, 4, Article 5.

[28] Sorva, J. 2007. Students' understandings of storing objects. *Proceedings of Seventh Baltic Sea Conference on Computing Education Research (Koli Calling 2007)*, Koli National Park, Finland.

[29] Sorva, J. 2008. The same but different. Students' understandings of primitive and object variables. *Proceedings of Eighth Baltic Sea Conference on Computing Education Research (Koli Calling 2007)*, Koli National Park, Finland.

[30] Spacco, J., Hovemeyer, D., Pugh, W. Emad, F. Hollingsworth, J. K., and Padua-Perez, N. 2006. Experiences with marmoset: designing and using an advanced submission and testing system for programming courses. *ACM SIGCSE Bull.* 38, 3 (June 2006), 13–17.

[31] Strauss, A. and Corbin, J. 1990. *Basics of Qualitative Research: Grounded Theory Procedures and Techniques*. Newbury Park, CS: Sage Publications.

[32] Titterton, N., Lewis, C., and Clancy, M. 2010. Experience with lab-centric instruction. *Computer Science Education*, 20(2), 79–102.

[33] Tobias, S. 1994. *They're Not Dumb, They're Different: Stalking the Second Tier*. Tucson, AZ: Research Corporation.

[34] Valentine, J. C., DuBois, D. L., and Cooper, H. 2004. The Relation Between Self-Beliefs and Academic Achievement: A Meta-Analytic Review. *Educational Psychologist*, 39(2), 111–133.

[35] Wiedenbeck, S. 2005. Factors Affecting the Success of Non-Majors in Learning to Program. *Proceedings of the first international workshop on Computing education research (ICER'05)*, October 1-2, 2005, Seattle, WA USA, 13–24.

Research Design: Necessary Bricolage

Sally Fincher
Computing Laboratory
University of Kent
Canterbury, CT2 7NF, England
+44 1227 824061
S.A.Fincher@kent.ac.uk

Josh Tenenberg
Computer Science & Systems
University of Washington, Tacoma
Tacoma, WA 98402-3100 USA
+1 253 692 5800
jtenenbg@uw.edu

Anthony Robins
Computer Science Department
University of Otago
Dunedin 9015, New Zealand
+64 3 479 8314
anthony@cs.otago.ac.nz

ABSTRACT
In this paper we suggest that in order to advance, the field of computer science education needs to craft its own research methods, to augment the borrowing of "traditional" methods such as semi-structured interviews and surveys from other research traditions. Two example instruments used in our recent research are discussed. We adopt the metaphor of "bricolage" to characterise not only what researchers do, but to argue that this may be a necessary step towards developing theory.

Categories and Subject Descriptors
K.3.2 [**Computer and Information Science Education**]: Computer Science Education

General Terms
Design

Keywords
Research methods, bricolage. research design.

1. INTRODUCTION
The methods that we use to investigate learning within the discipline embed assumptions about learning, human capabilities, social life, and the bio-physical world. For example, Eckerdal et al (2005) explored first-year student understandings of *object* and *class*, employing semi-structured interviews and a phenomenographic analysis. These interview studies take for granted that human speech provides an accurate account of an individual's phenomenological experience of a situation, and that research subjects will disclose their sentiments accurately to an interviewer with whom they have no prior relationship. Or consider the observational studies of Barker et al (2002) to gain insight into "the student experience of the social environment" in the Computer Science classroom. These methods embed the assumption that researchers immersed in (and taking contemporaneous field notes about) the ongoing cultural and material worlds of their research subjects will gain understanding of the social meanings of human interaction within the observed setting.

As educational researchers, methods are our toolbox, our stock in trade, the hammers and shovels that provide purchase for gaining insight into teaching and learning. As we have argued elsewhere (Fincher & Petre 2004, Tenenberg & McCartney 2010), there are a number of extant methods that we can borrow from, developed in other human sciences. In this paper, however, we make a different and contrasting argument: that there are cases when we need to craft our own methods, or reshape tools to better suit the phenomena that we wish to investigate.

When students are engaged in a task, whether learning new syntactic concepts, or practicing programming skills, there is a portion of the endeavour, maybe the largest portion, that is not externally visible. Yet we, as researchers, are interested in this. Exactly when does a student get their program working? What do they feel at that point—triumph? Success? A weary recognition of another step taken? And does what they feel affect their motivation for the next task? Do they work on problems alone, what scaffolding do they perceive in their environment—and what do they use? How does their knowledge build over time, and how does their understanding develop?

None of these tasks and processes (nor their associated research questions) are discrete enough to be studied in a controlled setting, none can be performed to order, and many happen outside of the gaze of others. As researchers, we have to find methods that permit us to examine these without our continuing presence.

The class of problems, then, that we are interested in concern ephemeral events, that may have occurred in the past, and are not amenable to direct observation. We think that these three characteristics, which we call *researcher-distant,* are present for many aspects of CSEd research, aspects that are currently served by less well-suited methods, such as semi-structured interviews or questionnaires. By *researcher-distant*, we mean not distant of influence – we are, after all, researchers actively pursuing questions – but distant of perspective. We want to allow the participants to expose their world as they see it; we don't want to focus on features which seem to us to be prominent, from our standpoint a rather long way away.

2. RESEARCH FOCUS
We were interested – as are many – to study novice programming students. We are in the process of exploring two central research questions, each informed by a research tradition. The first question concerns what cognitive strategies novice students pursue in programming, and how these are related to the material and social support that is available to them. We are pursuing this from a cultural-historical perspective (Vygotsky 1978, Rogoff 2003, Cole 1998) that takes activity as its focus, and examines how internal mental operations are mediated by external resources, including tools and symbolic representations, as well as social interaction.

Our other question concerns what narratives students tell about their programming activities, and how these are related to their identity as programmers. We seek not only descriptive accounts of activities, but also stories that relate individual identity to programming. Narratives of the self are an important genre of research into identity (e.g. Mishler 1991, Labov 1967). These narratives, according to Bruner (1987), have a reciprocal influence on the teller: not only do we tell the lives we live, "we *become* the autobiographical narratives by which we 'tell about' our lives" (Bruner 1987).

The current paper describes our growing realisation that exploring these questions requires new tools, and gives a preliminary description of two of the tools that we have developed, *My Programming Week* and *Emotional Timelines*.

3. MY PROGRAMMING WEEK

> "What happened here? Well let's see.
> On a central square, in a city of the sun rose a palace.
> It was high and handsome gleaming like the crown of a king."
> Adam Guettel, *Light in the Piazza*

Were we investigating these questions in the 1970's, when we learned to program, an obvious choice would be ethnographic observation and interviews in the centralized computing laboratories, since this is the only place where computers (and hence programmers) could be found. "Obvious" because of the taken-for-granted social interactions that might not be elicited through interviews off-site; because immersion *in situ* makes resources (both human and material) available to the researcher; because human interaction is ongoing, discursive, gestural, fluid, multi-valenced and meaning-laden, all features which are visible to the ethnographically-trained researcher.

But computing in the early 21st century is not physically constrained to centralized computing laboratories. The social, material, and technological organisation of learning has changed dramatically during the last several decades. Currently, the spaces and times where learning to program occurs, and the physical and social resources available vary by student, by time, by need, by opportunity. If we wanted to see where learning to program happens today, *where would we go*?

Although an ethnographic approach might still be useful, it would be infeasible for us, as researchers, to follow students around all the time, observing when and how they worked. This would not only be burdensome, but would face insurmountable issues of access and privacy. So we had to devise a proxy.

3.1 Recording

Without access to the relevant spaces, another option was to conduct retrospective interviews, where students recall what they do when they learn to program. This was methodologically attractive, but we were concerned that students would not have ready linguistic access to their own practices, particularly since practice knowledge is something that is often tacit and enacted, rather than rule-based and explicitly understood (Collins 2001, Polanyi 1966, Sternberg 1999). We thus augmented a retrospective interview with a student-generated representation of their programming activity designed to serve both as a record, and as a stimulus to recall.

In order to ground the study in concrete activity, we chose to focus on a single week centered around a single programming assignment, which we refer to as *my programming week*. We hoped to elicit students' natural patterns and rhythms of activity, to determine the resources they call on both in workaday activity and when they get stuck, and the stories they tell of their efforts.

Just after students were assigned a programming assessment (due one week later) we provided them with a grid, on a single side of a single sheet of paper, which had a cell for every hour of a seven-day week. The instructions we gave them were to note on the paper any time they did anything related to programming– thinking about it, talking over problems, consulting notes, creating design documents, reading textbooks, looking for material online, coding. We also asked them to note the *space* they were in when they did the noted activity, and, for each new space they encountered, to take a *photograph*.

At the end of the week–as close to the finish of the task as possible–we invited the students to a debriefing session. In this we asked them to talk through their week, from start to end. Unlike unstimulated recollection, the diary grid and photographs allowed them to index their episodic knowledge (Tulving 2002) about the activity represented.

3.2 Photo elicitation

Our use of photographs borrows from the use of visual methods in the social sciences (see (Pink 2007) and (Harper 2002)). In his ethnographic study of a handyman in rural, upstate New York, Douglas Harper (1987) wanted to record the complex interaction between Willie (the handyman) and the tools and materials with which he was so skillfully engaged. But Harper wanted as well to have a shared reference that Willie and he could both look at and from which Harper could probe more deeply into Willy's tacit, embodied knowledge. What then, was Harper to capture on film? "The question of what to photograph became, in fact, the question of how to see things at least roughly as Willie saw them"

Harper used a method that he borrowed from John Collier [1967] that Collier called *photo elicitation*. "In the photo elicitation interview the subject and the interviewer discuss the researcher's photographs, giving the interview a concrete point of reference. This approach is different from other sociological interviews because a photograph, rather than an interviewer's question (which may or may not make sense to the individual being interviewed), is the focus of attention. Roles are reversed as the subject becomes the teacher" (Harper 1987).

If the point is to see what the subject sees, and if access to the research site is off-limits or difficult to obtain, then the obvious solution is to place the camera into the hands of the research subject. *They* decide how little or how much to expose, they choose what to reveal and what to obscure. We were influenced in this choice, of putting the camera into the hands of research participant, by a set of data collection methods called *Cultural Probes* (Gaver et al 1998). Designers Gaver, Dunne, and Pacenti, asked participants to take photographs within their communities so as to better understand the local culture and tacit needs related to an exploratory design project "looking at novel interaction techniques to increase the presence of the elderly in their local communities."

3.3 Interview

At the end of the week, we interviewed participants, with their grids and photos to hand. Our interview protocol involved the following sequence of prompts and activities.

First, we asked them to annotate their photos with the resources available to them at that place. We considered a resource to be anything external to them that they made use of in their programming activities. These might include images and text (in textbooks, handouts, etc), media for writing these (pencils, paper), communication tools (cell phones, email), hardware/software systems (computers, IDE's, compilers, debuggers, web browsers). We expected that they would take many of the resources that they use for granted, so we used the photographs to gently probe, pointing to specific objects and asking about them. We then asked them which photos were associated with which times on their weekly grid.

We then asked them to note the people with whom they interacted in each of the locations. This interaction might be face-to-face or technologically-mediated: we asked them to indicate this as well.

We then elicited the specific programming-related activities they performed at different locations. This was achieved by means of questions such as "what were you doing in these four hours [pointing to a marked area of the calendar grid]?" and "what happened here [pointing to a photograph]?" In addition to asking descriptive questions about resources, people, and activities, we asked "why" questions to elicit the rationale that links these together. "Why did you choose to work here at this time?" "Do you recall why you emailed your tutor just then?"

At this point, we asked them to try to provide a *narrative* account of their programming week. Rather than a set of loosely-related locations, resources, and human interactions, we asked them to provide a coherent "story", told in chronological order.

Finally, if these had not already come out in the previous discussion, we asked two *critical incident* (Klein 1999) questions. The first highlighted the point of greatest tension or challenge, and if (and how) they overcame this challenge. The second critical incident question was concerned with any learning breakthroughs they might have had during their week of programming activity.

Our purpose here is not to provide a full analysis of this data, but rather to highlight the qualities of the material these instruments permit us to garner.

3.4 Stimulated recall

Unlike unstimulated recollection, the diary grid allowed participants to easily index back to the activity represented, they were able to recall not only where they were, but who they were with and what they were doing.

The *patterns* on the grid also allowed us easy access to less helpful practices. A grid with solid blocks of hours of students working alone often indicated that they were stuck on a problem (although not always).

INTERVIEWER: So the one thing I'm curious about is if this general shape of work, so it looks like fairly large blocks. Some amount at home, some amount at the labs. Is this what most weeks look like?

PARTICIPANT: Usually. I'm a night owl, so I prefer to do most of my work in the evenings, which kind of goes along with, you know, most of the computer industry, computing industry. Gaming industry. You know, that sort of thing.

3.5 The photographic window

In one interview, the student provided a photograph of their bedroom, where they do much of their programming work.

In the following sample of the interaction between interviewer and participant, the photo serves two purposes: it provides a point of mutual reference to which both attend at the same time, and it serves to stimulate recall from the research subject.

INTERVIEWER: What's up here [points to desk at top of photograph]?

PARTICIPANT: My notebook for when I take notes in class and just my folder with the various printouts and stuff for..

INTERVIEWER: Are there any other resources that you use here?

PARTICIPANT: I don't know if this really helps, but I guess I got a couple of my degrees there… like my high school… I don't know; right now it's a time where I'm stressed out about school and having those kind'a reminds me of the good ol' days when I was just a kid and having fun; just reminds me, when I'm doing any kind of homework, to just have fun and try to enjoy it. It's kind of just…it's symbolic to me; I don't know if it really…

The photograph provides a window into this student's activity that would have been impossible to achieve otherwise. Peering through this window at a distance allows access to the interviewer, and safety to the participant. As researchers we see things of unexpected importance, things we would not have thought to look for from a remote standpoint.

For this student, as for us when we were students, space had special meaning with regard to programming activity. The interview continues:

INTERVIEWER: Are there any other places where you do programming related work?

PARTICIPANT: Besides these two, not really.

INTERVIEWER: Okay. Let's go over to your calendar. ... Do you happen to recall, in these places [pointing to different marked places in the calendar grid], do you happen to recall which ones you did in which locations?

PARTICIPANT: That's kind of a funny story: I tried to work at my desk there, but for some reason it reminds you like a classroom. And it bothers me, so I always just go to my bed; just work on it...just that reminds you of like sitting at a desk, but most of the time...

INTERVIEWER: Okay. So when would you move over to here [pointing to the desk]?

PARTICIPANT: When I know that I really need to concentrate and that I know here I can get distracted by various things. If I'm at my desk I'll know that I mean business; I need to sit down and do this; I can't mess around.

Here we see how their space is imbued with meaning, how space becomes *place* for this student: how the evocation of place connects to individual identity: *here* I am a playful child, yet *there* I am a serious adult.

For other students, place is a more fluid concept. They started their assignment by reading an appropriate chapter from the textbook on the bus.

PARTICIPANT: And then, I continued to work on the assignment at home, late at night; from 1 to 3. And then, I finished the assignment also in the lab. So it went from the bus, to the lab, to home, back to the lab. Right here, where I finished it, and then went to class.

The photographs here illustrate a complex narrative of task and situation, of companionship and isolation:

PARTICIPANT: Well, in the lab, my friend...I specifically wanted to get help. I wanted meet up with my friend. And also I knew that a mentor was going to be there. So, all the time that I had people interaction, I sought them, or they sought me. 'Cause the second time I was here [in the lab], I knew what I was going to do. And that was finish it, and try the extra credit, but my friend called me. So it can go both ways. And for the beginning is where I sought it, and the end is where I actually gave help.

Looking back on these vignettes from the interviews, we can inquire: by what other means would we have achieved these insights? Would we have thought to put tick-boxes into a survey for all of the places that students revealed in photo and narrative ("Please select all locations where you do programming related work: in bed, on the bus, at your desk, at your dining room table, sitting on your computer tower, ...")? Would students reveal the times, locations, and resources in an interview *without* the diary grid and photographs to stimulate their recall?

They also reveal three key characteristics that our elicitation method afforded. First, they provided us access to places impossible to enter otherwise: the bus, the bedroom, the computing lab in the middle of the night. Second, they served as shared reference for student and researcher: "What happened here? What resources did you use? And third, they provided stimulus to recall, allowing mental access to things past that might otherwise be forgotten.

4. EMOTIONAL TIMELINES

My Programming Week examines cognitive strategies and narratives on a small time scale. We were also interested to examine these within the ecology of an entire academic course. In pursuit of this, we conducted an interview study of 20 students from an introductory programming course (approximately 10% of the number enrolled). We were interested in a phenomenological account of the course as a whole, a retrospective of a whole learning experience and in how students felt about it (not necessarily how successful they were in accomplishing it, although these are, of course, often closely linked).

4.1 Representing time

We again developed an instrument that both served as a stimulus for recall and as a shared reference to structure the interview. The inspiration for our instrument construction this time was not in methods from other disciplines, but methods from industry, specifically *project retrospectives* (Kerth, 2001). Project retrospectives are used where teams want to reflect on recently-past experience and learn from it to inform future work of the same kind. We appropriated three features of project retrospectives: timeline stimulus, recollection (and labeling) of significant events, and the creation of an "emotional seismograph".

In software project retrospectives, the (re)construction of the project timeline is a chance for everyone to recall what happened when, in what order: to create a shared representation. We approximated this by providing students with a single sheet of paper, with a vertical line down the middle representing time (see accompanying figure). On the left-hand side of the sheet, rows were labeled by week, lab, and lecture number, with the first week of the academic term at the top of the sheet and the last week at the bottom.

As researchers living in an industrialized social order (for those of us who do so), we take for granted "clock" time. Yet this public, socially shared demarcation of time is a relatively recent socio-cultural accomplishment. "In the United States alone, there were about 70 different time zones as late as the 1860's. ... In 1883 ... the railroads established the four time zones used in the United States today" (Levine 1997).

4.2 Remembrance of things past

> "For a long time, I went to bed early."
> Proust, *Remembrance of Things Past*

By contrast, experienced time has a different character: non-uniform, personal, subjective. We asked these students to annotate those weeks of the semester represented on the left-hand-side in which significant events occurred. Typical annotations were "This one was fun :-)" or "Hard. Intimidating code". We then turned the paper 90° (to a "landscape" orientation) and asked students to overlay a curve against the central timeline that represented their "emotional seismograph" for the course, where the x axis indicates their overall emotional reaction to the course at different times. As Levine et al (2006) note: "a person's memory of past emotional reactions plays a vital role in the construction of personal identity."

The *retrospective recall* of time is subject to a set of biasing influences. First, because of mental resource limitations, past events are not encoded completely, but partially in terms of prototypical or salient features. On recall, these memories are reconstructed, with the detail "filled in", often from information acquired after the remembered event so as to create a seamless whole (Gilbert 2006). Second, the affect associated with a remembered event is strongly influenced by both the peak intensity of the event, and the quality of the end of the event, the so-called *peak-end rule* (Do et al 2008) We thus deliberately constructed the timeline, labeling, and seismograph to contrast the "objective", socially shared scale of the calendar against the biased, affective, phenomenological experience of an individual as they recall their movement through the past.

4.3 The retrospective interview

Finally, we asked students to talk through the timeline, narrating it from start to finish, annotating the extreme peaks and troughs on the seismograph as they did so. Again, the shared representation allowed the interviewer to probe with particular questions: "What happened here?" The shape of their seismograph and the events they singled out for annotation afforded the opportunity for many *why* questions.

4.4 Emotional seismograph as narrative

For us, one of the surprising features of this technique was the narrative richness of the representation itself. The stories that students have to tell emerge not from transcribed dialogue, but powerfully from the page itself. Not only do these representations provide students access to memories of particular past events, but also these events—and their affect—can be viewed in relation to one another, as a coherent whole. It is not simply "the terrible time that I had with lab 6" but the fact that this was preceded and followed by a particular historical trajectory, all of which is evident to the researcher and the student, all available for perception, reflection, and explanation.

Two examples show the very different nature of experience of two students from the same course. The first student hardly recollects a negative moment: the only point the seismograph dips into negative is prior to the mid-semester test, and the student finishes the course more positive than they started.

> INTERVIEWER: There was a big dip right around the mid-semester, what was going on there?
>
> PARTICIPANT: Ah we did the test then - I missed a couple of lectures there ... I guess I wasn't a huge fan of having a lecture - was it the day before? I wouldn't recommend that. I didn't go,
>
> INTERVIEWER: That lecture the day before wasn't part of the expected test.
>
> PARTICIPANT: I know but, but you know.
>
> INTERVIEWER: So it's a big dip but a rebound?
>
> PARTICIPANT: We have the events I think about then, ... it was quite a useful thing and being able to respond to button clicks, that sort of thing, so you sort of get more happy with it then.

A second student, although they start off in a similarly positive position, rapidly sink into a negative decline and although there is a small mid-semester rally, it is short-lived. The seismograph finishes at Week 9 with the annotation "gave up". These representations thus "tell" and in so doing are subject to scrutiny and interpretation by both student and researcher.

As with the diary grid and photographs of *My Programming Week*, we do not believe we could have discovered this mix of learning and emotion in any other way, this coherent narrative of the phenomenology of an introductory programming course by individual students.

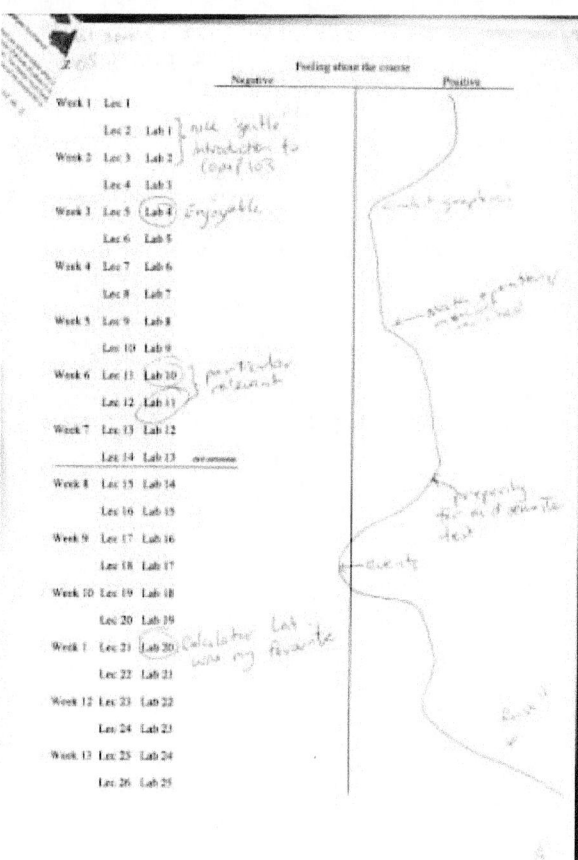

5. On *bricolage*

Denzin and Lincoln (2008) recognize our impulse to create appropriate instruments "The qualitative researcher as bricoleur, or maker of quilts, uses the aesthetic and material tools of his or her craft, deploying whatever strategies, methods and empirical material are at hand (Becker, 1998, p.2). If the researcher needs to invent, or piece together, new tools or techniques, he or she will do so."

As programming and computation are increasingly embedded in the contextual, situated, everyday world, in a complex ecology of inputs and activities, and if we as researchers are to inquire into how students learn within these contexts, it will require us to engage in methodological bricolage. Computing Education Research utilizes a relatively limited set of methods. Yet many research questions cannot be answered by the questionnaire, the experimental study, the semi-structured interview; rather, researcher distance—ephemerality, occurrences from the past, and outside the researcher's gaze—are important characterisitcs, and hence bespoke methods will be required. For us, these methods are also *researcher-distant*, that is to say that we are not putting ourselves in the frame, not biasing response with our questions ("When you program, at what point do you consult the textbook?") or expectations ("The work in week six was really very easy"). Instead, we craft instruments that let participants "speak for themselves" and allow us the insight to see the world as they do.

Peter Fensham (2004), in talking about the maturation of his own specialty (science education) into a field with a separate identity notes that one marker by which a field may claim identity is theory, and its development. He makes the argument (amongst others) that it may be too early in the disciplinary lifecycle for our sort of enquiry to develop theory and that we have "to live through a much longer adolescence of careful observation (as natural sciences like chemistry and biology have done)" (p.80). He puts the position that the kind of research needed is "extended systematic observation of the complexities of actual social situations" which may "yield valid descriptions of the multiple perspectives and consequent actions of those involved, and just possibly some tentative generalizing assertions" (p.103).

It is our hope that in seriously and thoughtfully engaging with questions specific to our field and our work, inventing and "piecing together" our own tools, rather than only adopting well-used methods from other disciplines, Computer Science education too may move tentatively towards our own theory.

6. Acknowledgments

We are grateful for financial support from the University of Washington, Tacoma's Chancellor's Fund, to the University of Otago's Research Committee, to the student research subjects who agreed to participate, and to the Helen Riaboff Whiteley Center of the Friday Harbor Laboratories of the University of Washington for providing the environment that enabled us to develop this paper.

7. References

Barker, L., Garvin-Doxas, K. and Jackson, M. (2002). Defensive climate in the computer science classroom. In *Proceedings of the 33rd SIGCSE technical symposium on Computer science education* (SIGCSE '02).

Bruner, J. (1987). Life as narrative. *Social Research* 54(1).

Cole, M. (1998). *Cultural Psychology: A Once and Future Discipline*, Harvard University Press.

Collins, H. (2001). What is tacit knowledge? In Schatzky, T., Knorr Cetina, K., and von Savigny, E. (Eds.) *The practice turn in contemporary theory*. Routledge.

Denzin, N. and Lincoln, Y. (2008). *Collecting and interpreting qualitative materials, 3e.* Sage.

Do, A., Rupert, A., and Wolford, G. (2008). Evaluations of pleasurable experiences: The peak-end rule. *Psychonomic Bulletin and Review* 15(1):96-98.

Eckerdal, A., Thuné, M., and Berglund, A. (2005). What does it take to learn 'programming thinking'?. In *Proceedings of the first international workshop on Computing education research* (ICER '05).

Fensham, P. J. (2004). *Defining an Identity: The Evolution of Science Education as a Field of Research.* Dordrecht, The Netherlands: Kluwer Academic Publishers.

Fincher, S. and Petre, M. (2004). *Computer science education research.* Routledge-Falmer.

Gaver, B., Dunne, T., and Pacenti, E. (1999). Design: Cultural probes. *interactions* 6(1): 21-29. Goody, J. (1977). *The domestication of the savage mind.* Cambridge University Press.

Harper, D. (1987). *Working knowledge: Skill and community in a small shop.*

Harper, D. (2002). Talking about pictures: A case for photo elicitation. *Visual studies* 17(1):13-26.

Kerth, N. L. (2001). *Project retrospectives : a handbook for team reviews.* New York: Dorset House.

Klein, G. (1999). *Sources of power.* MIT Press.

Labov, W. & Waletzky, J. (1967). Narrative analysis: Oral versions of personal experience. In J. Helm (Ed.), *Essays on the verbal and visual arts: Proceedings of the 1996 Annual spring Meeting of the American Ethnological Society* (pp12-44). Univeristy of Washington Press.

Levine, R. (1997). *A geography of time.* Basic Books.

Levine, L., Safer, M., and Lench, H. (2006). Remembering and misremembering emotions. In Sanna, L. and Chang, E. (Eds.) *Judgments over time: The interplay of thoughts, feelings, and behaviors.* Oxford University Press

Mishler, E. (1991). *Research Interviewing: Context and Narrative.* Harvard University Press.

Pink, S. (2007). *Doing visual ethnography: Images, media, and representation in research.* Sage.

Polanyi, M. (1966). *The tacit dimension.* Doubleday.

Rogoff, B. (2003). *The Cultural Nature of Human Development*, Oxford University Press.

Rogoff, B. and Lave, J. (1984). *Everyday cognition: its development in social context.* Harvard University Press.

Rose, Mike. (2004). *The Mind at Work.* Viking Adult.

Scott, J. (1999). *Seeing like a state.* Yale University Press.

Sternberg, R. and Horvath, J. (1999). *Tacit knowledge in professional practice: Researcher and practitioner perspectives.* Lawrence Erlbaum.

Tenenberg, J. and McCartney, R. (2010). Why discipline matters in computing education scholarship. *ACM Transactions on Compututing Educaction* 9(4): 18:1–18:7.

Tulving, E. (2003). Episodic Memory: From Mind to Brain. *Annual Review of Psychology.* 53:1–25.

Vygotsky, L. (1978). *Mind in Society*, Harvard University Press.

Exploring Programming Assessment Instruments: A Classification Scheme for Examination Questions

Judy Sheard
Monash University
judy.sheard@infotech.monash.edu.au

Simon
University of Newcastle
simon@newcastle.edu.au

Angela Carbone
Monash University
angela.carbone@monash.edu.au

Donald Chinn
University of Washington, Tacoma
dchinn@u.washington.edu

Mikko-Jussi Laakso
University of Turku
milaak@utu.fi

Tony Clear
Auckland University of Technology
tony.clear@aut.ac.nz

Michael de Raadt
University of Southern Queensland
deraadt@usq.edu.au

Daryl D'Souza
RMIT University
daryl.dsouza@rmit.edu.au

James Harland
RMIT University
james.harland@rmit.edu.au

Raymond Lister
University of Technology, Sydney
raymond.lister@uts.edu.au

Anne Philpott
Auckland University of Technology
aphilpot@aut.ac.nz

Geoff Warburton
RMIT University
geoffw@cs.rmit.edu.au

ABSTRACT
This paper describes the development of a classification scheme that can be used to investigate the characteristics of introductory programming examinations. We describe the process of developing the scheme, explain its categories, and present a taste of the results of a pilot analysis of a set of CS1 exam papers. This study is part of a project that aims to investigate the nature and composition of formal examination instruments used in the summative assessment of introductory programming students, and the pedagogical intentions of the educators who construct these instruments.

Categories and Subject Descriptors
K3.2 [**Computers and education**]: Computer and Information Science Education – *computer science education*

General Terms
Measurement

Keywords
Examination papers, CS1, introductory programming

1. INTRODUCTION
End of course formal examinations are one of the main techniques used for summative assessment of students in programming courses. Construction of an examination instrument is an important task, as the exam is used both to measure the level of knowledge and skill that students have reached at the end of the course and to grade and rank the students. A poorly constructed exam may not give a fair assessment of students' abilities, perhaps affecting their grades and their progression through their program of study.

Developing an examination paper is often an individual task, with the exam's format depending on the examiner's own preferences as well as on examination questions inherited from colleagues in previous offerings of the course. There are a number of ways that skills and knowledge may be assessed, and exams typically have a number of questions in a variety of styles, giving students different ways to demonstrate their knowledge and skills. In constructing an exam, educators must consider what they wish to assess in terms of the course content. They must consider the expected standards of their course and decide upon the level of difficulty of the questions. Considering the central role of the formal examination in assessing our students, it is important to understand the nature of the instruments we are using for this task. Tew [22] claims that "the field of computing lacks valid and reliable assessment instruments for pedagogical or research purposes" (p.xiii). This is a concern, because if the instruments we are using are neither valid nor reliable, how can we rely upon our interpretation of the results?

In this paper we report the development of an exam question classification scheme that can be used to determine the content and nature of introductory programming exams. We apply this instrument to a set of exam papers and report a sample of the results. We also explain the role of the scheme as part of a larger project which aims to investigate the nature and composition of formal examination instruments and the pedagogical intentions of the educators who construct these instruments.

2. ASSESSMENT BY EXAMINATION
Assessment is a critical component of our work as educators. In assessment we stand in judgment on our students to determine the level of learning that they have achieved in the curriculum of the course. It is critical that the instruments we use should give students the opportunity to demonstrate what they have learned about the course topics. However, assessment is also a strong influence on student learning behavior, as students tend to focus on and direct their efforts to the assessment tasks. As Ramsden maintains, "Students will study what they think will be assessed" [16] (p70). Biggs' theory of constructive alignment proposes an alignment of teaching and assessment and stresses the importance

of ensuring that the assessment tasks mirror the desired learning outcomes [3].

Given the importance of assessment, surprisingly few studies have investigated the content and characteristics of the instruments that we use [23]. A number of research studies have used examination instruments to measure levels of learning and to explore the process of learning. A body of work under the auspices of the BRACElet project has analyzed students' responses to examination questions [4, 11, 12, 18, 24]. Interest in this work stemmed from earlier studies (such as that of Whalley et al [25]) that attempted to classify responses to examination questions using Bloom's taxonomy [1] and the SOLO taxonomy [7]. The BRACElet project has focused on exam questions that concern code tracing, code explaining, and code writing. In an analysis of findings from these studies, Lister [10] proposed that a neo-Piagetian perspective could prove useful in explaining the programming ability of students.

Few studies were found that investigated the characteristics of examination papers and the nature of exam questions. A cross-institutional comparative study of four mechanics exams by Goldfinch et al [9] investigated the range of topics covered and the perceived level of difficulty of exam questions. Within the computing discipline, Simon et al [21] analyzed 76 CS2 (data structures) examination papers, but considered only questions on the topics of stacks and hash tables, which make up less than 20% of the marks available in those exams. Their analysis focused on the question style (e.g. multiple choice), the cognitive skills required and the level of difficulty of the questions. They further classified questions according to whether they required knowledge of the implementation of the data structure, the operations available with that data structure, or how to apply these operations. Following this study, a further analysis of 59 CS2 papers in the same dataset by Morrison et al [13] explored the *apply* questions, showing the range of question styles that can be used to test students' skill in applying data structures concepts.

Petersen et al [15] analyzed 15 CS1 exam papers to determine the concepts and skills covered. They found that there was a high emphasis on code writing questions, but much variation across the exams in the study. After finding that many questions required students to deal simultaneously with a high number of concepts, they proposed that single- or dual-concept questions might give students a better chance to demonstrate understanding. They suggested that more effort was needed to develop alternative types of question that focus on smaller sets of concepts,

A study by Shuhidan et al [19] investigated the use of multiple-choice questions in summative assessment, and found that the use of these questions remains controversial.

Like Petersen's, our study focuses on introductory programming examination papers: we develop a classification scheme for the purpose of analyzing these papers to give a comprehensive view of the course coverage, the styles of question employed, and the skills that students require to answer the questions.

3. RESEARCH APPROACH

This section describes how the exam question classification scheme was developed and applied, detailing the iterative process that was followed. After an introductory workshop, a project working team trialed the classification scheme on a single exam paper. This generated data that was used to refine the scheme with a view to achieving good inter-rater reliability results. Finally, a pilot study was conducted whereby the scheme was applied to a variety of exam papers.

3.1 Development of the Exam Question Classification Scheme

The idea of classifying exam questions stemmed from a BRACElet workshop following ICER 2008 in Sydney, a workshop funded by a fellowship of what subsequently became the Australian Learning and Teaching Council. The idea was formalized by a group of four project leaders, who produced a working draft of an exam question classification scheme.

Our intentions in developing a classification scheme are not unlike those of Bloom et al [1]: we wish to develop a common language to express the kinds of concepts and skills that students are expected to acquire in the first semester of studying object-oriented programming. As a first step we aim to discover, through analysis of actual CS1 exam papers, what questions instructors use to assess their students' mastery of concepts and skills.

Our initial scheme considered an individual question as the unit of analysis. The goal was to create a set of properties that describes different aspects of an exam question. We chose to characterize exam questions by the topic areas they cover, the style of the question, and the skills a student would need to have mastered to answer the question. We were also interested in a number of measures of complexity, such as the linguistic complexity of the question and its intellectual complexity as according to Bloom's taxonomy.

3.2 Presenting and Refining the Exam Question Classification Scheme at a Workshop

The exam question classification scheme was introduced to the computing education community at a half-day workshop at the 2011 Australasian Computing Education conference (ACE 2011) in Perth. The workshop was used to present the scheme and to obtain a sense of its usefulness to the broader computing education community. Sixteen participants attended, from eleven tertiary institutions. The workshop was conducted in four stages: description, trial, and refinement of the classification scheme, and discussion of its applicability and further development.

Following the introduction of the classification scheme, participants applied it to a selection of questions from a first-year introductory programming exam paper. Participants spent approximately 60 minutes classifying multiple-choice questions, code interpretation questions and small coding questions. During this time they discussed the categories of the classification scheme, clarifying their meaning and understanding, so that it became easier to approach consensus on the classifications.

3.3 A Revised Scheme, Trial Classification, and Inter-Rater Reliability

Following the workshop, 12 participants continued working on the project. Guided by feedback from the workshop, the project leaders refined the classification scheme and clarified some of the explanations behind the categories. Each member of the project working team then individually classified all of the questions on a single introductory exam paper using the refined question classification scheme, with a view to measuring the agreement among classifiers and thus the reliability of the scheme.

All categories but one of the trial classifications were analyzed using the Fleiss-Davies kappa for inter-rater reliability [8].

Because the scheme permits multiple topics to be recorded for a question, the Topics category could not be analyzed by this measure, which depends upon the selection of single values.

Table 1 shows the results of the inter-rater reliability test. On kappa measurements of this sort, an agreement of less than 40% is generally considered to be poor; between 40% and 75% is considered fair to good; and more than 75% is rated excellent [2].

Some members of the team found these reliability measures surprising or even alarming. When classifying a question we appear to be confident not only in our own classification but in the belief that like-minded people will choose the same values. The trial classification made it clear that this is not the case.

Perhaps most startling, but also most instructive, was the 73% rating for Percentage. This value is simply the percentage of the exam that each question is worth. The bulk of the disagreement was due to one member who neglected to complete this field at all. Once these values were added the reliability rose, but only to 98%, as two members had miscopied marks from the exam paper. The lesson from this is that even when raters agree, the measure of agreement can be reduced by data entry error.

The only excellent agreement was for Style of question, which most of the team expected to generate 100% reliability. Style of question has only five possible values, including multiple choice, short answer, and program code; yet still there was not complete agreement.

The cultural references question was simply whether the question included references that might be less meaningful to some groups of students than to others. In most cases such references were signaled by just one member, but others tended to agree when the references were explained. One question, for example, was based on a class for 'Chat'; one member observed that less computer-literate students might not be fully aware of what Chat is, and so potentially be disadvantaged by such a question unless the explanation was highly explicit. While others then agreed, the measured agreement was low because only one member had made this observation in the first instance.

3.4 Further Revision
Based on the results of the trial and inter-rater reliability

Table 1: Inter-rater reliability for 11 categories of the trial scheme; some categories are explained in the next section

Category	Reliability	Reliability range
Percentage	73%	fair to good
Skill required	73%	fair to good
Style of question	90%	excellent
Open/closed	60%	fair to good
Cultural references	15%	poor
Degree of difficulty	43%	fair to good
*Explicitness	31%	poor
*Operational complexity	52%	fair to good
*Conceptual complexity	34%	poor
*Linguistic complexity	47%	fair to good
*Intellectual complexity	27%	poor

* Use of these categories was discontinued for the pilot study

measurement, further clarifications were made to the scheme, and a number of categories – the last five in Table 1 – were dropped pending further consideration of how agreement might be improved. Participants reviewed their classifications in the light of these revisions and of other members' classifications. As these reclassifications were not independent it was not appropriate to recalculate the inter-rater reliability, but the new classifications did narrow the gap between the trial classification and full agreement.

3.5 Pilot Study
Following the clarifications and revisions, the next step was to pilot the scheme on a wider range of papers. Members of the project working team and two other colleagues supplied eleven exam papers from eight universities in five countries (Australia, Finland, New Zealand, UK, and USA).

The team formed pairs to apply the revised scheme to one or two exam papers each, as there is some evidence [20] that pairs classify more reliably than individuals. Members were required to classify the exam questions individually, then to discuss any differences and come to a consensus.

4. THE CURRENT CLASSIFICATION SCHEME
The refined scheme, as used to reclassify the first exam and classify the additional ten exams, is described briefly below.

Percentage of mark allocated. This represents the percentage of the entire exam that the question is worth. This category can be used as a weighting to determine what proportion of a complete exam covers the mastery of particular topics or skills.

Topics covered. An exam question can be assigned at most three of the following topics: data types and variables, constants, strings, I/O, file I/O, GUI design and implementation, error handling, program design, programming standards, testing, scope (includes visibility), lifetime, OO concepts (includes constructors, classes, objects, polymorphism, object identity, information hiding, encapsulation), assignment, arithmetic operators, relational operators, logical operators, selection, loops, recursion, arrays, collections (other than arrays), methods (includes functions, parameters, procedures and subroutines), parameter passing, operator overloading.

Note that in the list above, topics that follow 'assignment' tend to subsume data types and variables, so any question that is categorized with these later topics need not include data types and variables. Similarly, a topic such as selection or loops usually subsumes operators, and arrays generally subsumes loops. Having assigned one of these broader topics to a question, we would not also assign a topic subsumed by that broader topic.

The list of topics, which is probably not yet fixed, was compiled from the ACM curriculum, brainstorming among the project leaders, findings from the trial classification, and the computing education literature: a number of studies have investigated the topics taught in introductory programming courses. A survey of 351 CS academics by Dale [5, 6] explored the emphasis placed on different topics in CS1 courses and the perceived difficulty of these topics. Schulte [17] surveyed a similar number of teachers to determine the topics that they teach in introductory programming courses and their opinions about the importance, relevance and difficulty of these topics. Tew and Guzdial [23] analyzed the content of twelve CS1 textbooks to identify the concepts covered in CS1 courses.

Skill required to answer the question. The skills included in this category are: pure knowledge recall, trace code (includes expression evaluation), explain code, write code, modify code (includes refactor, rewrite), debug code, design program, test program. Only one skill can be chosen for a question. A question involving both design skills and coding would be classified as coding.

Style of question. This is a description of how the student's answer is represented. The choices are: multiple choice, short answer (includes definition, results of tracing or debugging, and tables), program code, Parsons problem [14], and graphical representation (for example, concept, flow chart, class diagram, picture of a data structure). A Parsons problem is a question in which a code segment is 'written' by correctly ordering the lines of code, which are provided in a jumbled order. Only one style can be chosen for each question. Similar categories were used by Petersen [15].

Open/Closed. A question that has only one possible answer is classified as closed. All others are classified as open.

Cultural references. Yes or no. Is there any use of terms, activities, or scenarios that may be specific to a cultural group and may influence the ability of those outside the group to answer the question? There might be references to a particular ethnic group and their customs, but a cultural reference need not be ethnic. A question might refer to a sport, such as cricket, using vocabulary or concepts that are specific to that sport.

Degree of difficulty. Low, medium, or high. This is an attempt to estimate how difficult the average student at the end of an introductory course would find the question. This classification is similar to that used by Simon et al [21] in their analysis of CS2 exam papers and Goldfinch et al in their analysis of mechanics examination papers [9].

4.1 Some Issues

A number of issues arose during the development and trial of the scheme. We describe a few of them here.

Multi-part questions. Some questions have multiple parts. Should these be classified as single questions or as multiple questions? This was left to the judgment of the people classifying the exam. A multi-part question asking students to "write down the results of evaluating the following expressions" could generally be classified as one question – although it might be difficult to remain within the limit of three topics. But a question that provides some code and asks students to do several distinct tasks such as explaining, refactoring, and writing additional code would have to be considered as multiple questions.

Skill required to answer question. It is sometimes difficult to determine whether a question involves pure knowledge recall or something more. For example, if a multiple choice question asks student to choose which of four lines of code constructs an object of some type and assigns it to a variable of a superclass of that type, does the question involve just knowledge recall, or might it be considered a code-tracing question?

Open/closed. There was need for resolution on whether a question that had essentially one answer (that is, there are multiple correct answers, but all express the same idea) should be considered open or closed. It was decided to consider such questions open, limiting the closed response to those questions that literally have only a single correct answer.

Degree of difficulty. This was perhaps the most subjective category to classify, as classifiers' judgments will be based on their own individual teaching experience and the pedagogy that they use. For example, a question on a concept or skill that is heavily emphasized in a class could be considered of low difficulty for that class, while in a different class it might be considered of medium difficulty.

Topics. The somewhat arbitrary limitation to three topics arose from the trial classification, where as many as 14 different topics were assigned to a single multiple-choice question. It was generally agreed that while all of these topics were pertinent, the restriction would force classifiers to choose the topics that were most pertinent to the question. It was also agreed that certain topics tended to subsume others – for example, arrays tend to subsume loops – and that there was no need to include both a subsumed topic and the one that subsumes it.

5. SAMPLE RESULTS

This section presents a taste of the results of the pilot analysis. The 11 exam papers comprised a total of 252 questions, with the number of questions in an exam ranging from 4 to 41. For each question the percentage mark allocated was recorded, and this was used as a weighting factor when calculating the contribution of each question to the values in each category.

5.1 Exam Paper Demographics

The 11 exam papers in the study were sourced from eight institutions in five countries. They were all used in introductory programming courses, ten at the undergraduate level and one at the postgraduate level, for classes from 25 students on a single campus to 800 students over four domestic and two international campuses.

The exams were mainly paper-based, though one had an online component, and mainly closed book, though one was open book and two were mixed. They were all of two or three hours' duration, and their weighting in the overall assessment for the course ranged from 25% to 80%. Some were for online students, some for on-campus students, and some for both. Most of them used Java, but Javascript, Alice, and C# were also represented.

5.2 Topics Covered

For each question we recorded up to three topics that we considered were central to the question. From our original set of 25 topics, three (recursion, GUI, and operator overloading) did not appear in the data set; and during analysis we added two further topics (events and expressions), giving a final list of 24 topics.

Table 2 shows the topics classified and their percentage coverage over the exams in the sample. Topics with the greatest coverage were OO concepts, loops, methods, arrays, program design, and selection. Ten topics had less than 2% coverage.

The study conducted by Tew and Guzdial [23] identified a set of eight concepts most commonly covered in CS1 courses; six of these appear in the top seven topics listed in Table 2. Tew and Guzdial's top eight concepts did not include program design but did include logical operators, which we found had low coverage (1.2%), and recursion, which we found had no coverage at all.

5.3 Skill Required

From a list of eight skills, each question was classified according to the main skill required to answer the question. Figure 1 shows the overall percentage coverage of each required skill over the 11 exams in the dataset. The most frequently required skill was code writing (45%). The five skills concerning code (writing, tracing, explaining, debugging, and modifying) together covered 81% of all exams, the remainder being taken by knowledge recall (7%), design (8%) and (4%) testing. We recognize that writing code often also involves a degree of program design, but we classified questions under program design only if they did not involve coding.

5.4 Cultural References

Cultural references were identified in only 15 of the 252 questions analyzed, making up a little more than 1% of the available marks. This is so small as to suggest that it might not be worth assessing or reporting – especially as the trial classification showed that any cultural references tended to be spotted first by a single classifier, and only then agreed to by others. However, one possible extension of this work will be to establish a repository of exam questions for the use of educators. In such a repository, this category would serve to alert users that somebody feels a particular question may cause problems for some students outside a particular context or culture.

6. DISCUSSION

The variation among raters in the trial raises some interesting questions. Most of the participants are or have been involved in teaching introductory programming courses, yet the agreement on level of difficulty was only 43%. Essentially, there was little or no consensus on whether questions were easy, moderate, or difficult.

Table 2: Topics and their coverage over the 11 exams

Topic	Percentage
OO concepts (includes constructors, classes, objects, polymorphism, object identity, information hiding, encapsulation)	39.0
Loops (subsumes operators)	36.4
Methods (includes functions, parameters, procedures and subroutines)	28.6
Arrays	28.1
Program design	22.4
Selection (subsumes operators)	12.2
Assignment	8.0
I/O	7.9
Parameter passing	7.8
File I/O	4.5
Strings	3.9
data types & variables	3.7
Collections (includes collections other than arrays)	3.6
Error handling	2.6
Arithmetic operators	1.8
Relational operators	1.7
Testing	1.6
Scope (includes visibility)	1.6
Logical operators	1.2
Events	1.1
Lifetime, Programming standards, Expressions, Constants	< 1 each

Discussion at the workshop and following the trial brought out some very good arguments for all the classifications, making it clear that what we are trying to determine is highly subjective, and depends not just upon the feelings of individual participants but on their knowledge of the courses that they teach and how their students would therefore respond to each particular question. Perhaps it is also influenced in some small way by aspects of the culture of the institutions at which the individual participants are employed.

7. CONCLUSION AND FURTHER WORK

We have established a number of categories to describe features of and variation among introductory programming exams, and have found that the 11 exams we have considered so far vary greatly in a number of aspects, from their broad characteristics to more specific details such as the topics covered. This is perhaps not surprising, when we consider that there is possibly a great variation in the pedagogic styles and beliefs of the people who set these exams. The next stage of this research will explore the pedagogical foundations of the exams through investigating the motivations and ideas of the educators who design these instruments.

In further analysis of the data we will explore the possibility of relationships between the categories of the classification system, such as between question style and skills required.

Ultimately, we plan to create a repository of introductory programming exams and exam questions for the use of educators. The variety that we have already found suggests that such a repository would be a rich source of material for academics seeking to inject change into their final assessments.

8. ACKNOWLEDGMENTS

Our thanks to the 2008 BRACElet workshop attendees who contributed to the initial brainstorming of ideas for classifying exams, and to the 2010 ACE Exam Taxonomy workshop attendees who provided feedback on the initial classification scheme. Thanks also to Jacqueline Whalley and Errol Thompson, who contributed exams for classification.

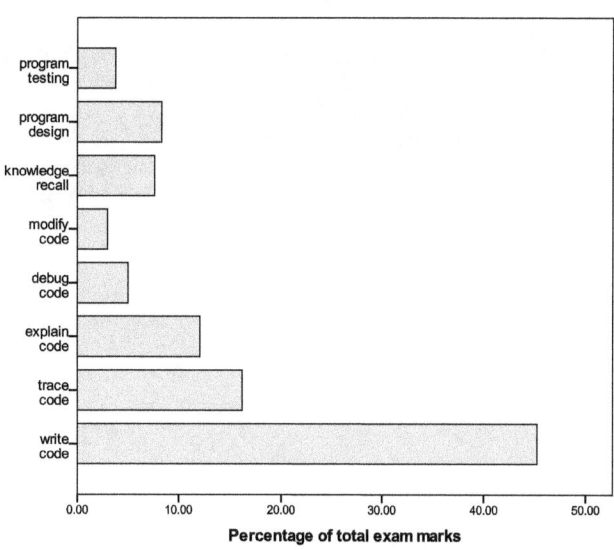

Figure 1: Skills required to answer questions

9. REFERENCES

[1] Anderson, L. W. and L. Sosniak, A., "Excerpts from the "Taxonomy of Educational Objectives, The Classification of Educational Goals, Handbook I: Cognitive Domain," in *Bloom's Taxonomy: A Forty Year Retrospective*, L. W. Anderson and L. Sosniak, A., Eds., ed Chicago, Illinois, USA: The University of Chicago Press, 1994, 9-27

[2] Banerjee, M., M. Capozzoli, L. McSweeney, and D. Sinha, "Beyond kappa: a review of interrater agreement measures," *Canadian Journal of Statistics*, 27:3-23, 1999

[3] Biggs, J. B., "What the Student Does: teaching for enhanced learning," *Higher Education Research and Development*, 18:57-75, 1999

[4] Clear, T., J. Whalley, R. Lister, A. Carbone, M. Hu, J. Sheard, B. Simon, and E. Thompson, "Reliably classifying novice programmer exam response using the SOLO taxonomy," in *NACCQ 2008*, Auckland, New Zealand, 2008

[5] Dale, N., "Content and emphasis in CS1," *inroads - The SIGCSE Bulletin*, 37:69-73, 2005

[6] Dale, N., "Most difficult topics in CS1: Results of an online survey of educators," *inroads - The SIGCSE Bulletin*, 38:49-53, 2006

[7] Dart, B. and G. Boulton-Lewis, "The SOLO model: Addressing fundamental measurement issues," in *Teaching and Learning in Higher Education*, M. Turpin, Ed., ed Camberwell, Victoria, Australia: ACER Press, 1998, 145-176

[8] Davies, M. and J. L. Fleiss, "Measuring agreement for multinomial data," *Biometrics*, 38:1047-1051, 1982

[9] Goldfinch, T., A. L. Carew, A. Gardner, A. Henderson, T. McCarthy, and G. Thomas, "Cross-institutional comparison of mechanics examinations: A guide for the curious," in *AaaE conference*, Yeppoon, 2008, 1-8

[10] Lister, R., "Concrete and other neo-piagetian forms of reasoning in the novice programmer," in *13th Australasian Computing Education conference*, Perth, Australia, 2011

[11] Lister, R., T. Clear, Simon, D. J. Bouvier, P. Carter, A. Eckerdal, J. Jacková, M. Lopez, R. McCartney, P. Robbins, O. Seppälä, and E. Thompson, "Naturally occurring data as research instrument: Analyzing examination responses to study the novice programmer," *inroads - The SIGCSE Bulletin*, 41:156-173, 2010

[12] Lopez, M., J. Whalley, P. Robbins, and R. Lister, "Relationships between reading, tracing and writing skills in introductory programming.," in *Fourth International Workshop on Computing Education Research (ICER '08)*, Sydney, Australia, 2008, 101-112

[13] Morrison, B., M. Clancy, R. McCartney, B. Richards, and K. Sanders, "Applying data structures in exams," in *SIGCSE'11*, Dallas, Texas, USA, 2011, 353-358

[14] Parsons, D. and P. Haden, "Parson's programmimg puzzles: A fun and effective learning tool for first programming courses," in *Eighth Australasian Computing Education conference (ACE2006)*, Hobart, Australia, 2006, 157-163

[15] Petersen, A., M. Craig, and D. Zingaro, "Reviewing CS1 exam question content," in *SIGCSE'11*, Dallas, Texas, USA, 2011, 631-636

[16] Ramsden, P., *Learning to Teach in Higher Education*. New York, NY, USA: Routledge, 1992

[17] Schulte, C. and J. Bennedsen, "What do teachers teach in introductory programming?," in *Second International Computing Education Research workshop (ICER'06)*, Canterbury, UK, 2006, 17-28

[18] Sheard, J., A. Carbone, R. Lister, B. Simon, E. Thompson, and J. Whalley, "Going SOLO to assess novice programmers," in *13th Annual Conference on Innovation and Technology in Computer Science Education (ITiCSE'08)*, Madrid, Spain, 2008, 209-213.

[19] Shuhidan, S., M. Hamilton, and D. D'Souza, "Instructor perspectives of multiple-choice questions in summative assessment for novice programmers," *Computer Science Education*, 20:229-259, 2010

[20] Simon, A. Carbone, M. De Raadt, R. Lister, M. Hamilton, and J. Sheard, "Classifying computing education papers: Process and results," in *4th International Workshop on Computing Education research (ICER 2008)*, Sydney, NSW, Australia, 2008, 161-171

[21] Simon, B., M. Clancy, R. McCartney, B. Morrison, B. Richards, and K. Sanders, "Making sense of data structure exams," in *International Computing Education Research workshop (ICER'10)*, Aarhus, Denmark, 2010, 97-105

[22] Tew, A., "Assessing Fundamental Introductory Computing Concept Knowledge in a Language Independent Manner. ," PhD Dissertation, 2010

[23] Tew, A. E., "Developing a validated assessment of fundamental CS1 concepts," in *SIGCSE'10*, Milwaukee, Wisconsin, USA, 2010, 97-101

[24] Venables, A., G. Tan, and R. Lister, "A closer look at tracing, explaining and code writing skills in the novice programmer. ," in *The fifth International Computing Education Research Workshop (ICER 2009)*, Berkeley, California, USA, 2009

[25] Whalley, J., R. Lister, E. Thompson, T. Clear, P. Robbins, P. K. A. Kumar, and C. Prasad, "An Australasian study of reading and comprehension skills in novice programmers, using the Bloom and SOLO taxonomies," in *Eighth Australasian Computing Education conference (ACE2006)*, Hobart, Australia, 2006, 243-252

Do Values Grow on Trees?
Expression Integrity in Functional Programming

Guillaume Marceau
WPI
100 Institute Road
Worcester, MA, USA
+1 (508) 831-5357
gmarceau@wpi.edu

Kathi Fisler
WPI
100 Institute Road
Worcester, MA, USA
+1 (508) 831-5357
kfisler@cs.wpi.edu

Shriram Krishnamurthi
Brown University
115 Waterman St
Providence, RI, USA
+1 (401) 863-7600
sk@cs.brown.edu

ABSTRACT
We posit that functional programmers employ a notion called expression integrity to understand programs. We attempt to study the extent to which both novices and experts use this notion as they program, discuss the difficulties that arise in measuring this, and offer some observational findings.

Categories and Subject Descriptors
D.1.1 [**Programming Techniques**]: Applicative Programming; H.5.2 [**User Interfaces**]: Evaluation/methodology

General Terms
Design, Human Factors, Languages.

Keywords
Programming for novices. Structured editing.

1. Programming with Values

Some people advocate the use of functional programming in computer science education, especially at the introductory level. Others oppose it on the grounds that it is not merely outside the mainstream but may even be unnatural (perhaps suggesting the latter as an explanation for the former). Unfortunately, this long debate has seen more heat than light. We believe curricula would be better served by rigorous studies that examine the purported advantages and weaknesses claimed by each side.

First, let us review the basic structure of functional programs. The central idea is that programs exist to consume and produce *values*, akin to functions in algebra. Most introductory books completely eschew side-effects in the student's programs (even though they can be described with some effort even in traditionally functional languages). As a result, students do not see *statements*, only *expressions*. A program is simply a series of definitions, each of which has an expression body. Each expression may, recursively, have many nested sub-expressions. The actual computation is triggered by one or more expressions presented either in the program source or in an interactive evaluator (sometimes colloquially called an "interpreter", even though the underlying implementation may employ a compiler, JIT, or other strategy).

The functional style raises many questions (as does its more traditional counterparts). For instance, one might ask how students relate to the decomposition of computation by statements versus expressions; how much the problems caused for program reasoning by side-effects are offset by benefits; at what depth of nesting students start to have difficulties; and so on. A broader set of issues is whether functional programming is indeed "natural" or not. If it is not, then perhaps it is unsuitable in education (though we must also then ask the same question about algebra itself, and understand how the answers relate). If it is, then perhaps some of the complaints about it stem more from instructor prejudice than from student behavior and perception.

To investigate such questions, we feel it is critical to first ask more foundational ones about students' ability to even relate to how functional programs compute. This paper reports on a first such investigation. From extensive discussions with experienced functional programmers, we find (anecdotally) that when reading, reviewing, and editing programs they *understand programs as trees of expressions, not as a sequence of characters*. We use the term **expression integrity** to capture this notion of understanding programs, and examine it in more detail. This concept is especially important in functional programs because everything other than a definition is an expression, even the control operations. We suspect, but don't study here, that this concept also applies to imperative programs that have shallow expressions but do have statements that can nest several levels (e.g., an assignment inside a conditional inside a loop inside a function).

Observe that "understand" has two senses: syntactic and semantic. Syntax is what users write (and hence it is what they have primary, direct control over), while semantics is what happens when the program runs (and hence reflects whether or not it met the user's goal). Computer scientists have long understood the tension between these two aspects of a language, and indeed movements such as *structured programming* grew precisely out of a direct desire to reduce the gap between the two. Thus, our investigation of functional programming should employ both syntactic and semantic angles.

This paper is about questions more than answers. It combines position (the importance of expression integrity) and discussion (how we might measure it).

2. Syntactic Studies

Expression integrity is presented in terms of how programmers understand programs. Of course, we cannot directly observe "understanding"; instead we must operationalize it. At a syntactic level, we postulate that there are certain behaviors we expect from programmers employing expression integrity, such as:

- They finish working with one expression before switching to another (for nested expressions, they may provide the

highest-level syntactic structure first, then fill in the sub-expressions, or they may complete sub-expressions in depth-first order). For languages with parenthetical syntax, they also maintain (relatively) balanced parentheses as they edit programs.
- They move and copy whole expressions.

These statements apply both to writing new code and to modifying existing code. For example, we would expect an expression-aware programmer to modify existing code by making edits as needed to a single (possibly nested) expression and restoring the surrounding expression structure (including parentheses) before moving on to another expression. Additionally, when modifying code, we would expect that

- They prefer reusing expressions to typing new code, even if the number of keystrokes is similar in each case.

Until a programmer has developed a sense of expression integrity, we would expect them to prefer edit paths with fewer keystrokes, and to apply edits without regard to the program's tree structure. (We observe in passing that these criteria are not limited to functional programs. A similar notion of integrity surely applies to statements also, though the rules are more complex.)

In other words, even when their editor permits character-wise editing (as most modern editors do), programmers with a sense of expression integrity conceptualize the syntax in terms of expression trees, and sometimes even avail of editor operations that atomically handle entire expressions at a time. These expression-oriented operations effectively endow programmers with the benefits of *structured* editing even in an unstructured editor, thereby avoiding the notorious inflexibility of fully-structured editors [1] without giving up their benefits.

Naturally, these are just claims (though based heavily on experience and anecdote). We set out to study these ideas in two populations: rank beginners, and experts. We first discuss our setup (Section 2.2), and our results for beginners (Section 2.3); then we step back and ask how our findings compare against expert behavior (Section 2.4). Before we get into these studies, however, it is worth examining the structure of expressions, since this affects what we can measure.

2.1 The Structure of Expressions

Observe that in a handful of languages (unlike Java, C, etc., where a program either parses or doesn't) there are multiple levels of "expression-ness". In XML, for instance, the levels are called *well-formedness* and *validity*. Well-formedness simply means that the basic rules of XML (pointy brackets, appropriate quotation of certain characters) are being followed, and that the opening and closing tags match and nest properly. However, a particular XML language will have additional rules. For instance, in XHTML (a version of HTML built atop XML), only certain tags are allowed, only some tags can nest within others, only certain attributes are legal, and so forth. This latter level of conformance is called validity. Thus all valid documents are well-formed, but not all well-formed documents are valid. Krishnamurthi [2] refers to languages with such a two-level structure as *bicameral*, since they mimic the bicameral legislatures of many countries.

Another language family famous for bicameral rules is Lisp. Well-formed terms (known as *s-expressions*) meet tokenization rules and have balanced parentheses, while valid terms are those that actually parse. In the Racket dialect, for instance, the term `(+ 1 2)` is both well-formed and valid, but `(lambda x)` is well-formed but not valid: it survives the "reader" (which converts a token stream into an s-expression) but fails to parse.

Our studies are conducted with students learning Racket. This gives us freedom to study programs at either level. While our tools support both, we chose to study well-formedness (which largely translates to whether programs are properly parenthesized) for two reasons:

1. It more closely corresponds to the level at which we believe *beginning* students think: they very quickly understand that programs must be properly parenthesized even though they do not understand the finer rules of grammar. Put differently, to beginners, balancing parentheses probably *is* what they imagine to be the primary form of validity.
2. When we study how student performance evolves over the course of the semester, it is valuable to quantify their progress. This requires that we can measure the degree of mis-parsedness of a program. This would presumably be based on the edit-distance to a properly parsed program, which is extremely sensitive to the editing operations available, and thus may be difficult for even experts to agree upon. In contrast, the degree of parenthetical imbalance (which, too, must deal with the fact that Racket programs have both parentheses and brackets) is a much more objective metric.

It is important to observe that, because every valid program is well-formed, a program that is not even well-formed is certainly not valid. Thus, any studies based on well-formedness would yield a lower-bound on what we would find by studying validity.

Of course, we must be careful when interpreting measurements. It is sometimes impossible to make edits without temporarily altering the validity—or even well-formedness—of a program. This can happen when fixing a typographical error. There are also edits whose entire point is to alter the way a program parses; in the process, it may be very difficult (or even impossible, given the structure of the language!) to make sure every intermediate state parses properly. We conjecture that programmers can easily tolerate such mal-formed intermediate programs provided they are not distracted during edits. Just as humans easily cope with poor spelling and grammar, a small amount of mis-parsedness seems entirely reasonable and perhaps cognitively preferable than trying to preserve parsability at all times.

More broadly, because most other programming languages do not have a bicameral structure, to generalize our results we must eventually examine validity also. Naturally, we should also study languages without a bicameral structure, to avoid confounding factors introduced by "lots of irritating, silly parentheses".

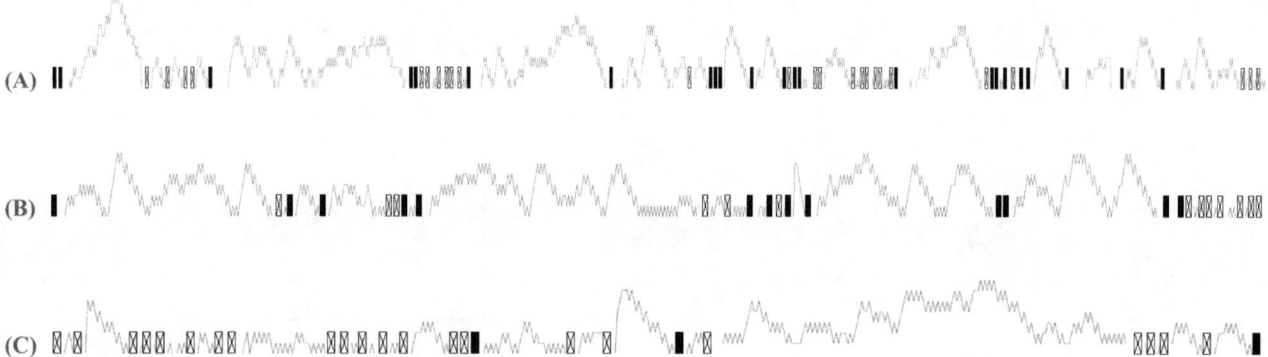

Figure 1. Different behaviors towards the maintenance of well-formedness and validity. The *y*-axes shows the amount of imbalance in the third lab (50 minutes) for an A-student, a B-student, and a C-student, respectively (same scale for all three). The highest peak is 9. Filled rectangles represent successful compilation attempts; x-ed rectangles are compilations that produced an error message.

2.2 Experimental Setup

We conducted our experiments in DrRacket, a modern (but intentionally spartan) interactive development environment. Three characteristics of DrRacket are noteworthy in this paper:

1. DrRacket runs identically (other than default key bindings) and as a native application on Windows, Mac, and Unix. Thus users can apply all the edit operations that they are comfortable with for the platform.
2. Whenever a cursor is placed (by mouse or keyboard) over a parenthesis, the environment highlights the entire parenthetical expression that begins or ends at that parenthesis. (If the parenthesis is mis-matched or dangling, DrRacket instead colors it pink.) This highlighting happens automatically without the need for a mode setting, as is necessary in some other editors.
3. Users can enable keystrokes for manipulating entire s-expressions, imitating those built into Emacs. Most of the advanced programmers described in this paper know these keystrokes, but none of the beginners were shown them (they are not easy to find without reading the manual, so most students never discover them).

Each user in our studies enabled logging software in DrRacket. This software logged all key and mouse events in the environment and could replay them, so we could study the precise evolution of the program source and watch a user's editing as a "movie". (The logger is a DrRacket plugin, so it does not capture any interaction outside the environment such as passwords, etc.).

2.3 Analysis of Student Data

In spring 2010 we collected detailed logs of students' interactions with DrRacket during the lab sessions of an introductory programming course. Each lab ran for 50 minutes. There were six lab sessions (one per week) over the duration of the course. Sixty students out of 120 consented to provide data.

Using these data, we asked three initial questions about students:

1. What is the pattern of well-formedness of their programs? Do they keep their parentheses mostly balanced, or are there wild fluctuations of imbalance?
2. When modifying existing code, as opposed to creating new code, is their behavior any different? For instance, is there a significant difference in their edits after error messages as opposed to edits after the successful passage of tests (which suggests they have completed a task and are moving on to new code)?
3. Do these behaviors change over the course of the semester, as they (a) become familiar with the language syntax, (b) acquire greater skill with the programming environment, and (c) realize (from experts such as professors and TAs) that letting programs become significantly imbalanced is likely to lead to more errors and make it harder to find and fix them?

To observe the extent of unbalancing over the course of a lab, we computed the amount of unbalancing after each change to the parenthetical structure. We used an A* search with alpha-beta pruning to compute the shortest edit distance to a balanced buffer. The search could either add a parenthesis to match a dangling one, remove a dangling parenthesis, or turn a parenthesis into a different kind (from round to bracket or vice versa).

Figure 1 shows the behavior of three students in the third lab. The label (A, B, C) reflects their final course grade. All three start with a balanced buffer (because it's empty), then compose some code. While doing so, the buffer becomes momentarily unbalanced. The students differ in how they manage this imbalance. Student A seems to have developed a habit of frequently returning to a balanced buffer; she also frequently compiles her code, possibly to confirm its well-formedness before going further. Student B also frequently restores the buffer's balance, but does not compile as often. Student C spends almost the entire second half of the lab with a deeply unbalanced buffer. Afterwards, he has to make four compilation attempts before returning to a valid program.

We sought to summarize these behaviors with a metric so that we could make aggregate comparisons across students, across time, and so forth. A natural first metric is:

1. Area under the curve: We could simply sum the total extent of imbalance the student's program demonstrates during an editing session.

This metric does not, however, capture whether or not a student regularly brought the buffer back into complete balance. Instead, we might want to measure:

2. Average length of runs between zeroes: On the premise that a long imbalanced edit is worse than a short one (since

(a)
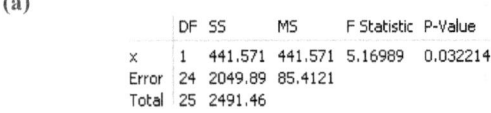
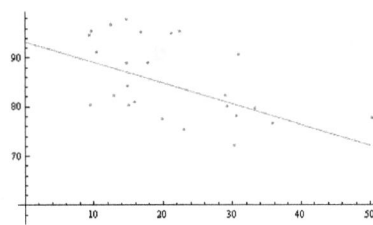

(b)
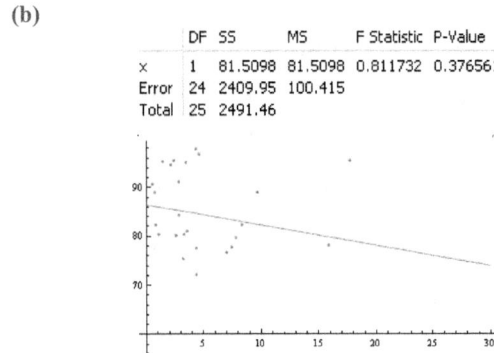

Figure 2. Correlation between the amount of imbalance (*x*-axis) and course grade (*y*-axis) when (a) writing new code (significant), and (b) fixing existing code (not significant).

the student must concentrate longer), we could emphasize the duration of imbalances over their size.

But this fails to capture our intuition that the more imbalanced a buffer is the greater the cognitive burden borne by the student (e.g., having to be conscious of the nesting depth). The summary measure we finally settled on combines the two previous metrics:

3. The mean of the areas under the curve between zeroes: Split at each point where the buffer returns to a balanced state; compute the area of each; average these areas.

This enables us to handle what might appear to be confounding data. For instance, suppose a student begins a program thus (where the arrow represents the cursor position):

```
(define (len l)
  (cond
    [(empty? l↑
```

The program has a nesting depth of four. It is unclear at this point whether the student will eventually balance everything. In contrast, a different student may always close every parenthesis they open right away, writing the above example as follows:

```
(define (len l)
  (cond
    [(empty? l↑)]))
```

By looking at sequences of edits, our metric lets us focus on the entire editing behavior, rather than trying to guess from an intermediate state what the final state will be.

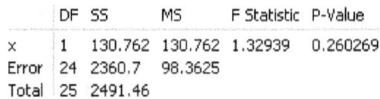
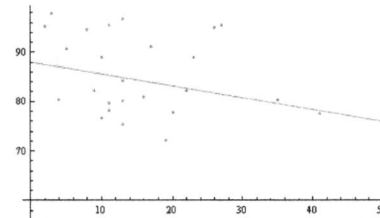

Figure 3. Correlation between the number of parenthesis errors and the final course grade (not significant).

Before analyzing the data, it is worth considering different styles of editing activity. In particular, writing new code is potentially quite different from changing existing code, since the former can much more easily be structural while the latter may necessitate non-structural changes. Thus, we choose to partition edits into those yielding new code versus those that were fixes to errors.

To classify edits, we assume (in line with prior work [3]) that edits after a successful compilation—until the next compilation—consist of new code. The one exception is when a compile returns a parenthesis error; in this case, we continue rather than terminate the edit sequence. Thus, new code sequences begin with a successful compilation, continue through any number of compilation attempts signaling a parenthesis error, and end on either another successful compilation or a non-parenthesis error. We classify all other edit sequences—starting at a non-parenthetical error—as fixing errors. We considered only edit sequences which added or removed at least one parenthesis.

Given this proposed operationalization of expression integrity, and our assumption that successful development of expression integrity is essential for student success in this programming course, we can then ask whether our metric correlates with the final course grade (unfortunately, individual lab assignments were not graded). We thus computed this correlation across the set of students who provided data for at least four labs during the course.

Figure 2 shows the result of the correlation. For episodes of writing new code (in (a)), the linear fit is statistically significant (p=0.032 albeit with an R^2 of 0.18). When fixing errors (b) it was not significant.

One might wonder whether this relationship occurs because better students make fewer parenthesis errors overall. But this is not the case. Figure 3 shows there is a slight correlation between the number of parenthesis errors and the final course grade, but this relationship is not statistically significant. We could also ask whether students' score on the metric improves over time. Unfortunately, because the difference in difficulty between labs is neither uniform nor monotonic, the between-task variability would mask any effects of learning. Indeed, we are not able to find any significant improvement effects across the term.

2.4 A Study of Experts

We believe that the buffer imbalance of experts can serve as a useful baseline for our expectations of students. We were able to conduct a small study of experts at the annual Racket user conference. Our study participants build large systems in Racket, ranging across academia, government, and industry. Some of them indeed use DrRacket on a daily basis.

Due to the limited availability of their time, instead of asking them to write full programs, we instead gave them a small correct, working program, and asked them to refactor it to remove some operations and use others instead; the change did not alter the program's behavior, only its syntax. All 10 participants successfully completed the task.

In designing the task, we ensured that the edit could be performed purely with the s-expression operations, so that it would be possible to never change the parenthetical balance of the program (and, in particular, keep the imbalance at zero). Some experts did strive to keep their buffer's parentheses balanced, and some seemed to use the compiler to confirm well-formedness of their program at intermediate points. Figure 4 shows the distribution of the metric for both students and experts (with experts in (c)). The students do score higher, but the difference could be attributable to the fact that students were creating new (and buggy) programs, not merely refactoring existing code.

In particular, our logging information suggested the experts made almost no use of the s-expression editing commands. As a follow-up, we conducted a survey to ask them whether

1. this was indeed true; if so,
2. whether their behavior in this study was representative of their usual DrRacket programming style; and, if so,
3. whether they mentally still viewed the program as a collection of trees or whether they viewed it as a sequence of characters.

All the participants confirmed that our observation of their behavior was correct. They stated that in general they made little to no use of the s-expression *editing* commands, though a few used the *traversal* commands. Despite this, they confirmed that they absolutely do view the program in terms of trees of expressions independent of which editor they are using, though some participants added that they sometimes also viewed the program in terms of lines (rather than characters), especially when they need to perform block edits. (We conjecture that so do the others, even though they did not say so explicitly.)

3. Semantic Studies

Different languages employ different computational models, which in turn rely on expression integrity in different ways. In functional programming, even control operators are expressions that return values to the surrounding computation. Each node in the "tree of expressions" corresponds to a value which substitutes for the node while reducing a program to a result. In imperative programming, expressions interleave with statements that store values in memory or specify control structure. The "tree of expressions" is insufficient for modeling semantics, in exchange for relying less on the tree model to explain computation.

In our functional programming context, then, we expect that students who lack expression integrity would struggle to understand how programs yield results. Operationally, we expect that students with a basic semantic sense of expression integrity

- Can explain how different expression types (arithmetic, data creation, control operators) reduce to values.
- Can explain what an individual expression contributes to a function's result.

A student with a strong sense of expression integrity should also reflect the following skills for maintaining and editing programs:

- They can identify the expressions whose values might change as a result of editing a particular expression.
- They can identify which sub-expressions need to be edited (and how) in order to change the result of an expression.

The metrics about the impact of edits point to a fundamental difference between functional and imperative programming. In the functional setting, all of our semantic metrics have an implicit *frame condition* [4]: if an expression changes, the values of its sibling expressions do not change. This is not true in an imperative setting, because the changed expression could have a side-effect that causes an unedited expression to produce a different answer. Put differently, in functional programming, the syntactic building block (the expression) corresponds directly to the semantic building block (the value). We would expect this difference to manifest itself in semantic studies of expression integrity within each programming style. However, space precludes us from discussing these issues more.

4. Related Work

Several works have sought to identify the component skills that novice programmers must learn. Mead et al. has an extensive survey of the topic [5], and identifies dependencies between skills. PROUST uses their skill decomposition to automatically detect which subgoals were intended to be met by a student's code [6].

Projects that attempt to operationalize the skills they identified are less common. Anderson and Reiser's LISP Tutor models the fine-grained goal-setting done by novices through 500 production rules [7]. These rules are then used to trigger automatic feedback, to select exercise sequences for the student, and to predict quiz performance.

Expression integrity (thinking of code as a tree) is an instance of *chunking*. Both Adelson [8] and Shneiderman et al. [9] find multiple lines of evidence that novice programmers transition

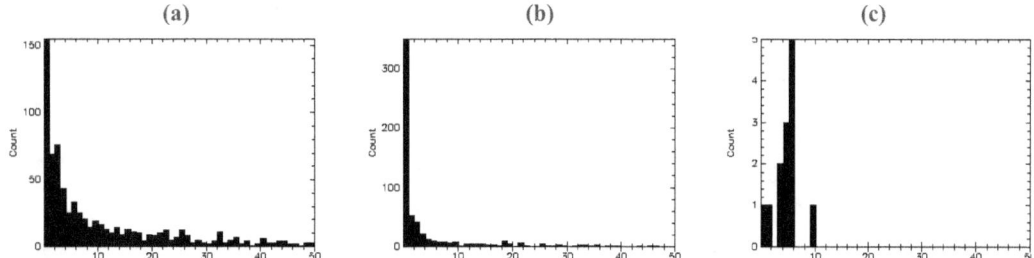

Figure 4. Histograms of the values of the metric of unbalancing for (a) students writing new code, (b) students fixing code, and (c) professionals during a refactoring exercise.

from syntactical chunking to some form of semantic chunking, but neither pinpoints the details. Fix, et al. give empirical support for five characteristics of how experts chunk the relationship between the functions and variables of a program, and to its goal [10]. We are not aware of any previous attempt to operationalize expression integrity specifically.

Some researchers have looked for patterns in beginners' editing behaviors. Rodrigo, et al.'s *error quotient* metric [3] summarizes the kinds and locations of errors a student makes, along with the locations edited in response. Like our metric of unbalancing, the error quotient correlates with final grades, but the two metrics satisfy different goals. The error quotient aims to detect where students struggle regardless of the conceptual cause, whereas we focus on the impact of expression integrity.

Dyke's work counts students' use of IDE features such as the multi-tab interface, breakpoints, and code auto-completion [11], and finds that these too correlate with final grades. In addition, the work finds that usage of more advanced features correlates with the rank difference between two members of a homework pair.

Ko, et al.'s study [12] of the editing behavior of expert Java programmers found patterns similar to those in Section 2.4: experts regularly pass through invalid buffer states while editing, but quickly repair the code and avoid prolonging the invalidity.

5. Perspective and Context

This paper outlines a research agenda centered around expression integrity, which in turn focuses on how students understand the structure of programs. We believe that understanding program structure, both syntactically and semantically, is a core skill in effective programming. We offer one preliminary (and language-sensitive) operationalization of expression integrity at the syntactic level. Naturally, we must address other syntaxes, study this concept at the semantic level, and correlate it with skills in debugging, maintenance, code reviews, etc.

Our preliminary findings, if borne out by more detailed studies, raise questions of what designers of programming environments should do in terms of syntax manipulation operations. On the one hand, fully-structured editors such as that of Scratch [13] are clearly popular and successful; indeed, the Scratch editor makes it impossible to create ill-formed programs. On the other hand, we are not aware of validation of the Scratch editor principle for large programs; any such studies would need to be reconciled with known data on structured editing [14]. What does seem apparent is that, given a free-form text interface, at least some experts employ this over structured commands. Whether it would still be worth teaching these commands to beginners to *instill* a notion of expression integrity needs further study.

Longer-term, expression integrity gives a foundation for studying the relative merits of functional and imperative programming for beginning students. Syntactically, programs correspond to trees in both styles. Semantically, the role of this tree differs significantly. By aligning the syntactic and semantic models through the tree structure, functional programming asks students to work with only a single mental model of programs. Imperative languages reduce semantic reliance on the tree model at the cost of introducing a second model with no framing condition. Understanding the cost-benefit tradeoffs of these models to each of program construction, debugging, and maintenance could provide significant input to the debate about suitable programming methods for novices.

Acknowledgments. We thank the US NSF for grant support, and appreciate comments from the anonymous reviewers and Matthias Felleisen. We thank the students and Racket users who participated in these studies.

6. References

[1] P. Miller, J. Pane, G. Meter, and S. Vorthmann, "Evolution of Novice Programming Environments: The Structure Editors of Carnegie Mellon University," *Interactive Learning Environments*, vol. 4, 1994, pp. 140-158.

[2] S. Krishnamurthi, "Programming Languages: Application and Interpretation," 2007.

[3] M.M.T. Rodrigo, E. Tabanao, M.B.E. Lahoz, and M.C. Jadud, "Analyzing Online Protocols to Characterize Novice Java Programmers," *Philippine Journal of Science*, vol. 138, 2009, p. 177–190.

[4] J. McCarthy and P.J. Hayes, "Some philosophical problems from the standpoint of artificial intelligence," *Machine Intelligence*, vol. 4, 1969, p. 463–502.

[5] J. Mead, S. Gray, J. Hamer, R. James, J. Sorva, C. St. Clair, and L. Thomas, "A cognitive approach to identifying measurable milestones for programming skill acquisition," *ACM SIGCSE Bulletin*, vol. 38, Dec. 2006, p. 182.

[6] W.L. Johnson and E. Soloway, "PROUST: Knowledge-Based Program Understanding," *IEEE Transactions on Software Engineering*, vol. SE-11, Mar. 1985, p. 267–275.

[7] J.R. Anderson, F.G. Conrad, and A.T. Corbett, "Skill acquisition and the LISP tutor," *Cognitive Science*, vol. 13, 1989, p. 467–505.

[8] B. Adelson, "Problem solving and the development of abstract categories in programming languages.," *Memory & cognition*, vol. 9, Jul. 1981, p. 422–433.

[9] B. Shneiderman and R. Mayer, "Syntactic/semantic interactions in programmer behavior: A model and experimental results," *International Journal of Computer & Information Sciences*, vol. 8, Jun. 1979, p. 219–238.

[10] V. Fix, S. Wiedenbeck, and J. Scholtz, "Mental representations of programs by novices and experts," *INTERACT '93 and CHI'93 conference on Human factors in computing systems*, ACM, 1993, p. 74–79.

[11] G. Dyke, "Which Aspects of Novice Programmers' Usage of an IDE Predict Learning Outcomes?," *Special Interest Group on Computer Science Education (SIGCSE)*, 2011.

[12] A.J. Ko and H. Aung, "Design requirements for more flexible structured editors from a study of programmers' text editing," *CHI*, 2005, p. 1557–1560.

[13] D.J. Malan and H.H. Leitner, "Scratch for budding computer scientists," *ACM SIGCSE Bulletin*, vol. 39, 2007, p. 223.

[14] A.J. Ko, "Designing a Flexible and Supportive Direct-Manipulation Programming Environment," *IEEE Symposium on Visual Languages Human Centric Computing*, 2004, p. 277–278.

Peer Instruction: Do Students Really Learn from Peer Discussion in Computing?

Leo Porter, Cynthia Bailey Lee, Beth Simon
Computer Science and Engr. Dept.
University of California, San Diego
La Jolla, CA USA
+1 858 534 5419
{leporter,clbailey,esimon}@ucsd.edu

Daniel Zingaro
Dept. of Computer Science
University of Toronto
Toronto, ON, Canada

daniel.zingaro@utoronto.ca

ABSTRACT

Peer Instruction (PI) is an instructional approach that engages students in constructing their own understanding of concepts. Students individually respond to a question, discuss with peers, and respond to the same question again. In general, the peer discussion portion of PI leads to an increase in the number of students answering a question correctly. But are these students really learning, or are they just "copying" the right answer from someone in their group? In an article in the journal Science, Smith et al. affirm that genetics students individually learn from discussion: having discussed a first question with their peers, students are better able to correctly, individually answer a second, conceptually-related question. We replicate their study, finding that students in upper-division computing courses (architecture and theory of computation) also learn from peer discussions, and explore differences between our results and those of Smith et al. Our work reveals that using raw percentage gains between paired questions may not fully illuminate the value of peer discussion. We define a new metric, Weighted Learning Gain, which better reflects the learning value of discussion. By applying this metric to both genetics and computing courses, we consistently find that 85-89% of "potential learners" benefit from peer discussion.

Categories and Subject Descriptors
K.3.2 [**Computer Science Education**].

General Terms
Algorithms, Human Factors

Keywords
Peer instruction, Clickers, PRS, Classroom response, Active learning.

1. INTRODUCTION
Based on observations that students learn very little in traditional physics lectures, Mazur and colleagues [4] developed and refined the active learning Peer Instruction (PI) pedagogy [2,4,7]. The core feature of PI is the multiple-choice question (MCQ): students begin by individually answering an MCQ (the individual vote), then discuss it with peers, and finally re-vote in light of that discussion (the group vote). Clickers–small, wireless keypads with buttons corresponding to response choices–are often used to allow a measure of student anonymity and accurate estimates of class ability by the instructor [2]; such estimates are useful for determining the direction of instructor-led discussion following each question.

The majority of early educational research in PI was done in physics. In that work, a commonly-reported metric is normalized gain (NG), which measures the improvement of students as a fraction of the total possible improvement. For example, if a student scores 60% on a pre-test and scores 80% on a post-test, their NG is 50%, meaning they learned 50% of what remained for them to learn". On the Force Concept Inventory (FCI), a standard physics concept inventory test, NG from pre- to post-course in PI classes were double that of traditional classes [4].

In computing, we have no widely-available concept inventories, so the above approach cannot be used to measure PI effectiveness. Instead, researchers have calculated NG on a per-question basis, and have found positive results. For example, one study found an NG of 41% in CS1 and 35% in CS1.5 [18], and a study of a remedial CS1 course reported an NG of 29% [22]. But, by measuring PI effectiveness in this way, the question must be asked: is this gain due to improved student understanding or due to students passively agreeing with neighbors [8]? In this replication and extension of [19], we seek to answer this question in the computing context by examining student performance on consecutive isomorphic questions (questions designed to exercise the same conceptual understanding). To the extent that students can individually answer an isomorphic question correctly, we have evidence of real understanding rather than peer-mirroring.

Isomorphic questions enable instructors to evaluate the learning gains provided by group discussion. Direct learning gains from discussion are demonstrated by students individually answering an initial question *incorrectly*, participating in a group discussion, answering that initial question *correctly*, and then, most critically, answering a new, conceptually-similar question *correctly*. In prior work [19], 16% of biology students in a class achieved these direct learning gains. Our work evaluates these gains in two different computer science classes: computer architecture and theory of computation, each taught by a different instructor. In these classes, the percentages of students who demonstrated these direct gains from the group discussion were 20% and 13% respectively.

In addition to demonstrating direct learning gains for students and thus reproducing results from Smith et al. [19], we identify differences between subject disciplines, define a new metric useful for exploring benefits of peer discussion, motivate the use of isomorphic questions in PI, and provide guidance for the development of isomorphic questions for computer science classes.

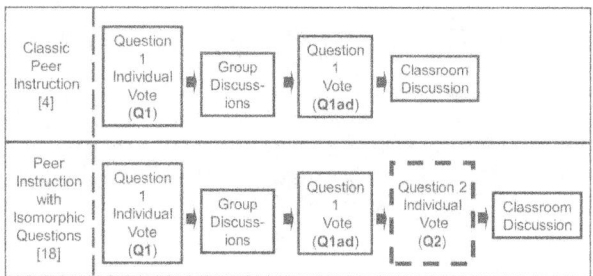

Figure 1. The Isomorphic Testing Process.

2. BACKGROUND & RELATED WORK

The core of classic PI (see Figure 1) is the in-class process of posing a deep conceptual question to students: having students answer the question individually, discuss it briefly with their seatmates, and vote again in light of increased understanding. However, to be most effective, PI requires other concordant course changes. In order to use class time most productively, many teachers require students to come prepared to discuss conceptual questions. Preparation can be solicited through pre-lecture reading and associated quizzes [4], pre-lecture screencasts [3], or clicker quizzes at the start of class [10]. Others suggest that PI-informed pedagogy should also occur in lab and tutorial sessions, not just lecture [4,22].

Key to the success of PI is the use of challenging conceptual questions that target common student misconceptions and core course concepts. Beatty et al. [1] offer helpful "tactics" for focusing student awareness, evoking cognitive processes, and promoting productive small-group and class-wide discussion. Other work provides best-practice tips for clicker use [2,21].

Several recent studies report the benefits of PI in computing [5,15,16,18,22]. In addition to consistently notable NGs, these studies use surveys to elicit student opinions and attitudes regarding PI. Students overwhelmingly support the effectiveness of PI for their learning, and recommend that it be used in further courses. In addition to student benefits, studies report various instructor benefits including a sharpened focus on student difficulties, an improved ability to adapt lectures, and an ability to involve students in teamwork and collaboration [16,18].

2.1 Isomorphic Questions in PI

Performance on individual MCQs and post-course student surveys tell us little about the long-term effects of answering MCQs. In the context of biology, Smith et al. [19] modified the classic PI format to assess the extent to which students were learning robust concepts, rather than copying peers or obtaining fragile, context-bound representations. Sixteen times throughout the term, students consecutively voted three times with no teacher intervention. Figure 1 contrasts classic PI with this variant where Q2 is a question isomorphic with Q1.

First, students answered a question individually (Q1). Next, they discussed that question in groups and voted again (Q1ad). Finally, and without seeing the answer to Q1, students were presented with a conceptually-similar isomorphic question (Q2) to which they responded individually. Isomorphic questions are questions that "look different" on the surface, but are simply "cover story" variations [19] that require students to adapt and apply the same core concept.

Smith et al.[19] found that the average correctness on Q2 was higher than the average correctness on both Q1 and Q1ad. Additionally, of those students who answered Q1 *incorrectly* and Q1ad *correctly* (i.e. those students who could have "copied" from their neighbors), 77% answered Q2 correctly. Finally, when looking at questions by difficulty, the increase from Q1ad to Q2 was more pronounced for the most difficult questions than for questions of other difficulties.

Similar research can be found in [17], where sequences of "rapid-fire" questions were used to free students from context-specific learning of concepts. The general finding is that on each subsequent question targeting the same concept, the student correctness rate increases.

2.2 The Value of Isomorphic Questions

One can evoke a social constructivist epistemology to understand the source of value in PI discussions [14]. Specifically, individual understanding arises powerfully in a context suffused both with opportunities to be active and opportunities to discuss with like-ability peers. Individually thinking about a question spurs the creation of an initial mental model, which can be refined through the ensuing peer discussion. Of importance is that these mental models be appropriate (i.e. match reality) and that students apply such models consistently in a variety of contexts [13].

Most commonly, teachers use one PI question per concept [17]. Students are expected to be able to apply that concept to a variety of situations. Unfortunately, a single MCQ may not be sufficient to alert teachers and students to potential difficulties in applying and abstracting concepts across situations. Ma et al. [13], for example, found that 41% of sampled CS1 students exhibited both a viable and a non-viable model for the same concept (reference assignment) on a course exam. On the specificity and rigidity of mental models, Jonassen notes: "What often makes human models weak and oversimplified is that they fail to identify relevant factors and are not dynamic, that is, they do not represent change in factors over time" [9]. Researchers have therefore investigated the use of multiple, sequential, isomorphic questions for both giving students more practice-per-concept and assessing mastery of concepts [17].

How are we to interpret the situation where students answer a first question correctly, but then answer a follow-up isomorphic question incorrectly? One hypothesis is that the students lack a coherent and generalizable model of the underlying concept. Research shows, however, that surface feature differences—the very features that we change in order to create isomorphic questions—can themselves substantially impact students' performance, even in the presence of robust conceptual understanding.

For example, several studies have found drastic differences in student performance on various versions of the Tower of Hanoi problem [11], where all versions are isomorphic regarding problem space and transformations between states. Two such isomorphisms include "move isomorphisms" (where discs are physically moved) and "change isomorphisms" (where discs do not move, but are made larger or smaller in-place). The general finding is that change isomorphisms are twice as difficult as move isomorphisms, and that this difference must lie in the way that subjects imagine or model the different situations. Kotovsky et al. [11] suggest several hypotheses; for example, that isomorphic questions differ linguistically, that they differ in the ease with which their "rules" can be applied, that they are more or less consistent with real-world knowledge, that they impose different cognitive demands, and that they elicit differing internal representations of problem state. This highlights an important caution: questions deemed isomorphic by instructors are not necessarily isomorphic to students.

We are interested in the extent to which the findings of Smith et al. [19] (biology) and Reay et al.[17] (physics) apply to computing. First, in a discipline with no agreed-upon concept inventory, to what extent can we create questions that are isomorphic? Second, if a student answers Q1 incorrectly, they presumably have a fragile understanding of the underlying concept. Given the tenacity of misconceptions and non-viable concepts reported in much computing literature, is it possible for students to grasp a concept in the mere minutes that elapse between Q1 and Q2?

3. METHODOLOGY

Isomorphic questions were tested in two classes under various administrative and experimental controls. In addition, students self-reported their beliefs and experiences with PI through surveys.

3.1 Courses Included in this Study

Two courses were included in this study. Both are upper-division required majors courses, taught at a large R1 institution during the summer of 2010.

Introduction to Computer Architecture (N=51) focuses on instruction set and processor design. The instructor, a senior graduate student in the area, had previously taught the course at a different institution, had been a teaching assistant (TA) for this course multiple times, but had not used PI. The course met for six contact hours per week (four 1.5-hour lectures), for five weeks. Class participation (answering at least 80% of the PI questions in each meeting) was worth five percent of the course grade and reading quizzes were worth three percent of the course grade.

Introduction to the Theory of Computation (N=45) focuses on automata and proof-writing skills. The instructor had some prior teaching experience (four courses), but no prior experience using PI, nor teaching this specific course. The course met for six contact hours per week (two three-hour lectures), for five weeks. Class participation (answering at least 80% of the PI questions in each meeting) was worth six percent of the course grade and reading quizzes were worth four percent of the course grade.

Both instructors had observed PI as adopted in an introductory computing course at their institution and received 1-2 hours of advice in creating questions from the instructor of that class. Recent evidence has been reported showing inexperienced teachers whose instructional practices are grounded in research-based methodologies can be highly effective [6].

3.2 Methodology for Creating Isomorphic Questions

To create isomorphic questions, instructors initially identified several core concepts for each course. Then they identified a common misunderstanding or key element of that concept to emphasize in an MCQ.

After designing one MCQ, a second was created, patterned after the first in both the concept being tested and the targeted misconception or key idea related to that concept. Typically, several iterations of edits to both questions were required to bring them into alignment in terms of equal difficulty, as well as to remove similarities that would render one answerable based superficially on the other.

Each instructor enlisted a colleague with experience in the course, either as instructor or TA, who reviewed final drafts of the questions for accuracy and equal difficulty.

3.3 Question Administration and Experimental Controls

In order to assess the learning value of peer discussion, in isolation from other aspects of the classroom experience such as instructor explanation, the following restrictions were observed:

First, the question order of Q1 and Q2 was determined by random coin toss. Although the instructors endeavored to create equally difficult questions, this precaution further eliminated potential for instructor bias toward presenting an easier or harder question first.

Second, between the start of Q1 and the conclusion of collecting student responses to Q2, the instructor did not provide guidance or explanation.

Third, students were not shown the correct response to Q1 prior to responding to Q2, and, moreover, were not shown graphs of the class' responses, from which they might deduce the likely correct response.

Fourth, student consultation with peers during Q1 and Q2 was prevented by enforcing strict silence at those times. No group was permitted to begin group discussion until all Q1 responses had been collected.

Finally, using experienced instructors from outside of our local context, a post-hoc analysis was performed to confirm the equal difficulty and content of the question sets in both courses.

3.4 Student Survey

At the conclusion of the term, students were asked to respond to a questionnaire about their experiences using PI, and their perceptions of its usefulness for learning. The survey was required for course credit. In the architecture course, all but three students participated; in the theory course, all students participated. In both cases, students were advised that instructors would not see their responses until after final grades were submitted.

The questions that were adopted verbatim from the replicated study [19] used a five-point Likert scale. Several additional questions were included, and these used a six-point forced-choice Likert scale (i.e, no neutral option).

4. RESULTS

There are three components of our results. The first is a motivating example to show how two similar individual and group votes can mask different learning gains which can be elucidated through a second isomorphic question. The second is an analysis that compares the isomorphic results from the two computing courses and the work of Smith et al. [19]. Lastly, an analysis of student perspectives is provided.

4.1 Value of Isomorphic Questions

Classic PI has a single individual vote followed by a group discussion and group vote. Typically, the instructor then adapts the classroom discussion and follow-on material based on the percentage of students correctly answering the group vote [16]. For example, although some instructors encourage students to explain their reasoning (not just the answer) for both correct and

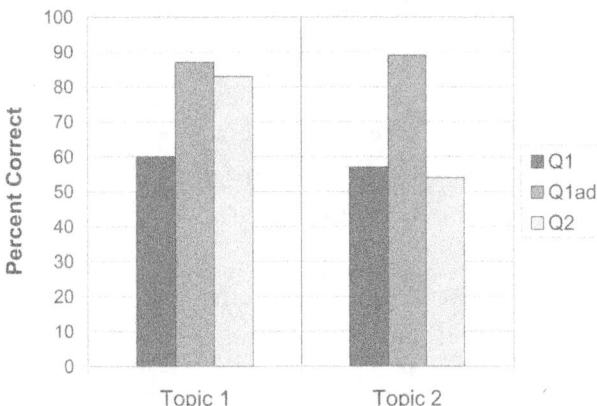

Figure 2: Percentage of students answering correctly for Q1, Q1ad, and Q2 for two topics from the architecture class.

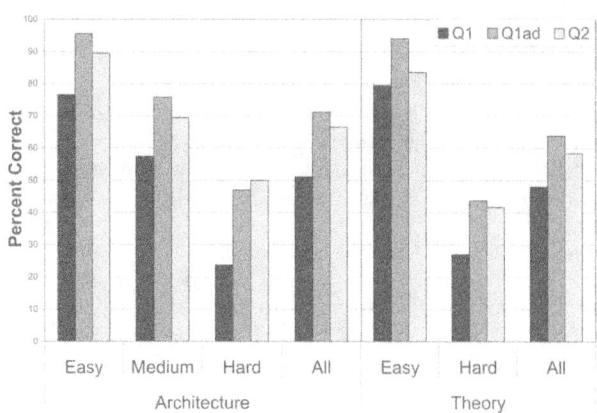

Figure 3: Percentage of students answering correctly for Q1, Q1ad, and Q2.

incorrect choices, it can be enticing for an instructor to hurry discussion in the presence of a compelling correct response rate.

Taken from the architecture class, two sets of questions with a high correct response rate on the group vote serve to illustrate the value of asking a follow-on isomorphic question. Figure 2 shows the average percentage of students responding correctly in Q1, Q1ad and Q2, for two different topics. In both cases, the percentage of students answering Q1 and Q1ad are comparable. The large percentage of students answering Q1ad correctly could indicate to the instructor that the students now understand the topic and the class-wide discussion can be brief. However, the Q1ad vote can be misleading. In Topic 1, the students demonstrate that their understanding of the material after the group discussion is strong enough that it can be applied to new topics. In the case of Topic 2, student understanding was not only fragile, but peer discussion may have confused some of the originally-correct students, or students may have been able to come up with the right answer without a deep understanding of the core issues. Without an isomorphic question, an instructor may struggle to determine whether a situation like Topic 1 or Topic 2 has occurred.

4.2 Student Learning Results

As presented in Section 4.1, the second isomorphic question is valuable in determining whether the group discussion resulted in generalizable learning. In that vein, Figure 3 provides the average percentage of students responding correctly to Q1, Q1ad, and Q2, in each of the two courses. Averages across Easy, Medium, and Hard question categories are provided. The classification of questions as Easy, Medium, or Hard was done according to the percentage of students responding correctly to Q1, as was done by Smith et al. [19]. All question categories in both courses show improved correctness from Q1 to Q1ad. The critical component— the component that demonstrates that the group discussion was helpful—is the gain from Q1 to Q2, which is positive for all classes. The difference between Q1ad and Q2 is also important as it may indicate fragile student understanding; i.e. they could understand Q1, but could not apply that understanding to Q2 [12]. In nearly all cases, there was some decrease in the percentage responding correctly between Q1ad and Q2, though Q2 was still higher than Q1. (The one exception is the Hard question category from architecture; on average, more students responded correctly

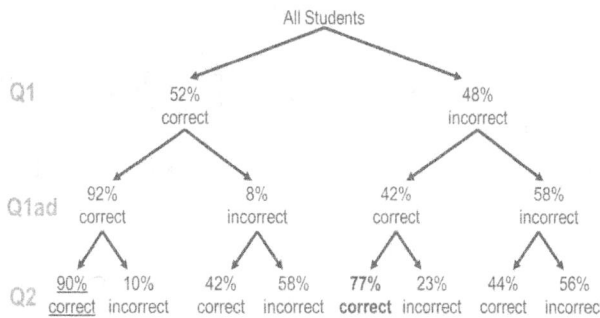

Figure 4: Flow chart from Smith et al.

to Q2 than Q1ad. Further discussion is in Section 5.) These data, demonstrating improvement between Q1 and Q2, are consistent with the finding that students learn from group discussion, and that not all of the Q1ad improvement was due to "copying" from a knowledgeable group member. The next set of diagrams further examines from which student populations these gains stem.

Figures 4-7 trace student response patterns over three-question isomorphic sequences. For each tree, the top two branches correspond to the percentage of all students responding correctly (left branch) and incorrectly (right branch) to Q1. The next layer down are the percentages (for each of the previously split groups) who answered correctly (left) and incorrectly (right) to Q1ad. Percentages are relative in these figures. In Figure 4, for example, *92% of the 52% of students who answered Q1 correctly* went on to answer Q1ad correctly again following the group discussion. Figure 4 contains the biology class results from Smith et al. [19]. Percentages are the average across all questions from the term that were reported in that study. Figure 5 provides the results from the architecture course, broken out into the averages of the Easy, Medium, and Hard questions, respectively, and the average of All questions. Figure 6 presents the average results for Easy, Hard, and All questions from Theory of Computation.

In Figures 4-7, the number in each tree which deserves the most attention is the one in bold font. This result depicts students who incorrectly answer Q1, then correctly answer Q1ad, and then correctly answer Q2. These students are gaining appreciable benefit from the group discussion as they did not understand the

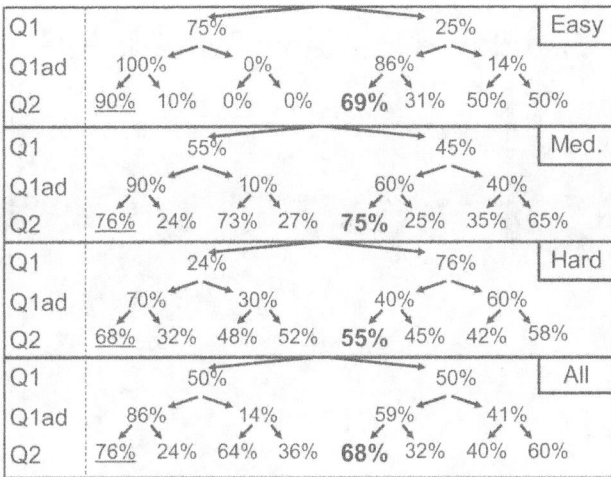

Figure 5: Flow chart for architecture grouped by easy, medium, hard, and overall average. Similar to prior results, left indicates correct, right indicates incorrect.

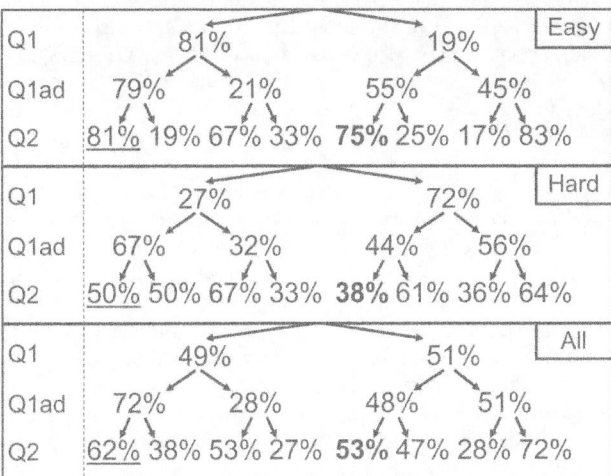

Figure 6: Flow chart for theory of computation grouped by easy, hard, and overall average. Similar to prior results, left indicates correct, right indicates incorrect.

concept at the first individual vote, learned from their group during the discussion, and then were able to apply that understanding to the next question. In each category, learning gains in computing are comparable to those provided for biology in Smith et al. [19].

Rather than using relative percentages, Figure 7 compares the all-question average for the three courses using absolute percentages. This helps capture the effect of the initial difficulty of the question–the fewer students getting Q1 incorrect, the greater potential benefit there is for discussion to be beneficial for students.[1] The most critical group (Q1 incorrect, Q1ad correct, Q2 correct) is again bolded. We can see that in each class (Smith's, architecture, and theory), somewhere between 13% and 20% of the students had demonstrable gains in learning from their discussion. One other notable difference between Smith's results

---
[1] There is no hard and fast rule for what defines a "good clicker question" based on how many students should get it right in the first vote, but Mazur recommends between 35-70% [4] and a faculty handbook advises against too easy of questions [21].

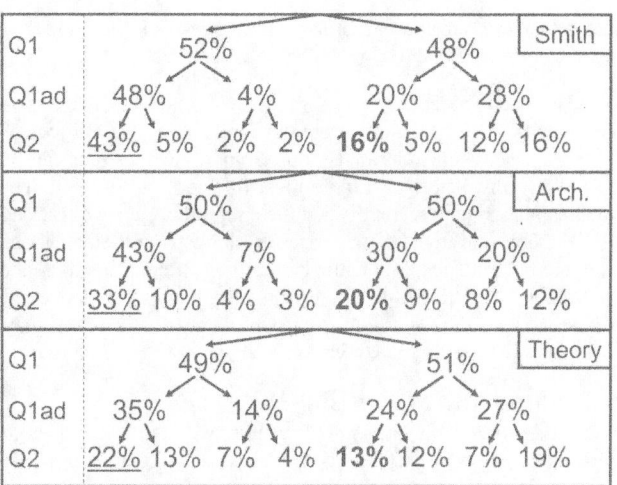

Figure 7: Flow chart for each class with percentage of students computed cumulatively.

in biology and those in computing is the percentage of students who answer Q1 correctly, Q1ad correctly, and Q2 incorrectly. The percentage of students in that group for Smith et al.'s biology class, the architecture class, and the theory class are 5%, 10%, and 13% respectively. These results will be discussed in more detail in Section 5.

4.3 Student Survey Results

Students broadly believed that "clickers with discussion is valuable for my learning" (80% and 86% agree for architecture and theory, respectively). They also believed that peer discussion caused them to learn more during lecture than they would otherwise. Responding to the statement: "If we completely took away the option for you to talk to your classmates during clicker questions, it would increase (or not change) the amount I learn during lecture," 73% in architecture and 82% in theory disagreed. Representative student comments include "I have learned different ways at approaching a question by the way group members explain it. To me, it has been highly valuable," and "Explaining why we think one answer is right over another helps us formalize the logic of why we chose that answer."

In architecture and theory (respectively), when asked if a knowledgeable group-mate was necessary to have a good discussion, 44% and 44% agreed, 25% and 34% were neutral, and 31% and 22% disagreed. Thus, in regard to learning in discussion, student opinion favored the necessity of having a knowledgeable group-mate. This is in contrast to the result in [19], where, responding to the same question, 47% of students disagreed. A typical comment from students who said it was necessary to have someone in the group who knew the correct answer was: "This is because at least one person is needed in order to explain how to obtain the correct answer." Representative comments from students who did not feel it was necessary include, "Sometimes just discussing the concept is important, even if nobody is sure," and "If neither of us knew the correct answer, we usually each knew enough about the question to collaborate and come up with a reasonable solution together."

Finally, students overwhelmingly supported the adoption of PI by other professors. In architecture and theory (respectively), 90% and 91% of students broadly agree that "I recommend that other instructors use our approach...in their courses." In both classes, 33% very strongly agree" with this statement.

5. DISCUSSION

The results and experiences from our study lead to a number of areas for discussion. The first is that isomorphic questions can be valuable to instructors as a tool to test for the fragility of student understanding. The second is that the computer science questions used in our study had different result characteristics than those presented in [19] and potentially require different metrics for evaluation. The third is that student qualitative responses elicited different views of discussion and group member roles which may factor into discussion effectiveness.

5.1 Isomorphic Question Design

As demonstrated in our initial example (Figure 2), a high percentage of students correctly answering Q1ad does not necessarily imply solid conceptual understanding. Students may be copying other student responses [8] or simply have a fragile understanding of the concept [12]. Evidence of such losses from Q1ad to Q2 occurred in questions from all difficulty levels. The losses in student correctness from Q1ad to Q2 for hard questions are likely attributable to fragile knowledge [12]. One hypothesis for the drop in easy questions is that students tended to have briefer, less in-depth discussions on questions self-deemed to be trivial. Further studies would be needed to confirm this hypothesis.

Regardless of the source of the drop in the percentage of students responding correctly, the existence of that drop motivates the use of isomorphic questions. By asking follow-up questions, the instructor can evaluate the level of student understanding. This is particularly important *for course topics where broad student understanding is crucial.*

Our instructors found that developing isomorphic questions can be difficult. Expert advice was useful as a means of feedback, but may be impractical or unavailable for other instructors adopting this pedagogical technique. In contrast, randomization of the questions was both highly useful and simple. Both instructors noticed an initial tendency to write a slightly easier question first, but when faced with the knowledge that the questions would be randomized, question difficulty became more consistent.

For the purposes of this study, students were not given any explanation by the instructor between Q1 and Q2. However, in a typical classroom, an instructor using isomorphic questions may wish to pose Q2 after leading a class-wide discussion and providing any further instruction as needed. Measuring student learning in this context would be an interesting area of exploration for future work.

5.2 Evaluating Learning Gained

In the context of isomorphic questions, a group of particular interest is the group of students who get Q1 incorrect and Q1ad correct. We define this group as the *potential learners*. This is not to say they are the only students learning from the PI process, but they define the set of students who appeared to learn through the peer group discussion[2].

---

[2] Also of interest, but beyond the scope of this paper, is the Q1 incorrect, Q1_ad incorrect, Q2 correct group which may have evidenced learning after seeing the concept in another context.

Amdahl's Law and Parallelism

- Our program is 90% parallelizable (segment of code executable in parallel on multiple cores) and runs in 100 seconds with a single core. What is the execution time if you use 4 cores (assume no overhead for parallelization)?

Execution time after improvement = Execution Time Affected / Amount of Improvement + Execution Time Unaffected

Selection	Execution Time
A	25 seconds
B	32.5 seconds
C	50 seconds
D	92.5 seconds
E	None of the above

Figure 8: Q1 from an isomorphic pair of "easy" questions in the architecture class.

When examining the results for all three classes, a notable difference appeared (as mentioned in Section 4.2). Smith et al. found that, of those students who correctly answer Q1 and Q1ad, 90% proceed to correctly answer Q2. For the two classes of this study, architecture and theory, those numbers are notably smaller, at 76% and 62% respectively.

One would expect that students who initially understand the concept (answer Q1 correctly) and hold onto that understanding (answer Q1ad correctly) would be capable of answering Q2 correctly. The relatively lower numbers of students in this category for the computer science classes caused the instructors to wonder—were our questions truly isomorphic in tested content? It was true that the computing instructors were both novice users of PI, teachers with less than five years of experience, and the theory instructor was teaching that course for the first time. However, our questions had been judged isomorphic by two outside experts (with significant related teaching experience) and delivery order had been randomized compared to the order of question development. This leads us to posit that, in computing, having questions that test the same knowledge" may be different than what is meant in biology. Anecdotally, computer science instructors hesitate to ask students plug and chug" questions; e.g., questions where a basic algorithm or set of steps can be applied to find the solution. Although PI questions in other STEM fields are commonly labeled ConcepTests", both our inexpert review of the isomorphic questions in [19] and our understanding of Smith's explanation of them [20] leads us to believe that differences exist in the kinds of questions computing instructors identify as isomorphic compared to those used by Smith et. al.

Examining the questions asked in computer science, the two sets of easy" questions from architecture were more similar to the biology questions in that they asked students to apply an algorithm to solve a problem. For those easy questions, the percentage of students who answer Q1 and Q1ad correctly, but then answer Q2 incorrectly, was the same as Smith et al.'s overall percentage of 10%. For example, an atypically easy isomorphic question from the architecture class was on the topic of Amdahl's Law (Q1 appears in Figure 8). In this question, students are asked to apply the Amdahl's Law equation (provided). The correct response is $90 / 4 + 10 = 32.5$ seconds (B). Q2 changes the question to 2 cores rather than 4. Q2 is entirely the same as Q1 except for the possible responses and the number of cores. If students understand the application of Amdahl's Law in Q1, they need only apply the same equation from Q2 to Q1 to achieve the correct result. For this question, 71%, 93%, and 93% of students responded correctly to Q1, Q1ad, and Q2 respectively. 100% of students who answered Q1 correctly and Q1ad correctly also answered Q2 correctly (these students represented 61% of the class). For further reference and for more typical examples, all questions from this study appear in supporting online text ([23]). The potential similarities (and differences) between these disciplines leads us to believe that this may be an interesting area for future study.

Regardless of the potential differences in questions from the two disciplines, the percentage of students who answer each of Q1, Q1ad, and Q2 correctly provides insight into the evaluation methodology and provides a useful metric for instructors. Let us define a *control group (CG)* as those students who seem to have mastered the concept by correctly answering Q1 and Q1ad.

The *potential learner group (PLG)* are those who learned the material from the group discussion (Q1 incorrect, Q1ad correct). We can use the CG's ability to answer Q2 correctly to assist in normalizing our expectation for the PLG to correctly answer Q2. That is, if the CG did not do well in correctly answering Q2, we should reduce (or weight) our expectations for the PLG to answer correctly.

We can use the percentage of the CG who correctly answer question Q2 as a measure of the maximum of available learning for the PLG. This metric provides us with Weighted Learning Gain (WLG)—weighted by the CG—expressed in Equation (1).

$$WLG = \frac{PLG\ \%\ correct}{CG\ \%\ correct} \qquad (1)$$

Using this metric, the three classes tell remarkably similar stories. The WLGs for Smith et. al's biology class, the architecture class, and the theory class are 86%, 89%, and 85% respectively. We believe this metric to be more representative of the value of discussion than the raw percentage increase.

5.3 Student Beliefs on the Nature of Discussion

As noted in the Student Survey Results (section 4.3), we found many students believed "having someone in the group who knows the correct answer is necessary in order to make the discussion productive" (69% and 78% agreed in architecture and theory respectively). We contrast this with the results in [19], where only 53% agreed. This disparity may be partially attributable to differences in the difficulty or style of questions used in each class. It may also be partially attributable to students' beliefs about what is normative in the nature of group discussion and roles within the group. Open-ended responses yielded two main categories of beliefs:

1. Students who believed it was necessary to have someone who knows the correct answer in the group often appeared to endorse a view that, *within the group, students replicate hierarchical teacher-student roles*. Representative comments include: "Someone [who] knows the answer will help others to learn," "Having someone that knows the concept is better to teach others in the group," and "…they corrected us."

2. Students who believed it was not necessary to have someone who knows the correct answer in the group often described *organizational structure and processes in which group member roles are undifferentiated*. Representative comments include: "Working together can also get you to the correct answer" and "Even if nobody knows the answer, each person might know different pieces of the answer that, together, could lead the group to the right answer". These responses were also more likely to attach value to the process, independent of the result: "There were a number of times that our group reached a wrong conclusion, but the discussion itself resulted in a better understanding of the relevant concepts" and "When people are throwing around ideas, you learn different approaches to a problem."

Many students expressed simply that they felt they could not progress without someone who knows the correct answer ("If nobody knows the answer, you get nowhere. Oftentimes, we just sit there and wait for the instructor because we're both confused"). There was not enough information to suggest whether these students endorse belief 1 or belief 2. Because this question was not designed specifically to elicit this information, more data would be needed to adequately characterize the prevalence of different beliefs about intra-group roles (e.g., targeted survey questions and follow-up interviews). This is a potential topic for further inquiry.

6. CONCLUSIONS

This paper replicates a key finding about the value of peer discussions for learning in the context of courses adopting the Peer Instruction pedagogy. Using matched-ability (isomorphic) questions, Smith et al. demonstrated that students learn from peer discussion in biology [19]. We replicate that result and find strikingly similar learning gains in two computing courses—architecture and theory of computation. During this study, we identified a phenomenon where questions deemed isomorphic by instructors were experimentally shown to be of different difficulty for students. To properly adjust for this phenomenon, we define a new metric, Weighted Learning Gain, that better measures student learning gains for isomorphic questions. We suggest that the use of this metric in future studies of isomorphic questions may not only lead to more comparable explorations of the value of peer discussion, but also illuminate issues surrounding fragile knowledge regarding specific disciplinary concepts. Lastly, we recommend that isomorphic questions be used for critical course concepts, where timely detection, acknowledgment, and discussion of misconceptions are most important.

7. REFERENCES

[1] Beatty, I. D., Gerace, W. J., Leonard, W.J., and Dufresne, R. J. Designing effective questions for classroom response system teaching. American Journal of Physics 74, 2006.

[2] Caldwell, J. E. Clickers in the large classroom: Current research and best-practice tips. CBE-Life Sciences Education 6, 2007.

[3] Carter, P. An experiment with online instruction and active learning in an introductory computing course for engineers: JiTT meets CS. 14th Western Canadian Conference on Computing Education, 2009.

[4] Crouch, C. H., and Mazur, E. Peer instruction: Ten years of experience and results. American Journal of Physics 69, 2001.

[5] Cutts, Q., Carbone, A., and van Haaster, K. Using an Electronic Voting System to Promote Active Reflection on

Coursework Feedback. In Proceedings of Intl. Conf. on Computers in Education, Melbourne, Australia, 2004.
[6] Deslauriers, L., Schelew, E., and Wieman, C. Improved Learning in a Large-Enrollment Physics Class. Science 332, 2011.
[7] Hake, R. R. Interactive-engagement vs. traditional methods: A six-thousand-student survey of mechanics test data for introductory physics courses. American Journal of Physics 66 (1), 1998.
[8] James, M.C., and Willoughby, S. Listening to student conversations during clicker questions: What you have not heard might surprise you! American Journal of Physics 79, 2011.
[9] Jonassen, D. H. Externally modeling mental models. In Learning and Instructional Technologies for the 21st Century, L. Moller, J. B. Huett, and D. M. Harvey, Eds. Springer US, 2009.
[10] Knight, J. K., and Wood, W. B. Teaching more by lecturing less. Cell Biology Education 4, 2005.
[11] Kotovsky, K., Hayes, J.R., and Simon, H.A. Why Are Some Problems Hard? Evidence from Tower of Hanoi. Cognitive Psychology 17, 1985.
[12] Lister , R., Adams, E.S., Fitzgerald, S., Fone, W., Hamer J., Lindholm, M., McCartney, R., Moström, J.E., Sanders, K., Seppälä, O., Simon, B., and Thomas, L. A multi-national study of reading and tracing skills in novice programmers, ACM SIGCSE Bulletin 36(4), 2004.
[13] Ma, L., Ferguson, J., Roper, M., and Wood, M. Investigating the viability of mental models held by novice programmers. In Proceedings of the 38th SIGCSE technical symposium on computer science education, 2007.
[14] Nicol, D. J., and Boyle, J. T. Peer Instruction versus Class-wide Discussion in Large Classes: a comparison of two interaction methods in the wired classroom. Studies in Higher Education 28(4), 2003.
[15] Pargas, R. P., and Shah, D. M. Things are clicking in computer science courses. In Proceedings of the 37th SIGCSE technical symposium on Computer science education, 2006.
[16] Porter, L., Bailey-Lee, C., Simon, B., Cutts, Q., and Zingaro, D. Experience Report: A Multi-classroom Report on the Value of Peer Instruction. In proceedings of the 16th Annual Conference on Innovation and Technology in Computer Science Education, 2011.
[17] Reay, N., Li, P., and Bao, L. Testing a new voting machine question methodology. American Journal of Physics 76, 2008.
[18] Simon, B., Kohanfars, M., Lee, J, Tamayo, K., and Cutts, Q. Experience report: Peer instruction in introductory computing. In Proceedings of the 41st SIGCSE technical symposium on computer science education, 2010.
[19] Smith, M., Wood, W., Adams, W., Wieman, C., Knight, J., Guild, N., and Su, T. Why Peer Discussion Improves Student Performance on In-Class Concept Questions. Science 323, 2009.
[20] Smith, M., Personal Correspondance, 2010.
[21] Wieman, C. and the staff of the CU and UBC Science Education Initiatives. Clicker Resource Guide, http://cwsei.ubc.ca/resources/clickers.htm.
[22] Zingaro, D. Experience report: Peer instruction in remedial computer science. In Proceedings of the 22nd World Conference on Educational Multimedia, Hypermedia & Telecommunications, 2010.
[23] http://cs.ucsd.edu/~bsimon/ICER2011_PI/

PeerWise: Exploring Conflicting Efficacy Studies

Paul Denny	Brian Hanks	Beth Simon	Spencer Bagley
Dept. Of Computer Science	BFH Educational Consulting	Computer Science and Engineering Dept.	Math and Science Education Doctoral Program
The University of Auckland	Seattle, WA 98119	Univ. of California, San Diego	UCSD/SDSU
Auckland, New Zealand	brianhanks@acm.org	La Jolla, CA 92093	La Jolla, CA 92023
paul@cs.auckland.ac.nz		bsimon@cs.ucsd.edu	sbagley@ucsd.edu

ABSTRACT
PeerWise (PW) is an online tool that allows students in a course to collaborate and learn by creating, sharing, answering and discussing multiple-choice questions (MCQs). Previous studies of PW at the introductory level have shown that students in computing courses like it, and report statistically significant learning gains in courses taught by the investigators at different institutions. However, we recently conducted three quasi-experimental studies of PW use in upper-division computing courses in the U.S. and failed to replicate these positive results. In this paper we consider various factors that may impact the effectiveness of PW, including instructor engagement, usage requirements and subject-matter issues. We also report several positive results from other STEM courses at the same institution, discuss methodological issues pertaining to our recent studies and propose approaches for further investigation.

Categories and Subject Descriptors
K.3.1 [**Computers and Education**]: Computer Uses in Education – *collaborative learning*.

General Terms
Experimentation, Human Factors.

Keywords
PeerWise, Multiple-Choice Questions, Assessment.

1. INTRODUCTION
PeerWise (PW) is an online tool that supports students in the authoring, sharing, and discussing of multiple-choice questions for a particular course. Since its first use in 2007, more than 150,000 questions and 3.5 million answers have been submitted by students from 100 institutions around the world. PW attempts to capitalize on student familiarity with social software and the value of user-generated content, by encouraging them to develop a shared learning resource. Placing the creation of the resource in the hands of the students represents a shift away from very traditional learning environments, in which the instructor is the single source of authority, and towards an environment in which students are responsible for supporting one another's learning [8].

Reported impact of PW on student learning in computing courses has been positive, but limited to a small number of introductory courses by PW investigators (i.e., Denny and Simon). Denny et al. [3] show positive correlation between PW activity and performance on a final exam (normalized using student performance data on a midterm before PW was introduced), where required usage was minimal and students were most active at the end of the term. In [4], Simon et al. show similar positive impact on learning in a course where students used the tool more extensively, with fortnightly requirements. We were interested in investigating whether such results would generalize to other courses, as the "instructor effect", where instructional innovations succeed best when accompanied by the enthusiasm or support of the developer of the innovation, is well recognized [13].

Here we report on the use of PW, and the subsequent analysis of student learning, using three quasi-experimental studies of upper division computing courses in the U.S.: operating systems, databases, and programming languages. For each study, we collected data for two terms of the course, taught during the same academic year, by the same instructor, and with the same final exam. In each case, in one term the instructor required PW use in the course multiple times (as a form of homework); the other term was taught similarly but without the use of PW. Analysis of the data from these courses shows no effect from using PW.

In addition to detailing these studies, we briefly report results from other disciplines in which outcomes were positive, and discuss issues that may account for our neutral results.

2. BACKGROUND
Although students are familiar with answering questions in an educational setting, challenging them to author questions and explanations presents many learning opportunities, such as focusing their attention on content and actively engaging them in processing and organizing the course material targeted by their questions. These and other benefits are well documented [15, 24], and sit alongside empirical evidence to support the inclusion of student-generated questions in the learning process [1, 20, 26].

The use of technology allows students to easily share their authored questions with one another, adding a social constructivist element [11]. A number of tools have been developed supporting a range of question types, from multiple-choice questions (AGQ [2], QPPA [25], QSIA [18], Questionbank [7]), to open-response questions [10], and programming questions [6]. In this paper we focus on a particular technology, PeerWise [3], which supports the multiple-choice question domain. While the MCQ format is familiar to students, it is also potentially challenging. First, creating good MCQs with plausible distractors that effectively target misconceptions is a difficult task [17]. Second, most students have no experience writing questions [22, 27], although

---

Permission to make digital or hard copies of all or part of this work for personal or classroom use is granted without fee provided that copies are not made or distributed for profit or commercial advantage and that copies bear this notice and the full citation on the first page. To copy otherwise, or republish, to post on servers or to redistribute to lists, requires prior specific permission and/or a fee.
ICER'11, August 8-9, 2011, Providence, Rhode Island, USA.
Copyright 2011 ACM 978-1-4503-0829-8/11/08...$10.00.

comprehensive guides on developing effective questions exist [23]. Finally, because students build a shared repository of questions, students acting maliciously or not participating seriously can compromise the quality of the resource.

PW enables students to answer one another's questions in a drill-and-practice fashion, providing immediate feedback. Students can also evaluate and critique each question they answer, bringing higher-level cognitive skills into play. In theory, because they are student-generated, the questions should be relevant to the content covered in a particular course. Students should be encouraged to test themselves frequently, as the benefits, particularly with respect to long-term retention, are well known [19]. Students who can successfully recall material they are tested on will remember it better in the future, and this effect holds in a range of educational contexts. In addition, the feedback received through regular question answering can help a student to develop accurate self-knowledge, which can then be used as a metacognitive control of their own learning [14].

The interface for the main menu of PW is shown in Figure 1. The page is organized into sections containing the questions authored by the student, the questions the student has answered, and all of the remaining unanswered questions. In this example, the screenshot also shows two notification messages. One of these indicates to the student that recent open-ended feedback has been written about questions they have authored. The other notification indicates that a question author has responded to open-ended feedback written by the student about a question they had previously answered. Displayed in the top right hand corner of the menu is a score that records an approximate measure of the extent to which other students in the course value the contributions of the student.

Figure 1. The main menu of PeerWise

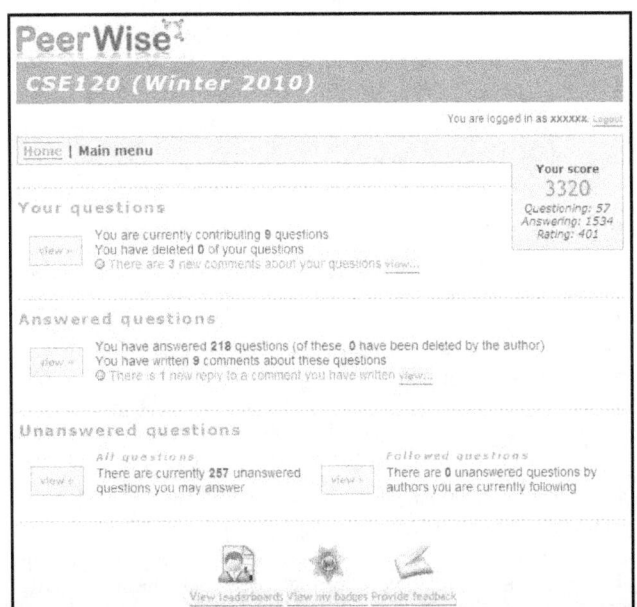

When searching for questions to answer, a student can choose to view only questions that have been associated (or "tagged") with a particular topic. The topics are defined by the question author at the time the question is created, and an initial list of course topics can be set up by the instructor. Figure 2 shows a list of available questions (from the Operating Systems course in our study) that have been tagged with the topic "mutual exclusion". When a student answers a question, they can select a quality and a difficulty rating for the question from a 6-point and a 3-point scale respectively. These ratings are aggregated per question and can be used by other students to find questions of interest. In the screenshot shown in Figure 2, the questions in the table are displayed in decreasing order of quality. Other information available in this table includes whether the author's answer is the most popular one selected, how many students have attempted the question, when the most recent comment about the question was written, how many students have requested specific help for the question, and the current difficulty rating of the question.

Figure 2. A list of questions available for answering

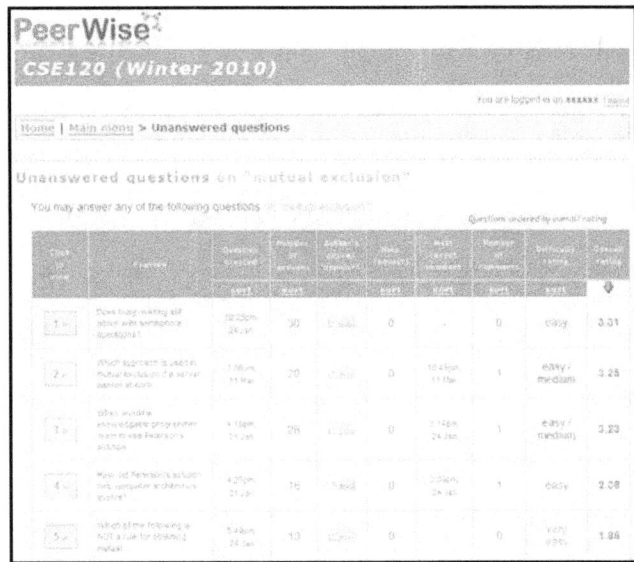

Previous studies of the use of PW in introductory programming courses have indicated that activity with the tool led to improved performance in formal examinations. While these studies have been conducted at different institutions, in each case the course instructors were involved with the development and investigation of the tool. A brief summary of two previous studies follows to highlight the methodological differences.

PW was used in a 12-week CS1 course taught at the University of Auckland in 2007 [3]. A mid-term test was held approximately half-way through the course, prior to PW being introduced. Students were able to use PW throughout the second half of the course (approximately 6 weeks) and were required to author 2 questions and answer 10 questions prior to a single deadline before the final exam. The mid-term test results were used to group students into quartiles, and the exam performance of the most and least active students on PW within each quartile were compared. A range of different measures of activity were considered, and for the most part the more active students outperformed the less active students on the final exam but not on the mid-term test.

In 2009, two 10-week CS1.5 courses taught at the University of California, San Diego (UCSD) were the focus of a similar analysis [4]. PW was introduced at the beginning of each course, and students were required to make contributions roughly every second week. Students were ranked based on their final course grade in the prerequisite CS1 course and ranked again based on their final course grade in the CS1.5 course. Students were organized into quartiles based on their activity with PW (measured as the number of questions answered), and the difference in rank was calculated for each student and averaged for each quartile. The data showed a positive relationship between increased PW activity and change in class rank. In both courses studied, students who used PW more tended to improve their class rank compared with their less active peers.

3. METHODOLOGY

As a follow-up to these studies, we were interested in investigating the impact of PW on student learning in computing classes not taught by the investigators. As both previous studies were at the introductory level, we were also interested in analyzing upper division courses. Therefore, we conducted a set of quasi-experimental classroom studies during the 2009-2010 academic year in three upper-division courses at UCSD: CSE 120 (operating systems), CSE 130 (programming languages), and CSE 132A (database principles). In each case, we studied two sections of the course: once without PW and once (in the following academic term) with PW. The two sections of each course were as similar as possible; they were taught by the same instructor using the same educational approach, the same assignments, and the same exams (although in some cases the questions were re-ordered). These instructors had not used PW previously, and were not invested in its success as developers or researchers. The instructors were offered a small payment for participating and helping us to collect data.

This design led to two methodological differences from previous work. First, students in the PW sections were required to author and answer questions on a weekly basis. This decision was motivated by a desire to encourage students to reflect on course material frequently and to regularly test their understanding. Roediger et al. [19] extol the benefits of regular testing on long-term retention and illustrate that more than simply assessing learning, testing can be a powerful means of improving it. Second, we did not have accurate norming data for students prior to using PW, as in previous studies. As students used PW throughout the course, mid-term grades were not appropriate for normalizing. Grades in prerequisite courses were not deemed particularly useful because students may not have taken these courses in the same sequence or from the same instructor. Consequently, we used the paired-sections approach to allow us to compare the performance of the classes.

In the three courses, we collected student performance data, including grades on homework assignments, laboratory exercises, and the final exam. In the sections in which PW was used, we also collected usage data, including the number of questions authored and answered by each student. Students were asked to author 1 question and answer 5 questions each week, and for meeting these requirements they were rewarded with 2% of their final grade. A short attitudinal survey was also conducted in each section using PW.

Finally, we invited students from these courses to participate in one-on-one interviews that were recorded and transcribed. Our invitations targeted students who were highly active with PW as well as students who were minimally active. The interviewers were in no way affiliated with the teaching of the course, and a total of 20 interviews were conducted, each lasting between 30 and 60 minutes. The interviews were semi-structured, and explored the way that students authored, answered and evaluated PW questions. In this paper, we have used the interview data to inform our discussion section, however we do not formally analyze the data.

For each pair of courses, we examined the impact of PW in the section in which it was used. If there appeared to be an impact that could potentially be attributed to PW use, we compared student performance in that section with its non-PW counterpart. We were interested in two aspects of PW use and their potential impact on student performance: question answering and question writing.

4. RESULTS

First, we report on the results of our data analysis in the three courses. We then report attitudinal results from student surveys and compare them to previous work. Finally, we provide high-level summaries of studies by others in other disciplines including bioengineering, structural engineering, biology and physics.

4.1 CSE 120

The 72 students in the PW section of this course answered between 1 and 477 PW questions, with a mean of 115.1 and a median of 82. Although there was a positive relationship (Pearson r = .19) between the number of PW questions answered and performance on the final exam, this relationship was not statistically significant (ANOVA: F = 2.63, p = .109).

Students in this section wrote between 0 and 12 PW questions, with a mean of 5.93 and a median of 7. There was a statistically significant relationship between question writing and exam performance (F = 6.66, p = .012). Despite this, the students in this section of CSE120 did not do as well on the final exam as those students in the prior term, who did not have access to PW. Table 1 compares the final exam scores of these cohorts.

Table 1. Final exam score

Term	n	Mean	Median
Fall 2009 (PW not used)	56	43.3	44
Winter 2010 (PW used)	72	39.3	40

This difference in final exam performance was statistically significant (F = 8.60, p = .004). For a possible explanation, we examined the cumulative grade point average (GPA) measured on a 4-point scale of the students in the two sections. We found that the students in the fall section had higher cumulative GPAs than the students in the winter section, as shown in the following table (we were unable to obtain cumulative GPAs for a few students):

Table 2. Cumulative GPAs

Term	n	Min	Mean	Median	Max
Fall 2009	46	2.39	3.26	3.30	4.0
Winter 2010	63	2.03	3.06	3.09	3.82

This difference in cumulative GPA was statistically significant (F = 4.91, p = .029). Assuming there is a relationship between a student's cumulative GPA and their performance on the final exam in CSE 120, it is not surprising that the students in the winter term did not do as well as those in the fall term. For the two sections, we analyzed the relationship between cumulative GPA and final exam performance. In both sections, the relationship was highly significant (p < .001). There was no secondary effect associated with the course section.

Further analysis of the winter section showed that a student's cumulative GPA was not a predictor of the student's likelihood to answer PW questions, suggesting that all students answered PW questions regardless of their GPA. However, there was a significant interaction between a student's GPA and the number of PW questions authored. This relationship was highly significant (ANOVA F = 7.62, p = .008) and suggests that students with higher GPAs were more likely to write PW questions. Further examination of the relationship between cumulative GPA, PW question authoring, and final exam performance showed that GPA and question authoring explained 31.0% of the variance in final exam score, but GPA alone explained 30.6% of the variance. This suggests that writing PW questions had no impact on a student's performance on the final exam in this course, but that students who had higher GPAs were more likely to write PW questions.

4.2 CSE 130

The PW section of this course was offered in the spring 2010 term. We examined the relationship between PW activity and final exam performance for the 128 students who took the final. Students answered between 0 and 243 questions, with a mean of 33.0 and a median of 20. They wrote between 0 and 14 questions, with a mean of 2.5 and a median of 2. There were 20 students who did not use PW.

There was no evidence that PW activity was correlated with final exam performance. Although there was a slight positive relationship between the number of questions answered and final exam score, this was not statistically significant ($p = .42$). There was a slight negative correlation between question authoring and exam performance, suggesting that students who wrote more PW questions did worse on the final, but this relationship was not statistically significant ($p = .46$).

There were also no statistically significant differences in performance among the students who used PW at least once, or between the students who never used it and those who did. We did not find any evidence that PW use had an effect on student performance on the final exam in this course.

4.3 CSE 132A

Fifty-three students took the final exam in the PW section of this course, which was offered in the winter 2010 term. Students answered between 0 and 232 PW questions, with a mean of 41.6 and a median of 33.5. They wrote between 0 and 13 questions, with a mean of 5.5 and a median of 7. There were seven students who did not answer or write any PW questions during the course.

Although there was a positive relationship between answering PW questions and final exam performance, this relationship was not statistically significant ($p = .15$). There was also no difference between the most and least active students in terms of question answering. The students who answered more than the median of 33.5 questions did slightly better on the final exam than the students who answered fewer questions, but this difference was not significant ($p = .19$). There was also no difference between the students who answered at least one question and those who did not answer any ($p = .95$).

There was a positive correlation between writing PW questions and final exam performance, but again this relationship was not statistically significant ($p = .08$). The half of the students who wrote at least 7 questions (the median contribution) did better on the final exam than those who wrote fewer, but this difference was not statistically significant ($p = .11$). There was also no difference in performance between the group of 11 students who did not write any PW questions and the 42 students who wrote at least one ($p = .10$).

Overall, although the trends were positive, we did not find any evidence that using PW had any statistically significant impact on student final exam performance in this course.

4.4 Student Attitudinal Surveys

To investigate student attitudes regarding PW, we conducted surveys in these courses. Unfortunately, the response rates in CSE132 (8 of 53 students) and CSE120 (18 of 72 students) were very low. In CSE 130, we received more vigorous instructor support and conducted two surveys: one at the class mid-term (response rate of 94% of students active with PW) and a follow-up survey at the end of the course (73% response rate). Both surveys included the Likert-type question, "I find PeerWise valuable for my learning" which was also asked on a survey conducted in the CSE8B class in which previous learning gains had been reported [4]. The surveys also included several open-ended response questions including "What do you believe is the biggest problem with PeerWise?".

The responses to the three surveys exhibit a large spread (Figure 3). Statistical analysis using a Kruskal-Wallis test (a non-parametric equivalent of ANOVA) indicated that there was a significant difference between the response distributions in the three surveys ($p < .001$). Follow on analysis using a pairwise Wilcoxon rank sum test indicated that there was no difference in the response distributions in CSE 130 between the midterm and the end of the course ($p = .31$), but the difference between the two CSE 130 responses and the CSE8B responses were both significant at the $p < .001$ level. Student valuation in CSE 130 is clearly much less positive than previously reported results from author Simon's CSE8B course.

Figure 3. Likert scale responses

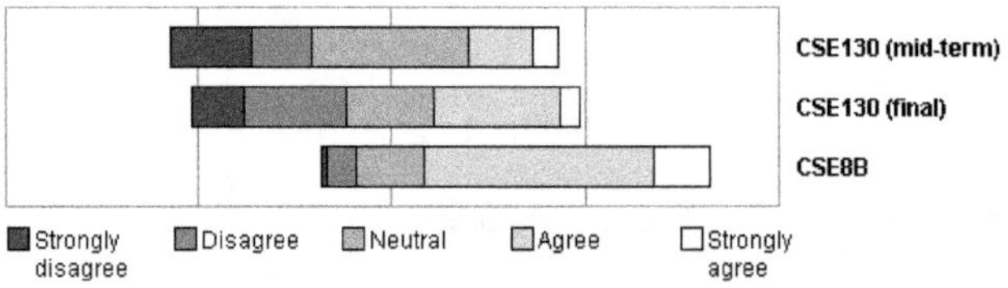

Informal analysis of the open-ended responses to the "What do you believe is the biggest problem with PeerWise?" question revealed that low-quality questions were the biggest concern for students in the CSE130 course (e.g. "The quality of questions are usually poor", "Some students provide poor questions or explanations"). The other two common themes were the fact that the activity was mandatory, and the fact that some students did not take the activity seriously, both of which may impact question quality.

4.5 Results in Other Disciplines

PW has also been used in several other disciplines at UCSD. Some instructors have done their own studies [5], and others have shared data from their classes with us for analysis. We see a much greater positive impact of PW outside the CS discipline at UCSD. The disciplines and courses in which it has been used include Bioengineering (Design), Biology (Organismic/Evolutionary Biology), Physics (Mechanics) and Structural Engineering (Dynamics).

In Bioengineering a midterm was conducted prior to PW being introduced, and students were required to author two questions with answering questions being voluntary. Students were divided into highly active (HA) and minimally active (MA) groups based on the number of questions answered. The HA and MA students performed similarly on the mid-term exam, indicating that no measurable self-selection effect existed, but HA students performed significantly better on the final exam ($p < 0.05$) [5].

PW was implemented similarly in Organismic/Evolutionary Biology; it was introduced after a midterm, with students required to author two questions and answer five for a token amount of extra credit. Students who used PW increased their score from their midterm to their final by an average of 7 percentage points, whereas students who did not only increased by 2 percentage points ($p < 0.01$). The normalized gain (a measure of the proportion of available points a student gains or loses from the pre- to the post-test, as described in [21]) was 11.6% greater for students who used PW compared with those who did not. There did not appear to be a self-selection bias, as no significant difference between the midterm scores of each group existed.

PW was also used in a lower-division physics class at UCSD. Students were given 0, 1, 2 or 3 points of extra credit at the end of the term, based on their PW usage level. The difference in mean scores on the final was not significantly different between levels of extra credit. However, when those who received any extra credit were separated out, their scores on the final were approximately 3 percentage points higher than those of their peers. One possible explanation for this observation is a self-selection effect; it appears that *how much* students used PW was not as important as *whether* students used PW.

PW was used twice in Dynamics, once in 2009 and again in 2010. In 2009, students who wrote at least 2 questions and answered 10 received 2% extra credit on the overall course grade. Students who used PW scored an average of 4 points higher on the final exam, which was statistically significant ($p=0.036$). No norming data (e.g., midterm scores) was available, so it is possible that other effects may account for this difference. In 2010 the same Dynamics instructor sought to more carefully explore the potential for PW to support student learning. 5% extra credit was offered on the final exam, but only half the course was randomly offered PW participation to earn this; the other half was offered a "cumulative" set of homework questions reflecting the entire term (homework was otherwise not required, collected, or graded that term, only "recommended"). In this case students who did either extra credit option scored 6 points better on the final than those who didn't ($p < 0.01$). However, these extra credit options were not equally effective: students who did the homework outperformed those who did nothing by 8.7 percentage points, whereas those who used PW only outperformed the inactive group by 3.4 percentage points ($p < 0.01$). Although the instructor estimate of the time required to do the homework thoroughly was 10 hours, we do not have an accurate measure of how long students actually took, or how this compares to the time spent by those students participating with PW.

5. DISCUSSION

While we were hopeful of replicating the results of earlier studies of PW in computing courses, we did not find similar positive impacts on learning in upper-division CS courses. In two cases there was no clear relationship between PW activity and exam performance. In the third case, the student cohort using PW did not perform better than the cohort who did not use it. These results lead us to ask, "Should we recommend PW to instructors and students in computing courses?"

In our discussion we consider three topics: the challenges of measuring the impact of PW on learning in in-situ university classroom settings, the potential "instructor" effect whereby tool developers or self-selected innovators find tools successful, but success is not replicated in "general" adoption, and the impact of course context and logistical factors on effectiveness.

5.1 Challenges of In-Situ Studies

Studies of the impact of PW on student learning are ideally carried out in-situ in real university-level courses, modeling its use in practice. However, the reality is that in such scenarios there exist a multitude of factors that are difficult to control. For example, did the time students spent using PW replace time they may have spent doing some other form of studying or learning? If so, which was more beneficial for them? Which was more efficient? Did PW's online, social and lightweight aspects engage students in studying more than they would have otherwise? Were students motivated by seeing how their answers compared to those of their peers? Did PW use enable students to recognize they needed to seek help from other resources or simply study more? Was it only the students who were interested in "doing better" in the course (regardless of their absolute performance level) who self-selected to use PW? On the other hand, are we happy that a resource exists for those students seeking improvement to use? Some of these questions can be informed by student self-reports, but others would be hard for students (or researchers) to measure accurately.

In the studies reported here, we were concerned that we did not have effective data for measuring students' learning prior to PW use. This was the initial motivation behind the design of the quasi-experimental studies, in which we considered the results of a previous cohort of students for comparison purposes. As it turned out, because we did not find significant correlations between student activity with PW and exam performance in the CSE130 and CSE132A courses, we did not examine the data for these courses from previous terms. We note that the levels of participation by students in the CSE130 and CSE132A courses was lower than in CSE120 (both in terms of authoring and answering questions), making it less likely for the data to exhibit a relationship. In the CSE120 course, where we found a significant relationship between authoring questions and exam performance, our comparison with the previous term was not valid due to students that term having higher cumulative GPAs.

In addition, it is worth emphasizing that the analyses we performed here are quantitative. Our metrics include the number of questions authored and answered, yet we haven't examined the quality of these questions. It is highly plausible that a student who spends an hour researching and writing a question that targets material they are initially unfamiliar with will benefit more than the student who rushes to complete a poorly worded question in a few minutes; our analysis in this paper does not differentiate these cases. An ongoing challenge is how to effectively motivate students to apply themselves to this task.

To avoid the difficulties associated with comparing different student cohorts, a better study design would model the one used in the Dynamics 2010 class. This involves randomly assigning students into two groups, one of which uses PW and the other having access to some other activity requiring a similar investment in time (which was likely not true in the reported case). These studies can be difficult to run for several reasons, including a) sufficient class size to enable statistical power and b) concern by instructors over offering different learning resources to students in the same course. Faculty may feel more comfortable performing such a randomized study on "extra credit" material – which brings its own self-selection effect to the study.

5.2 Instructor Effect

Previous PW studies in computing classes involved those taught by the investigators. The instructors' enthusiasm in these courses may lead to a phenomenon known as the "instructor effect" which may lead to un-replicable results. Various work in the STEM disciplines have explored the factors impacting instructional practice adoption issues; Henderson et al. give a review of the literature [9]. Although the instructors of the computing courses reported here were not invested in the success of the PW activity, neither were those of the physics or biology courses in which PW seemed to work well. It should be noted that both engineering faculty, teaching the Bioengineering and Design courses, were deeply interested in student learning and approached the authors with requests to use PW.

Beginning this study, we believed that instructor "buy-in" and transfer of that buy-in to the students in the class would be critical to the potential of PW to improve learning. Although the activity is primarily student-driven, the instructor plays an important role as a motivator. To this end, we asked our computing instructors to require PW use for a grade regularly throughout the term, find (or have a TA find) and review in class at least one good and one poor question each week to show students they value PW use, and to suggest to students that PW questions might be selected for use on the final exam. In reality, it was hard to ascertain the extent to which these directions were followed, or whether they had the desired effect on students. It may, in fact, not be as important as we initially thought, given the success of PW in classes in physics and biology where the instructors did not particularly promote the use of PW.

5.3 Context and Logistical Issues

A number of issues seem to affect PW value that derive from specific contextual and logistical aspects of the specific course in consideration. Some of these seem to have a disciplinary flavor that lead us to wonder if computing, specifically, is not as valuable a venue in which to utilize PW.

5.3.1 Difficulty of Authoring Questions

Although it didn't come across as a major theme in the surveys, a few students indicated that the process of authoring questions was difficult: "I've worked with [PW] before [in author Simon's class], and I think the main problem is that it is just hard to write questions for other people. Much harder than simply studying directly", "We don't have time to come up with correct questions when we are trying to understand concepts ourselves". As we discuss in the next section, this might be exacerbated when students are time limited or don't feel the need to take it seriously.

It may be that students would benefit from formal instruction on how to write good quality, relevant questions for their course. In an independent report of the use of student-authored questions in physics, McGregor et al. [12] devoted significant class time to setting the ground work for the activity, acknowledging the fact that students are unfamiliar with designing and authoring assessment questions. Instructors for the courses reported here were provided with a generic presentation to display in class that outlined a few ideas for writing good questions, including checking questions for errors and writing a detailed explanation for the answer, but no concrete ideas for authoring good questions relating to the course content.

Providing instruction and support for students on how to author good questions is likely to be course-specific. Future work might compare the quality of existing questions for the courses studied here, with those authored by students who have been given some formal training and support in question writing.

5.3.2 Workload and Existing Feedback Mechanisms

In follow-up interviews with students in the upper division computing courses, we identified a great deal of concern regarding the integration of PW into an existing "known" course. Specifically, the upper division computing courses at UCSD have well-known and almost universally replicated structures; students know that Class X is a programming-intensive class and that Class Y requires answering textbook open-ended questions, a small programming project, but no weekly programming and no proofs.

In our courses, students were aware that PW was a "new" part of the course and, moreover, that it was "added" to the course with no removal of other required work. The mandatory nature was grating, especially because they knew students "last term" didn't have to do it.

Combined with the previous concern of difficulty of writing good questions, this likely contributes to the problem of having a poor-quality question set. This may be reflected in the following student comments from surveys: "When it is mandatory to submit questions for a class, many students end up submitting questions with little work or thought put in", "Do not make it mandatory, this will keep people who do not want to be involved (and make bad questions) out". One student also commented that if they wanted to learn something, they'd write a program, not a multiple-choice question. Indeed, one advantage computing students may have over students in other disciplines is that they have the computer at their disposal to provide immediate feedback. The value of an activity like PW may be greater in subject areas for which correct answers cannot be verified so easily.

With particular regard to programming courses, tools which enable students to practice writing code may provide more useful drill-and-practice opportunities than a tool such as PW can offer. Several examples of such tools exist. CodingBat [16] is a well-known practice tool supporting both Java and Python that includes a database of exercises expressed as short descriptions of the specification for a single method. Students create an implementation for the method, and receive immediate feedback on the correctness of their code. Similarly, CodeWrite [6] allows students to practice implementing single methods and provides the same type of feedback as CodingBat. However, in the style of PW, the exercises available in CodeWrite are authored by the students themselves. Mirroring the challenge of authoring plausible distractors for MCQs within PW, students authoring exercises in CodeWrite must create a set of test cases that are used to verify other students' solutions. Tools such as CodingBat and CodeWrite may help students learning programming to build skill and confidence before they tackle larger programming projects.

5.3.3 Match with Exam Type

The PW tool currently supports only the MCQ format; however, this was not the format of the questions used on all exams. The CSE132A exam, for example, was comprised mainly of open-ended questions, with less than one-quarter being true/false questions. CSE 130 also used no MCQs on the final, though CSE 120 did. However, in the Biology class, the exams consist mainly of MCQs. The mismatch between question types used on the final exam and those supported by PW may have some impact on the usefulness of the activity as perceived by students.

6. CONCLUSION

In this paper we detail conflicting efficacy studies exploring the use of PeerWise in university STEM classes. We show no clear impact on learning for three upper-division computing courses, but positive results in five other STEM courses. We look in greater depth at the challenges in controlling these studies and discuss whether students in other disciplines may benefit more from PeerWise than those in computing.

7. ACKNOWLEDGMENTS
This work is supported in part by NSF DUE 0942397. We thank all the instructors who used PW and provided data: Lelli Van Den Einde, Melissa Micou, Benjamin Grinstein, Josh Kohn, Ranjit Jhala, Joseph Pasquale, Victor Vianu, and their TAs.

8. REFERENCES

[1] Barak, M. and Rafaeli, S. 2004. On-line question-posing and peer-assessment as means for web-based knowledge sharing in learning. Int. J. Human-Computer Studies, 61:84-103.

[2] Chang, S-B., Huang, H-M., Tung, K-J., and Chan, T-W. 2005. AGQ: a model of student question generation supported by one-on-one educational computing. CSCL '05. International Society of the Learning Sciences 28-32.

[3] Denny, P., Hamer, J., Luxton-Reilly, A., and Purchase, H. 2008. PeerWise: students sharing their multiple choice questions. ICER '08. ACM, USA, 51-58.

[4] Denny, P., Hanks, B., and Simon, B. 2010. Peerwise: replication study of a student-collaborative self-testing web service in a u.s. setting. SIGCSE '10. ACM, USA, 421-425.

[5] Denny, P., Simon, B., and Micou, M.K. 2010. Evaluation of PeerWise as an Educational Tool for Bioengineers, in ASEE Annual Conference and Exposition 2010: Louisville, KY.

[6] Denny, P., Luxton-Reilly, A., Tempero, E., and Hendrickx, J. 2011. CodeWrite: supporting student-driven practice of java. SIGCSE '11. ACM, USA, 471-476.

[7] Draaijer, S., and Boter, J. 2005. Questionbank: Computer Supported Self-Questioning. In M. Danson (Ed.), 9th Int. Comp. Assisted Assessment Conf. (pp. 235-250). Loughborough, UK.

[8] Hamer, J., Cutts, Q., Jackova, J., Luxton-Reilly, A., McCartney, R., Purchase, H., Riedesel, C., Saeli, M., Sanders, K., and Sheard, J. 2008. Contributing student pedagogy. SIGCSE Bull. 40, 4 (November 2008), 194-212.

[9] Henderson, C., Beach, A., & Finkelstein, N. (submitted) Facilitating Change in Undergraduate STEM Instructional Practices: An Analytic Review of the Literature, Submitted June 2010. Submitted for Journal Publication and Downloaded from http://homepages.wmich.edu/~chenders/Projects.htm

[10] Luxton-Reilly, A., Plimmer, B. and Sheehan, R. 2010. StudySieve: a tool that supports constructive evaluation for free-response questions. CHINZ '10. ACM, USA, 65-68.

[11] Mayes, T., and Fowler, C. 2006. Learners, learning literacy and the pedagogy of elearning. In A. Martin & D. Madigan (Eds.), Digital literacies for learning (pp. 26-33). London: Facet Publ.

[12] McGregor K. M. and Merchant A. R. 2005, Student authored questions encouraging a deeper learning in physics, Proc. of the Science Learning and Teaching Conference 2005, UK Centre for Materials Education, The Higher Education Academy, UK

[13] Mitra, A. 1994. Instructor-effect in determining effectiveness and attitude towards technology-assisted teaching: Report of a case study. Journal of Instruction Delivery Systems, 8(3), 15-21.

[14] Murphy, L. and Tenenberg, J. 2005. "Do computer science students know what they know?: a calibration study of data structure knowledge". SIGCSE Bull. Vol. 37, (3), 148-152, ACM

[15] Nicol, D. 2007. E-assessment by design: using multiple-choice tests to good effect. Journal of Further and Higher Education, 31(1):53-64.

[16] Parlante, N. Nifty reflections. SIGCSE Bull., 39(2):25-26, 2007.

[17] Pritchett, N. 1999. Effective Question Design. In S. Brown, P. Race & J. Bull (Eds.), Computer-Assisted Assessment in Higher Education (pp. 29-37). London: Kogan Page.

[18] Rafaeli, S., Barak, M., Dan-Gur, Y., and Toch, E. 2004. QSIA: a web-based environment for learning, assessing and knowledge sharing in communities. Comput. Educ. 43, 3 (Nov 2004), 273-289.

[19] Roediger, H. L., and Karpicke, J. D. 2006. Test-enhanced learning: Taking memory tests improves long-term retention. Psychological Science, 17, 249-255.

[20] Rosenshine, B., Meister, C., and Chapman, S. 1996. Teaching students to generate questions: A review of the intervention studies. Review of Edu. Research, 66(2), 181-221.

[21] Simon, B., Kohanfars, M., Lee, J., Tamayo, K., and Cutts, Q. 2010. Experience report: peer instruction in introductory computing. SIGCSE '10. ACM, USA, 341-345.

[22] Vreman-de Olde, C., and de Jong, T. 2004. Student-generated assignments about electrical circuits in a computer simulation. Int. J. of Science Education, 26(7), 859-873.

[23] Woodford, K. and Bancroft, P. 2004, Using multiple choice questions effectively in information technology education, in Proc. of the 21st ASCILITE Conference', Perth, pp. 948-955.

[24] Yu, F. Y., and Liu, Y. H. 2005. Potential values of incorporating multiple-choice question-construction for physics experimentation instruction. Int. J. of Sci. Ed., 27(11), 1319-1335.

[25] Yu, F. Y., Liu, Y. H., and Chan, T. 2005. A web-based learning system for question posing and peer assessment. Innovations in Education and Teaching Int., 42(4):337-348.

[26] Yu, F. Y., and Hung, C. C. 2006. An empirical analysis of online multiple-choice question-generation learning activity for the enhancement of students' cognitive strategy development while learning Science. Lecture series on computer and computational sciences: Recent progress in computational sciences and engineering (pp. 585-588). Chania, Crete, Greece.

[27] Yu, F. Y., and Liu, Y. H. 2008. Creating a psychologically safe online space for a student-generated questions learning activity via different identity revelation modes. British Journal of Educational Technology.

Students' Perceptions of the Differences Between Formal and Informal Learning

Jonas Boustedt
Division of Technology and Environment
University of Gävle
Gävle, Sweden
jbt@hig.se

Anna Eckerdal
Department of Information Technology
Uppsala University
Uppsala, Sweden
Anna.Eckerdal@it.uu.se

Robert McCartney
Department of Computer Science and Engineering
University of Connecticut
Storrs, CT USA
robert@engr.uconn.edu

Kate Sanders
Mathematics and Computer Science Department
Rhode Island College
Providence, RI USA
ksanders@ric.edu

Lynda Thomas
Department of Computer Science
Aberystwyth University
Aberystwyth, Wales
ltt@aber.ac.uk

Carol Zander
Computing & Software Systems
University of Washington Bothell
Bothell, WA USA
zander@u.washington.edu

ABSTRACT

Research has shown that most learning in the workplace takes place outside of formal training and, given the swiftly changing nature of the field, computer science graduates more than most workers, need to be able to learn computing topics outside of organized classes.

In this paper we discuss students' perceptions of the difference between formal and informal learning of computing topics, based on three datasets: essays collected from a technical writing course at a single university; the results of a brainstorming exercise conducted in the same course; and semi-structured interviews conducted at six institutions in three countries.

The students report strengths and weaknesses in informal learning. On the one hand, they are motivated, can choose their level of learning, can be more flexible about how they learn, and often retain the material better. On the other hand, they perceive that they may miss important aspects of a topic, learn in an ad hoc way, and have difficulty assessing their learning.

Categories and Subject Descriptors

K.3.2 [**Computers and Education**]: Computers and Information Science Education—*Computer Science Education*

General Terms

Measurement, Experimentation

Permission to make digital or hard copies of all or part of this work for personal or classroom use is granted without fee provided that copies are not made or distributed for profit or commercial advantage and that copies bear this notice and the full citation on the first page. To copy otherwise, to republish, to post on servers or to redistribute to lists, requires prior specific permission and/or a fee.
ICER'11, August 8–9, 2011, Providence, Rhode Island, USA.
Copyright 2011 ACM 978-1-4503-0829-8/11/08 ...$10.00.

Keywords

informal learning, self-directed learning

1. INTRODUCTION

Given the rapidly changing nature of computing, our students will have to continue learning after they graduate. The ACM Code of Ethics makes this explicit, requiring members to "acquire and maintain professional competence." [2] To keep current, most graduates will need to acquire at least some knowledge through informal learning, outside of formal classroom settings. Even before they graduate, many students learn computing topics informally.

In this paper we look at how students themselves characterize the differences between formal and informal learning and consider the implications of the students' perceptions for formal instruction. We further discuss the implication of these findings for computing educators, and for students moving into the world of work.

We base our analysis on three datasets: essays collected from a technical writing course at a single university; the results of a brainstorming exercise conducted in the same course; and semi-structured interviews conducted at six institutions in three countries.

The background to this study is presented in Section 2, the methodology in Section 3, and results are outlined and analyzed in Section 4. A discussion of the students' experiences and the implications for educators may be found in Section 5. The paper ends with conclusions and future work.

2. BACKGROUND

Informal learning is an umbrella term for several kinds of learning, including experiential learning, workplace learning, self-directed learning, and learning in informal environments, among others. Experiential learning is "the process whereby knowledge is created through the transformation of experience." [10, p. 41] Moon [14] gives the example of a student who sees and touches limestone at a quarry after hearing a lecture on its properties. In computing, experiential knowledge might be derived from hands-on projects, which are found in both informal and formal settings, from internships, or from other interactions with professionals.

Considerable attention has been paid to informal learning in the workplace, for example design engineers at automotive companies in Britain [8], K12 teachers in the United States [11], and Malaysian managers [7]. These professionals could be considered expert "informal students," and may serve as a point of comparison for beginners. This kind of research has shown the importance of informal and lifelong learning in workplaces. Cross [3] argues that informal learning is more efficient for learning skills than formal courses given by employers. Cross claims that formal training only represents 10 - 20 % of all learning at workplaces.

Self-directed learning is informal learning where the student is in control. A more intentional, planned type of informal learning, it has been defined by Knowles as:

> a process in which individuals take the initiative, with or without the help of others, in diagnosing their learning needs, formulating learning goals, identifying human and material resources for learning, choosing and implementing appropriate learning strategies, and evaluating learning outcomes. [9, p. 18] as quoted in [6]).

Self-directed learning is the best fit for the type of learning we are investigating.

Informal environments such as museums and galleries might be seen as places of extremely self-directed learning: they present visitors with carefully organized information, but visitors choose whether to go there, and what to learn when they do. On the other hand, children are often taken to museums on school trips, and there is a body of work by researchers seeking to ensure that the students learn during their visits, for example by integrating visits with pre- and post-visit activities. [1] These efforts may suggest ways in which computing educators might also integrate formal and informal education. In Section 5, we present a few suggestions, suggested by our data, that educators can help students prepare for informal learning.

In the Computing Education community, Dorn and Guzdial [4, 5] surveyed end-user programmers, few of whom had any formal computing education, about their knowledge of scripting and related computing topics. Our area of interest is different in that we seek to see how informal and formal learning play out in the context of computing education. Most closely related to this paper is [13], which provides background on informal learning in general and reports on a preliminary study of informal learning. Its main observation was that many students' informal learning experiences were related to project work.

3. METHODOLOGY

For this paper, we examined three different datasets. First, students at one university were asked to write a 350 to 400-word essay "describ[ing] an experience of informal learning in Computer Science (as opposed to formal educational learning, such as at [home university])." The students were told that "This experience will be one in which you learned something not taught in a university degree program, although it could be in relation to something from a course." In addition, questions were provided to guide the students:

> How did you learn it? How much did you learn about the CS subject? Why did you choose to learn it informally? Were there any other people involved in your learning? If so, what parts did they play? How did you use it once you learned it?

The essay was assigned in Fall 2009 and Spring 2010 as part of a technical writing course that is required for computing students. The Fall 2009 group received an additional instruction: "This experience must have left an emotion that remained with you." A total of 58 essays were collected.

Second, the 30 students from the Spring 2010 section of the technical writing course were asked to brainstorm about the differences between formal and informal learning, as an example of how to set up a "Compare and Contrast" paper. The result of this brainstorming, which took place after the students had written their essays, was Table 1. The list of criteria was arrived at very rapidly (within two minutes), and the table likewise (in approximately 30 minutes).

Third, during 2009-10, fifteen students at six institutions in three countries were interviewed about their informal learning experiences in computing. These semi-structured interviews were organized around a range of questions: what they learned, how they learned it, why they chose to learn it, how they had used what they learned, and so forth. One of the questions asked explicitly for comparisons with formal learning: "How did your informal learning compare with more traditional experience of learning something in school or University?" The students interviewed ranged from sophomores to graduate students, including eleven undergraduate and four graduate students. When it became obvious that this was not reflecting students who did little or no informal learning, we sought out 2 students who filled this gap, using the technique of theoretical sampling as suggested by Corbin and Strauss. [15]

We chose to perform a qualitative study, because we are exploring a new area, computing students' informal learning of computing. As a result, we selected interviewees who were likely to represent as broad as possible a variety of perspectives within that space. The essays and interviews[1] were analyzed using inductive content analysis. [12] The authors identified parts of the texts where students contrasted formal and informal learning, categorized these segments, and resolved any differences through discussion. The analysis of the results of the brainstorming exercise was more informal, but that entire dataset is presented in Table 1.

4. RESULTS AND ANALYSIS

The range and ambition of the informal learning described by our participants is very impressive. Students used informal learning not just to extend their formal learning, but also to learn completely new topics on their own. Several students echoed E42: "Each summer I like to choose a project that will enhance my knowledge of computers."

The participants reported strengths in both formal and informal learning. Some common themes included practical,

---

[1] The 58 participants who wrote essays included both men and women. Given the large number and the fact that we did not have names or genders, we arbitrarily assigned numerical IDs to each essay (1-58), and identify each essayist by their essay number: the author of the nth essay is referred to as En. Odd-numbered IDs are referred to as "he" and even-numbered ones as "she." In the case of the interviewees, we refer to them by changed names of the correct gender.

Table 1: Compare and Contrast Formal and Informal Learning.

This table presents the result of a brainstorming exercise that took place in a technical writing class in Spring 2010. The purpose was to compare and contrast students' thoughts on formal and informal learning. The eight criteria as well as the related properties are results that were established during the brainstorming discussion.

Criteria	Formal Learning	Informal Learning
Access to information	In-class lectures Lectures build progressive levels of disclosure Class hrs/class time	Web/Internet lectures (if available) Information not filtered or pre-organized (requires sorting) Available 24 hrs day/7 days week
Availability of help	Professor website & office hours Lab-tech/tutor hours	Forums, chat rooms, instant messengers, videos (youtube), book appendices, hired tutor, friends/coworkers/etc
Setting	Classroom/lab For Homework: (same as Informal Learning) Wherever you can connect to info (e.g., Library)	Wherever you can connect to info (e.g., Library)
Cost	Tuition + books + lab For Homework: (same as Informal Learning) Internet connection + laptop/computer (or library fees)	Internet connection + laptop/computer (or library fees)
Time	Set class hours + study hours (formula)	When you spend the time is based on your schedule How much depends on level of understanding & amount of info
Quality of information	Scholarly, tested, accurate, comprehensive, up-to-date	Variable based on author/organization & the amount of info Possibly outdated, not always accurate
Effort to learn	Based on individual learning style Premade assignments focus learning Assisted by instructor	Based on individual learning style Exercises may not be at student's current level On your own
Recognition	Credits, grade, etc (skills implied)	Satisfaction, self-confidence (to achieve your goals)

external factors; and also the control, structure, and pace of learning; confidence; the depth of learning; the instructor's role; and inter-relationships between formal and informal learning.

4.1 Control, Structure, and Pace of Learning

With informal learning, students noted that they were in control of what they learned and could focus on learning itself, as opposed to passing exams. Sebastian speaks very positively about this sense of control:

Sebastian: It's – wow, for the first time in my school career, my entire learning is in my hands and at my discretion ...

For Penelope, that sense of control seems to result in a feeling of *safe* as opposed to *anxious* learning:

Penelope: With informal learning I get to be in the space where I'm building on what I know, and in formal learning I have on more than one occasion found myself in a space where it feels like I'm on a slippery slope because all the concepts - I mean the professor may lecture and during - it's all in short term memory right?

Kyle noted the absence of structure in informal learning:

Kyle: So again, the thing that I missed is the practice part. Now there are no homeworks to do, there's no deadlines, there's no penalties for not doing anything, so the discipline part comes into play there.

Nevertheless, despite the lack of structure – or perhaps because of the discipline required by informal learning – he is confident that it would take less time to learn the material the second time:

Kyle: And now because I have no use for what I'm learning, my learning - the tricks are getting weaker, so now I have to go back and look it up. But at least I know it won't take as much time as I learned it before.

Both essayists and interviewees observed that informal and formal learning move at a different pace. Sebastian reported that it was easier to learn algorithms informally from a book, because it would give him more time to "crunch" through the algorithms. On the other hand, Ryan felt that some material was better learned in a course:

Ryan: ...the Big O, induction, proof by induction and stuff like that would be very difficult to learn by yourself, ...and the soft skill classes about the things, for me, I would want the conversation there, the discussion of it.

The difference in pace can mean that less time is spent on informal learning. Ryan, Sebastian, and Tanner were part of a group of students working together to learn Artificial Intelligence informally (as part of an independent study). Sebastian reported that, in the absence of perceived necessity, the students spent more time on other courses with tougher deadlines:

Sebastian: I know I can comfortably say, though shamefully admit, that I did not work as hard in

AI as I did in other classes; but I can also very confidential and joyfully say that I learned just as much. I just didn't have to work as hard.

Tanner agreed about not working as hard, but saw that as a negative, taking the view that learning comes through work:

> *Tanner:* Yeah, the biggest difference is obviously the pacing. Sometimes a classroom setting is really good at forcing you ... if you're not in the mood to do something, that's tough, you got to do it anyway. That can be really helpful in getting work accomplished.

4.2 Confidence

Informal learning can provide a great sense of accomplishment. As E18 said, "I believe no classroom or teacher may be able to successfully reproduce the feeling of accomplishment that I acquired by learning and succeeding on my own." E45 repeated and expanded on this theme:

> *Essay 45:* It is empowering to know I can teach myself a programming language, without needing to take a class for it. The language itself probably will not be of much use in the future, but the knowledge I can be proactive in achieving a goal is invaluable. In the past, I have been a very passive person, putting the bare minimum of effort needed to complete tasks. This experience shows me, that I can change myself for the better.

None of the students described losing confidence as a result of failing at some Informal Learning project, but the nature of our methodology may have made this unlikely. This is discussed further in Section 5.3.

4.3 Depth of Learning

Some of the students compared the different types of learning based on their outcomes. E52 contrasted her experiences learning Perl on her own unfavorably with her later experiences learning Java and C++:

> *Essay 52:* However, not long after I took some advanced computer programming classes, like; Java and C++, and I felt like I did not know anything about PERL. ...Through this experience of informal learning, I notice that without specific guidelines, I would miss many important concepts that I would not miss otherwise in a formal environment.

Others found that informal learning worked better, for example E25: "Learning topics by on your own [sic] has plenty of benefits. Information is retained better, and self-directed learning can also lead to researching other topics that you might not have otherwise searched for."

Students found gaps in both informal and formal learning. Ryan's informal-learning experience was more task-driven, and led to a narrower focus than he preferred:

> *Ryan:* For the most part, it was just figuring out what I needed to do, how much I needed to know to be able to do what I wanted and not have ramifications that would cause problems, and that did bother me, honestly. ...I want to understand all of the concepts that have to deal with this and then eventually understand how to implement my specific solution.

George learned PHP independently on-line, but did not think learning Java with tutorials would be optimal due to tutorials' narrow and pragmatic emphasis on programming:

> *George:* I think you COULD learn Java but again not so good as when you study at the University. With the tutorials, mostly they just show how to program, how to write programs. But there is nothing about how to make efficient programs. How does it work inside? There is nothing about that.

Finally, as alluded to earlier, there is always the practical matter of learning more in a traditional course "or you won't pass the exam":

> *Tanner:* Well, I don't think I learned as much as I would have in a traditional class. ...in a regular class, you have sort of an obligation to learn the material or you won't pass the exams.

On the other hand, with formal learning, students talked about cramming material into short term memory for exams. In addition, formal learning sometimes just doesn't cover all the topics the student is interested in. Anders, for example, took a course in Operating Systems and felt it was "very theoretical," but not very practical:

> *Anders:* Yeah, I have a course in operating systems. That is very theoretical how they're built up and what kind of functions they have. But then how you install them and how you run programs in them and stuff like that you have to learn by yourself.

In the process of comparing formal and informal learning, one student perceived something about her own learning style:

> Essay 48: During my reflections upon this learning experience I realized something about how I learn: I need a larger purpose. Whether learning in an informal way or otherwise, I need to have an immediate reason or way to apply it. In some of my previous programming courses this took the form of a pet project where I could play around with what we were learning. In the case of learning Lua, this purpose took the form of helping other people solve their scripting problems.

Not unusually, E48 reported benefiting from hands-on projects, but took a broader view than many, including not only her own projects but the opportunity to help others debug their programs.

4.4 Instructor's Role

One way informal learning is different from formal learning is the lack of an instructor. Molly pointed out that the experience and deeper knowledge of the instructor is an important advantage of formal learning:

> *Molly:* I learn nicely in a class. I enjoy that, I enjoy the insights of the person who is teaching it, the greater experience.

Other students observed that instructors can make learning more efficient by focusing attention on essentials or by providing definitive answers that may be unavailable in informal learning:

Nathan: I would say if I learned it in the class, it would be more structured ... [T]he more important concept would have been given to me initially rather than I have to figure out what's important and what is not.

Tanner: When you have a more traditional authority figure in the professor, you have the voice of reason that says, no, this is the answer and now we can move on.

Not all students miss the instructor, however; Sebastian found the independence that comes with informal learning to be a very positive experience. (See quotation from Sebastian above in Section 4.1).

4.5 Informal and Formal Learning Interactions

Informal and formal learning are interrelated for many students. For example, E52 resorted to informal learning because she found her formal class to be unsatisfactory:

Essay 52: Although, the teacher recommended a good PERL book, my experience with him was not pleasant, mainly because his lectures deviate off topic frequently, which makes his lectures hard to follow. Because of this, my only option was to tackle PERL by reading and playing with PERL codes on my own.

E56, on the other hand, was inspired by a formal class to pursue the same topic in more depth informally:

Essay 56: During a class...I was introduced to a program called Alice. During this class, I learned how to use the basic functions that Alice is able to perform. After I had completed my final project for the class, I still wanted to know what else I could get Alice to create...From this point forward, rather than frustrating [sic] over a topic that was not fully explained to me, I will take it upon myself to learn more about it through informal education.

Molly, like E56, found that formal learning led to informal learning. She studied algorithms informally, and when asked why she replied:

Molly: Cause it got referenced in some other course and I wasn't understanding what was going on. It was being used often as an example to clarify something, which then made something clear as mud for me.

For other students, the informal learning came first and motivated them to study computing formally. E47 for instance said, "Not only did the [software engineering skills] help me manage to save my father around $1000 dollars a year, but also increased my desire to pursue a career in computer science."

Conversely, informal learning can affect formal learning. Cedric gained confidence through informal learning, which led to increased confidence in formal learning as well:

Cedric: ...the experience in terms of a reflection on how I move forward in my formal classes, I guess, would be that - I guess it just made me more confident in terms of if I can learn this on my own and overcome that, then I shouldn't really have as much of a difficult time or I shouldn't worry as much in terms of when I meet a problem that I don't know how to solve right away. I'd be less likely to get really overwhelmed and just sort of go at it from any angle that I can.

Sometimes a topic learned informally is directly applicable to a student's formal education. One student (Oscar) describes learning C (chosen because "systems are C driven") and found it "useful immediately" in a systems course. On the other hand, George reported that he didn't learn much by taking a PHP course after learning PHP informally:

George: (laughs) It was just a repeat to be honest. The feedback on the assignment was just "well done excellent" and almost the highest possible marks.

Cedric reported that he learned to go about learning based on his formal education:

Cedric: Well, definitely from my formal classes, I learned how to sort of piece together this process of what to look for or what things to start off with and then built it from there ...I think my formal classes gave me a good idea on how to formulate or assemble my knowledge of what I'm trying to work on.

Kyle went further and reported "trying to simulate" the formal learning environment when learning informally:

Kyle: I've always taken classes and there's homework, there's somebody to present it, there's some exam. Can I do that with a book – but at my own pace and at my guidelines? So I make my own exams, I make my own homework problems, and I choose which problems to do and which not to, and I grade my own.

4.6 Externally observable factors

There are a number of obvious, externally observable differences between formal and informal learning: how much it costs, whether there is a professor, whether you get a grade for it, and so on. These factors were barely mentioned in the essays and interviews, but were the main focus of the in-class brainstorming exercise (as shown in Table 1).

4.7 Formal without Informal

The nature of our methodology made it difficult to investigate cases where informal learning failed or was not used. The essays formed part of the assessment for the technical writing class, and so all the students had to be able to complete them. Initially, interview opportunities were taken up by students who had experience of informal learning.

Of the 58 essays, 29 students reported on projects that were completed entirely for their own interest, i.e. completely outside the formal curriculum. Nine students discussed projects completed at work, and the other 20 students related stories where their informal learning was motivated in some way by their formal learning, mainly: following up on a class, getting a jump on a class, and learning another IDE that was suggested by an instructor. We do not know whether these students also had projects that they could have written about that had less formal, or work related, 'coercion' associated with them.

Students who do not attempt informal learning were not likely to be interviewed for this project, as we solicited volunteers to be interviewed about their informal learning experiences. To remedy this, we used the technique of theoretical sampling [15] in order to find out more about this group of students. The ones we were particularly interested in were good students who nevertheless did not participate in informal learning. Two students were identified and interviewed.

Jessica is currently a PhD student and now does a considerable amount of informal learning, but she identifies herself as a person who did not do much as an undergraduate: "I'm not a tinkerer." She did no background reading and says that she "responded very well to the classroom environment."

She sees no reason to make her life hard but, in her final year, she came "unstuck" and says that "everyone reaches the point where they have to figure things out for themselves." She now has to learn informally in order to do her research. But with regard to non-research informal learning, she says that if she does it at all "it is utility that makes it happen" and "it has to be something short with payoff."

Helena is similar to Jessica but at an earlier stage of her university career. She describes her experience before coming to the university:

> *Helena:* I tried to learn Java before I came here – I didn't – although I got all the books. It was partly because I had so many other things on but I basically never got round to doing it. [But] I thought 'oh well if I don't get into this I'm sure I'll be okay as long as I work hard'.

She agrees that formal education mainly works for her, but has already realized (using exactly the same words as Jessica) that "you reach a point where you have to work." She acknowledges the importance of informal learning, saying, "I have always got away with doing not quite as much work as I maybe should have."

Both of these young women have a realistic idea of their own ability to manage well within the formal educational system. They do not see themselves as informal learners but do see that they may need to be at some point. They are what we might consider to be 'classic students' except that in the context of our study they appear to be in the minority.

5. DISCUSSION

In order to triangulate, we collected three sorts of data: the essays, the brainstorming session, and the interviews. As expected, there was overlap, but some differences as well.

There were qualitative and quantitative differences between the essays and the interviews: the ability to ask follow-up questions led to deeper, less ambiguous responses in the interviews, the interviews were a good bit longer than the essays, and the essays were somewhat more structured, as they had presumably been edited before submission. The essays were submitted by two classes as assignments, while the interviews were done with volunteers. The essayists and interviewees spoke as individuals (with the partial exception of Ryan and Sebastian, who were interviewed together), while the brainstorming-exercise table was written by a group. Moreover, the speed with which the table was produced (thirty minutes in total, with the criteria chosen in the first two minutes) suggests a strong consensus.

The essays and interviews reinforced the same points, particularly when discussing depth of learning, effects on confidence, and the interactions between formal and informal learning. Both focused on internal factors, such as motivation, emotions, effects on confidence, and learning outcomes, and were much more like each other than either was like the brainstorming results, even though the brainstorming was done by a subset of the essay students and the interview students were much more diverse in age, background, and geographical location.

The brainstorming exercise was done by students who had already reflected on and written descriptions of their informal learning experiences. The results do not conflict with those from the essays and interviews, but they are on a different level: strongly focused on externally observable factors, not the internal factors that were emphasized in the essays and interviews. This may reflect more on the methodology than on the students' perceptions, as they wrote about those factors in their submitted essays; it is possible that they felt more comfortable discussing external factors in a group setting.

In the rest of this section, we discuss the results of this paper from three perspectives: the students' view of informal learning vs. formal education; what that suggests to us as educators; and the relationship of informal learning to students' working lives.

5.1 The students' perspective

The good news is that many computing students are already beginning to develop valuable informal-learning skills. Some of this learning is a side effect of completing assignments; some is designed to fill in perceived gaps in lectures or coursework. Students also learn computing topics completely outside their formal learning, for self-directed projects or simply to advance their knowledge.

The many benefits of informal learning that the students identified include:

- In informal learning, the learner can choose the level of learning (conceptual/specific).
- Things learned informally are often better retained.
- There is a sense of accomplishment from informal learning (e.g., satisfaction, self-confidence)
- Informal learning is motivating and can make a topic interesting.
- Informal learning can be more flexible – takes place at a time and place at a pace that suits the learner.
- Informal learning can facilitate formal learning and vice versa.
- Informal learning can be used to add depth or breadth to what is learned in a formal course.

Students also recognize that there are problems with informal learning. If all material was learned informally, their breadth and depth of knowledge would suffer; specifically:

- With informal learning there is a risk that students miss important aspects of a topic.
- Informal learning is often ad hoc and stops when the task can be solved using the knowledge acquired so far.
- Informal learning can be difficult for the learner to assess – how can a learner know when enough is learned?
- Some students need the structure provided by teachers and deadlines.
- An informal learner may miss the opportunity to have classroom discussions and other social interactions important for learning.
- Without concrete rewards and deadlines, too little time may be spent on the informal learning.

5.2 The educators' perspective

First of all, it was heartening to see that the students recognized both advantages and disadvantages of learning informally. Students were able to see the strength of having a structure and a guide through complex material. But if we want to enhance students' opportunities to practise informal learning - be the "guide on the side" – what can we do as curriculum designers and instructors?

We suggest that self-directed learning, as defined by Knowles in Section 2, should be part of our students' formal training. This definition suggests some questions that we could encourage our students to reflect on to help develop their informal learning skills:

- What do I need or want to learn?
- What are my specific learning goals?
- What resources are available, and which should I use?
- What learning strategies should I employ?
- How will I assess my progress, and how will I know that I am done?

Besides having our students reflect on informal learning, we could also design "semi-formal" learning experiences: informal learning that is required as part of a course. For example, in Programming Languages, students could be required to learn a new language on their own, but following a standard sequence (What are the datatypes? How are variables declared? What are the built-in operators? Etc.) In a project course, students could be required to learn a new technology independently or given freedom to define a part of the project that must bring in something not in the curriculum. Given how often students refer to project-related informal learning in the essays and interviews, this type of assignment could help to scaffold informal learning.

5.3 Implications for our students' working lives

When we came to analyze these data we found a number of aspects of informal learning that relate to working life. This section discusses the issues identified in the data that have an impact on students' lifelong, informal learning in the workplace.

Self confidence. For many students, informal learning was important for building confidence in their ability to learn new material on their own. In Essay 45, discussed in Section 4.2, the student talks about the informal learning experience as "empowering", saying that after the experience of informal learning "I [know that I] can teach myself ... without needing to take a class for it." Edmund discusses the pressure he initially felt in his new job because he did not know everything, until he learned that he could learn what he needed to know. He says that he sees many newly employed graduates go through the same intimidating process.

Conversely, one might ask, if successful informal learning experiences build confidence, what about failures – would they decrease confidence? We did not find examples of this in our data. It's certainly possible that someone could attempt to learn a topic that's beyond their reach; on the other hand, the fact that the learner is in control of what they learn and how fast they learn it may help to limit the potential damage. This remains an interesting question for future work.

The sense of control. The students in our study emphasize that in informal learning they felt a sense of control regarding what they learned and the pace at which they learned it. This might not be the case for informal learning in working life where it is more likely that they have to learn specific material relevant to a project, as fast as possible. An important aspect of informal learning is thus to learn to decide what is adequate material to learn, i.e. to limit the material in relation to the task and time given, which might mean to exclude interesting material not relevant for the task. How much of a new knowledge area is needed, and how deep is the knowledge needed for the present task?

Finding good sources. The students discuss problems related to finding relevant sources, and judging their credibility, particularly on the Internet where information is not filtered, maybe not pre-organized, and might be outdated and inaccurate.

Using Internet based resources. Forums, chat rooms, and tutorials on the Internet are mentioned among other resources. Do all our students know where to find these resources, how to use them, and do they have the confidence to be active in a forum or chat rooms with unknown people (who the students might believe are more experienced than themselves?) Tanner notes, for example, that while he has found some forums helpful, "especially in the old-timer sort-of open-source communities, you get some people that are really amazing and some people that are really sort of elitists, you if you don't already know it ... you're barred from the club effectively."

Getting help. The students discuss the problem of having no formal teacher. Most students are used to having someone who is there to answer their questions. and asking others is an important resource in informal learning. Different companies may however have different cultures for how much you can ask colleagues, or how much you are supposed to colaborate and help others. This is a problematic question which we believe is good to raise with students. We have seen in interviews that newly employed graduates feel concerned that they do not know as much as their more experienced colleagues.

These issues, which came up in this investigation of formal vs. informal learning, deserve further investigation. Computing is an unusual academic discipline in that our students frequently begin its study informally as children, move through formal study at University while also pursuing informal learning at the same time, and then pursue it as a career, where they often learn informally again. We would like to examine these progressions in more depth through further interviews with people working in industry.

6. CONCLUSIONS AND FUTURE WORK

In this paper, we report on an empirical investigation of students' comparisons of formal and informal learning. Our data included essays; a brainstorming exercise by students in a technical writing class required of all computing majors at one university; and interviews with undergraduate and graduate students at six different universities.

Students reported strengths in both formal and informal learning. Informal learning provided a strong sense of accomplishment. Students noted that with informal learning, they were in control of what, how, and when they learned. When studying a difficult topic, they reported that the slower pace of informal learning was helpful. In addition, having control over the pace of learning was reassuring. Informal learning also enabled them to make sure the topics they were interested in were included.

Formal learning, on the other hand, was perceived as broader and less task-driven. Some students valued the experience, deeper knowledge, and structure provided by an instructor. They observed that instructors can make learning more efficient by focusing attention on essentials, or by providing definite answers. Moreover, formal classes' deadlines tend to take priority over informal learning activities.

Formal and informal learning are inter-related activities. Formal learning provided both a model for how to go about learning informally and motivations to do so, either to fill in gaps in formal coursework or to extend knowledge of a subject that had caught a student's interest. Conversely, some students were motivated by their informal learning in high school or at work to study computing formally. Sometimes a topic learned informally was directly applicable to a student's formal education. Increased confidence, gained through informal learning, could lead to increased confidence in formal learning as well.

The students' observations led us to further examine informal learning in two ways: from the perspective of Computing educators wishing to help students with the difficulties they identify with informal learning; and from the perspective of how the data, outlined above, relates to students' future (or current) working lives.

We note that students themselves are aware of the pitfalls of informal learning, and suggest some ways that educators can help students to develop their informal learning skills.

In the data we were able to identify some important aspects related to informal learning in the workplace. The most salient are: informal learning can build self-confidence; practice in informal learning can help with evaluation of resources such as forums and chat rooms; and a discussion needs to take place about the culture of informal learning within organizations.

In future work, we plan to build a general picture of informal learning as practiced by computing students. This theory will address learning strategies – how students learn informally, self-assessment – how students evaluate their progress, and outcomes – how successful are students in learning informally. Longer term goals include expanding this study to an examination of informal learning among computing professionals.

Acknowledgments

This work was supported by a SIGCSE special projects grant. The authors would also like to thank Jan Erik Moström, who participated in the initial discussions of this project, the Department of Information Technology at Uppsala University for providing us with workspace and facilities in Uppsala, Umeå University for virtual meeting space, Laurie Anderson for gathering the essay data, and our participants for their time and insights.

7. REFERENCES

[1] D. Anderson, K. B. Lucas, and I. S. Ginns. Theoretical perspectives on learning in an informal setting. *Journal of Research in Science Teaching*, 40(2):177–199, 2003.

[2] Association for Computing Machinery. Code of Ethics. http://www.acm.org/about/code-of-ethics, 1992. (Accessed 4 Sep 2010).

[3] J. Cross. *Informal Learning: Rediscovering the Natural Pathways That Inspire Innovation and Performance.* Pfeiffer, 2006.

[4] B. Dorn and M. Guzdial. Graphic designers who program as informal computer science learners. In *ICER '06: Proc. of the second intl. workshop on computing education research*, pages 127–134, 2006.

[5] B. Dorn and M. Guzdial. Discovering computing: perspectives of web designers. In *ICER '10: Proc. of the sixth intl. workshop on computing education research*, pages 23–30, 2010.

[6] L. M. Guglielmino, H. B. Long, and R. Hiemstra. Self-direction in learning in the United States. *Intl. J. of Self-directed Learning*, 1(1):1–17, 2004.

[7] J. Hashim. Competencies acquisition through self-directed learning among malaysian managers. *Journal of Workplace Learning*, 20(4):259–271, 2008.

[8] Y. James-Gordon and J. Bal. The emerging self-directed learning methods for design engineers. *The Learning Organization*, 10(1):63–69, 2003.

[9] M. S. Knowles. *Self-directed learning: A guide for learners and teachers.* Association Press, New York, 1975. Quoted in [6].

[10] D. A. Kolb. *Experiential learning: Experience as the source of learning and development.* Prentice-Hall, 1984.

[11] M. C. Lohman. Factors influencing teachers' engagement in informal learning activities. *Journal of Workplace Learning*, 18(3):141–156, 2006.

[12] P. Mayring. Qualitative content analysis. *Forum: Qualitative Social Research*, 1(2), 2000. http://www.qualitative-research.net/fqs-texte/2-00/2-00mayring-e.htm. (Accessed 10 Apr 2010).

[13] R. McCartney, A. Eckerdal, J. E. Moström, K. Sanders, L. Thomas, and C. Zander. Computing students learning computing informally. In *Proc. of the 10th Koli Calling International Conference on Computing Education Research*, 2010.

[14] J. A. Moon. *A Handbook of Reflective and Experiential Learning: theory and practice.* RoutledgeFalmer, 2004.

[15] A. C. Strauss and J. M. Corbin. *Basics of Qualitative Research: Grounded Theory Procedures and Techniques.* Sage, Thousand Oaks, 2nd edition, 1990.

ScriptABLE: Supporting Informal Learning with Cases

Brian Dorn
University of Hartford
200 Bloomfield Ave
West Hartford, CT 06117
bdorn@hartford.edu

ABSTRACT

Informal learning resources have the potential to reach millions of currently underserved learners teaching themselves about the basics of computing using the Web, example code, peer networks, books, and other materials. In this paper, we investigate the effectiveness of case-based learning aids (CBLAs) as a resource to scaffold informal education in scripting for web and graphic design. We present the design of a new CBLA called ScriptABLE and outline initial evaluation results with respect to its ability to foster both programming ability and more expert understanding of computing concepts.

Categories and Subject Descriptors

K.3.2 [**Computers and Education**]: Computer and Information Science Education—*computer science education*

General Terms

Design, Human Factors

Keywords

end-user programmers, informal computing education, Web/graphic design

1. INTRODUCTION

The vast majority of the CS education research community's efforts to enhance learning center on formal instructional environments. We study students in and develop new tools/resources for elementary, secondary, and post-secondary classes. In so doing, we may be missing an opportunity to reach the millions of people who find computing outside of academia's hallowed halls and are left to teach themselves through informal educational activities.

Informal education, or the lifelong acquisition of knowledge through day-to-day interactions with family, peers, and other sources of instruction in one's natural environment, poses a unique set of challenges for those who seek to build resources to promote it. However, with the increasing ubiquity of computational devices, opportunities for informal learning about computing are more abundant than ever. There are no doubt countless people learning about computing "in the wild." In this paper we focus on one particular subgroup: Web and graphic designers who have acquired knowledge of scripting primarily through self-instruction.

Prior studies of users in this particular end-user population have highlighted the nature of their current learning practices and the difficulties that may arise in developing tools to support them. These users exhibit a strong proclivity for example-driven learning, with designers seeking out code examples related to a current project of interest [3, 10]. Further, the Web often serves as a first line of defense against knowledge gaps, despite inherent difficulties in formulating good search queries. In a study of web and graphic designers involving introductory concepts, Dorn and Guzdial [10] noted a strong correlation between frequency of use and concept difficulty; the most difficult concepts (e.g., recursion, exception handling) were least often used and most misunderstood by designers. Unfortunately, these same concepts were also least likely to appear in existing online scripting resources written for this audience [11].

A recognized problem of highly context-oriented learning, like what informal learners do, is that knowledge can become "context-bound," making it difficult to transfer to or from other similar settings [4]. Thus, there is a great opportunity for researchers to explore how to foster conceptual knowledge growth in such communities while at the same time recognizing existing practices favoring example-driven learning. We propose that one particularly effective way to balance these two issues is through the use of collections of annotated scripting examples, or case-based learning aids. Each example project (i.e., case) in such a library presents a solution to a realistic programming task for web/graphic designers. Central to each case is a narrative description of the process by which someone else solved the task. We hypothesize that informal learners can effectively acquire conceptual knowledge from such case libraries through interactions with these narratives as they search for new information related to their current (potentially different) tasks.

The primary goal of this work is to evaluate the extent to which case libraries containing projects written with a narrative form can indeed support informal learning. Specifically, to what extent do users engaged in task-oriented scripting activities with access to a narrative case library:

(**RQ1**) write more correct code, and

Permission to make digital or hard copies of all or part of this work for personal or classroom use is granted without fee provided that copies are not made or distributed for profit or commercial advantage and that copies bear this notice and the full citation on the first page. To copy otherwise, to republish, to post on servers or to redistribute to lists, requires prior specific permission and/or a fee.
ICER'11, August 8–9, 2011, Providence, Rhode Island, USA.
Copyright 2011 ACM 978-1-4503-0829-8/11/08 ...$10.00.

(RQ2) produce better conceptual explanations about programming tasks?

In order to evaluate these two questions, we also will discuss the design and implementation of a new case library system that was prototyped as part of this research effort.

In the remainder of this paper, Section 2 outlines literature regarding case studies, their use in computing education, and relevant cognitive theories. Next, Section 3 provides an overview of a new case library called ScriptABLE, designed specifically as an educational resource for informal learners who build scripts for Photoshop. We then discuss our methodology for evaluation of this system (Section 4) and the study's results (Section 5). Lastly, Section 6 concludes the paper with additional discussion and future work.

2. RELATED WORK

Case studies have promoted learning in many educational settings. A case provides a narrative description of the process by which experts devise solutions to problems. Students learn from cases by examining their content, asking questions, making predictions, considering alternatives, and comparing them to other cases.

In computing, case studies have been used to foster programming language knowledge acquisition and development of problem-solving skills [15]. Clancy and Linn's *Designing Pascal Solutions: A Case Study Approach* provided a general structure for the presentation of programming cases and outlined a course-length set of examples for teaching computer science [8]. Each case includes a problem statement, a narrative description of an expert's solution, a complete code listing of the solution, a series of questions for the learner to consider about the case, and a number of related assessment questions. Empirical results suggest the narrative commentary about the solution is a key feature of cases that increases the amount one learns [15].

Built on the concept of cases, Kolodner et al. [14] define a case-based learning aid as "a support that helps learners interpret, reflect on, and apply experiences ... in such a way that valuable learning takes place" [14, p. 829]. In practice, these learning aids often take the form of case libraries (i.e., collections of cases) that enable learners to compare and contrast interrelated cases. Such comparison increases the likelihood that a learner will be able to infer the conditions under which solution approaches are applicable [4]. In software design, Guzdial and Kehoe [12] created STABLE, which contained multiple correct solutions to problems by previous undergraduate students in the same course on similar assignments. Evaluation results showed that students used STABLE to find code fragments related to their current assignments, but in doing so, they gained insights into object-oriented design.

Three primary instructional models and theories inform our application of case-based learning aids to informal education for web and graphic designers: Case-Based Reasoning (CBR) [13], Cognitive Load Theory [16], and Minimalist Instruction [5].

CBR was originally developed to further reasoning abilities of expert systems [13]. This model was appropriated by education and the learning sciences as a way to think about the design of learning environments [14]. CBR's implications for promoting learning align with a number features common to case libraries [14]. Their explanatory discussion of problem solutions can incorporate failure points and guidance for others in similar situations. A library's user interface can explicitly provide indexes of the library's content and link related cases together. The case structure, if well designed, provides an example for learners in how to organize their own knowledge and experiences.

Cognitive Load Theory (CLT) [16] seeks to guide instructional design based on underlying cognitive architectures and the inherent limitations of working memory. "Worked examples," an instructional resource well-aligned with CLT, are a description of the process by which a problem is solved focusing on various problem states and steps needed in the solution [7]. Cases are, by definition, a form of worked example. A case's narrative externalizes the mental schemas employed by the author for direct inspection by novices. In theory, learning by studying cases reduces the amount of information which must be inferred by the learner about the problem solution, and should therefore reduce the burden on working memory.

Minimalist instruction [5] emphasizes realistic scenarios in which users are learning by doing. Recognizing that people naturally seek information in order to achieve a task, tutorials and documentation designed in the minimalist fashion present information around activity, in contrast to materials that favor alternative concerns like logical decomposition and conceptual ordering. Carroll and Rosson [6] argue that case-based learning aids can naturally serve as minimalist information sources. "They provide guidance and encouragement for user action by describing specific activities, events, and problems from real world practice" [6, p. 4].

3. SCRIPTABLE

This section introduces the design of ScriptABLE, a new case-based learning aid for end-user programmers who script Photoshop. We sought to provide explicit scaffolding for the difficult, and often misunderstood, introductory programming concepts that are not typically well supported in online resources (e.g., exception handling, recursion [11]). At the same time, we wanted to design our tool to align with the known learning strategies employed graphic and web designers [10]. Given this design space and our theoretical foundations, we had five overarching goals in building ScriptABLE:

1. Project-driven activities should set the context for content in the system;
2. Conceptual instruction for computing concepts should be explicitly presented alongside example code from projects;
3. Instruction should emphasize errors and recovery from them;
4. Concepts must be tagged or labeled with names at multiple levels to promote recognition, particularly at both the syntactic and conceptual levels (e.g., `if-else` and "selection"); and
5. Highlight unfamiliar or often misunderstood introductory content for the target audience.

These criteria lend themselves quite naturally to a case-based learning aid.

ScriptABLE is a Web-based case library of Photoshop scripting projects presenting code written in JavaScript.[1]

---
[1] Accessible at http://cases.scriptable.org

The system itself is implemented using a customized installation of the MediaWiki[2] content management system. While implemented using wiki software, open editing of ScriptABLE's pages is prohibited and users access the content anonymously. From ScriptABLE's home page users may browse available projects by name or by index term (i.e. tag), or perform a search of the library.

At the heart of the ScriptABLE library are individual project pages. Each project page presents the development of a solution to a particular scripting problem from conceptualization of an algorithm, outlining testing scenarios, and refinement of incremental solutions. These project pages make up the individual cases in ScriptABLE from which users can learn, and importantly, every project page uses a standardized form in its presentation.

3.1 Case Structure

ScriptABLE's individual case structure is based on Clancy and Linn's *Designing Pascal Solutions* [8]. We adapted and extended their basic case format discussed earlier to meet the needs of online, informal learning environments. Our final case format can be seen in the excerpt from one ScriptABLE project shown in Figure 1. It consists of the following seven components:

Project Description: Each project begins with a brief description outlining the goal or problem statement for the script to be written (see marker 1 in Figure 1). This serves to motivate the project with a real-world problem situated within the context of typical Photoshop activities that a graphic or Web designer would likely encounter, providing a sense of authenticity for the case.

Primary Tags: Next, each case lists the tags, or index terms, that are most relevant to the content of the project (see marker 2). Tags are shown in three separate groups: Concepts, Syntax, and Photoshop Tasks. Thus, the primary tags can be viewed as an indication of the programming concepts, JavaScript syntax, and Photoshop tasks addressed in a project. Primary tags are limited to only the concepts, syntax, and tasks are explicitly discussed and explained in the body of the project narrative.

Use Scenarios: Each project contains one or more use scenarios (marker 3) describing different circumstances in which the script can be run. Scenarios provide step by step instructions for how to run the script in the desired manner and detail the expected result of doing so. Thus, these serve as test cases. Each use scenario is selected for conditions that illustrate potential bugs in the script. Recovering from those errors is used as motivation for additional versions of the code, iteratively approaching a final result that functions correctly for all scenarios.

Script Development: The bulk of each project page consists of the script development section (marker 4 in Figure 1). It provides a narrative description of how the code for this project is developed, interleaving discussion of the necessary conceptual content within the context of the project. This section first discusses a basic algorithm for accomplishing the particular task based on the way a user might do the same task manually in the Photoshop interface. The informal algorithm is then translated into the first script version.

Throughout the development section, each code version is followed by an attempt to execute the program as described by one of the use scenarios and the resulting out-

---
[2] http://www.mediawiki.org/

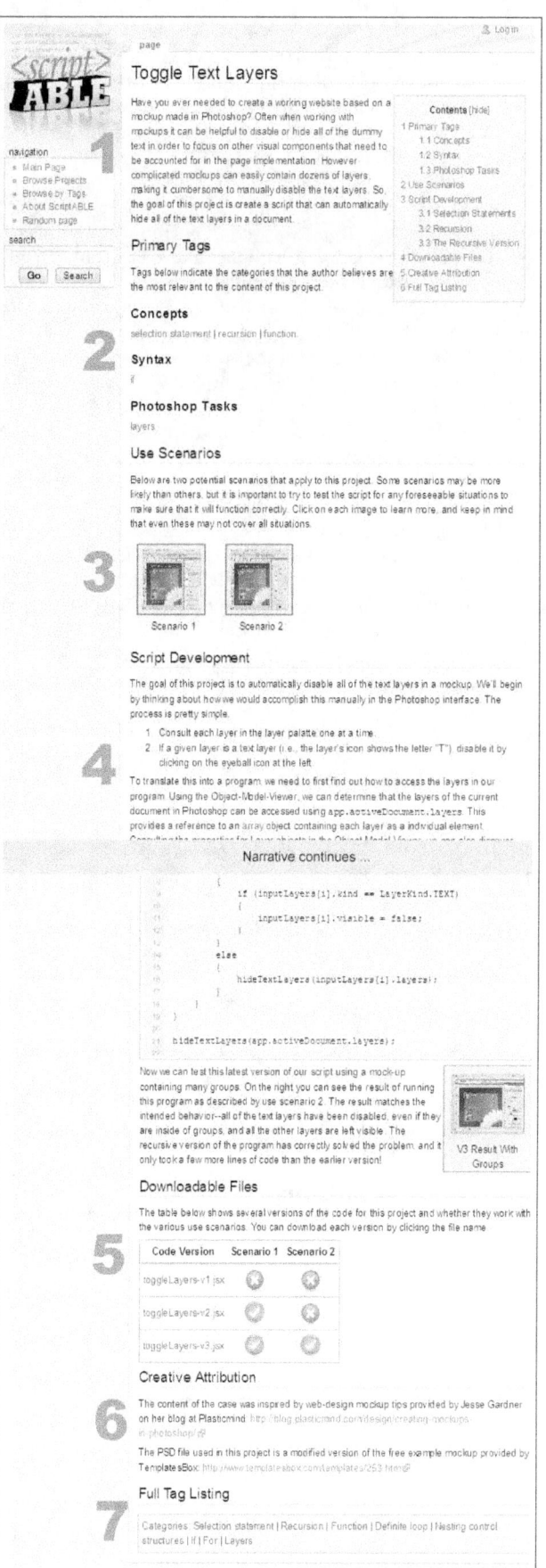

Figure 1: Example ScriptABLE Project with Numeric Annotations

put is shown. Typically, the code works for some, but not all scenarios, prompting further refinement of the script. In each refinement step a new computing concept is introduced to enable a more sophisticated solution. For example, the project shown in Figure 1 discusses how to disable all text layers within a Photoshop document. The narrative moves from a naïve iterative solution to a fully-functional recursive one that can properly handle tree-like layer structures within documents. Along the way it introduces the necessary concepts of selection, functions, and recursion.

Downloadable Files: A tabular summary of code presented in the narrative is given in the downloadable files section (marker 5). The table shows whether a version of the script passes or fails each use scenario. Users can download versions of the scripts using the links presented here.

Creative Attribution: The creative attribution section (maker 6) provides additional authenticity by linking to a source of inspiration for each project—for example, graphic design rules of thumb or questions posed in online forums.

Full Tag Listing: Finally each project page ends with a full tag listing that shows all of the tags relevant to this project. As mentioned, the primary tags section only includes concepts and syntax explicitly discussed in the script development section. However, there are often other syntactic concepts used throughout the project. For example, a project can make use of an `if` statement in the code without explicitly discussing the concept of selection; nonetheless, the code is still an example of selection. Accordingly, the full tag listing provides a comprehensive list of index tags.

ScriptABLE's structure and style is what uniquely distinguishes it from other online resources a graphic or Web designer might encounter. Tutorial sites, like W3schools[3], often strive for coverage of scripting syntax and make use of several small ($\approx$ 10 lines), independent code snippets to illustrate the language's syntax. By contrast, ScriptABLE's narratives set code examples within the context of larger projects, revisiting code multiple times with increasing sophistication while connecting to conceptual instruction. Other project-oriented sites like blogs or online magazines (e.g., Smashing Magazine[4]) do interleave code with explanations, but the degree to which any article contains intentional instruction about the syntax or semantics of the code used varies widely based on the author's purpose. ScriptABLE, on the other hand, is designed as an educational aid for introductory programming and maintains a consistent style and tone throughout its projects.

3.2 Tags and Indexing

A simple hierarchy of tags is used within ScriptABLE to meaningfully annotate, categorize, and cross-index projects. The three basic categories for all tags are Concepts (e.g., array, exception handling), Syntax (e.g., `if`, `try-catch`), and Photoshop Tasks (e.g., compute grayscale, paste, crop). A user may navigate through the hierarchy to a specific tag (e.g., selection statement) to see all of the relevant projects. In addition to displaying a list of corresponding projects, all concept tag pages provide a brief definition of the concept and example code snippet (see Figure 2) adapted from earlier work by Dorn and Guzdial [10]. Further, all syntax oriented tags direct users to corresponding general concept tag pages.

---

[3] http://www.w3schools.com
[4] http://www.smashingmagazine.com

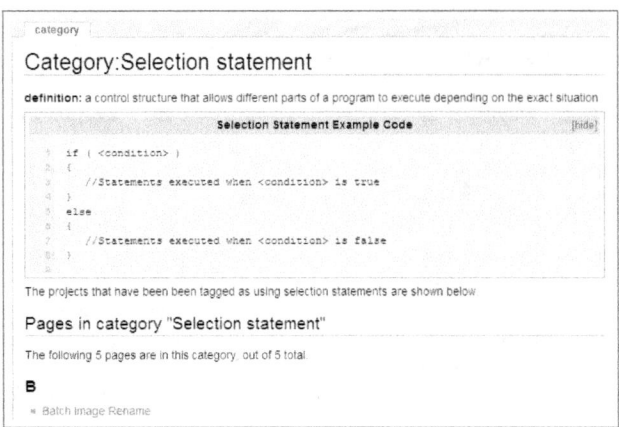

Figure 2: Concept Tag Page for Selection

3.3 Conceptual Coverage

For this evaluation, ScriptABLE contained a limited number of projects targeting six concepts identified elsewhere as least frequently used, most difficult, and least well understood by graphic and Web designers [10]. The concepts incorporated were: selection statement, functional decomposition, exception handling, indefinite looping, importing code, and recursion.

ScriptABLE projects were developed such that there were at least two projects which included explicit coverage of each of these six topics. Further, most projects were complex enough that their narratives covered at least two concepts. In the end, the ScriptABLE library evaluated in this study contained 7 unique projects covering these concepts. Further it included pages for 26 concept tags, 5 syntax tags, and 7 Photoshop task tags. Full details on the design and implementation of ScriptABLE can be found in [9].

4. STUDY METHOD

Our evaluation of ScriptABLE consisted of a multi-part lab study examining the role the script development narrative plays on improving participants' code quality and their conceptual understandings. In the study, participants were given a series of project-oriented Photoshop scripting tasks related to the activities, projects, and tools used in the Web and graphic design profession.

All participants completed two 2-hour study sessions in a controlled usability lab. In each session, participants were asked to complete a series of tasks in an existing Photoshop scripting project written in JavaScript. These tasks consisted of a combination of code comprehension, bug fixing, and feature extension. The first session was designed to establish a baseline for participants' performance on the tasks using only their pre-existing knowledge and current information seeking behaviors on the Web. Then, performance during the second session, in which they had access to a version of ScriptABLE, could be compared as a measure of learning. In session 2, half of the participants used a version of ScriptABLE with the narrative explanations, while the other of half received a version lacking the narrative. The "no-narrative" group still had access to all of the code examples from projects and the definitions contained in the tag pages. In this way, the "no-narrative" version provided materials similar to typical online code repositories currently used (e.g., the Photoshop Scripting Exchange). By comparing relative improvement in performance between these groups we can determine what role the narrative itself may play in the development of expertise.

At the outset of the first session, participants were asked to complete a demographic survey about their scripting expertise and background. Participants were then introduced to the specific project they would be working on in this task and shown the programming IDE provided with Photoshop. This project involved the automatic extraction of meta-data from a collection of photos to produce a comma-delimited file with the data. Participants were given time to review the provided materials and then were asked to complete two warm-up tasks to familiarize themselves with the project and programming environment. Research personnel assisted as necessary during the warmup tasks to build confidence. After completing warm-up tasks, participants were given 90 minutes to complete 6 individual tasks using only information found on the Web or in the documentation materials accessible through the IDE's help menu.

Approximately two weeks following the first session, participants completed a second session involving another Photoshop scripting project. The project and tasks used in the second session were comparable to that given in the first session; they required knowledge and use of the same programming concepts, and the code necessary for their solutions was the same length and overall complexity. Resources in the second section were restricted to the IDE's documentation and one version of the ScriptABLE tool. Participants were purposely sampled into treatment groups (narrative and no-narrative) based on observed performance in the first session. This ensured an even distribution of pre-existing ability levels between the treatment groups. Following a brief introduction to the ScriptABLE interface, the format of the second session mirrored that of the first.

4.1 Tasks

The six assigned tasks in both sessions were designed to require the use of one of the concepts covered by ScriptABLE's projects. Each task targeted exactly one unique concept, with the exception of one task involving both functional decomposition and importing code modules. The tasks were divided into two or more related sub-tasks designed to assess the intended construct from different levels of sophistication along Bloom's Taxonomy [1]. Subtasks were classified as "describe," "strategize," or "code" questions based on the nature of the prompt. Describe subtasks asked participants to run the script in a particular manner and describe what happened. Strategize subtasks asked participants to devise a strategy for preventing the error that occurred and outline the programming technique they would use in plain English. Lastly, code subtasks asked participants to implement their given strategy within the project.

The three question types make it possible to investigate both conceptual knowledge about a topic in addition to practical code development ability. This is important because it was foreseeable that a participant could correctly understand what was needed to complete a task, but struggle with elements of JavaScript syntax in implementing their idea.

4.2 Recruitment

Participants were primarily recruited from emails to local interest groups related to professional Web/graphic design and classified advertisements. A minority of participants were also recruited from undergraduate (non-Computer Science) groups. Volunteers were screened via email to confirm that they met study criteria, ensuring our pool of participants were familiar with scripting, involved in the field of Web/graphic design, but not professionally trained in software development. All participants were compensated with a $75.00 Amazon gift card upon completion of the study.

4.3 Participant Demographics

Eighteen participants, 11 men and 7 women, completed the study, and they represented a wide cross-section of the recruitment pool. A third of participants (6/18) indicated a primary occupation in the Web or graphic design industries, about 40% (7/18) were full-time post-secondary students, and the remaining 5 participants reported a combination of the two (e.g., a part-time student with an industry position). A variety of job titles were given, but careers in photography, Web development, graphic design, or other design disciplines accounted for over 70% (13/18) of the total.

Participants had a variety of prior experience with image editing and scripting tools. Experience with Photoshop ranged from 1 to 18 years with an average of 5.9 years ($\sigma = 4.8$), with participants reporting that they used it 9.6 hours per week, on average ($\sigma = 14.9$). Participants had less exposure to scripting or programming with an average of 4.5 years ($\sigma = 4.1$) of prior experience. On a scale from one (novice) to five (expert), the average self-reported rating of scripting expertise was 2.5 ($\sigma = 1.1$). Thus, on the whole, participants were experienced Photoshop users with at least basic knowledge of programming.

5. RESULTS

Our evaluation of ScriptABLE's effectiveness as a scaffold for learning computing concepts is divided into two parts. First we examine participants' ability to complete syntactically and semantically correct coding tasks, then we present findings related to their ability to answer conceptual questions about the tasks.

5.1 Code Quality

There were four "code" subtasks completed by each participant. To analyze the quality of the code produced for these subtasks we developed a simple rubric with four ordered categories to be applied to each of the final scripts. The categories, from most correct to least, were: (4) Code functions correctly; uses the intended construct; closely resembles the ideal solution. (3) Code functions correctly; uses the intended construct; but also includes unnecessary additional constructs that could be removed or otherwise simplified. (2) Code does not function correctly but uses the intended construct. (1) Code does not function correctly and does not use the intended construct. (0) No code edited or inserted.

Two independent raters applied the rubric to all 144 script excerpts produced in the two sessions (4 excerpts per participant per session). Ratings were compared and any disagreements were collaboratively reconciled between the raters to produce the final value. We then aggregated ratings for each of the four coding questions to produce a single value between 0 and 16 for each participant's code quality in a given session. The top half of Table 1 presents summary statistics for participants' code performance during session one and session two, and it also indicates the degree to which aggre-

Table 1: Code and Conceptual Performance Statistics

Variable	Treatment Group	Mean	Median	Mean Rank	Mann-Whitney U	Mann-Whitney p-value
Session 1 Code	narrative	7.78	6	9.83	37.50	0.812
	no-narrative	7.33	5	9.17		
Session 2 Code	narrative	10.11	13	9.28	38.50	0.872
	no-narrative	10.11	8	9.72		
Code Improvement	narrative	2.33	2	8.72	33.50	0.558
	no-narrative	2.78	3	10.28		
Session 1 Concept	narrative	7.44	7	9.22	38.00	0.862
	no-narrative	7.67	8	9.78		
Session 2 Concept	narrative	10.22	10	10.56	31.00	0.426
	no-narrative	8.78	9	8.44		
Concept Improvement	narrative	2.78	2	11.78	20.00	0.071*
	no-narrative	1.11	1	7.22		

gate code scores improved (calculated simply as session two score minus session one score). The rightmost columns show Mann-Whitney U test results for between-subjects comparisons of the two treatment groups on a given measure.

The statistics for the "session 1 code" variable illustrate that the purposeful balancing of participants based on session one performance yielded treatment groups with very similar performance distributions; session one performance was not significantly different ($p = 0.812$). Thus, it is reasonable to consider these two groups as comparable in their demonstrated coding ability going into the second session.

Participants' code scores improved across the board from session one to session two. The mean and median scores for both the narrative and no-narrative groups increased markedly. A Wilcoxon signed-rank test confirmed a significant positive shift in scores within-subjects ($Z = -3.172$, $n = 18$, $p < 0.001$). However, we did not observe significant between-subjects differences comparing the groups' overall code quality on the second task ($U = 37.50$, $n1 = n2 = 9$, $p = 0.872$) nor in the degree to which their code improved across the sessions ($U = 33.50$, $n1 = n2 = 9$, $p = 0.558$). In other words, code scores improved for both groups, but neither group improved significantly more than the other.

There are several likely explanations for these observations about coding ability. For example, there may have been learning effects from session one, or there may have been differences between the project contexts that made the second session's code easier to understand and/or edit. However, the primary result for the research questions posed earlier is that, while participants did better on the second session, these gains were not attributable to the version of ScriptABLE that they used during that session.

5.2 Conceptual Response Quality

Having examined participants' ability to write code, we now turn to an analysis of participants' ability to complete open-ended questions about programming concepts. For this analysis, we focus on performance on the five "strategize" subtasks; these serve as our indicators of conceptual understanding. Recall that these prompts asked participants to outline a programming technique or concept that would be applicable in the current situation and would allow them to overcome an issue in the code. Responses to these prompts were handwritten in English.

Similar to the analysis of code performance, we developed a rubric for judging the quality and correctness of conceptual responses. Again, two independent raters applied the rubric to all 180 responses gathered during the two sessions (five responses per participant per session) and collaboratively reconciled any disagreements. The final rubric used for each question had the following four categories, from ordered most to least correct: (3) Response correctly identifies the intended construct by name, using normative terminology. (2) Response correctly describes an approach that makes use of the intended construct, but does not explicitly use normative terminology in the answer. (1) Response does not address the intended construct, but does exhibit an algorithmic or programmatic approach to solving the problem that could work under limited conditions. (0) No answer given, or response was nonsensical or wholly unrelated to the issue being addressed.

We again combined conceptual performance scores for individual sub-tasks in a session to create a single value for each participant ranging from 0 to 15. This aggregate value was used as the overall measure of each participants' performance on conceptual questions. Summarized statistics for conceptual performance are given in the bottom half of Table 1. This table illustrates the mean and median conceptual performance values in sessions one and two and the observed improvement in the answers disaggregated by treatment group. Statistics for between-subjects comparisons on these three variables appear in the rightmost columns.

The treatment groups again performed quite comparably on conceptual questions in the first session as a result of our intentional balancing. The data in Table 1 show that the mean and median values for session one performance were very similar, and a Mann-Whitney U test indicates a non-significant result ($U = 38.00$, $n1 = n2 = 9$, $p = 0.862$). Thus, the groups were alike enough following session 1 to permit meaningful comparisons in relative improvement.

There was a statistically significant within-subjects increase in the quality of conceptual responses from session one to session two (Wilcoxon signed-rank, $Z = -3.135$, $n = 18$, $p = 0.001$). That is, participants' responses were more technically accurate and were more likely to make use of normative computing terminology. However, unlike the code measures, there were detectable differences in conceptual performance tied to which version of ScriptABLE participants received. Simply looking at the average values for session two it appeared that the narrative group outperformed the no-narrative group (see Table 1). We noted a difference in the degree to which answers improved between the treatments that approached statistical significance at the 0.05 level ($U = 20.00$, $n1 = n2 = 9$, $p = 0.071$). Our relatively small sample size reduces our statistical power, but that we were able to observe a marginally significant difference in conceptual understanding in spite of that is encouraging.

Looking at the data another way, participants who used the full narrative form of ScriptABLE improved, on average, about 2.5 times more than those who used the version lacking the narrative. Every participant in the narrative group improved by at least one point in the rubric, and several people improved by three or more points. Those in the no-narrative condition improved with much less regularity and four participants showed either negative or no improvement.

These results suggest the presence of a difference in the quality and correctness of conceptual responses that can be attributed, in some part, to the version of ScriptABLE used. Participants who used the full version with project narrative exhibited more growth in the technical correctness of their responses and their use of normative terminology to describe their proposed solutions. As an objective indicator of conceptual learning, this serves as initial evidence that the case library can promote transfer of normative computing knowledge from ScriptABLE's projects and indexes, at least in the short term. Whether participants retain this knowledge beyond the study session is beyond the scope of this study.

6. DISCUSSION

Looking back at the original research questions, we note somewhat mixed results. The presence or absence of a narrative explanation in provided resource did not appear to have significant impact on the overall correctness or quality of code produced by participants (RQ1). However, we did note a marginally significant difference when it came to conceptual responses (RQ2). These results are promising and provide initial evidence in support of the proof of concept case-based approach embodied by ScriptABLE.

It is natural to wonder why the case library users with access to the narrative showed increased gains in conceptual performance but not in performance on code measures. Consider two types of participants at opposite ends of the spectrum: advanced users who already have a fairly solid understanding of the concepts being studied and beginners whose knowledge of JavaScript is largely the product of simple copy/paste operations of pre-existing code.

Advanced users need resources to look up unfamiliar functionality or, most often, to remind themselves about small syntactic details that they have forgotten [2]. The underlying concepts have already been learned. For these users, either version of ScriptABLE provides enough information through the tag pages and example code to help them with such tasks as remembering how to write a function header in JavaScript—they are simply seeking small hints about specific syntax elements. Thus, these users are able to create code that works just as well given either ScriptABLE version. Their conceptual answers are strong in the first session because they already know of the various constructs, and they perform equally well in the second session.

On the other hand, beginners must attend to many more details in the two study sessions. We observed that some participants had never heard of many of the concepts (e.g., `while` loops, exception handling, recursion). Lacking strong understanding of the relevant concepts in the first session, these participants often provided non-specific answers for the strategize subtasks. They often wrote little or no code to solve the problems in the first session, and later remarked that they had trouble figuring out how to get the specific JavaScript code right. In the second session, their improvement on these factors was influenced by the version of ScriptABLE they received. With sparse instructional content, those in the no-narrative group improved little on their understanding of the concepts, and were still unable to get started with selecting the necessary JavaScript syntax in the code. However, those who used the full case library were often able to identify the correct concept for a given task based on the explanations given in ScriptABLE's project text. The script development narrative helped them confirm that the concept they were reading about could help solve their problem, and they used this in their responses to the strategize prompts. This resulted in pronounced improvements in their conceptual performance scores. However, when they were required to put their strategy into code, they still struggled to transfer knowledge about the concept to write completely new code in their project—by design, none of the code examples presented in ScriptABLE could be directly copy/pasted to solve a subtask. In unsuccessfully transferring between the concrete details of the ScriptABLE project and the assigned task, their code performance scores did not improve by the same margin. One might imagine that users with access to the narrative would eventually demonstrate code performance gains given repeated use of the system beyond the time constraints imposed by this study.

6.1 Limitations

Recruitment for this study yielded fewer participants than desired. While the limited sample size impacts the strength of our statistical analysis, it does not preclude meaningful application of non-parametric tests like those used here. We were able to detect indications that narrative explanations can be used to support informal learning in a case library. Replication of this study with a larger population would be warranted to confirm the effect of narrative explanations in ScriptABLE.

As mentioned in the results section, participants in both conditions improved significantly on both coding and conceptual responses, but it cannot be fully determined how much of that was simply the result of a rehearsal effect or differences in the difficulty of the assigned projects. Accordingly, our interpretation of the findings is constrained. In subsequent replication studies, it would be beneficial to add a third treatment group whose members have access to identical resources on the Web in both sessions, thus mitigating this confound.

6.2 Future Work

Beyond replication studies to confirm our findings, one next step would be to explore case-based learning aids in other settings where informal computing education takes place. Due to diversity of end-user programming tools and the important role that domain knowledge plays in such settings, there is a need to build and evaluate additional tools like ScriptABLE to support different groups of end-user programmers. Comparing results of different studies may allow us to distill generalizable principles applicable across informal learning environments. Further, conducting a large-scale deployment of ScriptABLE could explore how CBLAs are adopted as online resources (or not) in daily practice.

Based on our observations during this study, we pose two other areas of future work. Despite the fact that ScriptABLE projects are written in a narrative format, our observations were that few participants read these projects in a linear fashion. Anecdotally, participants navigated a project by jumping around the narrative body and skimming for a keyword. While we did not gather eye-tracking data in this study, doing so in the future would provide fine grain detail about how a case is "consumed", revealing implications for how cases and/or narratives should be best structured.

Lastly, we observed interesting behavior patterns with respect to searches during our study. In session one, where participants had access to the Web, we saw repeated struggles in formulating search queries and evaluating the relevance of results. Searching was less common with ScriptABLE, but we did not conduct a detailed analysis of the nature of query strings. Doing so could provide additional data about common information foraging strategies and how those strategies change when given a case-based learning aid.

6.3 Concluding Remarks

In this paper, we have presented ScriptABLE, a prototype of a novel case-based learning aid. ScriptABLE can serve as a model of instructional resources for informal learners of computing, especially for end-user programmers like those in our study population. From its tagging and indexing system to the content of its project pages, ScriptABLE draws on both educational theory and practical research evidence about what resources informal learners in Web and graphic design use and how they engage with them. It serves as an example of how to present conceptual instruction about computing while leveraging existing information seeking habits of informal learners.

Our evaluation study provides initial evidence in support of the case-based approach used in ScriptABLE. We demonstrated that learners engaged in project-oriented tasks are able to make use of such a case library for their inquiries. Qualitative feedback from users gathered during the study was largely favorable towards the system. Importantly, our data suggest that the narrative commentary about script development, which is a hallmark of case-based learning aids, can foster deeper understanding about computing concepts for users engaged in task-oriented activities. These findings provide justification for the future development and study of case-based learning aids for informal computing learners.

7. ACKNOWLEDGMENTS

This material is based upon work supported by the National Science Foundation under Grant Nos. 0613738 and 0618674. Any opinions, findings, and conclusions or recommendations expressed in this material are those of the author and do not necessarily reflect the views of the NSF.

References

[1] L. W. Anderson, D. R. Krathwohl, P. W. Airasian, K. A. Cruikshank, R. E. Mayer, P. R. Pintrich, J. Raths, and M. C. Wittrock, editors. *A Taxonomy for Learning, Teaching, and Assessing: A Revision of Bloom's Taxonomy of Educational Objectives*. Longman, New York, NY, abridged edition, 2001.

[2] J. Brandt, P. J. Guo, J. Lewenstein, M. Dontcheva, and S. R. Klemmer. Two studies of opportunistic programming: Interleaving web foraging, learning, and writing code. In *Proc. CHI '09*, pages 1589–1598, 2009.

[3] J. Brandt, M. Dontcheva, M. Weskamp, and S. R. Klemmer. Example-centric programming: Integrating web search into the development environment. In *Proc. CHI '10*, pages 513–522, 2010.

[4] J. D. Bransford, A. L. Brown, and R. R. Cocking. *How People Learn: Brain, Mind, Experience, and School*. National Academy Press, Washington, D.C., expanded edition, 2000.

[5] J. M. Carroll. *The Nurnberg Funnel: Designing Minimalist Instruction for Practical Computer Skill*. MIT Press, Cambridge, MA, 1990.

[6] J. M. Carroll and M. B. Rosson. Cases as minimalist information. In *Proc. HICSS'05*, 2005.

[7] M. E. Caspersen and J. Bennedsen. Instructional design of a programming course—a learning theoretic approach. In *Proc. ICER '07*, pages 111–122, 2007.

[8] M. J. Clancy and M. Linn. *Designing Pascal Solutions: A Case Study Approach*. W.H. Freeman & Co., New York, NY, 1995.

[9] B. Dorn. *A Case-Based Approach for Supporting the Informal Computing Education of End-User Programmers*. PhD thesis, Georgia Institute of Technology, 2010.

[10] B. Dorn and M. Guzdial. Learning on the job: Characterizing the programming knowledge and learning strategies of web designers. In *Proc. CHI '2010*, pages 703–712, 2010.

[11] B. Dorn, A. E. Tew, and M. Guzdial. Introductory computing construct use in an end-user programming community. In *Proc. VL/HCC'07*, pages 27–30, 2007.

[12] M. Guzdial and C. Kehoe. Apprenticeship-based learning environments: A principled approach to providing software-realized scaffolding through hypermedia. *Journal of Interactive Learning Research*, 9(3/4):289–336, 1998.

[13] J. L. Kolodner. *Case-Based Reasoning*. Morgan Kaufmann Publishers, Inc., San Mateo, CA, 1993.

[14] J. L. Kolodner, J. N. Owensby, and M. Guzdial. Theory and practice of case-based learning aids. In D. H. Jonassen, editor, *Theoretical foundations of learning environments*, pages 215–242. Lawrence Erlbaum Associates, Mahwah, N.J., 2nd edition, 2004.

[15] M. C. Linn and M. J. Clancy. The case for case studies of programming problems. *CACM*, 35(3), 1992.

[16] J. Sweller. Cognitive load during problem solving: Effects on learning. *Cognitive Science*, 12:257–285, 1988.

What Students (should) Know About Object Oriented Programming

Peter Hubwieser
Technische Universität München
Boltzmannstr. 3, D-85748 Garching
+49 (89) 289 17350
peter.hubwieser@tum.de

Andreas Mühling
Technische Universität München
Boltzmannstr. 3, D-85748 Garching
+49 (89) 289 17352
muehling@in.tum.de

ABSTRACT
In order to explore and validate suitable methods for investigating learning processes, we are currently conducting a case study, exploring the mental models of novice students in the field of object oriented modeling and programming. After abstracting and systemizing the information that was presented to the students of our introductory CS 1 course for non-majors we have asked them to draw concept maps at four points in time. Additionally, we conducted a small midterm exam, where the students had to implement some of the most important concepts and a regular final exam. We found that learning progress can be observed in detail by evaluating the concept maps.

Categories and Subject Descriptors
K.3.2 [**Computers and Education**]: Computer and Information Science Education, *Computer science education.*

General Terms
Measurement, Human Factors, Languages.

Keywords
Learning process, mental model, concept maps, object-orientation, objects first.

1. INTRODUCTION
The research in the field of Computer Science education is just taking the first steps towards a systematic investigation of learning processes by developing competency models [15], whereas e.g. in Mathematics such models were developed already in the early 80ies [21]. As Malmi et al. stated 2010: "However, after decades of research, we still have only a vague understanding of why it is so difficult for many students to learn programming, the basis of the discipline, and consequently of how it should be taught" [16]. Despite the current focus on competencies we are still interested in the investigation of knowledge elements, as these might be preconditions for certain competencies (following e.g. [31]). For example, knowledge about algorithmic structures is suggested to be a precondition for programming competencies. Apparently it is crucial for learning, particularly when following modern constructivist teaching approaches, that the learners gain exactly the necessary prerequisite knowledge, because otherwise their attempts to acquire a certain competency are not likely to be successful. Thus, if the prerequisite knowledge is well known, it is possible to support these learning processes in a very efficient way by presenting it at an early stage to the students. Therefore, our long-term goal is to find out (empirically) which cognitive structures are preconditions for programming competencies. Searching for methods that might help to detect this, we are currently exploring and trying to validate evaluation methods for cognitive structures. To this purpose, we have closely evaluated the knowledge structures of a CS1 lecture for students of engineering. We chose this lecture because its learning content is quite similar to a central part of the recently introduced compulsory subject of Informatics, namely the part of OOM/OOP in the 10th grade, which is the focus of our educational research activities [10].

The course of lessons was investigated very closely concerning the knowledge that the students are supposed to acquire. We asked the students to draw concept maps anonymously (marked with a random unique code number) at different points in time during the course. Until now, we have evaluated four generations of these maps. Additionally, we asked them to voluntarily complete a small midterm exam and to mark their final exam with the code number of their maps, allowing us to match the maps of each student to his/her exam solutions.

2. THEORETICAL BACKGROUND
Our teaching concept follows the "objects-first" approach that was introduced about 10 years ago as a reaction to problems students faced in writing their first object-oriented programs [4]. We have presented a quite radical version of this approach for our compulsory subject of Informatics in Bavaria [9], similar to the approach that was presented later in [8]. Recently, Ehlert and Schulte have compared the objects-first and the objects-later [6] approaches empirically.

Particularly in science education there are many research activities that use concept mapping techniques in order to investigate cognitive structures (regarded as "mental models"), see [14], [30]. The students have to draw a graph, with nodes representing concepts with edges symbolizing associations between these concepts, e.g. "is part of". There is a variety of measures for the assessment of concept maps (as graphs) and many corresponding research results that validate these measures, e.g. [28], [1], [29]. Some years ago, Sanders et al. compared the knowledge of students in several nations using concept mapping techniques [25]. Goldsmith and Davenport developed a graph-theoretical measure for the similarity of graphs based on neighborhood structures [7]. McClure et al. [18] validated this measure by correlating it with several scoring techniques. Hereby, they also detected that the scoring of locally correct edges using a master map is the most convincing scoring technique for concept maps.

By drawing concept maps, the students externalize parts of their knowledge. Due to the structure of the maps, this is restricted to *factual* and *conceptual* knowledge following the categorization of Anderson and Krathwohl [2]. According to [24] mental models are changed by *assimilation* or *accommodation*. Assimilation means including new information into an existing mental model by activating an adequate schema or by adjusting it by means of accretion (accumulation of new information) or tuning (changing of single components). If these processes are not successful, new information will only be accommodated by the process of reorganization, which is realized by constructing a new mental model. In [26] and [27] Seel describes closely which methods might be applied to explore or assess mental models.

Concerning the evolution of mental models, we refer to the theory of Conceptual Change, which was discussed in detail in [22] by comparing two competing theoretical perspectives regarding knowledge structure coherence: *knowledge-as-theory* vs. *knowledge-as-elements*. Following the first one, the students' knowledge is "most accurately represented as a coherent unified framework of theory-like character", following the latter it is "more aptly considered as an ecology of quasi-independent elements". The usage of concept maps offers direct access to the "ruggedness" of the knowledge of a student [13].

Nevertheless, it's crucial to remember that a concept map does not represent the knowledge of its author directly. Instead, it has to be regarded merely as an externalization of this knowledge that might be influenced by the motivation to draw an extensive map, by the focus of current attention or by many other external influences, as already stated by [20].

Concerning the representation of subject domain knowledge of object-oriented programming, [23] proposed to organize it in *Trucs*, (testable, reusable units of Cognition) which are collections "of concepts, operational skills and assessment criteria". The drawing of concept maps usually starts with a list of given concepts that the students have to arrange and to connect by associations. Such a list might be formed e.g. by the 39 concepts that [3] identified as "quarks of object oriented development" by exploring relevant textbooks. Mead et al. compared several criteria for identifying very important knowledge elements and propose to search for *anchor concepts* that are either fundamental or integrative and transformative [19].

3. THE COURSE OF LESSONS

For our investigation we chose one of our currently running courses that introduces freshmen of engineering (major in geodesy) into the fundamentals of object-oriented programming (OOP), attended by about 40 students. The course comprises two weekly hours of lecturing and two more hours of practice in two groups of 20 students. It runs over one semester (usually 15 weeks).

As pointed out in [11], there is a fundamental didactical dilemma in teaching OOP: On the one hand, modern teaching approaches postulate to teach in a "real life" context [5], i.e. to pose authentic problems to the students. Therefore, it seems advisable to start with interesting, sufficiently complex tasks that convince the students that the concepts they have to learn are really helpful in their professional life. On the other hand, if we start with such problems, we might ask too much from the students, because they will have to learn an enormous amount of new, partly very difficult concepts at once, as discussed in [12].

Following a "strictly objects first" approach [8], we solved this problem by distributing the learning objectives over the parts of the course that precede the "serious" programming-part and thereby avoiding to confront the students with too many unknown concepts when they have to write their first program. Basically, we suggest to the students to look at an object as a state machine [10]. In order to realize this in a student oriented way, the students need to be able to understand a simulation program of a typical state machine, e.g. a traffic light system.

Please note that the course was taught in German language, thus all the text material, the concepts and the concept maps had to be translated from German to English for this paper.

As it is not possible to understand the results of our survey otherwise, we shortly summarize the curriculum of the course:

Chapter 1 – Modeling. Informatics: main subject areas, typical working methods; Functional modeling: data flow diagrams; modeling techniques in Computer Science.

Chapter 2 – Object Oriented Modeling. Objects in documents: object, class, attribute, method, class card, object card; artificial languages: grammars, BNF; states of objects: state, transition, state diagram, real and program objects; object diagram, association, class diagram, multiplicity of associations, compound objects: creation of objects as values of attributes.

Chapter 3 – Algorithms. The concept of Algorithms: programming languages, class definition: definition and declaration, signature of methods, access modifier, attribute declaration, definition of methods; structure of Algorithms: graphical representation of algorithms, structural components of algorithms, nesting of components, input and output of algorithms; properties of Algorithms: terminating, deterministic, determined.

Chapter 4 – Object Oriented Programming. Definition of classes: structure of object oriented programs, definition and declaration, signature of methods, access modifier, attribute declaration, definition of methods; assignment statement, ring exchange, assignment in constructor methods, encapsulation, equality; translation of computer programs, compiler vs. interpreter, execution of programs, course of events of a program; communication by methods: input, output, side effects, local and global variables/attributes; creating objects at runtime, constructor method, references, removal of objects; implementation of Algorithms: structure elements in programming languages: sequence, conditional statement, repetition; arrays, index..

Chapter 5: State Modeling. Finite automatons, triggering and triggered action, state chart; Implementation of automatons: switch statement; conditional transitions: complete state modeling, implementation of conditional transitions

Chapter 6: Interaction and Recursion. Implementation of associations: unidirectional, bidirectional, 1:1, 1:n, m:n multiplicities, association class; sequence charts: calling of methods, sequence charts; Recursive algorithms: linear and cascading recursion;

Chapter 7: Generalization: Sub- and super classes, specialization, inheritance; implementation of specialization, overriding of methods, generalization, class hierarchies; polymorphism: calling methods of foreign classes, abstract classes.

4. SUBJECT DOMAIN KNOWLEDGE

In order to compare the knowledge that was externalized by the students with the knowledge they *should* acquire by studying the course material, we tried to find representations of the relevant information that are as compact and as formal as possible. For that purpose we have summarized all learning elements that we expect the students to know by reducing the slides and the textbook for the course to a list of statements without any examples or explanations, looking e.g. like the following:

"If an attribute is marked as private, only objects of the same class are allowed to read or write its value."

These statements (called *knowledge elements*) filled about 13 pages of text. To derive a list of concepts that should form the possible nodes of the concept maps, we reduced these statements in the following steps. Using the feature *word frequency* in the module *MaxDictio* of the software package *MaxQDA* (www.maxqda.de), we produced a list of keywords of the text. Then we sorted this list alphabetically (case-sensitive) and removed all words starting with a lower case letter. In German, this condition assures that the deleted words are all non-nouns. Finally, we removed all remaining non-nouns that were written in upper case (e.g. because they opened a sentence). In the next step, we reduced all words to a standard form (singular nominative) and removed all variations or abbreviations of the same noun. The following steps were based on the meaning of the words in the given context. We separated combinations of nouns that have an independent meaning in our context (in German e.g.: *Attributwert* was separated to *Attribut*, *Wert*), combined words that have no independent meaning (*garbage*, *collection* was combined to *garbage_collection*) and removed all words with a too general (*Informatics*, *model*), too specific or too technical (*Pascal*, *RAM*) meaning. Finally, all proper nouns and all purely didactical, organizational and pedagogical keywords were omitted. The whole process turned out to be quite objective and reproducible.

Afterwards we re-imported the resulting list of words into *MaxQDA*, coded and categorized it following the rules of qualitative research [17], obtaining finally the following list of 40 concepts (shortly called CL): *aggregation, algorithm, array, assign statement, association, attribute, class, condition, conditional statement, data encapsulation, data type, data, default value, execution, function value, function, generalization, identifier, inheritance, initialization, input parameter, instantiation, interface, method call, method, object, operation, polymorphism, program, reference, repetition, specialization, state, state machine, state transition, structural elements, subclass, transition, value, variable*.

Compared to the list of the 39 "quarks" that were elaborated in [3], there are 9 exact (verbatim) correspondences, 6 terms of CL have a very similar meaning to 7 of the quarks and 25 terms of our list have no apparent correspondence to any quark. The reason for the minor overall correspondence might be that the (more abstract) quarks are selected concerning their importance for object orientation as a technique, while CL represents just the basic concepts of our lecture which is not restricted to object orientation.

We asked the students to draw their maps in the following way. We presented the concepts of CL in the form of a checklist. At first the students should check all the concepts that they believed to know something about. Following this, they should draw a graph, using the checked concepts as nodes and connecting these by associations, which all should be denoted by suitable labels. For the evaluation of the maps we have removed all associations that were not labeled, assuming that these did not reflect any precise knowledge.

Following [18] the scoring technique "relational with master map" has the highest reliability and validity of the 6 strategies they have tested. It is performed by scoring every association in a student map as *correct* or *incorrect* by comparing it to a master map that was drawn by an expert, depending on a comparison of the labels that were given to the regarded association by the student or the expert, respectively. In order to get such an expert map that is as objective as possible, we derived it from the same material that we have used for the derivation of our CL. For that purpose, we coded all sentences of the list of the knowledge elements (see above) by the occurrences of one or more of the 40 concepts of CL using *MaxQDA*. Afterwards, we produced a list of all sentences that were marked with two or more concepts of CL, assuming that these sentences might suggest associations between those concepts. As concept maps can represent binary associations only, we checked the arity of these associations. Among the 161 sentences that contained more than one concept, we found 101 containing 2, 40 containing 3, 17 containing 4 and 3 containing five concepts. Therefore we could assume that most of the associations (63%) are binary and consequently could be represented in a concept map directly. Following this, we translated the information that was contained in these 161 sentences in associations by qualitative means. It turned out that this was not possible in some cases, e.g. because the regarded statement was structurally too complicated. We ended up with a set of 98 associations which formed our *objective expert map* (OEM) that was used e.g. to score the student maps.

5. DATA COLLECTION

At the beginning of the course, every student was asked to provide some personal information. Afterwards we asked them to draw a first concept map ("pre-test", PT) using pencil and paper. To ensure anonymity, we identified each student by a code number given to them randomly at this pre-test. In the subsequent tests, the students were asked to give their code number, so we could assign the maps or exercises to the other artifacts of each student.

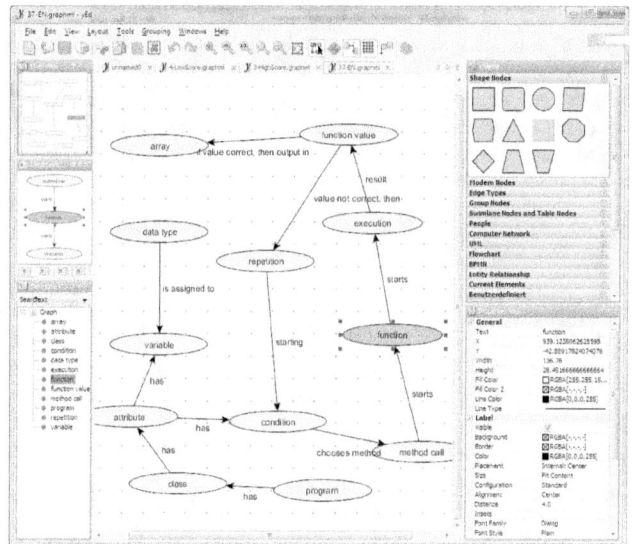

Figure 1. Exemplary map in the yEd graph editor.

Altogether, we collected four generations of concept maps at four distinct points in time. As the drawing was done partly in the main lecture and partly in the tutorials (and was voluntarily), we had varying numbers of participants. The pre-test was done by 39 students before the course started. The first mid-test (MT1) was done by 38 students after 4 weeks, right after chapter 2 had been taught to the students.

A small midterm exam (MX) was completed by 26 students after 7 weeks, in which the students should implement some of the most important concepts: *assign statement, attribute, class, data encapsulation, data type, identifier, initialization, method call, method, object, program, value*. The students were asked to write the definition of a simple class *City* with given attributes for *name*, *population*, *area* and a simple method that calculates the population density out of these attributes. Additionally, the attributes should be initialized with given values.

At the time of the exam, the course had finished chapter 4 almost completely (with the exception of arrays). One week after the exam, another collection of concept maps (MT2) yielded 19 student maps. Up to MT1, the tests were conducted on paper. From MT2 on, the students used the freely available graph editor *yEd* (see www.yworks.com and Fig. 1 for a screen-shot), starting from a template containing our list of concepts, CL. This has been done to counter an increasing "laziness" of the students when drawing the maps (since they had to redraw all the concepts and edges already drawn previously). Finally, immediately after the end of the lecture and some weeks before the final exam, there was a last test (post-test, POST), that was attended by 17 students. In the final exam (FX), 13 students gave us their code number and hereby allowed us to correlate their maps with their scoring in the exam.

6. DATA ANALYSIS

The collected data (we digitalized all maps that were collected on paper using *yEd*) consisted of 107 maps from students, the results of the midterm exam and the results of the final exam.

6.1 Naming of Associations

Before analyzing the students' maps, we normalized the labels of the edges (which were freely chosen by the students) in the following way: all verbs were transformed to a standard form (first person singular indicative), all isolated prepositions and articles were deleted, all auxiliary verbs were removed, isolated nouns or adjectives were deleted and all multiplicity specifications ("some", "many" etc.) were removed. In the next step we categorized the resulting names from all surveys following the rules of qualitative text analysis [17].

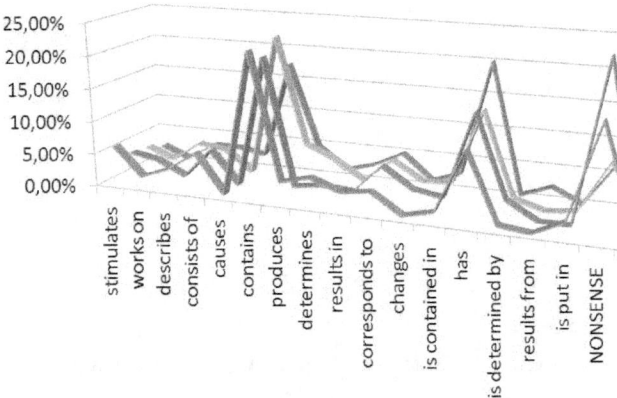

Figure 2. Frequency of categories of association labels (PT in front, MT1, MT2, POST at back).

We found that the number of (categorized) edge labels with more than one occurrence was quite low and stayed nearly constant (PT: 24, MT1: 28, MT2: 29, POST: 31) over the four surveys. Thus, apart from single occurrences, the students only used about 30 (semantically) distinct names in each survey to express the associations between the concepts. This is very interesting, as it shows that the restriction of edge labels to a predefined list, which would make the automatic collection and evaluation of maps much easier, would not result in a considerable loss of the gathered information.

Additionally, it turned out that the relative frequency of these categorized associations was quite constant over the four surveys. Fig. 2 shows the result for those concepts that were used at least in one survey for more than 2% of the edges. The most frequent categories by far were *contains* and its opposite form *has*. In contrast to this, the frequency of usage of the 40 concepts (CL) was quite different over the four surveys.

Subsequent to normalization and categorization, all associations were scored by the lecturer of the course with points (0 points for "totally incorrect", 0.5 points for "partly correct" and 1 point for "totally correct"). This was done by comparing it to the *objective expert map* (see section 4) following the technique "relational with master map" suggested by [18]. The edges were scored "totally incorrect" only if the suggested relation between these two concepts was apparently wrong and "partly correct" if it did not describe the relation totally correct, but a certain aspect of it in an acceptable way.

6.2 Graph-theoretical Measures

Two very basic measures of a concept map are the number of edges (as approximation for its "complexity") and the number of (weakly) connected components, leaving out isolated concepts. In other words, we treat the concept map as an undirected graph and count the connected components (clusters of nodes that are reachable from another). Both measures are used and validated, for example, in [13], where the latter measure is called *ruggedness*. Additionally, we can calculate the average score (using the edge scores 0, 0.5, 1 described above) over all edges of a given map. Table 1 summarizes the results of the surveys regarding these measures.

Table 1. Ruggedness (R), edge count (EC), correct edge count (CEC) average score (AS).

Test	Mean (Std. deviation)			
	R	EC	CEC	AS
PT	1.6 (57%)	8.1 (63%)	3.0 (73%)	0.5 (36%)
MT1	1.8 (54%)	11.9 (48%)	5.9 (71%)	0.6 (33%)
MT2	2.7 (63%)	17.6 (34%)	11.1 (43%)	0.7 (17%)
POST	3.3 (58%)	18.1 (49%)	10.9 (54%)	0.7 (20%)

6.3 Midterm (MX) and Final Exam (FX)

For evaluation, all mistakes that were made by students were closely described, provided with a unique identifier, counted and assigned to one of the concepts of CL. This test was completed by 26 students, who made a total of 105 mistakes. The distribution of the mistakes over the concepts was the following: *assign statement* 26%, *method* 12%, *method call* 12%, *class* 11%, *initialization* 10%, *data type* 8%, *program* 8%, *data encapsulation* 6%, *value* 5%, *attribute* 3%.

The most frequently occurring mistakes were purely syntactical: *String constant without quotation marks* 13%, *String type written lower case* 8%, *missing semicolon at end of line* 8%, *incorrect string concatenation in output method* 8%.

Next, we took a closer look at the relationship between a students' concept map and his/her result in MX. To this end, we isolated the maps of MT1 of the 17 students that both drew this map and gave their code number on MX. When correlating the number of correct edges with the achieved score in the exam, we get an effect of 0.68 with a p-value of 0.002. Apparently, on average, a student with good results in the exam will also have a high number of correct associations in the concept map. This indicates that there is some correspondence between the declarative knowledge of a student and his /her ability to apply that knowledge in the context of an examination.

As the final exam took place very short before the deadline of this conference, we had not the time to investigate possible correlations between the performance of the students in this exam and the quality of their concept maps in detail. At a first glance we were not able to find correlations between the graph measures presented in this paper and the results of the exam at any relevant level of significance, which is mainly due to the very low number of students that took part in POST and also gave their map code number at FX.

6.4 Evolution of the Students' Knowledge

Our aim was to find concepts and associations (in the OO context) that were understood very well or, in contrary, have caused remarkable problems to the students. Because it is very hard to keep an overview over the evolution of graphs with too many concepts, we concentrated this analysis on concepts that have a close relationship to object orientation, which was the focus of the course. Therefore, we selected those 9 concepts of CL that are contained in the list of quarks [3], added *generalization*, *specialization* and *subclass*, because they represent the quark *class hierarchy* and finally *method call* because it is a special form of the quark *message passing*. The result was the following list (OCL):

aggregation, association, attribute, class, instantiation, generalization, inheritance, method call, method, object, polymorphism, specialization, subclass.

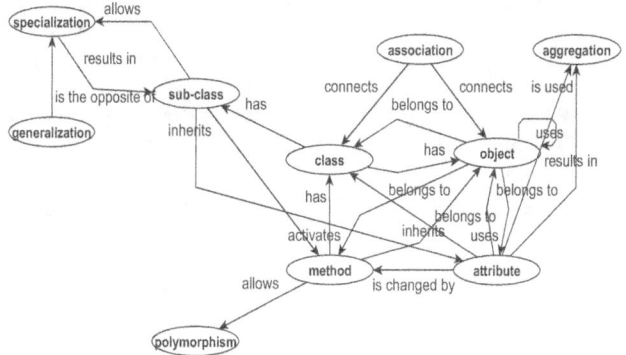

Figure 3. Partial objective expert map of OO-concepts.

Restricted to these 13 concepts, we could draw a *partial objective expert map* based on the associations we had derived from the course texts for the total OEM (see section 4). Nevertheless, only 10 of these concepts actually appear in this graph, because 3 of them were not connected by the total OEM at all. The partial map is shown in fig. 3.

When summing the edge scores for each edge over all student maps for a given survey, we get a value that describes how well this particular association was understood. For easier analysis, we used -1, 0, 1 as score values (in contrary to 0, 0.5, 1 as above). Thus, all "partly correct" edges were ignored in the summation. From this list of edge scores we extracted those that were particularly low or high. We defined a *high score* to be not lower than the 3rd quartile and a *low score* to be not higher than the 1st quartile of the score values. Based on these limits we could draw a map each for the corresponding *high scored* respectively *low scored* associations for each survey and hereby get an overview over concepts and associations that were understood well or badly, respectively. Figures 4 (*high scored* associations) and 5 (*low scored* associations) show the development of those "landscapes" over the four surveys.

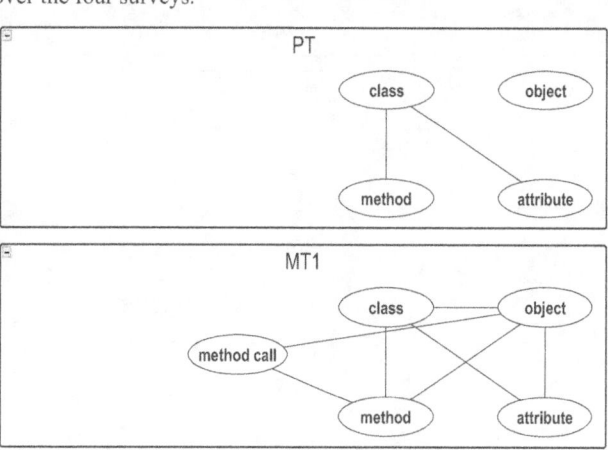

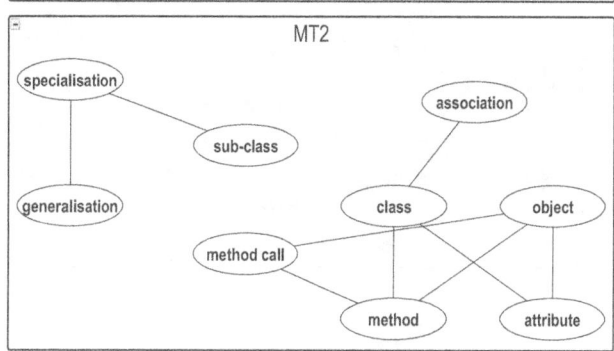

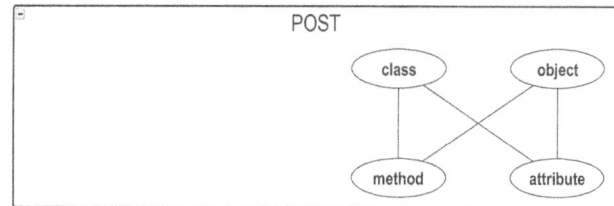

Figure 4. Frequently correct (high scored) associations.

Finally, we investigated the similarity of the connections (by associations without respect to their labels and their correctness) of the single OO related concepts in the student maps compared to the expert maps. We applied the similarity measure for graphs proposed by [7]. It is built upon the set of neighbors of a given node, computed locally for each node and then – if necessary - averaged over all nodes for the whole graph. It basically measures the similarity of the set of neighbors of a concept in the two compared maps. Its value is always within the interval [0; 1]. We were interested in concepts that show a very high (respectively very low) degree of similarity to the expert maps. However, the extreme measures of 0 and 1 are difficult to interpret. Isolated nodes, for example, will always get a rating of 0 and nodes with very few edges in the expert map (like *generalization*) tend to produce a rating of 1 very often. Therefore we left out the nodes with exact values of 0 and 1, i.e. we don't make any statement about the similarity of these concepts. When taking every map of every student into account, taking the average of the similarity for each of the OO related concepts - compared to the partial *objective expert map* - we get the ranking that is shown in table 2.

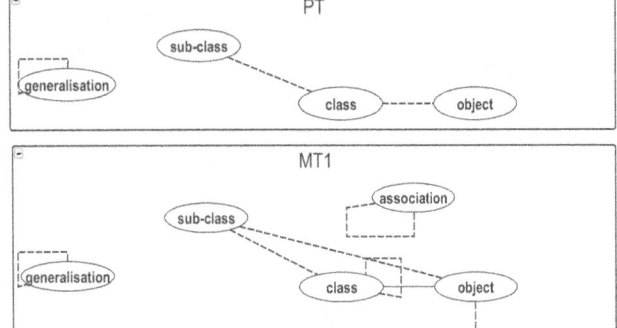
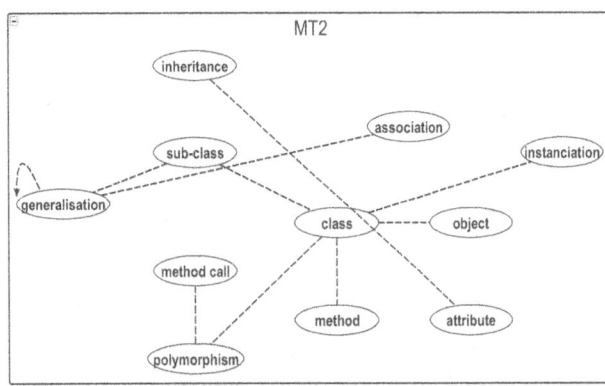
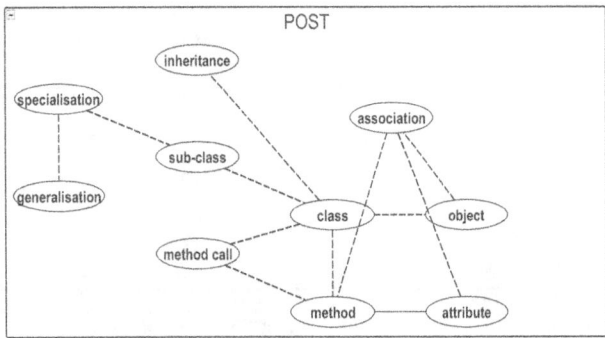

Figure 5. Frequently incorrect (low scored) associations.

7. DISCUSSION

The score values show that the average number of correct edges per student map increases clearly up to MT2. Looking at the quartiles (not shown in Table 1) of the CEC, both the 1st and the 3rd quartile (as well as the median, consequently) show a monotonically increasing trend (from 1 to 6 and from 4.8 to 15 respectively) over the four tests. This is to be expected and shows that the students are indeed gaining relevant knowledge.

We can also observe that the spread in the scores is the largest at PT, followed by MT1. The spread in PT is easy to explain by the varying of already existing subject-domain knowledge of the freshmen. Nevertheless, an average of 3 correct edges shows, there was already some amount of knowledge before the lecture had started. Given that MT 1 was the first "real" test (where the course had already begun) the high standard deviation shows that some students pick up the new material quickly, whereas others seemingly have major difficulties in creating a mental model for the presented concepts. Obviously, from a teachers' point of view, one hopes for this discrepancy to diminish as the course progresses. Exactly this can be observed in Table 1. The only exception to the trend is a small increase in the standard deviation at the POST test, which might have been caused by an increasing laziness of some students.

Table 2. Similarities of the connections of OO concepts

instantiation	0.97
inheritance	0.91
class	0.31
object	0.25
attribute	0.23
subclass	0.15
association	0.13
method	0.13
method call	0.12
specialization	0.07
generalization	0.06
aggregation	0.03
polymorphism	0.01

Interestingly, the average score AS (edge count divided by edge score of each map) is not increasing similarly. Nevertheless, looking at the quartiles of AS, both the 1st and the 3rd quartile show a monotonically increasing trend (from 0.43 to 0.69 and from 0.64 to 0.83 respectively) over the four surveys similar to CEC. This shows again that the students are learning actually.

When correlating ruggedness and edge count, no (or only a very weak negative) effect shows. This implies that those measures are somewhat independent. We can see that the mean of the edge count in table 1 clearly shows an increasing trend, while the standard deviation is quite high overall, decreasing from PT to MT2 and increasing again at POST. This shows that the maps are getting more complex, on average, which is to be expected. Interestingly, however, the average ruggedness also increases. We could interpret this result as in favor of the *knowledge-as-elements* theory [22]. However, it might also have simpler reasons. For example, the students might be too lazy to redraw the complete map and just focus on "new" edges, thus increasing the number of connected components. Or they might not see the connection between the different chapters yet.

Concerning figures 4 and 5, it is very interesting to see, how the knowledge of the students is developing. Starting from nearly no relevant knowledge, the incorrect associations are growing seemingly more than the correct ones (which, indeed, stay nearly constant until the last test). That means, the students were actively drawing edges in the concept maps, yet the labels were clearly incorrect (edge score of -1). So, the students knew what the main concepts of the lecture had been before the corresponding tests and they seemingly had a mental representation of their interconnections. Otherwise they most probably wouldn't have drawn any edges.. As the material of object-orientation is rather complex and also completely new to the students, it is not surprising that, at the beginning (i.e. MT1, when they were first presented the material), there are more misunderstandings than correct associations. However, as this trend continues throughout MT2 and even into POST, we can identify clear problem areas of the covered material. For instance, the association between *class* and *object* remains a misconception throughout every test. MT1 is the only test, where this association is also present among the "correct" edges. This lends itself to the interpretation, that a number of students were able to recall some factual knowledge about the relation of classes and objects at MT1, whereas in subsequent tests, they neither seemed to recall it, nor gained some deeper understanding about those two very central concepts of object-orientation.

Another interesting example is the association between *class* and *subclass*. Basically, the understanding of this association requires knowledge about inheritance, which wasn't present in the lecture until the very last chapter 7. Still, students seemed to have a (incorrect) mental representation of the meaning that led them to draw an edge in the concept map. For example, one of the incorrect edges in MT1 between *class* and *subclass* was labeled "contains". Interestingly enough, when the material was finally presented in the lecture (before MT2), *subclass* appeared for the very first time in the list of correct associations, even in the context of inheritance, but still, a large enough number of students had misconceptions (as the association *class-subclass* is also present in the list of incorrect associations of MT2).

Trying to locate problem areas, we are searching for concepts/associations that:

- were present in the lecture prior to the test (otherwise we cannot expect the students to know anything about it),
- are present only in the list of incorrect associations (this indicates the most troublesome areas) and
- remain that way for more than one test (so it's clear that the misconceptions remain).

For this lecture, this leads to the concepts of *inheritance, generalization* and *association,* which, interestingly, participate in different associations in each test – clearly indicating that the students did not have a well formed mental model about it. Also, the already mentioned *class-object* association and the association *attribute-method* fulfill these requirements.

However, when contrasting the evolution to the ordered list of similarities in Table 2, we get a slightly different picture. *Class* and *object* are remarkably high in the ranking, even though their absolute values are not remarkably high. Thus, even though there are related misconceptions concerning those concepts, many students seem to have drawn correct edges around these two concepts. So, in the overall structure, students seem to have got a grasp on how the concepts are interconnected with the rest. And indeed, *class* is the center of both the incorrect and correct landscapes in the figures.

8. CONCLUSION AND FUTURE WORK

We presented several measures that can be applied to analyze static and dynamic aspects of concept maps, when observing students over a larger time frame. So far, these measures seem plausible; however, they need to be investigated more closely. In particular, we will explore the relation between the changes in the maps of a student and the schemata of knowledge they have learned in order to distinguish assimilation and accommodation processes. In our next step we will investigate the results of the final exam (FX) more closely in order to find knowledge patterns in the maps that are corresponding with the ability to apply the knowledge in the exam. These might be candidates for the prerequisite knowledge elements that we have addressed in the introduction of this paper.

Additionally we are developing a web-based software tool that allows drawing concept maps using any web-browser (*CoMapEd*), storing them together with all relevant information about the survey in a relational data base on a server and evaluating the maps using all measures discussed above. We aim to use this tool for the first time for a survey among the informatics teachers in our state that is scheduled for the end of 2011. The goal is to investigate the knowledge of the teachers in a similar way as presented in this paper. After this survey, we plan to offer access to the tool for students and teachers in schools and universities.

9. REFERENCES

[1] Albert, D. and Steiner, C. M. 2005. Empirical Validation of Concept Maps: Preliminary Methodological Considerations. In Proceedings of the Fifth IEEE International Conference on Advanced Learning Technologies (ICALT'05), IEEE, Ed.

[2] Anderson, L. W. and Krathwohl, D. R. 2001. A taxonomy for learning, teaching, and assessing. A revision of Bloom's taxonomy of educational objectives. Longman, New York.

[3] Armstrong, D. J. 2006. The quarks of object-oriented development. Commun. ACM 49, 123-128.

[4] Cooper, S., Dann, W., and Pausch, R. 2003. Teaching objects-first in introductory computer science. In Proceedings of the 34th SIGCSE technical symposium on Computer science education. SIGCSE '03. ACM, New York, NY, USA, 191-195.

[5] Cooper, S. and Cunningham, S. 2010. Teaching computer science in context. ACM Inroads 1, 5-8.

[6] Ehlert, A. and Schulte, C. 2009. Empirical comparison of objects-first and objects-later. In Proceedings of the fifth international workshop on Computing education research workshop. ICER '09. ACM, New York, NY, USA, 15-26.

[7] Goldsmith, T. E. and Davenport, D. M. 1990. Assessing structural similarity of graphs. In Pathfinder associative networks. Ablex Publishing Corp, 75–87.

[8] Gries, D. 2008. A principled approach to teaching OO first. In Proceedings of the 39th SIGCSE technical symposium on Computer science education. SIGCSE '08. ACM, New York, NY, USA, 31-35.

[9] Hubwieser, P. 2003. Object Models of IT-Systems: Supporting Cognitive Structures in Novice Courses of Informatics. In Informatics and the digital society: Social, ethical and cognitive issues ; IFIP TC3/WG 3.1 & 3.2 Open Conference on Social, Ethical, and Cognitive Issues of Informatics and ICT, July 22 - 26, 2002, Dortmund, Germany. IFIP / International Federation for Information Processing. Kluwer Academic Publishers, Boston, Mass., 129-140.

[10] Hubwieser, P. 2006. Functions, Objects and States: Teaching Informatics in Secondary Schools: Invited talk. In Informat-

ics Education - The Bridge between Using and Understanding Computers. Lecture notes in computer science. Springer.

[11] Hubwieser, P. 2007. A smooth way towards object oriented programming in secondary schools. In Informatics, Mathematics and ICT: A golden triangle: Proceedings of the Working Joint IFIP Conference: WG3.1 Secondary Education, WG3.5 Primary Education; College of Computer and Information Science, Northeastern University Boston, Massachusetts, USA 27th - 29th June 2007, D. Benzie and M. Iding, Eds., Boston,MA.

[12] Hubwieser, P. 2008. Analysis of Learning Objectives in Object Oriented Programming. In Informatics Education - Supporting Computational Thinking, Third International Conference on Informatics in Secondary Schools - Evolution and Perspectives, ISSEP 2008, Torun, Poland, July 1-4, 2008. Lecture notes in computer science. Springer, 142–150.

[13] Ifenthaler, D. 2010. Relational, structural, and semantic analysis of graphical representations and concept maps. Educational Technology Research and Development 58, 81–97.

[14] Kern, C. and Crippen, K. J. 2008. Mapping for Conceptual Change. The Science Teacher, 9/1/2008, 32–38.

[15] Magenheim, J., Nelles, W., Rhode, T., Schaper, N., Schubert, S., and Stechert, P. 2010. Competencies for informatics systems and modeling: Results of qualitative content analysis of expert interviews. In Education Engineering (EDUCON), 2010 IEEE, 513–521.

[16] Malmi, L., Sheard, J., Simon, Bednarik, R., Helminen, J., Korhonen, A., Myller, N., Sorva, J., and Taherkhani, A. 2010. Characterizing research in computing education: a preliminary analysis of the literature. In Proceedings of the Sixth international workshop on Computing education research. ICER '10. ACM, New York, NY, USA, 3-12.

[17] Mayring, P. 2000. Qualitative Content Analysis. http://qualitative-research.net/fqs/fqs-e/2-00inhalt-e.htm.

[18] McClure, J. R., Sonak, B., and Suen, H. K. 1999. Concept map assessment of classroom learning: Reliability, validity, and logistical practicality. Sci Teach 36, 475\textendash492.

[19] Mead, J., Gray, S., Hamer, J., James, R., Sorva, J., St. Clair, C., and Thomas, L. 2006. A cognitive approach to identifying measurable milestones for programming skill acquisition. SIGCSE Bulletin 38, 4, 182–194.

[20] Norman, D. A. 1983. Some observations on mental models. In Mental models :, D. Gentner and A. L. Stevens, Eds. Lawrence Erlbaum Associates, Hillsdale, NJ, 7–14.

[21] Ohio State Board of Education. 1991. Model Competency-Based Mathematics Program. http://www.eric.ed.gov/PDFS/ED359024.pdf.

[22] Özdemir, G. and Clark, D. B. 2007. An Overview of Conceptual Change Theories. Eurasia Journal of Mathematics, Science & Technology Education 3, 4, 351–361.

[23] Pedroni, M. and Meyer, B. 2010. Object-Oriented Modeling of Object-Oriented Concepts. In Teaching fundamental concepts of informatics. 4th International Conference on Informatics in Secondary Schools - Evolution and Perspectives, ISSEP 2010, Zurich, Switzerland, January 13-15, 2010 ; proceedings, J. Hromkovic, R. Královic and J. Vahrenhold, Eds. Lecture notes in computer science 5941. Springer, Berlin, 155–169.

[24] Piaget, J. 1950. *The psychology of intelligence*. Harcourt, New York NY.

[25] Sanders, K., Boustedt, J., Eckerdal, A., McCartney, R., Moström, J. E., Thomas, L., and Zander, C., Eds. 2008. Student understanding of object-oriented programming as expressed in concept maps. SIGCSE '08. ACM, New York, NY, USA.

[26] Seel, N. M. 1995. Mental Models, Knowledge Transfer, and Teaching Strategies. Journal of Structural Learning and Intelligent Systems 12, 2, 197–213.

[27] Seel, N. M. 2008. Empirical perspectives on memory and motivation. In Handbook of research on educational communications and technology, J. M. Spector, Ed. Erlbaum, New York, NY.

[28] Shavelson, R. J. and Ruiz-Primo, M. A. 1999. On the psychometrics of assessing science understanding. In Assessing science understanding, J. Mintzes, J. H. Wandersee and J. D. Novak, Eds. Academic Press, San Diego, 304–341.

[29] Steiner, C. M. and Albert, D. Investigating Application Validity of Concept Maps. In Concept Mapping: Connecting Educators. Proceedings of the Third Int. Conference on Concept Mapping. Tallinn, Estonia & Helsinki, Finland., A. J. Cañas, P. Reiska, M. Åhlberg and J. D. Novak, Eds., 2008, 469–476.

[30] Vanides, J., Yin, Y., Tomita, M., and Ruiz-Primo Maria Araceli. 2005. Using Concept Maps in the Classroom. , Vol. 28, No. 8, Summer 2005. Science Scope 28, 8, 27–31.

[31] Weinert, F. E. 2001. Concept of Competence: A conceptual clarification. In Defining and Selecting Key Competencies, D. Rychen and L. Salganik, Eds. Hogrefe and Huber, Seattle.

Predicting At-Risk Novice Java Programmers Through the Analysis of Online Protocols

Emily S. Tabanao
Department of Information Technology
MSU-Iligan Institute of Technology
Iligan City, Philippines
emily.tabanao@g.msuiit.edu.ph

Ma. Mercedes T. Rodrigo
Department of Information Systems and Computer Science
Ateneo de Manila University
Quezon City, Philippines
mrodrigo@ateneo.edu

Matthew C. Jadud
Department of Computer Science
Allegheny College
Meadville, PA, USA
matthew.c@jadud.com

ABSTRACT

In this study, we attempted to quantify indicators of novice programmer progress in the task of writing programs, and we evaluated the use of these indicators for identifying academically at-risk students. Over the course of nine weeks, students completed five different graded programming exercises in a computer lab. Using an instrumented version of BlueJ, an integrated development environment for Java, we collected novice compilations and explored the errors novices encountered, the locations of these errors, and the frequency with which novices compiled their programs. We identified which frequently encountered errors and which compilation behaviors were characteristic of at-risk students. Based on these findings, we developed linear regression models that allowed prediction of students' scores on a midterm exam. However, the models derived could not accurately predict the at-risk students. Although our goal of identifying at-risk students was not attained, we have gained insights regarding the compilation behavior of our students, which may help us identify students who are in need of intervention.

Categories and Subject Descriptors

K.3.2 [**Computer and Information Science Education**]: Computer Science Education

General Terms

Human Factors

Keywords

Novice Programmers, Achievement, Compilation Behavior, Java programming, CS1

Permission to make digital or hard copies of all or part of this work for personal or classroom use is granted without fee provided that copies are not made or distributed for profit or commercial advantage and that copies bear this notice and the full citation on the first page. To copy otherwise, or republish, to post on servers or to redistribute to lists, requires prior specific permission and/or a fee.
ICER'11, August 8–9, 2011, Providence, Rhode Island, USA.
Copyright 2011 ACM 978-1-4503-0829-8/11/08...$10.00.

1. INTRODUCTION

Learning to program is hard. In a study conducted by McCracken et al., researchers found that as many as 35% of students fail their first programming course, while in the United Kingdom and the United States approximately 30% of computer science students did not understand programming basics [18]. This has led to a growing concern among computer science educators over the lack of programming comprehension of first-year computer science students.

Novice computer programmers are of special interest to the computer science education community. Computer science education researchers have conducted investigations into the kinds of problems novice programmers encounter when learning to program. Novices' knowledge has been found to be limited and shallow, hence they struggle with writing syntactically-correct programs [18]. They typically lack detailed mental models of various programming constructs [4,9], and tend to organize knowledge based on superficial similarities. Novices use general problem solving strategies instead of problem specific or program specific strategies, and approach programming "line by line" rather than at the level of meaningful program structures [21,25]. Novices have been observed to have poor program comprehension as evidenced by activities involving the tracing of their code [19]. They had a poor grasp at how a program executes and have problems with understanding that each instruction is executed in the state that has been created by the previous instructions [1].

Over the years, computer science educators and researchers have also conducted studies to identify the causes of these problems and to find possible solutions. One such method used is the collection and analysis of online protocols, which typically involve gathering information by augmenting the programming environments students use to write, compile and test their programs, thus allowing for automated data collection and subsequent analysis. In this study, we collect students' interactions with the Java compiler (mediated by the BlueJ IDE), which include the error message, the line number where the error appeared, the source code, and the time the compilation occurred.

The goal of this study was to determine whether at-risk novice Java programmers can be accurately identified through the analysis of online protocols. We quantified the compilation behavior of the students by computing what Jadud calls the Error Quotient (Section 2.1) [14]. We also derived the errors encountered and time between compilations from the data logs. From this, we built a linear regression model based on the EQ, errors encountered and time between compilations and the students' achievement in class as represented by students' midterm exam scores.

This present study has several potential benefits to educators teaching programming. Identifying at-risk students early in the semester can help educators provide targeted help and proper intervention to those who need it the most. By knowing the errors students typically incur in their programming, educators can better address concepts that students find difficult to grasp or are having misconceptions about. The EQ score can tell who among the students are struggling with syntax errors, prompting teachers to intervene to mitigate frustration. Spotting at-risk students early may also help reduce the dropout rates in computer science classes.

1.1 Research questions

From the online protocols of our students, we ask the following questions:
1. How do students with different achievement levels differ in terms of:
   a. Error profiles?
   b. Average time between compilation profiles?
   c. EQ profiles?
2. What factors predict the students' midterm scores?

2. REVIEW OF RELATED LITERATURE

Many studies have been conducted that identified factors related to success in the learning of programming. Among the identified student characteristics that may contribute to student success in introductory programming courses are prior programming experience, gender, secondary school performance and dislike of programming, intrinsic motivation and comfort level, high school mathematics background, attribution to luck for success/failure, formal training in programming, and perceived understanding of the material [5, 11, 12, 24].

Other studies have investigated teaching and learning approaches in relation to success in learning programming. Byckling and Sajaniemi developed the concept of *roles of variables* and a visualization tool to support the concept. Initial experiments with the visualization of variable roles helped novices in their learning of programming [7]. A subsequent experiment that tested the tool showed that visualization significantly improved the debugging skill of the students [2].

Mayer stated that mental models are crucial to learning and understanding programming [8]. To this end, Dehnadi designed an instrument to reveal the learners' mental models regarding assignment of values to variables and to evaluate the consistency and viability of those mental models. He believed that consistency of mental model is more important than viability of the model. That is, if the learner believes there is one and only one rule that applies, and consistently applies that rule, then the consistent application of the rule can have a strong effect on success in early learning of programming [8]. However, after several experiments the instrument failed to accurately deliver expected results [6].

It is generally accepted that programming is not easy. When novices were interviewed about their experience while performing their programming assignments, students clearly recalled emotional experiences and reactions. One of the most harmful of these emotions is frustration [16]. Some students learned from the bugs they encounter in their programs, but others get frustrated every time they encounter a problem and tend to view bugs as a measure of their performance. Labeled by Perkins as *stoppers*, these students have a tendency to get discouraged by their mistakes and give up [19]. Recently, Rodrigo & Baker was able to build a model that predicted frustration from the online protocols of the students [22]. In another study, Rodrigo et al. found confusion, boredom and IDE-related on-task conversation had negative effect on achievement in an intro to programming course [23].

Other attitude and behavior that were found to have positive effect on achievement in early programming course are perfectionism and self-esteem, and high states of arousal or delight [15]. Negative attitude such as disliking programming was found to be associated with lower success in early programming courses [3].

2.1 Error Quotient

In an attempt to represent student compilation behavior as a single scalar quantity, Jadud developed the Error Quotient (EQ). EQ is a function of error type, location, and proximity in time relative to other errors. It was intended as an indicator of how well or poorly a student was progressing.

Every record in the online protocol represents one compilation event. Stored in each record is the error message (if there was an error at the time of compilation), the location (line number) of the error in the file, and the source code. To compute the EQ, we examine the error message, the line number and the text of the source code. Given two compilation events, we first check whether both compilations ended in error. If they did, we assign a penalty. We then compare the error messages encountered. If they are the same, another penalty is imposed. If the errors occurred on the same line numbers, a third penalty is imposed. Finally, the programmer incurs a fourth penalty if the edit location of the source code on both events are the same. The penalties are normalized and averaged across all pairs of compilations to arrive at the final EQ score of the session.

An EQ score ranges from 0 to 1.0, where 0 is a perfect score. An EQ score of 0 means that at no point did the student encounter errors in consecutive compilations. A score of 1.0 means that every compilation resulted to the same syntax error in the same location.

3. METHODOLOGY

This study was conducted in the Department of Information Systems and Computer Science (DISCS) of the Ateneo de Manila University on the First Semester of School Year 2007-2008. The course *CS21A - Introduction to Computing 1* (CS1 in the literature) is the first computer programming course offered by the department to students studying Computer Science or Management Information System, and it is a required course for students in both degree programs. The Computer Science students take the course during their first year in the program, while the MIS students take it during their second year. It is presumed that students taking the course do not have prior knowledge of programming, but it is expected that they know basic operations of how to use a computer.

The participants of this study were the students enrolled in CS21A on the first semester of 2007-2008 at the Ateneo de Manila University. Of the 143 subjects participating, 35% were female and 65% were male; 18% were students in the Computer Science program, and 82% were students in Management Information Systems.

On the first day of classes students were informed about the study. A consent letter was given to each of the students. Each student affixed their signature and the signature of their parent/guardian if they were willing to be part of the study. They were not, however, obliged to join the study.

The students perform laboratory exercises in the computing laboratories that also served as lecture rooms. All the machines were installed with the same operating system, Java standard development kit, and BlueJ. The machines were connected to a local area network and the Internet. The laboratories have one-to-one student-to-computer ratios.

Over the first nine weeks of the semester, we scheduled five days during which students performed laboratory exercises. The lab exercises followed the lectures of the topics covered in the class and were designed to be finished in a one hour laboratory session. The exercises were given to the students on the day of their scheduled laboratory. A driver program was also given in each exercise for the students to test their code. Data gathering of the compilation logs was completely automated. Data was gathered only on the scheduled laboratory when the standard exercises were given.

3.1 Tools for collecting data

The data gathering tool was implemented as an extension to the BlueJ programming environment [14]. The focus of this study was on the compilation activities of the students inside the BlueJ IDE. A compilation event data was captured every time a student clicked the Compile button. Compilation events were recorded and stored in an SQlite database. Each record in the database represents one compilation event. We only retained data for students who consented to participate in the study.

3.2 Data pre-processing

Once the data had been gathered, it was pre-processed for analysis. For each study participant, all compilation records not related to the lab exercise were deleted. Students whose online protocol records were incomplete because of absences or technical problems were deleted from the dataset as well. After all the deletions, the sample was reduced from 143 to 124 students; 79 were male and 45 were female.

4. RESULTS AND DISCUSSION

The tools that we used for data collection allowed us to capture a copy of the students' work in progress every time they compiled their code. Here we present the errors encountered, the time between compilations, the computed Error Quotients, and linear regression modeling results. Computed results for the entire five lab sessions will be presented.

Using the midterm exam score, we categorized our students into three groups to determine behaviors of different student categories. Students who were one standard deviation below the mean were called the AtRisk group. Those who were one standard deviation above the mean were the HighPerforming group and those who were within one standard deviation from the mean are the Average group. Twenty-three out of 124 students were in the AtRisk group. They received a score of 62 or below. Twenty-five out of 124 students were in the HighPerforming group. They received scores of 89 and above. The Average group was composed of 76 students.

For each student, we extracted the timestamps, the errors encountered if there were any together with the line number and the contents of the file compiled. We computed the average time between compilations, total compilations, the EQ and the sum of all errors encountered for the five lab sessions. We also made a tally of the frequency of compilations per ten second bins and the top ten errors encountered.

A total of 24,151 compilation events were collected during the five laboratory sessions, 14,470 of these events or 60% ended in error. Table 1 shows the breakdown of these compilation events among the three student groups. Notice that the AtRisk group incurred the highest percentage of errors among the three groups even if they only made up 19% of our participants.

Table 1. Total Compilation Events per student group

Student Group	Total Compilation Events	Events with Errors	Percentage of events with errors
AtRisk	4,822	3,169	66%
Average	15,720	9,532	61%
HighPerforming	3,609	1,769	49%
Total	24,151	14,470	60%

4.1.a. Do different groups of students have different error profiles?

Using the total error events, we compared the groups using a one-way ANOVA to determine whether there were significant differences between the groups in terms of the errors they encountered. When the F test was significant, we proceeded with post-hoc analysis using Tukey HSD to check which among the groups had significant differences.

There was a significant difference among groups on the Total Errors, $F(2,121)=8.97$, $p<.001$. Post-hoc test results showed that the HighPerforming group had a significant lower number of errors encountered from the AtRisk group at $p < .001$. The HighPerforming group also had a significant lower number of errors compared to the Average group at $p < .01$, and the Average group was not significantly different from the AtRisk group. Post-hoc test results also revealed that students in the AtRisk group encountered the most errors among the three groups.

We were also interested to know what kinds of compilation errors each group encountered most frequently. We disaggregated the total errors into the top ten errors incurred by all the subjects. Figure 1 shows the top ten errors encountered over five lab sessions broken down by group.

We then performed a one-way ANOVA on each error type to determine whether the incidence of these errors among the different groups were significantly different. For the errors where significant differences were found, another post-hoc test was performed. ANOVA revealed five errors where significant differences between the three groups were found.

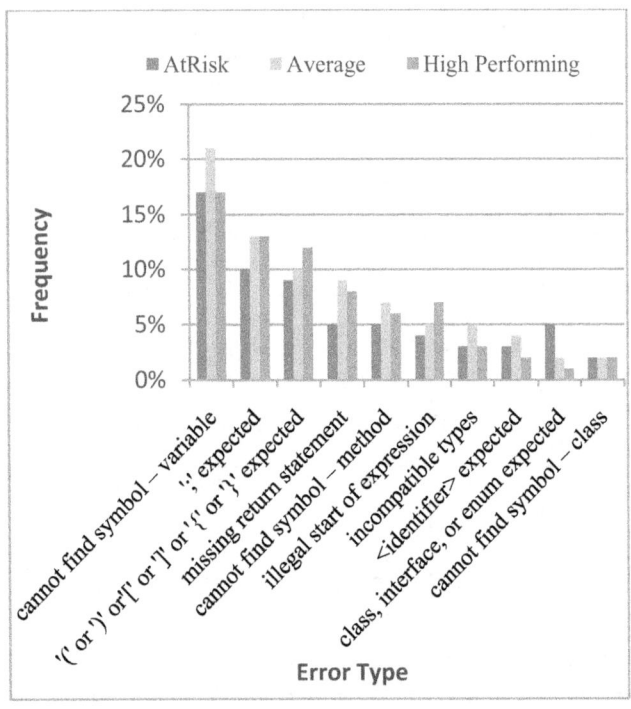

Figure 1. Top Ten Errors over Five Lab Sessions broken down by Student Group

Table 2 shows the results of the post-hoc test on these errors.

Table 2. Tukey HSD test on Error Types with Significant F test at 95% confidence interval

Error Type	Groups Compared	p adj
cannot find symbol-variable	Average-AtRisk	0.02
	HighPerforming-AtRisk	0.00
	HighPerforming-Average	0.01
incompatible types	Average-AtRisk	0.91
	HighPerforming-AtRisk	0.08
	HighPerforming-Average	0.06
identifier expected	Average-AtRisk	0.33
	HighPerforming-AtRisk	0.00
	HighPerforming-Average	0.01
class, interface, or enum expected	Average-AtRisk	0.00
	HighPerforming-AtRisk	0.00
	HighPerforming-Average	0.70
cannot find symbol-class	Average-AtRisk	0.68
	HighPerforming-AtRisk	0.04
	HighPerforming-Average	0.09

Table 2 shows that:

1. the HighPerforming group was significantly different from the AtRisk group on only four errors: `cannot find symbol-variable`, `identifier expected`, `class, interface, or enum expected`, and `cannot find symbol-class` errors. The mean differences show that the HighPerforming group encountered fewer instances of these errors compared to the AtRisk group;

2. the HighPerforming group was significantly different from the Average group on only two errors the `cannot find symbol-variable` and `identifier expected` errors. The HighPerforming group encountered fewer instances of these two errors as compared to the Average group; and

3. the Average group was significantly different from the AtRisk group on only two errors the `cannot find symbol-variable` and `class, interface, or enum expected` errors. The AtRisk group encountered more instances of these two errors when compared with the Average group.

4.1.b. Do different groups have different average time between compilations profiles?

Every time students compiled their code, our data collection program recorded a timestamp, the time the event happened. Timestamps were precise up to the millisecond level. We did not attempt to categorize students based on the precise time between compilations—this level of granularity was too fine-grained for our purposes. Instead, as in Jadud's study [13], we arranged the time between compilations into 10 second bins and performed a one-way ANOVA on the three student groups to determine if there were differences in their compilation behavior in terms of how rapidly they compiled their programs. Figure 2 shows a comparison of the compilation of the groups of students.

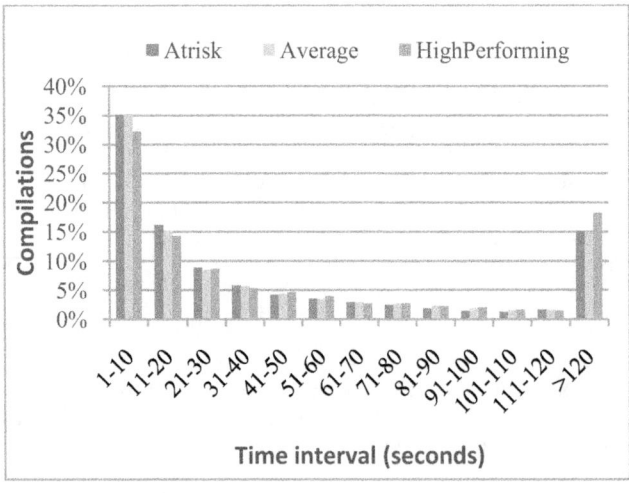

Figure 2. Time between compilations over Five Lab Sessions broken by Student Group

Table 3 summarizes the time interval in seconds at which there was a significant difference among the three student groups. Further analysis using Tukey HSD was performed and results are also shown in Table 3, from which we can see that:

1. there was no significant difference between the Average and AtRisk group in terms of time between compilations;
2. there was a significant difference between the HighPerforming and the Average group except on the time intervals 21-30, 111-120 and >120 seconds. The HighPerforming group performed fewer compilations in all time intervals compared to the Average group; and
3. the HighPerforming group was significantly different from the AtRisk group except on the time interval 81-90 seconds.

The AtRisk group performed more compilations in all time intervals compared to the HighPerforming group.

Table 3. Tukey HSD test on time intervals with significant F test at 95% confidence interval

Time interval (seconds)	Groups Compared	p adj
1-10	Average-AtRisk	0.71
	HighPerforming-AtRisk	0.04
	HighPerforming-Average	0.05
11-20	Average-AtRisk	0.25
	HighPerforming-AtRisk	0.00
	HighPerforming-Average	0.01
21-30	Average-AtRisk	0.35
	HighPerforming-AtRisk	0.01
	HighPerforming-Average	0.06
31-40	Average-AtRisk	0.53
	HighPerforming-AtRisk	0.00
	HighPerforming-Average	0.01
61-70	Average-AtRisk	0.66
	HighPerforming-AtRisk	0.02
	HighPerforming-Average	0.04
81-90	Average-AtRisk	0.81
	HighPerforming-AtRisk	0.31
	HighPerforming-Average	0.04
111-120	Average-AtRisk	0.53
	HighPerforming-AtRisk	0.02
	HighPerforming-Average	0.10
>120	Average-AtRisk	0.21
	HighPerforming-AtRisk	0.01
	HighPerforming-Average	0.10

These results suggest that we cannot differentiate an Average from an AtRisk student based on the timing of when they click the compile button. The HighPerforming group, on the other hand, can always be differentiated from the Average and the AtRisk groups. Though there is one time interval where the HighPerforming group is not significantly different from the AtRisk group, particularly the 81-90 seconds interval, overall, the difference is significant at p <.05. There is a need to further examine the data to check what the AtRisk group was doing exactly. We suspected they could be doing something not related to the assignment or maybe they seemed lost or got stuck and did not know what to do as uncovered by the study of [16]. It is possible that although the AtRisk group spends a significant amount of time between compilations, the time between compilations is not spent productively.

4.1.c. Do different groups of students have different EQ Profiles?

We took the average Error Quotient (EQ) of the students for the five lab sessions and used as our data for this analysis. We wanted to see how different the EQ scores were of the three student groups. Figure 3 shows the EQ scores and percentage distribution among our participants.

Result of one-way ANOVA showed that there was a significant difference in the EQ scores among the groups, $F(2,121) = 20.528$, $p < .001$. After performing post-hoc analysis, we found that the Average group is significantly different from the AtRisk group at

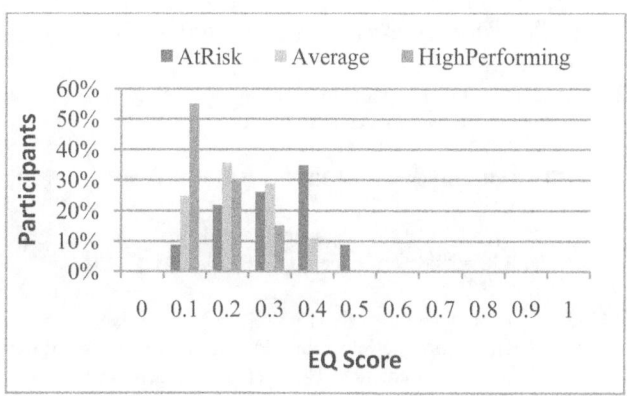

Figure 3. EQ Score distribution by Group

$p < .001$ and the mean difference show that the AtRisk group have higher EQs compared to the Average group. The HighPerforming group was significantly different from the Average group at $p<.01$ and the mean difference show that the HighPerforming group have lower EQs compared to the Average group. The AtRisk group was significantly different from the HighPerforming group at $p<.001$ and the mean difference show that the AtRisk group had higher EQs compared to the HighPerforming group (Table 4).

Table 4. Tukey HSD test on EQ at 95% confidence interval

Groups Compared	Mean difference	p adj
Average-AtRisk	-0.11	0.00
HighPerforming-AtRisk	-0.19	0.00
HighPerforming-Average	-0.08	0.00

4.2. What factors predict the midterm score?

In this part of our data analysis, we first correlated the Total Errors encountered and average time between compilations with the Midterm Score. It was important to get a correlation from these variables first in order to see if there was any relationship between them. If there was no relationship existed between them, linear regression would fail. Pearson's product-moment correlation showed the following results:

1. there was a significant negative relationship between the total errors encountered and the Midterm Score, $r = -.41$, $p<.001$;
2. there was a significant positive relationship between average time between compilations and the Midterm Score, $r = .27$, $p< .01$; and
3. there was a significant negative relationship between EQ and the Midterm Score, $r= -.55$, $p <.001$.

Results revealed that there was a correlation between the errors encountered, average time between compilations and the Error Quotient. We then proceeded with performing linear regression to determine whether any of these were predictors of achievement as represented by the students' scores on the midterm exam. To test the generalizability of our models we also computed each model's Bayesian Information Criterion for Linear Regression (BiC'). The BiC' is used to assess the tradeoff between model fit and the number of parameters (which can spuriously increase model fit). Values of BiC' less than -6 signify that the model has significantly better fit than chance, given the number of model parameters [20].

4.2.a. Predicting midterm score using the errors encountered

Using the Total Errors encountered from the five lab sessions and the Midterm Score we arrived at the following model:

Model 1: MidtermScore = 84.29698 - 0.07304*TotalErrors

Multiple R^2=0.1457, Adjusted R^2=0.1387
$F(1,122)$=20.81, p-value<.001, BIC = -7.8

Model 1 accounted for only 13.87% of the variance of the Midterm score. From the intercept of Model 1, we concluded that the model could not predict the HighPerforming group. However, this could also mean that the errors encountered by the HighPerforming group of students did not affect their MidtermScore.

We performed multiple regression by inputting the top ten errors into our modeling tool. Only three out of the ten errors were significant as seen in Model 2.

Model 2:
MidtermScore = 83.50274-0.25632*UNKNOWN_VARIABLE
- 0.42035*CLASS_INTERFACE_EXP
- 0.75506*UNKNOWN_CLASS

Multiple R^2=0.2645, Adjusted R^2=0.1994, $F(10,113)$=4.063, p-value<.001, BiC'=-10.2635

Model 2 seemed to apply only to the Average and the AtRisk groups. It could not predict HighPerforming students but it is much better compared to Model 1 in terms of predicting the AtRisk students.

From the results in Section 4.1.a, we found that among the top 10 errors, there were only five errors where the three groups had significant differences. And out of the five, three came out in Model 2 that significantly affects the Midterm Score. As added information and to help us further understand Model 2, we generated the means of the error types per group. Table 5 shows the computed means.

Table 5. Group mean values on error types

Error Type	Mean Values		
	High-Performing	Average	AtRisk
cannot find symbol - variable	12.0	23.3	33.6
incompatible types	1.3	5.6	6.3
identifier expected	1.9	4.2	5.6
class, interface, or enum expected	0.8	2.2	7.8
cannot find symbol-class	1.1	2.7	3.3

Table 5 shows that the HighPerforming group incurred the least number of errors, which implies that the HighPerforming group's Midterm Score was not affected by the errors they encountered. However, the Midterm Scores of the students in the Average and AtRisk group may be negatively affected by the following errors: cannot find symbol-variable, class, interface, or enum expected and cannot find symbol-class. Model 2 indicates that the more cannot find symbol - variable, class, interface, or enum expected and cannot find symbol-class errors the AtRisk and Average group encounters, the lower their midterm scores will be. Also, we could notice in Table 5 that the AtRisk and Average groups had closer means and were higher compared to the HighPerforming group.

4.2.b. Predicting the midterm score using Time between compilations

To determine if time between compilations was a good predictor of the Midterm score, we took the mean of the average time between compilations of the five lab sessions and came up with Model 3.

Model 3: MidtermScore = 65.04788
+ 0.12107*AverageTBC_seconds

Multiple R^2=0.07272, Adjusted R^2=0.06512
$F(1,122)$=9.568, p-value<.01, BIC = -1.97243

Model 3 suggests that average time between compilations had a positive effect on the Midterm score. The longer the time intervals between compilations, the higher the Midterm score will be. Although this finding was intuitive, the model itself was quite weak at an R^2 value of .06 and with a BiC' value of -1.97. When we computed the predicted Midterm Scores the model was not able to predict AtRisk students and all students were predicted to belong to only one group.

4.2.c. Predicting midterm score using EQ scores

We computed the average EQ score for the five laboratory sessions and together with the Midterm Score arrived at Model 4.

Model 4: MidtermScore = 92.918 - 64.396*EQ

Adjusted R^2 = 0.2971, $F(1,122)$ = 52.98,
p-value = 3.591e-11, BIC' = -17.3303

In all the models that we have, Model 4 has the highest R^2 value. The BiC' value suggests that the model has significantly better fit than chance given the EQ parameter. Model 4 suggests that EQ has a negative effect on the Midterm score. The higher the EQ, the lower the Midterm Score will be.

We combined all factors in Models 1 to 4 to see if we can come up with a better model. These factors are the errors UNKNOWN_VARIABLE, CLASS_INTERFACE_EXP and UNKNOWN_CLASS and the EQ. We arrived at Model 5. The EQ came out to be a highly significant predictor of the Midterm score.

Model 5: MidtermScore = 90.58643-43.33380*EQ

Adjusted R^2 = 0.3073, $F(7,116)$= 8.795,
p-value=1.202e-08, BIC' = -20.8326

The UNKNOWN_VARIABLE error had p=.06, an indication to look for in determining AtRisk students. We can see from Model 5 that the EQ accounted for about one-third of the variance of the Midterm Score based on the adjusted R^2 value. The BiC' value indicates that our model has a significantly better fit than chance given the parameters.

5. CONCLUSION AND FUTURE WORK

In this paper, we attempted to determine whether there were differences among groups of students in terms of their error profiles, compilation profiles and Error Quotient profiles. We also tried to determine whether any of these indicators could predict the midterm scores. Based upon students' online protocols we found that errors encountered by novices in Java programming can negatively affect their midterm score. We have shown that High Performing novices encountered similar errors with the rest of their peers. However, when compared against the Average and AtRisk novices, High Performing novices encountered these errors less frequently. The Average and AtRisk novices encountered more errors, and these two groups differed significantly on only three types out of the top ten errors. We found that errors did not affect the Midterm Scores of the HighPerforming novices but there were three types of error that negatively affected the Midterm Scores of the Average and AtRisk novices: `cannot find symbol - variable`, `class, interface, or enum expected` and `cannot find symbol-class` errors.

We also found that higher time between compilations yielded positive effect on the Midterm Score. The average time between compilations performed by the High Performing novices was higher than those of the Average and the AtRisk novices. The HighPerforming group spent more time on their programs and wrote more lines of code compared to the other two groups. There was a significantly high incidence of recompilations in less than 30 seconds among the AtRisk and Average novices. The compilation behavior of the two groups was the same.

We generated linear regression models that predicted the Midterm Score of a student given the errors encountered, time between compilation and the EQ across five lab sessions. The model with EQ as a factor could significantly predict Midterm Scores better than would-be-expected by chance. However, our models came out to be poor at predicting AtRisk students.

From the significant findings of this study, we identify several possible avenues for further investigation. We could use other achievement indicators such the grade for lab exercise where data were collected to strengthen our models. We can also improve on the basis of grouping the students. Instead of just one group to represent the average students, we can break them into high-average and below-average students. We can use the standard cut-off in the grading systems for A, B, C and D. We surmised that high-average students had similar compilation behavior with the high performing students and that below average and at-risk students may have had similar behaviors as well.

The models derived from the errors encountered suggest that we look out on students who struggle with errors. Additional investigations can be undertaken to explore the conceptual errors that generate these syntax errors. The differences in the types of errors encountered by AtRisk and HighPerforming students, for example, may say something about the students' mental models and where their understandings are flawed. Insight into these flaws can help computer science educators design interventions to correct these mental models.

Finally, we believe there is potential to use IDEs intelligent systems that offer help or guidance to students or gives signal to the teacher for provision of help to some students. Support systems of this type may help mitigate student frustration and confusion, increase programming comprehension, and raise achievement. They may also contribute to greater student retention in computer science and related disciplines.

In conclusion, this study has shed light on the differences of the profiles of novice programmers. Using the compilation logs we can spot who among the novices are performing well. Though we have not successfully attained our goal of identifying at-risk students, the study has given us clues on which compilation behaviors at-risk students are exhibiting. Our suggestions on improving the study might give us better models in the future.

6. ACKNOWLEDGMENTS

We thank Arvin Guingguing, Anna Christine Amarra, Ramil Bataller, Andrei Coronel, Darlene Daig, Jose Alfredo de Vera, Thomas Dy, Maria Beatriz Espejo-Lahoz, Dr. Emmanuel Lagare, Sheryl Ann Lim, Ramon Francisco Mejia, Shiela Pascua, Dr. John Paul Vergara, and the technical and secretarial staff of the Ateneo de Manila's Department of Information Systems and Computer Science for their assistance with this project. We thank the Ateneo de Manila's CS21A students, school year 2007-2008, for their participation. We thank the Department of Science and Technology's Philippine Council for Advanced Science and Technology Research and Development for making this study possible by providing the grants entitled Modeling Novice Programmer Behaviors Through the Analysis of Logged Online Protocols and Observation and Diagnosis of Novice Programmer Skills and Behaviors Using Logged Online Protocols. Finally, Dr. Rodrigo thanks the Philippine American Educational Foundation and the Council for International Exchange of Scholars for her 2008-2009 Advanced Research and University Lecturing Fulbright Scholarship.

7. REFERENCES

[1] Ahmadzadeh, M., Elliman, D. and Higgins, C. An analysis of patterns of debugging among novice computer science students. In Proceedings of the 10th annual SIGCSE conference on Innovation and technology in computer science education (ITiCSE '05). ACM, New York, NY, USA, 84-88. http://doi.acm.org/10.1145/1067445.1067472

[2] Al-Barakati, N., Al-Aama, A., 2009. The effect of visualizing roles of variables on student performance in an introductory programming course. SIGCSE Bull. 41, 3 (July 2009), 228-232.
http://doi.acm.org/10.1145/1595496.1562949

[3] Bennedsen, J., Caspersen M. E. 2008. Optimists Have More Fun, But Do They Learn Better? - On the Influence of Emotional and Social Factors on Learning Introductory Computer Science. Computer Science Education, 18, 1, 1-16.

[4] Ben-Ari, M. 1998. Constructivism in computer science education. ACM Press New York, NY, USA. Vol. 30(1).

[5] Bergin, S., Reilly R.: Programming: Factors that influence success. SIGCSE 2005. Proceedings of the thirty-fifth SIGCSE technical symposium on Computer Science Education. St. Louis, Illinois, US. February 2005, 411-415.

[6] Bornat, R., Dehnadi, S., Simon. 2008. Mental models, consistency and programming aptitude. In *Proceedings of the tenth conference on Australasian computing education - Volume 78* (ACE '08), Simon Hamilton and Margaret Hamilton (Eds.), Vol. 78. Australian Computer Society, Inc., Darlinghurst, Australia, Australia, 53-61.

[7] Byckling, P., Sajaniemi, J., 2006. Roles of variables and programming skills improvement. *SIGCSE Bull.* 38, 1 (March 2006), 413-417. DOI=10.1145/1124706.1121470
http://doi.acm.org/10.1145/1124706.1121470

[8] Dehnadi, Saeed. A Cognitive Study of Learning to Program in Introductory Programming Courses [Doctoral Thesis]. Retrieved from http://eprints.mdx.ac.uk/6274/1/Dehnadi_A_Cognitive_Study_of_Learning.pdf

[9] duBoulay, B. 1986. Some difficulties of learning to program. Journal of Educational Computing Research, Vol. 2, pp. 57--73.

[10] Fenwick, J.B.Jr., Norris, C., Barry, F.E., Rountree,J., Spicer,C.J. and Cheek, S.D. 2009. Another look at the behaviors of novice programmers. SIGCSE Bull. 41, 1 (March 2009), 296-300. DOI=10.1145/1539024.1508973 http://doi.acm.org/10.1145/1539024.1508973

[11] Goold, A. and Rimmer, R. (2000): Factors affecting performance in first-year computing. ACM SIGCSE Bulletin, 32(2): 39-43.

[12] Hagan, D., Markham, S., 2000. Does it help to have some programming experience before beginning a computing degree program?.*SIGCSE Bull.* 32, 3 (July 2000), 25-28. http://doi.acm.org/10.1145/353519.343063

[13] Jadud MC. (2005). A first look at novice compilation behavior using BlueJ. Computer Science Education, 15(1), 25-40.

[14] Jadud, M.C., 2006. Methods and tools for exploring novice compilation behaviour. Proceedings of the 2006 international workshop on Computing education research. New York, NY, USA : ACM Press. pp. 73--84.

[15] Khan, I., Hierons, M., Brinkman, W. 2007. Mood independent programming. In *Proceedings of the 14th European conference on Cognitive ergonomics: invent! explore!* (ECCE '07). ACM, New York, NY, USA, 269-272. http://doi.acm.org/10.1145/1362550.1362606

[16] Kinnunen, P., Simon, B. 2010. Experiencing programming assignments in CS1: the emotional toll. In Proceedings of the Sixth international workshop on Computing education research (ICER '10). ACM, New York, NY, USA, 77-86. http://doi.acm.org/10.1145/1839594.1839609

[17] Lahtinen, E., Ala-Mutka, K. and Jarvinen, H.M. 2005. A study of the difficulties of novice programmers. ACM Press. ACM SIGCSE Bulletin. New York, NY, USA. Vol. 37(3), pp. 14--18.

[18] McCracken, M., Almstrum, V., Diaz, D., Guzdial, M., Hagan, D., Kolikant, Y.B., Laxer, C., Thomas, L., Utting, I., and Wilusz, T. 2001. A multi-national, multi-institutional study of assessment of programming skills of first-year CS students. In Working group reports from ITiCSE on Innovation and technology in computer science education (ITiCSE-WGR '01). ACM, New York, NY, USA, 125-180. http://doi.acm.org/10.1145/572133.572137

[19] Perkins,D.N., Hancock, C., Hobbs, R., Martin, F. 1986. Conditions of Learning in Novice Programmers. Journal of Educational Computing Research, N. 1, Vol. 2, pp. p37--55.

[20] Raftery, A. E.. Bayesian model selection in social research. *Sociological Methodology*, 25, 111-163, 2003.

[21] Robins, A., Rountree, J. &Rountree, N. 2003. Learning and Teaching Programming: A Review and Discussion. Taylor & Francis, Computer Science Education,13(2), pp. 137-172.

[22] Rodrigo, M.M.T., Baker, R. 2009. Coarse-grained detection of student frustration in an introductory programming course. In *Proceedings of the fifth international workshop on Computing education research workshop* (ICER '09). ACM, New York, NY, USA, 75-80. http://doi.acm.org/10.1145/1584322.1584332

[23] Rodrigo,M.M.T., Baker R.S.J.d., Jadud, M.C., Amarra, A.M., Dy, T., Lahoz,M.B.E., Lim, S.L., Pascua,S.A.M.S., Sugay, J.O., and Tabanao, E.S., 2009. Affective and behavioral predictors of novice programmer achievement. *SIGCSE Bull.* 41, 3 (July 2009), 156-160. http://doi.acm.org/10.1145/1595496.1562929

[24] Wilson, B. (2002): A study of factors promoting success in computer science including gender differences.Computer Science Education, 12(1-2):141-164.

[25] Winslow, L.E. 1996. Programming pedagogy - A psychological overview. SIGCSE Bulletin, 28(3), pp. 17-22.

Explaining Program Code:
Giving Students the Answer Helps – But Only Just

Simon
University of Newcastle, Australia
simon@newcastle.edu.au

Susan Snowdon
University of Newcastle, Australia
susan.snowdon@newcastle.edu.au

ABSTRACT
Of the students who pass introductory programming courses, many appear unable to explain the purpose of simple code fragments such as a loop to find the greatest element in an array. It has never been established whether this is because the students are unable to determine the purpose of the code or because they can determine the purpose but lack the ability to express that purpose. This study explores that question by comparing the answers of students in several offerings of an introductory programming course. In the earlier offerings students were asked to express the purpose in their own words; in the later offerings they were asked to choose the purpose from several options in a multiple-choice question. At an overseas campus, students performed significantly better on the multiple-choice version of the question; at a domestic campus, performance was better, but not significantly so. Many students were unable to identify the correct purpose of small fragments of code when given that purpose and some alternatives. The conclusion is that students' failure to perform well in code-explaining questions is not because they cannot express the purpose of the code, but because they are truly unable to determine the purpose of the code – or even to recognize it from a short list.

Categories and Subject Descriptors
K3.2 [**Computers and education**]: Computer and Information Science Education – *computer science education*

General Terms
Measurement

Keywords
Introductory programming, assessment, code-explaining questions, multiple choice

1. INTRODUCTION
Many students in introductory programming courses appear unable to correctly explain the purpose of very small code fragments [7]. In an earlier paper one of us wondered whether this is because students cannot determine the purpose of the code or because they simply cannot express it correctly [17].

Multiple-choice questions can help to resolve this question. If we actually give students the answer, along with suitable distractors in a multiple-choice question, the question of expression no longer arises. If students can determine the purpose of the code, they need only choose the correct answer from those provided, and that answer is already expressed correctly.

Even if students cannot determine the correct answer by working forward from the code, they have the option of determining it by working back from each of the options. Students are generally allowed more time in an examination than they need to answer the questions, so most students will have time to spare. If students know and understand the concepts being tested, a simple desk-check of the code will determine which option is correct, so long as they can take the intuitive leap of providing some initial values for the checking.

Multiple-choice questions are not universally approved of [16], but they are reasonably widely used, and there is some evidence in the literature of their use to assess skills well beyond the knowledge recall with which they are traditionally associated. When using them for code-explaining questions, as indeed when using them in any other context, the examiner will possibly require assurance that providing the correct answer, along with some incorrect ones, will not result in the whole class choosing the correct answer. While there are many valid uses for multiple-choice questions, it is unlikely that they include guiding incapable students to the correct answer.

2. CODE-EXPLAINING QUESTIONS
Following the explicit realization that students in a first programming course are unable to read simple programs [7], much work has been done to quantify this phenomenon in order to better understand it and to work out what it might be telling programming teachers [8, 10, 21].

The SOLO taxonomy (Structure of the Observed Learning Outcome) [1] classifies students' answers to written questions in a way that incorporates what the students know and how they integrate that knowledge into a structural pattern [20].

A code-reading or code-explaining question presents students with a small piece of code and asks them to explain it, not line by line but in terms of its overall purpose. An example would be the question:

> What is the purpose or outcome of the following piece of code?
> ```
>     x = a1;
>     a1 = a2;
>     a2 = x;
> ```

The BRACElet project has conducted much research on the inclusion of code-explaining questions in programming exams and their analysis according to the SOLO taxonomy [2, 9, 15, 22]. Of particular interest to the project is whether students' answers to code-reading questions are *multistructural* (essentially, explaining a piece of code line by line) or *relational* (explaining the purpose of a piece of code). A correct multistructural answer to the question above would be that the code gives x the value of a1, then gives a1 the value of a2, then gives a2 the value of x. A correct relational answer would be that the code swaps the values of a1 and a2.

Despite increasing efforts to encourage students to provide relational explanations, many appear incapable of explaining code in that manner, falling back instead on multistructural explanations. Perhaps as a consequence, students tend not to perform well on code-explaining questions.

An open question in this endeavor is whether students' poor performance on code-explaining questions is because they have failed to understand the type of answer that is being asked for, because they do not comprehend the code at the level of abstraction required to provide such an answer, or because they cannot express themselves sufficiently well in English to provide such an answer [17].

3. MULTIPLE-CHOICE QUESTIONS IN PROGRAMMING EXAMS

Many programming teachers consider multiple-choice questions to be unsuitable for the assessment of programming skills and knowledge. A survey respondent in a study by Shuhaida et al expresses what appears to be a typical belief: "I feel that multiple choice is a completely inappropriate tool for judging deep understanding and comprehension of programming concepts" [16]. This belief is not, however, universal, and there is some evidence of the effective use of multiple-choice questions to test more than simple knowledge recall in programming exams [6, 11, 24].

Those who do use multiple-choice exam questions agree on the need for the questions to be carefully constructed [4, 5], and for the distractors (the incorrect answers) to be plausible, so that students will not be able to answer a question simply by eliminating the implausible answers [3, 4, 24].

4. THE COURSE AND THE EXAM

The analysis described in this paper is conducted in the context of an introductory programming course at a university in Australia. The course is taught at three campuses, two in Australia and one overseas.

The final examination for the course incorporates 'traditional' multiple-choice questions, code-tracing questions, code-explaining questions, code-writing questions, and debugging questions. The BRACElet project [23] recommends that to permit comparative analysis, examiners include code-tracing, code-explaining, and code-writing questions of three specific types: a code fragment with no looping; a code fragment with a simple loop; and a code fragment with some logic control within a loop. The examination in this course follows that recommendation. Of particular interest to this analysis, it includes three code-explaining questions, one at each of the specified levels.

In early versions of the examination the code-explaining questions were standard open-answer questions of the form typically used in the BRACElet project, and the students' answers supported the project's finding that students do not answer these questions well. Consideration of the possible reasons led to the idea of replacing the open-answer questions with multiple-choice questions in which all of the answer options were in the relational form. Of the three possible reasons for poor performance given in Section 2, this would eliminate failure to appreciate the type of answer that was required, and would eliminate inability to express the explanation sufficiently well in English. If students could not choose the correct answer from the four plausible answers provided, it would seem reasonable to conclude that they do not comprehend the code at the level of abstraction that is required to deduce, or indeed to recognize, its purpose.

The exam included only three code-explaining questions, one each of the three types recommended by the BRACElet project [23]. The first of these questions was changed significantly between offerings of the exam, and so is not a good candidate for comparison. The other two questions were identical except for having written-answer form in the early offerings and multiple-choice form in the later offerings. The analysis that follows is a comparison of these two questions across several offerings of the exam.

The principal comparisons will be made between the written and multiple-choice versions of the question in successive years (2009 and 2010) at one of the domestic campuses and the overseas campus. Results are also available for the other domestic campus in 2010, but in 2009 insufficient students gave their consent to the use of their results for this research, so no comparison can be made at that campus.

5. THE QUESTIONS AND MARKING

The two questions that can be compared across offerings of the exam ask students to explain a simple loop and a loop that contains an *if* statement. In the 2009 exams students were asked to explain these pieces of code, with wording that made it clear they were being asked to explain the purpose of the code, not its detailed working.

When it was decided to reformulate the questions as multiple choice, the problem arose as to what distractors students might find plausible. Fortunately, a recommended source of distractors is students' misconceptions [4, 19], and the students' answers to the 2009 exams were a rich source of misconceptions. All of the distractors for the multiple-choice questions were chosen from common wrong answers to the previous year's written-answer questions.

In deference to the research of the BRACElet project, if students felt that none of the provided answers correctly expressed the purpose of the code, it would be interesting to know what they thought the purpose was. To this end, each question was given a 'none of the above' answer, and students choosing that answer were asked to write what they thought was the purpose of the code. This would make the question less amenable to automatic marking, but this was not an issue for these exams, which already have a large number of questions that require manual marking.

There were two further deviations from standard multiple-choice marking practice. First, each question was worth five marks, not one mark. The written questions in 2009 were worth five marks each, and it was expected that answering the multiple-choice question would take the same amount of time and require the same knowledge and skills, so it seemed reasonable to allocate them the same marks. Second, just as some incorrect answers to the written questions would be awarded part marks, so selecting the same incorrect answers to the multiple-choice questions would be awarded the same part marks. While this decision was made so as not to disadvantage the students in 2010, it does have the added benefit of facilitating comparison of the results from the two years. These two deviations from normal multiple-choice practice are examined in detail in another paper [18].

The multiple-choice versions of the two questions are as follows. The digit to the left of each answer indicates the mark allocated to selection of that answer. The query to the left of option e indicates that these answers would be marked on their own merit, in just the same way as the written answers from the previous year's exam.

---

25. What is the purpose or outcome of the following piece of code?

```
For i = 0 To dPayment.Length - 1
    dBalance = dBalance + dPayment(i)
Next
```

1 (a) to add a payment to a balance
0 (b) to count the payments
3 (c) to add all payments except the last to the balance
5 (d) to add all payments to the balance
? (e) something else – please write the purpose

---

26. What is the purpose or outcome of the following piece of code?

```
sOne = sTitle(0)
For i = 1 To iTitleLastIndex
    If sTitle(i).Length > sOne.Length Then
        sOne = sTitle(i)
    End If
Next
```

5 (a) to find the longest title in the array of titles
2 (b) to find the length of the longest title in the array of titles
2 (c) to move the longest title in the array of titles to the first place in the array
1 (d) to sort the array of titles according to title length
? (e) something else – please write the purpose

---

6. COMPARISON OF THE OFFERINGS

The principal goal of this analysis is to compare the students' performance on the written-answer questions in 2009 with their performance on the multiple-choice questions in 2010. For each of questions 25 and 26 we have four distinct populations, as follows:

Written-answer questions		
aInt09	International campus, 2009	57 students
cDom09	Domestic campus, 2009	34 students
Multiple-choice questions		
bInt10	International campus, 2010	67 students
dDom10	Domestic campus, 2010	40 students

It is customary to use Analysis of Variation (ANOVA) to determine whether populations are different, which is essentially the same as determining whether their means are significantly different. However, while an ANOVA will indicate whether there are differences between some populations in a group, it will not indicate which populations differ from which, and a further test is required to determine this. A suitable test for this purpose is Dunnett's test, which is effective when the sample sizes are small, the separate populations are not normally distributed, and their variances are not equal (as determined by separate tests) [12]. Dunnett's test compares a single control population against the other populations to determine which are significantly different from the control. Taking each population in turn as the control, this will eventually find any significant differences between populations.

In the figures that follow, the diamond shapes represent the different populations. The mean of the measured sample of each population is at the line across the widest part of the diamond. The diamond itself represents the 95% confidence interval; that is, there is a 95% confidence that the mean of the whole population lies somewhere within the diamond. The short lines near the top and bottom are called the overlap lines: two means are significantly different when any overlap between their diamonds is limited to the small tips beyond these lines [13].

The circles to the right of the diamonds are provided for ease of comparison: it is often easier to see whether the circles overlap than to see whether their respective diamonds overlap. However, it is important to remain aware that populations with a small overlap between their circles can still be significantly different, depending on whether the overlap includes the overlap lines of the corresponding diamonds. It is perhaps needless to add that the diamonds and the circles are simply visual aids, and the final determination of significance is made by examining the numerical output of the analysis.

Figure 1 shows the distribution of marks for question 25 for each of the four populations, and the result of applying Dunnett's test with aInt09 as the control population.

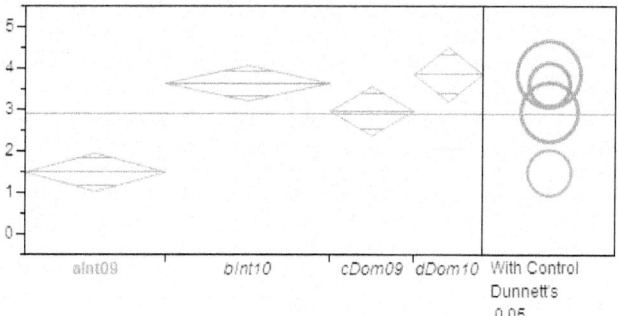

Figure 1: marks for Q25 for each of four populations

Figure 1 tells us that population aInt09 is significantly different from all of the others (its circle doesn't overlap any of the others). The figure suggests, and further applications of Dunnett's test confirm, that there are no other significant differences in the group (the circles of all the other populations do overlap). Of particular interest to the question being considered, at the overseas campus the mean mark for the written-answer question is 1.49, the mean mark for the multiple-choice question is 3.64, and the difference is significant. On the other hand, at the domestic campus the mean mark for the written-answer question is 2.97, the mean mark for the multiple-choice question is 3.85, and the difference is not significant.

Also of interest is that on the written-answer version of the question, in 2009, the mean mark of students on the domestic campus is significantly higher than that of students on the overseas campus. On the other hand, there is almost no difference between campuses on the multiple-choice version in 2010.

Figure 2 shows the distribution of marks for question 26 for each of the four populations, and the result of applying Dunnett's test with aInt09 as the control population.

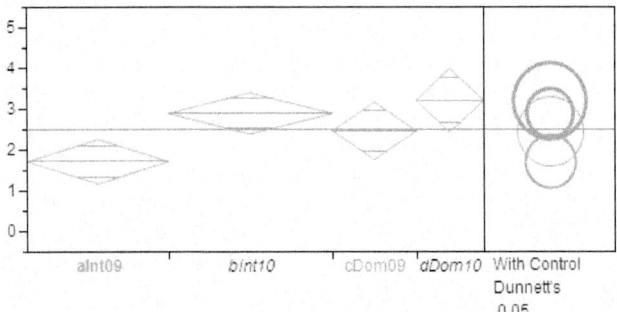

Figure 2: marks for Q26 for each of four populations

Figure 2 tells us that population aInt09 is significantly different from populations bInt10 and dDom10, but not from population cDom09. There are no other significant differences in the group. Of particular interest to the question being considered, at the overseas campus the mean mark for the written-answer question is 1.72, the mean mark for the multiple-choice question is 2.90, and the difference is significant. At the domestic campus the mean mark for the written-answer question is 2.47, the mean mark for the multiple-choice question is 3.45, and the difference is not significant.

As with question 25, on the written-answer version of the question, in 2009, the mean mark of students on the domestic campus is noticeably higher than that of students on the overseas campus; however, for this question the difference is not significant. There also appears to be a difference between campuses on the multiple-choice version, that is, in 2010, but again the difference is not significant.

While data from the other domestic campus were not available for 2009, Figure 3 introduces that campus for 2010, this time showing the distribution of the combined marks for question 25 and question 26.

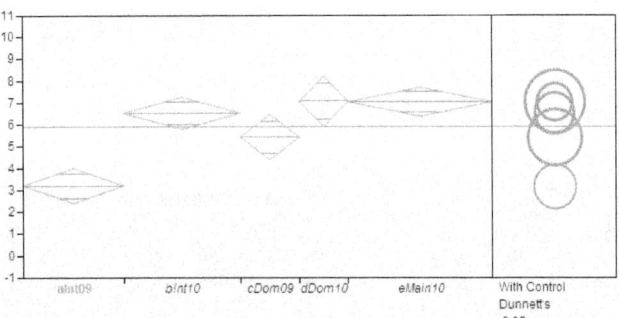

Figure 3: marks for Q25 + Q26 for each of five populations

In addition to echoing the findings of Figures 1 and 2, Figure 3 shows that the second domestic campus (mean 7.05) shows a 2010 distribution very much like that of the first domestic campus (mean 7.3) and the overseas campus (mean 6.53).

While an increase in the mean mark for these questions is a worthwhile result, another feature of interest is how many students actually got the right answer for a question, as measured by how many scored the maximum possible five marks for the question. Table 1 shows this for each question in each population, as a proportion of the students in that population. At both campuses, on both questions, the proportion of students scoring full marks increases, sometimes markedly, in the move from written-answer questions to multiple-choice questions. However, in none of the populations is the proportion close to 100%, which it would be if the multiple-choice nature of the question made it trivially easy for the students.

Table 1: proportion of students in each population who scored full marks for the question

		Written answer	Multiple choice
International	Q25	19%	51%
	Q26	32%	43%
Domestic	Q25	32%	58%
	Q26	38%	53%

7. ADDRESSING POSSIBLE CONFOUNDS

At all three campuses the form of the code-explaining questions changed from written answer in 2009 to multiple choice in 2010, but it is unlikely that this was the only change, and it is possible that the observed variation in results might have arisen from other differences between campuses.

In a full experiment students would be allocated randomly to classes and each class given a different experimental treatment. This work is based on students' end-of-course examinations, and it would be impractical and unethical to have different students undertake different exams: all of the students in a single offering of the same course must clearly be given the same assessment items. This is therefore a *quasi-experiment*. Shadish, Cook, and Campbell explain that "quasi-experiments share with all other experiments a similar purpose – to test descriptive causal hypotheses about manipulable causes ... But, by definition, quasi-experiments lack random assignment" [14 p13]. Shadish and Campbell go on to explain what can be done to help overcome this drawback. Essentially, "the researcher has to enumerate alternative explanations one by one, decide which are plausible, and then use logic, design, and measurement to assess whether each one is operating in a way that might explain any observed effect" [14 p14].

One alternative explanation for the observed effect is a difference in marking between campuses. In particular, might there be a difference between the way the written answers were marked at the overseas campus (aInt09) and the domestic campus (cDom09)? Like the exams, the marking rubrics were identical at both campuses. Furthermore, as part of the standard quality assurance process the marked exam scripts from the overseas campus were sent to the domestic campus, where the marking was checked thoroughly by the same person who marked the scripts at the domestic campus. A difference in marking therefore seems fairly implausible.

Another alternative explanation is a difference in capability between the various classes of students. This explanation can be examined by further measurement.

Question 25 asks students to read and explain a piece of code with some simple arithmetic inside a loop, and question 26 asks students to read and explain a piece of code with a logical test inside a loop. Two further questions in the exam ask students to write highly comparable pieces of code: question 28 asks for code to calculate the product of the integers from 1 to a specified integer, and question 29 asks for code to count the non-negative integers in an array of integers. If the observed variation for questions 25 and 26 is due to differences in the students' capabilities, we might reasonably expect the same variation with questions 28 and 29.

Figure 4 shows the distribution of the combined marks for questions 28 and 29 for the four course offerings being compared. If the variation in the code-explaining questions were due to differences in the capabilities of the groups, we would expect to see a similar pattern to that in Figures 1-3. In fact we see a suggestion that at the overseas campus the students in 2009 were stronger than those in 2010 – the converse of the effect in Figures 1-3. It therefore seems unlikely that their worse performance in code-explaining is due to a lesser capability.

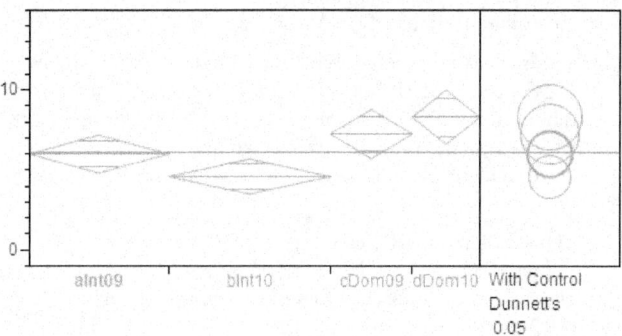

Figure 4: marks for Q28 + Q29 for each of four populations

Pursuing this possibility a little further, Figure 5 shows the distribution of the marks of each class on the whole exam. This figure shows that the two overseas groups aInt09 and bInt10 are virtually identical, the two domestic groups cDom09 and dDom10 are virtually identical, and there are no significant differences between any of these groups.

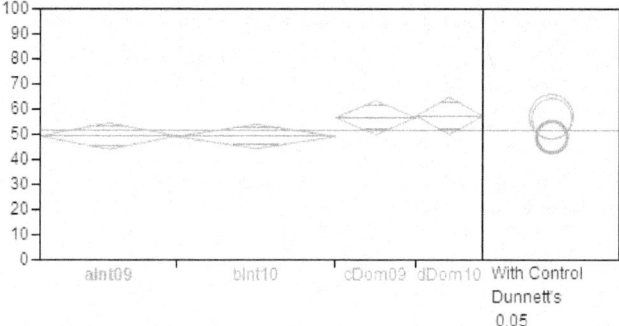

Figure 5: marks for the whole exam for each population

A final alternative explanation for the poorer performance of students at the overseas campus in 2009 is a difference in teacher emphasis. Code-explaining questions of this type were introduced to the course and its assessment in 2008, with 'practice' questions provided almost every week in tutorials. Teaching staff at all campuses formed the general impression that students tended to ignore these questions, preferring to go directly to questions that required them to write code. However, it is possible that staff at the domestic campus were more insistent, and therefore that the students at that campus actually did more practice on these questions. It is also possible that, after marking the 2008 and 2009 exams, the staff at the overseas campus decided to devote more attention to these questions in the tutorial.

As there is no way of exploring this possibility by logic or measurement, it will have to remain speculative. However, with Figure 4 suggesting that students of aInt09 might be slightly more capable than those of bInt10, a difference in teaching emphasis does offer one plausible explanation for the significantly worse performance of aInt09 on the code-explaining questions 25 and 26.

That worse performance was the only significant difference between any of the four classes being considered. As we now have a plausible alternative explanation for that difference, it is possible that while the change from written-answer to multiple-choice appears to have brought about a perceptible improvement in students' marks for the code-reading questions, that difference is not significant.

8. WHAT'S BEEN LOST

Code-explaining questions were introduced to programming examinations by the BRACElet project, and that project has done a great deal of analysis on the SOLO form of students' answers to these questions. Casting these questions in multiple-choice form means that such analysis is no longer possible, as all of the answer options are in the SOLO relational form. The principal loss in this change is the richness of the students' written answers, especially as research data. The loss is not absolute, though, because of the inclusion of option e, the answer for students who were unwilling to choose any of the relational explanations provided. It is perhaps appropriate at this point to briefly analyze the answers that some students gave under option e.

From a total of 190 students across the three campuses, option e was chosen by just six students for question 25 and sixteen students for question 26.

Answers provided with option e are often somewhat confused. For example, this student appears to have chosen a combination of option a (to add a payment to a balance) and option c (to add all payments except the last to a balance):

> The purpose of the code is to count up how many payments there are for dblPayment then for the total of the number you have to subtract one as the coder doesn't want the last payment to be added to dblBalance. The code will then find the value of dblBalance by the sum of dblBalance and dblPayment(i).

Given the confusion expressed here, it is not surprising that the form of the answer is more multistructural than relational: it is hard to imagine that such a confused purpose could ever be expressed in a relational manner.

One of the option e answers to question 26 captures superbly the distinction between SOLO relational and multistructural answers. The correct answer to the question is option a, to find the longest title in the array of titles. One student who chose option e wrote the following answer:

> To find the longest title in the array of titles and assign that title's string value to strOne. It does this by continually comparing the next string to the previous and if its length is greater than the last strOne's value changes to the greater/longer string.

It is interesting that this student appears to have grasped what the code does, both at the detailed multistructural level and at the more abstract relational level, yet for some reason was unwilling to answer the question by choosing option a.

Fully half of the option e answers to question 26 say, more or less clearly, that the purpose of the code is to sort the titles in the array according to their length. Once again, one of the given answers, option d, says exactly the same thing. One student uses almost exactly the same wording as option d:

> To order the title arrays from shortest to longest

while others prefer a more multistructural explanation:

> The code will compare the strTitle(i).Length with strOne. Length to see if strTitle is greater than strOne. If so then strOne equals the value of strTitle(i). The first strOne will be 0. It will sort the titles by length and eventually find which title has the longest and shortest length out of the array.

Answers such as these clearly provide much food for thought, but the change from written-answer questions to multiple-choice questions effectively removes them from the pool of data available for research. Even if it is decided to continue providing an open-ended option e for questions of this type, the low number of students selecting that option means that the written answers will be highly atypical of the class, and will therefore have a research status not greatly different from anecdotal.

9. DISCUSSION

The principal conclusion of this analysis is even when students are given the answer to a code-explaining question, they are no better at finding it among the alternatives than they are at working it out for themselves. At both the domestic and overseas campuses, there was a noticeable improvement in the average performance on these questions as their form changed from written-answer to multiple-choice; but at the domestic campus the improvement was not significant, and the significant difference at the overseas campus might be due in part to the alternative explanation discussed in section 7.

It is interesting to note that if the poor performance of aInt09 on questions 24 and 25 can be attributed to a difference in teacher emphasis, there is no significant difference between the domestic campus, where most of the students speak English as a first language, and the overseas campus, where most speak it as a second language. Few people would argue that a computing degree should be independent of the language in which it is delivered, and it appears to be generally accepted that a degree from an English-speaking university implies some reasonable facility with English as a means of communication. Examiners might therefore be reluctant to moderate their language expectations of their students in order to give them more chance of passing. The findings presented here suggest that such moderation is unnecessary, and there is no significant difference in performance between the domestic and overseas campuses.

Perhaps of most interest, though, is that these results explicitly address a hitherto unanswered question from the BRACElet project: when students cannot explain the purpose of a piece of code, is it because they cannot read and understand the code, is it because they understand the code but cannot abstract their understanding to a suitable (relational) level, or is it because they lack the English skill to explain their understanding of the code? The multiple-choice questions used in the 2010 offerings of this exam remove both of the answers that involve English expression, leaving just one conclusion: when students cannot explain the purpose of a piece of code, it is because they cannot read and understand the code.

10. ACKNOWLEDGMENTS

We are grateful to the BRACElet leaders, Raymond Lister, Tony Clear, and Jacqui Whalley, for initiating the project, for developing it, and particularly for publishing their research design and inviting other researchers to implement it. We are also grateful to the BRACElet members on whose examination questions some of our own are based. Finally we express our appreciation to the anonymous reviewers of this paper, whose insightful observations have led to considerable improvements.

11. REFERENCES

[1] Biggs, JB & KF Collis (1982). Evaluating the quality of learning: the SOLO taxonomy (Structure of the Observed Learning Outcome). New York: Academic Press.

[2] Clear, Tony, Jacqueline Whalley, Raymond Lister, Angela Carbone, Minjie Hu, Judy Sheard, Beth Simon, & Errol Thompson, (2008). Reliably classifying novice programmer exam response using the SOLO taxonomy. 21st Annual NACCQ Conference, NACCQ, Auckland, New Zealand, 23-30.

[3] Hansen, James D & Lee Dexter (1997). Quality multiple-choice test questions: item-writing guidelines and an analysis of auditing testbanks. Journal of Education for Business 73(2):94-97.

[4] Isaacs, Geoff (1994). Multiple choice testing. HERDSA Green Guide No 16. Higher Education Research and Development Society of Australasia Inc, Campbelltown, Australia.

[5] Lister, Raymond (2000). On Blooming first year programming, and its Blooming assessment. Fourth Australasian Computing Education Conference (ACE2000), 158-162.

[6] Lister, Raymond (2005). One small step toward a culture of peer review and multi-institutional sharing of educational resources: a multiple-choice exam for first semester programming students. Seventh Australasian Computing Education Conference (ACE2005), 155-164.

[7] Lister, Raymond, ES Adams, Sue Fitzgerald, W Fone, John Hamer, M Lindholm, Robert McCartney, E Moström, Kate Sanders, Otto Seppälä, Beth Simon, & Lynda Thomas (2004). A multi-national study of reading and tracing skills in novice programmers. SIGCSE Bulletin, 36(4):119-150.

[8] Lister, Raymond, Colin Fidge, & Donna Teague (2009). Further evidence of a relationship between explaining, tracing and writing skills in introductory programming. 14th Annual SIGCSE Conference on Innovation and Technology in Computer Science Education (ITiCSE'09), July 3-8, 2009, Paris, France.

[9] Lister, Raymond, Beth Simon, Errol Thompson, Jacqueline L Whalley, & Christine Prasad (2006). Not seeing the forest for the trees: novice programmers and the SOLO taxonomy. SIGCSE Bulletin 38(3):118-122.

[10] Lopez, Mike, Jacqueline Whalley, Phil Robbins, & Raymond Lister (2008). Relationships between reading, tracing and writing skills in introductory programming. Fourth International Workshop on Computing Education Research (ICER '08), Sydney, Australia, 101-112.

[11] Roberts, Tim (2006). The use of multiple choice tests for formative and summative assessment. Eighth Australasian Computing Education Conference (ACE2006), 175-180.

[12] Rudolph, PE (1988). Robustness of multiple comparison procedures: treatment versus control. Biometrical Journal 30(1):41-45.

[13] Sall, John, Ann Lehman, & Lee Creighton (2001). JMP start statistics. Duxbury, Pacific Grove, CA, USA.

[14] Shadish, William R, Thomas D Cook, & Donald T Campbell (2002). Experimental and quasi-experimental designs for generalized causal inference. Houghton Mifflin Company.

[15] Sheard, Judy, Angela Carbone, Raymond Lister, Beth Simon, Errol Thompson, & Jacqueline L Whalley (2008). Going SOLO to assess novice programmers. SIGCSE Bulletin 40(3):209-213.

[16] Shuhidan, Shuhaida, Margaret Hamilton, & Daryl D'Souza (2010). Instructor perspectives of multiple-choice questions in summative assessment for novice programmers. Computer Science Education 20(3):229-259.

[17] Simon (2009). A note on code-explaining examination questions. Ninth International Conference on Computing Education Research – Koli Calling 2009, Koli, Finland, November 2009.

[18] Simon (2011). Wrong is a relative concept: part marks for multiple-choice questions. Thirteenth Australasian Computing Education Conference (ACE2011), Perth, Australia, 47-53.

[19] Tew, Allison Elliott & Mark Guzdial (2010). Developing a validated assessment of fundamental CS1 concepts. 41st ACM Technical Symposium on Computer Science Education (SIGCSE 2010), 97-101.

[20] Thompson, Errol (2009). How do they understand? Practitioner perceptions of an object-oriented program. Dissertation, Massey University, Palmerston North.

[21] Venables, Anne, Grace Tan, & Raymond Lister (2009). A closer look at tracing, explaining and code writing skills in the novice programmer. Fifth International Workshop on Computing Education Research (ICER '09), Berkeley, California, USA.

[22] Whalley, Jaqueline L, Raymond Lister, Errol Thompson, Tony Clear, Phil Robbins, PJ Ajith Kumar, & Christine Prasad (2006). An Australasian study of reading and comprehension skills in novice programmers, using the Bloom and SOLO taxonomies. Eighth Australasian Computing Education Conference (ACE2006), Hobart, Australia, 243-252.

[23] Whalley, Jacqueline L & Raymond Lister (2009). The BRACElet 2009.1 (Wellington) specification. Eleventh Australasian Computing Education Conference (ACE2009), pp-pp.

[24] Woodford, Karyn & Peter Bancroft (2005). Multiple choice questions not considered harmful. Seventh Australasian Computing Education Conference (ACE2005), 109-115.

CAL Programming Tutors that Guide Students in Solving Problems and Help Students Building Skills

Wei Jin
Dept. of Computer Information Sciences
Shaw University
Raleigh, NC 27601
(919) 546-8376
wjin@shawu.edu

Albert Corbett
Human-Computer Interaction Institute
Carnegie Mellon University
Pittsburgh, PA 15213
(412) 268-8808
corbett@cmu.edu

ABSTRACT

In this paper, we describe our approach in addressing learning challenges students experience in introductory programming courses. We combine two effective instructional methodologies to help students learn to plan programs prior to writing code: Cognitive Apprenticeship Learning (CAL) and Cognitive Tutors (CT). In the CAL component, the instructor models program planning in class and paper handouts are used to scaffold program planning in homework assignments. In CAL-CT, the program-planning process is also supported by a computer tutor which provides step-by-step feedback and advice. The results show that the combined CAL-CT approach yielded substantial gains over traditional instruction. Its advantage over the CAL-Only approach is also significant.

Categories and Subject Descriptors

K.3.2 [**Computers & Education**]: Computer & Information Science Education – *Computer Science Education, Curriculum.*

General Terms

Design, Experimentation, Human Factors

Keywords

CS1, Cognitive Apprenticeship Learning, Cognitive Tutors, Introduction to Programming, Pedagogy, Scaffolding

1. INTRODUCTION

Shaw University is the oldest Historically Black University in the south and its mission is to provide higher education to those who otherwise would not have such an opportunity. Since there are substantial performance gaps among students and many students are not well-prepared for college, it faces special challenges in helping all students to learn and progress.

Many educators have observed the difficulties that students have with mastering programming [19] and many innovative approaches have been proposed. For example, cooperative learning and peer programming utilize students themselves as resources to help each other in learning [4, 25].

Our approach is to use computer tutors that help students develop problem solving and program writing skills. These tutors simulate a human instructor who demonstrates how to approach a programming problem and guides students through problem solving processes. Through numerous guided practices, we hope that eventually the problem analysis and solving process will become students' habits and they can use them automatically in their independent problem solving.

Our approach is most effective at helping students who have difficulties in starting, especially those who would specifically "freeze" at, a programming assignment. Similar problems were documented in [21], where the authors categorize some students as "stoppers" who would, while working on a program in class, constantly ask for help every step of the way. From our experience, many students have such difficulties for new programming concepts. Some students may quickly overcome them with some practice, while some other students may take much longer. Guidance tutors, which start students off with a problem analysis, then guide students through an expert problem-solving process in a step-by-step fashion, seem to be the most appropriate in addressing the above mentioned challenge. With practice, as students develop proficiencies, they may opt out some of the help the tutors can provide and move forward more on their own. However, the tutors are always ready to provide guidance or hints whenever they are needed.

Our approach is a combination of the Cognitive Apprenticeship Learning (CAL) model and Cognitive Tutors (CT). CAL involves a task analysis of expert problem solving processes and the design of scaffolding techniques. CT programs interact as personal coaches with students during their problem-solving practice. Both have been shown effective at helping students improve problem solving skills in domains that require abstract thinking and both are adaptive in nature (see Section 2 for detail).

The study presented in this paper is an extension of previous work [16], which focused on the very basic programming concepts – variables and basic statements. First, in addition to variables and basic statements, currently we have developed computer tutors for if statements and for loops. Second, the tutors in the previous report [16] only provide students with planning guidelines on how to solve a problem (writing a program). In contrast, our current tutors will help students step-by-step in planning and writing complete programs.

In this paper we report an evaluation of three learning approaches, CAL-CT (CAL with Cognitive Tutor support), CAL-Only (CAL with paper worksheets) and no-CAL (conventional problem

---

Permission to make digital or hard copies of all or part of this work for personal or classroom use is granted without fee provided that copies are not made or distributed for profit or commercial advantage and that copies bear this notice and the full citation on the first page. To copy otherwise, or republish, to post on servers or to redistribute to lists, requires prior specific permission and/or a fee.
ICER'11, August 8–9, 2011, Providence, Rhode Island, USA.
Copyright 2011 ACM 978-1-4503-0829-8/11/08...$10.00.

solving), based on student test scores collected over several semesters. In addition, we also compare how effective the tutors are for students at different skill levels. The data show that both the CAL-CT and the CAL approach have improved student test scores. On average, test scores for students in the CAL-CT group are 53% higher than students that benefitted from CAL-Only instruction and 64% higher than students in the no-CAL group.

The remainder of the paper is organized as follows: In Section 2, we discuss the rationales for our approach in the context of CAL and CT. We describe the CAL component in Section 3 and the CT component in Section 4. We evaluate the effectiveness of CAL and CAL-CT in Section 5. We then describe our plan in making the CT component more adaptive in Section 6 and our approach to tutor authoring in Section 7. We will conclude in Section 8.

2. RATIONALES AND RELATED WORK
2.1 Cognitive Apprenticeship Learning (CAL)
Cognitive apprenticeship learning (CAL) models traditional apprenticeship learning, which has successfully trained individuals in various trades and professions [8]. Students learn complex skills by practicing in real life problem-solving settings. In addition to explaining how to perform a task, the teacher demonstrates how to perform the task (modeling), gives individualized guidance and feedback to the apprentice during practice (coaching), and gradually reduces the amount of help given as the apprentice develops proficiency in the task (fading). During this process, the teacher also provides scaffolding tools to guide the apprentice in the performance of the task, which are discarded as the apprentice becomes more adept.

The cognitive apprenticeship learning model helps students acquire abstract skills. Since abstract skills engage thinking processes that are "invisible," the teacher articulates expert thought processes to students. The description of these problem-solving processes and strategies provides organizational scaffolds for students and helps them acquire higher-level skills. In addition, instructors may use other materials, such as specially designed problems or worksheets to guide the student during practice [14]. In contrast, traditional forms of instruction are much less explicit with the problem-solving process. They often present students with models of complete answers that give no indication of the decision-making process and have no coaching component.

2.2 Cognitive Tutors (CT)
Cognitive tutors are an educational technology with characteristics similar to human tutors. They are most effective at developing skills that can only be gained through applying knowledge in a problem solving context. These skills are often the higher-level skills in Bloom's Taxonomy [5], such as knowledge application and synthesis, which are the skill levels that students need to reach to master programming.

Cognitive tutors pose complex problem-solving tasks to students and provide the individualized advice students need to succeed [1, 2, 9, 17]. Cognitive tutors are based on an understanding of both domain knowledge and problem-solving strategies. This knowledge is represented as a "cognitive model" in the cognitive tutor, an expert system that can solve the problems in the many ways that students solve them. As a student works, the cognitive model is used to follow the student's step-by-step solution and provide accuracy feedback. The tutor does not automatically provide detailed advice; instead students have the opportunity to reflect on and correct their own mistakes. However, if the student asks, the cognitive model is also employed to provide advice on how to accomplish each problem-solving step.

Cognitive tutors have been shown to speed learning by as much as a factor of three and yield an achievement effect size of about one-standard deviation compared to conventional instruction [2]. This is about twice the effect of typical human tutors [10] and about half the effect of the best human tutors [6].

2.3 Our Approach: CAL-CT
To make the CAL approach work, instructors have to devote much time and attention to each student, which is a very challenging task to manage with even a modest number of students. A specially designed software system, such as STABLE [13], can provide comparable support by using an annotated case library and a structure of peer support through online discussions.

Our approach is to combine the cognitive apprenticeship learning model and cognitive tutors. The advantages of CAL-CT are: (1) Cognitive tutors make it possible for students to receive more individualized "coaching" outside of classrooms/office hours; (2) Use of automatic tutors encourages students to actively participate in learning by limiting the fear of mistakes; (3) Availability of help is immediate, which is made possible by the hints made available to students by automatic tutors.

2.4 Other Related Work
There have been various related approaches to automatic tutoring in programming. For example, natural language dialog to help students develop pseudo code had some success [18], but the evaluation was limited in scope. Reverse engineering has been used to determine whether a program satisfies goals and then provide relevant hints [24], however, there was no evaluation of how this tool had improved student learning. In [20], crucial parts of a program were made into blanks for students to fill and a tool would compile the completed program and report errors or run the test cases. It was shown that this tool helped reduce the amount of help students needed from teachers, but it did not show much improvement in student learning. In [12], debugging tutors automatically generated programs with errors for students to identify. The focus was to help students master certain programming concepts (e.g. scope of names) but not to write

---

Problem: Write a program to calculate the time needed to mow a lawn around a rectangular house sitting inside a rectangular lot.

Variable Analysis

	Purpose of the Variable	Variable Name	Variable Type
Input Variables	the length of lawn in feet	*length*	float
	the width of lawn in feet	*width*	float
	the mowing speed in sqft/min	*mowingSpeed*	float
Output Variables	mowing time in minutes	*mowingTime*	float

Flow Analysis

Input Section	Prompt the user to enter the values for variables *length*, *width* and *mowingSpeed*.
Computation Section	Calculate the value for *mowingTime*.
Output Section	Display the value of *mowingTime*.

Figure 1: Pre-programming Analysis for Basic Statements

complete programs. In [23], machine learning was used to determine grasp of knowledge and present learning materials adaptively. The goal was not, however, to develop students' skills in writing programs. Similar to [23], [3, 7] are both web-based systems for delivering homework problems, but in these systems, students write code and the code is then compiled and tested. However, even though students are pleased to receive grades immediately, they are generally disappointed with the lack of specific feedback [3]. In addition, these tools do not specifically target students' problem analysis skills nor do they address the problem of students not knowing how to start a programming assignment. Finally, some enhanced IDEs also have tutoring features, such as identifying syntax/logic/style errors and providing feedback that is more meaningful [15, 22].

3. THE CAL COMPONENT

The CAL component is a step-by-step problem solving process to guide students in the right direction and help them develop habits to think as experienced programmers. We have developed instruments (e.g. worksheets) that help students follow this process. We emphasize that these worksheets are effective only if instructors model how to use them in problem solving through multiple examples and demonstrate how to convert information in a worksheet into a program.

3.1 Variables and Basic Statements

Problem solving involves three steps: (1) mental visualization of how the program interacts with a user, (2) variable analysis, and (3) flow analysis. Step 2 extracts essential information from step 1: the inputs the user will provide for the program and the outputs the program will calculate and give to the user. Step 3 determines the order of data processing. Figure 1 shows the worksheet that explicitly supports variable analysis and flow analysis. The problem description and the shaded areas are provided to students and the rest are blanks that students need to fill out. The worksheet provides the framework for students to think. It is most effective to introduce the worksheets in the classroom where an instructor models their use and summarizes after students spend some time working on a sheet.

Problem: If a student is first-year and GPA is 3.0 and up, he gets *good starter* award. If GPA is 3.5 and up, he gets *dean's list* award.

Case Analysis

ID	Categorization of the Cases	Actions of the Cases
1	Student is a first-year and GPA is 3.0 or up	Student gets good starter award.
2	Student's GPA is 3.5 or up	Student gets dean's list award.

Exclusiveness/Order Analysis

Are the above cases exclusive to each other?	No
If no, please list the order of cases:	Order does not matter.

Logic Expressions and Actions

ID	Logic Expressions	Actions
1	classification==1 && gpa >= 3.0	cout << "Good Starter Award." << endl;
2	gpa >= 3.5	cout << "Dean's List Award." << endl;

Put the If Statement(s) Together

If the cases are exclusive, please use one multi-branch if-else statement. Otherwise, use independent if statement for each case.

```
if (classification == 1 && gpa >= 3.0) {
    cout << "Good Starter Award." << endl;
}
if (gpa >= 3.5) {
    cout << "Dean's List Award." << endl;
}
```

Figure 2: Pre-programming Analysis for Ifs

3.2 If Statements

Figure 2 shows a correctly completed CAL worksheet for an If statement. This worksheet also divides the program planning process into several sections: (1) Case analysis: A case is the set of situations under which the program should perform the same actions. Eventually a case will be specified by a logic expression, but during step 1, students describe each case in plain English. (2) Exclusiveness/order analysis: Students indicate if the cases in the program are exclusive of each other (that is, if only one can be true at any given situation). Exclusive cases can be implemented as one multi-branch if statement. If cases are non-exclusive, they should be implemented as independent if statements. (3) Logic expressions and actions: Students convert their English case descriptions into formal symbolic expressions for the tests and actions and at the bottom of the page assemble these components into one or more if statements.

Since variables are a topic for Basic Statements, when students reach the topic of If statements, they already achieved certain fluency. Here students have freedom to choose a proper variable name for a data item as long as consistency is maintained throughout the worksheet. Students also need to bring their work product (in the last blank space) into a program to compile, debug, and test. The worksheet itself only provides a framework for students to think and it is still up to students to figure out the details themselves.

3.3 Loops

Iteration is a challenging topic. Students have trouble condensing actions into a compact loop format. The problem is not with loop syntax, but with how to abstract the sequential actions into a set of statements that will be executed repeatedly.

Our problem solving process helps with this abstraction. Figure 3 shows a correctly completed worksheet for loops. It involves the following steps: (1) Students describe the solution as a sequence of actions in English. (2) Then students specify a sequence of C++ statements that implement the actions identified in step 1. (3) In the next, key phase, students find the patterns among the sequence

Problem: Calculate 2 + 4 + 6 + ... + 10000 and display the result.

Describe the solution in sequence of actions (plain English):

Add 2 to sum
Add 4 to sum
...
Add 10000 to sum

Translate the above actions into C++ statements:

```
sum = sum + 2;
sum = sum + 4;
...
sum = sum + 10000;
```

Abstract into a set of same statements that can be repeatedly executed:

```
sum = sum + num;
num += 2;
sum = sum + num;
num += 2;
```

Condition that the loop should stop:

num > 10000

The condition that the loop should continue (reverse condition):

num <= 10000

Variables to set up before the loop:

sum = 0;   num =2;

Actions after the loop:

```
cout << "2+4+6+...+10000 = " << sum << endl;
```

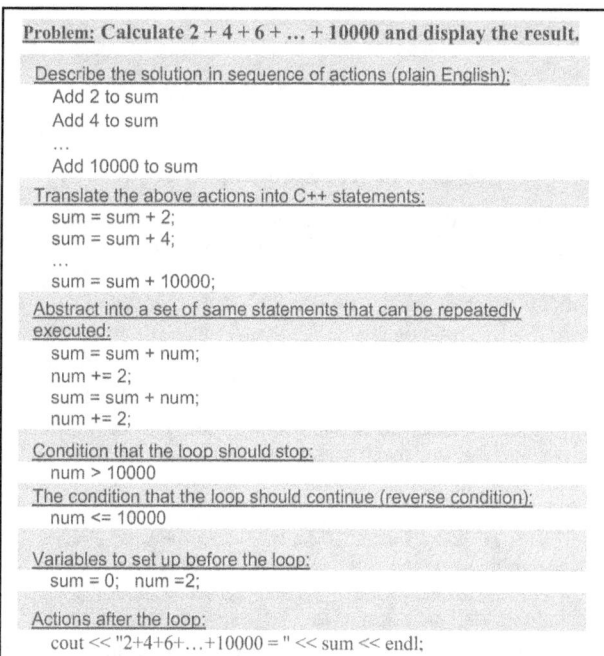

Figure 3: Pre-programming Analysis for Loops

of C++ statements and abstract them into a set of C++ statements, which can be executed repeatedly to produce the same behavior as the sequence in step 2. Finally, students (4) determine how to stop the loop, and (5) determine how to set up the variables before the loop and the actions to perform after the loop. Students have freedom to choose a proper variable name for a data item as long as consistency is maintained throughout the worksheet.

Challenges: The problem solving processes and the accompanying worksheets provide scaffolding for modeling and coaching on how to construct programs to solve problems. They guide students and scaffold them in following a good analytical process. However, our classroom experience is that while some students can make good progress, some required additional help and some still didn't know what to do. For the last group, it is difficult to conduct one-on-one coaching during a class period. In addition, in our instructional experience, worksheets would not be effective at all outside the classroom for this group of students. Frequently these students failed to submit homework assignments due to their inability to use these worksheets independently.

4. THE CT COMPONENT: STEP-BY-STEP ITERATIVE REFINEMENT

Our approach to address the challenges described at the end of Section 3 is to use Cognitive Tutors that interact with students within the framework of the cognitive apprenticeship learning model. The tutors provide the step-by-step support each student needs to complete each planning/programming task successfully. The tutor indicates whether each student action is correct. If incorrect, students can request a hint as to why it is wrong.

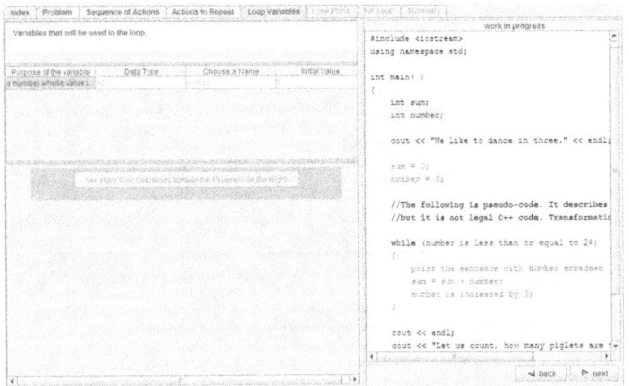

Figure 4: Screenshot of a Loop Tutor

We have adopted an iterative refinement approach, an approach advocated by TeachScheme [11]. Program construction is divided into several stages. A program is gradually constructed or refined based on students' decisions at each stage. The tutor will also preserve all intermediate stages. This allows students to go back to previous stages to review and reflect on how the final program has been constructed.

Each stage is represented as a tab in the tutor interface. Each tab is divided into the left panel and the right panel. The left panel is where students make guided decisions. Some decisions, such as variable names and logical expressions, could require students to type in the answers, but most decisions are multiple-choice. The right panel displays the work-in-progress program. After students make correct decisions on the left panel, the tutor displays an updated program on the right panel that incorporates the decisions made. Students will observe how their decisions in each stage contribute to the construction of the program.

```
#include <iostream>
using namespace std;

int main( )
{
    int sum;
    int number;

    cout << "We like to dance in three." << endl;

    sum = 0;
    number = 3;

    //The following is pseudo-code. It describes what is going on,
    //but it is not legal C++ code. Transformation needed.

    while (number is less than or equal to 24)
    {
        print the sentence with number embedded
        sum = sum + number;
        number is increased by 3;
    }

    cout << endl;
    cout << "Let us count, how many piglets are there?" << endl;
    cout << "Wow, " << sum << " piglets dance hand-in-hand!" << endl;

    return 0;
}
```

(a)

```
#include <iostream>
using namespace std;

int main( )
{
    int sum;
    int number;

    cout << "We like to dance in three." << endl;

    sum = 0;
    number = 3;

    while (number <= 24)
    {
        cout << "Look! Here come " << number << " little piglets. How
        sum = sum + number;
        number = number + 3;
    }

    cout << endl;
    cout << "Let us count, how many piglets are there?" << endl;
    cout << "Wow, " << sum << " piglets dance hand-in-hand!" << endl;

    return 0;
}
```

(b)

Figure 5: The Right Panel of the Loop Tutor at the Beginning (5a) and End (5b) of Tutor Stage (4)

Figure 4 shows the screenshot of a loop tutor. The loop tutor consists of five stages. In stage (1), students figure out a systematic but sequential solution to the problem. In stage (2), students abstract and condense the sequential solution into actions that can be executed repetitively. Usually variables have to be introduced, but at this stage, the actions are described in plain English. In stage (3), students specifically decide what loop variables need to be introduced. As displayed in Figure 4, the student enters variable names, data types and initial values. In the left side of the figure, the student has specified an integer variable, *number*, with an initial value of 3. The tutor has inserted the corresponding (highlighted) statements in the program window to the right. In stage (4), students determine various loop parts, including the loop control logic expression, loop variable updates, and etc., to finalize loop implementation. Finally, in stage (5) the students transform the *while* loop into a *for* loop.

Figure 5a and 5b show how the content in the right panel changes in a stage. Figure 5a shows the work-in-progress program at the beginning of stage (4) and Figure 5b represents an updated program at the end of the stage, which has incorporated students' decisions regarding what each loop component should be.

5. EFFECTIVENESS EVALUATION

These CAL and CAL-CT learning activities were incorporated into introductory programming courses at Shaw University and in this report we use student test scores to evaluate these interventions for each of the three programming topics across semesters (Fall 2007 – Spring 2010). For each of the three constructs, Variables & Basic Statements, Ifs, and Loops, all the students in the same semester used one of the learning approaches: No-CAL (the baseline), CAL-Only, or CAL-CT. Table 1 shows student assignment by semester. All classes had the same instructor except for the Spring'09 No-CAL Basic and If cells in Table 1.

Table 1: Student Assignment by Semester

	Basic Statements	If	Loops
Fall'07	CAL-Only	No-CAL	
Spring'08	CAL-Only	CAL-Only	No-CAL
Fall'08	CAL-Only	CAL-Only	CAL-Only
Spring'09	No-CAL	No-CAL	No-CAL
Fall'09	CAL-CT	CAL-CT	CAL-Only
Spring'10	CAL-CT	CAL-CT	CAL-CT

For each topic, the instructor introduced the programming construct in class and then students completed some program-tracing and syntax-debugging activities. At this point, a pretest was given to students. That is, at this point, students had learned the syntax of a programming construct but had not any programming experience for that construct. After the pretest, students worked on some programming problems in class. In the CAL-Only and CAL-CT conditions, the teacher demonstrated the use of the CAL worksheets in completing these example programs. Students then completed a homework assignment consisting of a set of problems in which they wrote programs.

- In the No-CAL condition, students completed the set of programming homework problems without any additional scaffolding.
- In the CAL condition, CAL worksheets were made available for the homework assignment and students were encouraged, but not required, to use the worksheets to help design the programs.
- In the CAL-CT condition, students completed a small set of homework problems and CAL worksheets were made available for that purpose. Students then completed a set of programming exercises in the CAL-CT environment. Note that there is no CT-Only approach for two reasons: (1) the classroom use of worksheets is in common to CAL and CAL-CT by design, and (2) we wanted to conduct a within-student analysis of the "added value" in going from CAL worksheets to the CT environment, as discussed under section 5 "Learning Progress in the CAL-CT condition."

Following each homework assignment, the instructor reviewed the answers in class in all conditions. Finally, students completed a posttest in class. The test questions were equivalent to the homework assignments; they were all problem-based, asking students to write complete programs. We collected student test data over multiple semesters and tried to keep the test problems for each construct as similar as possible across semesters. We used self-developed and expert-inspected grading rubrics to evaluate student tests and generate test scores. Since our focus is problem solving, our rubrics give more weight (points) to students' approach to solving problems than to program syntax. Table 2 shows the number of students in each condition who participated in the study.

Table 2: Number of Students in Each Group

Condition	Basic Statements	If Statements	Loops
No-CAL	7	35	36
CAL-Only	55	35	19
CAL-CT	39	31	9

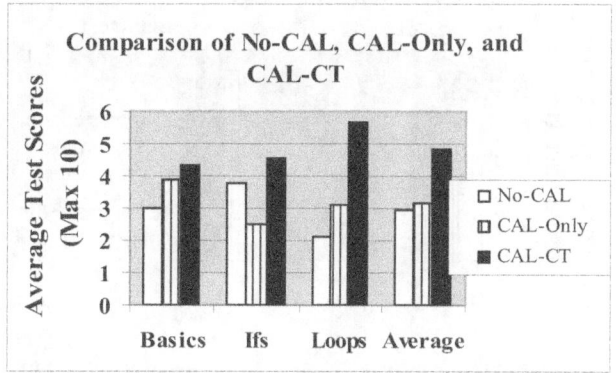

Figure 6: Posttest Comparisons among Three Groups

Figure 6 displays average posttest scores for the three learning conditions for each of the three programming topics and overall. As expected, students in the CAL-CT group scored higher than students in the other two conditions for each of the three topics and this overall result is significant by a non-parametric test of independent probabilities, $p < 0.04$.

For the Loop construct, the differences among the groups were quite large. Posttest scores in the CAL-CT group were 82% higher than in the CAL-Only group, which in turn were 48% higher than the No-CAL baseline group. In a between-subject ANOVA, the main effect of learning condition is reliable, $F(2, 61) = 5.02$, $p < .01$. In pair-wise comparisons, the difference between CAL-CT and CAL-Only is reliable, $p < .04$, as is the difference between CAL-CT and No-CAL $p < .01$, while the difference between CAL-Only and No-CAL is not significant.

For the If construct, posttest scores for the CAL-CT group were 22% higher than in the No-CAL condition and 82% higher than in the CAL-Only condition. In a between-subject ANOVA, the main effect of group type is marginally significant, $F(2, 98) = 2.22$, $p < .12$, and the only significant pair-wise difference is between the CAL-CT and CAL-Only groups, $p < .05$. We believe that the close similarity of an example with the posttest solution led to the high posttest scores for Fall'07 (part of No-CAL), which caused the "skew" that No-CAL outperforms CAL.

Finally, for Variable & Basic Statements, the differences among the three groups were much smaller and in a between-subjects ANOVA, the main effect of group is not significant. In fact, the CAL-Only group for basic statements is not strictly CAL only because this group has used preprogramming analysis tutors as reported in [16]. These tutors are much simpler. They helped students fill out the preprogramming analysis worksheet without leading students to the final solutions (complete programs).

Learning Progress in the CAL-CT condition. In the CAL-CT condition, pretests and intermediate tests were used to examine how students made progress in learning. Students completed programming problems on these tests analogous to the posttest problems. For the Variables & Basic Statements construct, each student took a pretest before the homework assignment and completed an intermediate test after working on the initial set of problems with CAL worksheets and before beginning the CAL-CT problems. For the If construct, each student completed either a pretest or an intermediate test. For the Loop construct, each student completed an intermediate test.

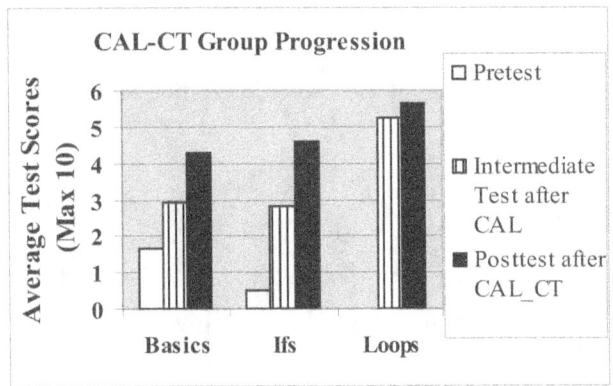

Figure 7: Student Performance Progression (CAL-CT)

Figure 7 displays the results of the pre-, intermediate and post tests. For both the Variables & Basic Statement constructs and the If construct, the learning activities with off-line CAL worksheets alone yielded substantial learning gains between the pretest and the intermediate test. This gain for Variables & Basic Statements is reliable in a paired-sample t-test, $t(20) = 2.75$, $p < .02$ and the gain for Ifs is marginally reliable in an independent-sample t-test, $t(26) = 2.61$, $p < .08$. For these two constructs, the Cognitive Tutor CAL-CT activities yielded substantial additional learning between the intermediate test and posttest. These respective gains were reliable in paired-sample t-tests, $t(35) = 3.34$, $p < .01$ and $t(19) = 2.62$, $p < .02$. In contrast, for the Loop construct, CAL-CT problem solving yielded little additional learning between the intermediate test, which followed the use of off-line CAL worksheets, and the posttest, and the difference between the two tests is not significant. This latter result is surprising since, as we've seen, the CAL-CT group posttest scores are reliably higher than the CAL-Only posttest scores (Figure 6).

Effectiveness of the CT Component for Different Students.
Automatic tutors provide a way for students to get additional help outside of classrooms, so they could be useful resources for weaker students to utilize to catch up with or narrow the gap with stronger students.

Figure 8 displays the benefits of the CT for students in different GPA ranges. Figure 8a displays average intermediate test scores and posttest scores for five GPA ranges. Each data point in the figure is the average of the average scores for three different constructs (the Variables & Basic Statements construct, the If construct and the Loop construct). Figure 8b displays the learning gains that resulted from CT use for the five GPS ranges.

We can see that students in the middle range benefitted most from using automatic tutors. Students with high GPAs scored close to the ceiling on the intermediate test and had little room to improve on the post test. In fact their scores declined slightly, perhaps because students were instructed that the highest score of the three tests would be used as the score for a learning unit. Since students with high GPAs got high scores early on, they might not put as much efforts into the posttests as those who did not do well. For example, one such student who did very well for the Loop intermediate test only attempt one of the three questions at the Loop posttest.

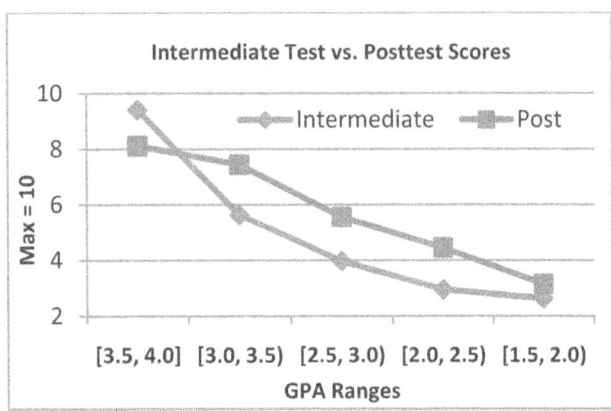

Figure 8a: Performance Gap Narrowed at Posttest

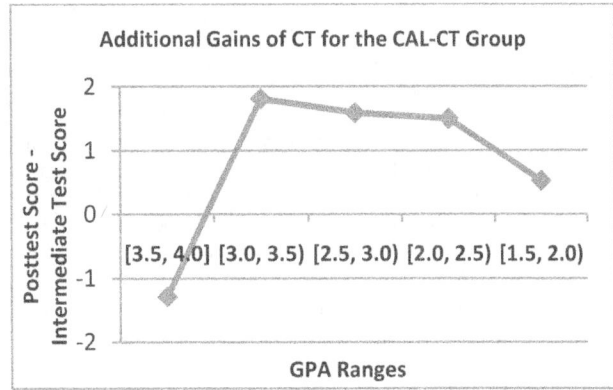

Figure 8b: Additional Gains from CT for Different GPAs

We can also see that students with low GPAs did not benefit as much from the tutors as those in the middle range. To explore this further, we examined how much the students in the 5 groups had used the tutors. For each concept, the CT assignment consisted of a series of programming problems. For each problem, the tutor would help students as needed to complete a correct program. As long as the students put in the necessary time, they should get 100% correct. Each submitted tutor program was graded using the same rubrics that were used to obtain test scores. If no program was submitted for a question, that question got zero points. The scores for the tutor assignments really reflect how much effort students had put in using the tutors.

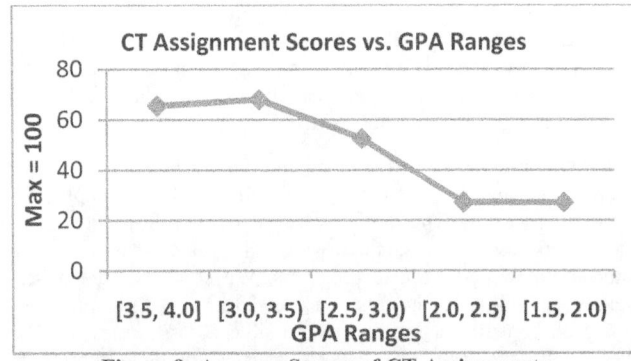

Figure 9: Average Scores of CT Assignments

Figure 9 shows the average CT assignment scores for students in each GPA range. As in Figure 8, each data point is the average of the average CT scores for the three constructs. We can see that the students in the two lowest GPAs showed lower efforts in utilizing tutors than other students. Another observation is that, even with similar efforts, students in the higher of these two GPA ranges [2.0, 2.5) gained more from using the tutors than those in the lower GPA range [1.5, 2.0).

We had hoped that the students with low GPAs could have used the tutors to narrow the gap with other students. The results, however, show otherwise. The main reason may be the low engagement of these students in coursework. It is not uncommon for these students to miss an assignment altogether. Second, these students may have already gotten lost when we were introducing the basic concepts (e.g. syntax) before we started writing programs. If we have tutors in all aspects of learning, including learning syntax, these students may become more engaged.

Student Attitudes. Finally, Table 3 shows student survey data collected during Spring 2009 (No-CAL) and Spring 2010 (CAL-CT). Students rated their agreement with each statement on a 5-point scale. Table 3 displays the percentage of students who "fully" or "highly" agreed with each statement. Clearly CAL-CT students tend to have more positive attitudes toward the course activities. A higher percentage of CAL-CT students than No-CAL students fully or highly agreed with every statement. The biggest differences between the two groups were for the 4th and 5th questions, "The instruction in this course was high quality," and "The course materials were excellent," and both of these differences are significant at the .05 level in a z-test of the difference between two independent samples.

Table 3: Student Surveys – Full or High Agreement

Survey Questions	No-CAL (28)	CAL-CT (24)
Felt motivated to come to every session.	57%	75%
Felt motivated to complete all hw assignments.	64%	79%
The instruction was very different from other courses.	67%	71%
The instruction was high quality.	68%	92%
The materials were excellent.	57%	88%
The course increased the excitement I have on learning C++ programming.	54%	71%
This course convinced me to stay a computer science major or to become on.	46%	50%
This course kept me or made me become interested in a CS career.	64%	71%
This was the best course I took this sem.	29%	33%

6. ADAPTIVE EXTENSION

Currently, the way that the tutor interacts with the students includes two important components of apprenticeship learning: modeling and coaching. In a true cognitive apprenticeship learning environment, however, the tutor will determine how much help a student needs. As the student develops proficiency, the tutor will reduce the amount of help given. This section discusses our plan to include the fading aspect of apprenticeship learning.

The current CT emphasizes program planning and off-loads the task of code generation. That is, the tutor generates the necessary changes to the actual C++ program code on the right panel, based on the student's evolving plan in the left panel. In a planned iterative development, the students will perform both the planning and coding roles. Instead of a tutor updating the work-in-progress program on the right panel, the tutor will ask students to try to make the necessary changes to the program to reflect the decisions they have just made. The tutor will provide feedback and advice as students write the program.

The tutors will also be extended to track students' actions. Self-directed actions, such as updating a work-in-progress program on the right panel will earn students higher scores for a tutoring assignment than letting the tutor generate the necessary updates to the program. The amount of decisions students have to make on the left could also be adaptive. If the tutor thinks that a student needs more help, the tutor will provide more guidance by asking students to make more decisions on the left panel. The tutor will automatically have the student start writing the code only after they have demonstrated that they can do the planning and are ready to focus on the coding.

We also plan to enhance our tutors so that they will present a more IDE-like interface with structured editors on the right panel. When a program is done, students can also compile, run and test the program.

7. TUTOR AUTHORING

The CAL-CT tutors are based on Java Swing technology and can be delivered to students easily online through either Java Applets or Java Web Start. Tutor authoring addresses the issue of how to create these tutors. Our approach has evolved over the last couple of years.

Initially, tutors for each type of programming constructs, such as Variables & Basic Statement, If and Loop, were developed (programmed) separately. Tutor questions and actions were specified by text files. For each type of tutors, they have different interfaces and the formats for tutor action specification are also different. We found that this approach required repetitive efforts. Even though these tutors shared lots of similarities in interface and functionality, they had to be programmed separately.

Then we decided to use a unified approach to specify both tutor interface and tutor actions, for which we chose to use XML as the tutor specification language. A tutor engine program interprets the tutor specification and interacts with students. The tutors use a tabbed tutor interface as shown in Figure 4. This way, teachers can specify programming problems/solutions and tutor behaviors using XML text files. They do not have to do any programming.

However, specifying tutors using XML is a tedious and time-consuming process. It is also easy to make mistakes, such as missing XML tags. One loop tutor may take one to two days to develop. Our solution is a GUI based tutor authoring tool. Through this tool, teachers can specify the widgets to use for each tab and the contents and behaviors of each widget. This tool then converts the GUI description to a corresponding XML file, which can be interpret by the tutor engine described in the previous paragraph. This tool has greatly sped up our tutor development process and made our approach feasible for adoption.

8. CONCLUSION

CAL-CT combines two effective approaches for developing problem solving skills. The CAL-style preprogramming analysis allows students to model experts' analytical thinking and problem solving processes and helps them to mature as programmers. Online tutors give students individual attentions which are usually not available outside classrooms and keep them moving forward.

Our ultimate goal is to develop an engaging CAL-CT curriculum to help students master programming skills. In the near future, we will focus on develop adaptive features mentioned in Section 6.

We will also implement adaptive problem delivery mechanisms to better fit individual student's needs. We will pay special attention to how to engage low-performing students, either through incorporating new tutors or through other type of interventions.

9. ACKNOWLEDGMENTS

This material is based upon work supported by the National Science Foundation under Grant No. 0837505.

Our thanks to Yingqi Wang for assistance in developing the tutors, Susan Rodger and Sung-Sik Kwon for their tutor-interface suggestions and Barry Nagle for designing student surveys.

10. REFERENCES

[1] Anderson, J. R., Conrad, F. G., and Corbett, A. T. 1989. *Skill Acquisition and the LISP Tutor*. Cognitive Science 13(4), 467-505.

[2] Anderson, J. R., Corbett, A. T., Koedinger, K. R., and Pelletier, R. 1995. *Cognitive Tutors: Lessons Learned*. J. of the Learning Sciences, 4(2), 167-207.

[3] Baldwin, J., Crupi, E., and Estrellado, T. 2006. *WebWork for Programming Fundamentals*. ITiCSE'06: Proceedings of the 11th annual SIGCSE conference on Innovation and technology in computer science education, 361-361, June 26-28, 2006, Bologna, Italy.

[4] Beck, L. L., Chizhik, A. W., and McElroy, A. C. 2005. *Cooperative learning techniques in CS1: design and experimental evaluation*. SIGCSE'05: Proceedings of the 36th SIGCSE technical symposium on Computer Science Education, 470-474.

[5] Bloom, B. S. 1984. *The 2 sigma problem: The search for methods of group instruction as effective as one-to-one tutoring*. Educational Researcher, 13(6), 4-16.

[6] Bloom, B. S. and Krathwohl, D. R. 1956. *Taxonomy of Educational Objectives: The Classification of Educational Goals, by a committee of college and university examiners*. Handbook I: Cognitive Domain. New York, Longmans, Green.

[7] *CodeLab®: A Powerful Tool for Programming Instruction*. http://www.turingscraft.com/.

[8] Collins, A., Brown, J. S., Newman, S. E. 1989. *Cognitive Apprenticeship: Teaching the Crafts of Reading, Writing and Mathematics*. In L. Resnick (Eds.), Knowing, Learning and Instruction, Essays in Honor of Robert Glaser. Erlbaum, Hillsdale, NJ.

[9] Corbett, A. T. and Anderson, J. R. 1995. *Knowledge tracing: Modeling the acquisition of procedural knowledge*. User Modeling and User-Adapted Interaction, 4, 253-278.

[10] Corbett, A. T., McLaughlin, M. S. and Scarpinatto, K. C. 2000. *Modeling student knowledge: Cognitive tutors in high school and college*. User modeling and user-adapted interaction, Volume 10, 81-108.

[11] Felleisen, M., Findler, R. B., Flatt, M. and Krishnamurthi, S. 2004. *The TeachScheme! Project: Computing and Programming for Every Student*. Computer Science Education (CSE) 14(1): 55-77, March 2004. (25)

[12] Fernandes, E. and Kumar, A. N. 2004. *A Tutor on Scope for the Programming Languages Course*. ACM SIGCSE Bulletin, Volume 36, Issue 1 (March 2004), 90-93.

[13] Guzdial, M. and Kehoe, C. 1998. *Apprenticeship-based learning environments: A principled approach to providing software-realized scaffolding through hypermedia*. Journal of Interactive Learning Research 9(3/4): 289-336. (24)

[14] Heller, P., Keith, R., and Anderson, S. 1992. *Teaching Problem Solving Through Cooperative Grouping. Part 1: Group versus Individual Problem*. American Journal of Physics, Volume 60, Issue 7 (July 1992), 627-636.

[15] Hristova, M., Misra, A., Rutter, M., and Mercuri, R. 2003. *Identifying and Correcting Java Programming Errors for Introductory Computer Science Students*. SIGCSE'03: Proceedings of the 34th SIGCSE technical symposium on Computer science education, 486-490.

[16] Jin, W. 2008. *Pre-programming Analysis Tutor Helps Students Learn Basic Programming Concept*. SIGCSE'08: Proceedings of the 39th SIGCSE technical symposium on Computer Science Education, 276-280.

[17] Koedinger, K. R. and Corbett, A. T. 2006. *Cognitive Tutors: Technology brings learning science to classroom*. In K. Sawyer (Ed.), the Cambridge Handbook of the Learning Sciences, Cambridge University Press, 61-78.

[18] Lane, H. and VanLehn, K. 2003. *Coached Program Planning: Dialogue-Based Support for Novice Program Design*. SIGCSE'03: Proceedings of the 34th SIGCSE technical symposium on Computer science education, 148-152.

[19] McCracken, M. et al. 2002. *A multi-national multi-institutional study of assessment of programming skills of first-year CS students*. SIGCSE Bulletin, Volume 34, Issue 1 1 (March 2002).

[20] Odekirt-Hash, E. and Zachary, J. L. 2001. *Automated Feedback on Programs Means Students Need Less Help from Teachers*. SIGCSE'01: Proceedings of the 32nd SIGCSE technical symposium on Computer Science Education, 55-59.

[21] Perkins, D., Hancock, C., Hobbs, R., Martin, F. and Simmons, R. 1989. *Conditions of learning in novice programmers*. Studying the Novice Programmer. Lawrence Erlbaum Associates. (23)

[22] Shaffer, S. C. 2005. *Ludwig: An online programming tutoring and assessment system*. Inroads --- The SIGCSE Bulletin, Volume 37, Issue 2 (June 2005), 56-60.

[23] Soh, L. K. 2006. *Incorporating an Intelligent Tutoring System into CS1*. SIGCSE'06: Proceedings of the 37th SIGCSE technical symposium on Computer science education, 486-490.

[24] Song J. S., Hahn, S. H., Tak, K. Y., and Kim, J. H. 1997. *An intelligent tutoring system for introductory C language course*. Computers & Education, Volume 28, Issue 2 (February 1997), 93-102.

[25] Williams, L., Kessler, R. R., Cunningham, W., and Jeffries, R. 2000. *Strengthening the Case for Pair-Programming*. IEEE Software, Volume 17, Issue 4 (July/Aug 2000), 19-25.

Personifying Programming Tool Feedback Improves Novice Programmers' Learning

Michael J. Lee and Andrew J. Ko
The Information School I DUB Group
University of Washington
{mjslee, ajko}@uw.edu

ABSTRACT

Many novice programmers view programming tools as all-knowing, infallible authorities about what is right and wrong about code. This misconception is particularly detrimental to beginners, who may view the cold, terse, and often judgmental errors from compilers as a sign of personal failure. It is possible, however, that attributing this failure to the computer, rather than the learner, may improve learners' motivation to program. To test this hypothesis, we present *Gidget*, a game where the eponymous robot protagonist is cast as a fallible character that blames itself for not being able to correctly write code to complete its missions. Players learn programming by working *with* Gidget to debug its problematic code. In a two-condition controlled experiment, we manipulated Gidget's level of *personification* in: communication style, sound effects, and image. We tested our game with 116 self-described novice programmers recruited on Amazon's Mechanical Turk and found that, when given the option to quit at any time, those in the experimental condition (with a personable Gidget) completed significantly more levels in a similar amount of time. Participants in the control and experimental groups played the game for an average time of 39.4 minutes (SD=34.3) and 50.1 minutes (SD=42.6) respectively. These finding suggest that how programming tool feedback is portrayed to learners can have a significant impact on motivation to program and learning success.

Categories and Subject Descriptors

K.3.2 Computer Science Education: Introductory Programming, D.2.5 Testing and Debugging.

General Terms

Design, Human Factors.

Keywords

Programming, Education, Personification, Motivation, Debugging

1. INTRODUCTION

For most beginners, the experience of writing computer programs is characterized by a distinct sense of failure. The first line of code beginners write often leads to unexpected behaviors, such as syntax errors, runtime errors, or program output that the learner did not intend. While all of these forms of feedback are essential to helping a beginner understand what programs are and how computers interpret them, the experience can be quite discouraging [28,29] and emotional [25].

These findings have significant implications for computing education. To many learners, error messages are not perceived as

Permission to make digital or hard copies of all or part of this work for personal or classroom use is granted without fee provided that copies are not made or distributed for profit or commercial advantage and that copies bear this notice and the full citation on the first page. To copy otherwise, or republish, to post on servers or to redistribute to lists, requires prior specific permission and/or a fee.
ICER'11, August 8–9, 2011, Providence, RI, USA.
Copyright 2011 ACM 978-1-4503-0829-8/11/08...$10.00.

Figure 1. Runtime error highlighted in the instruction pane (*rear*), with corresponding error messages in the control

actionable facts, but as evidence that they are incompetent and that the computer is an all-knowing, infallible authority on what is right and wrong [6]. Even in programming environments designed for beginners such as Alice [24] and Scratch [35], where syntax errors are impossible and most runtime errors are avoided by having the runtime do something sensible rather than fail, the communication between the learner and the computer is framed as one-way: the computer does not express its interpretation of the code, it simply acts upon it without explanation. These relationships between learners and programming tools are more command-and-control than collaboration.

And yet, how people perceive their relationship to a computer is a critical determinant of not only their attitudes towards computers, but also their performance in using them to accomplish tasks [27]. Moreover, studies have shown that people expect computers to behave with the same social responses that people do [41]; for example, automated systems that blame users for errors negatively affect users' performance and their attitudes toward computers [17].

If negative feedback from computers affects people's performance on conventional computer tasks, does programming tool feedback also affect novice programmers motivation and learning success? To investigate this question, we designed Gidget, a web-based programming game in which the user helps a damaged robot correct its faulty code completing its missions (which are expressed as test cases). To investigate the role of feedback on learners' motivation, we designed two versions of the game, manipulating the robot's level of *personification*, changing communication style, sound effects, and appearance. As seen in Figure 1, the control version of the game used conventional, impersonal messages and appeared as a faceless terminal; the experimental version used personified language with personal pronouns, taking the blame for syntax and runtime errors, and had a face. In each condition, the information content conveyed through messages was the same. We then recruited a total of 250 individuals from all over the world using Amazon's Mechanical Turk [1], with 116 of them meeting our criteria as rank novice programmers. With this latter pool of participants, we found that those in the experimental group finished significantly more levels than those in the control group, meaning they successfully used more commands in the programming language. Participants in the control and experimental played the game for an average time of 39.4 minutes (SD=34.3) and 50.1 minutes (SD=42.6), respectively. However, there was no significant difference between conditions in the total time played, nor the number of times an individual executed a version of their code overall. Our findings also show that the experimental group completed more levels in fewer program executions than the control group, suggesting they were attending more to the steps of program execution explained by the robot.

In the rest of this paper, we discuss prior work on feedback in programming tools, detail our game and study design, and then discuss our results and their implications on computing education.

2. RELATED WORK

The role of feedback and critique in learning has long been studied in education [2,3,4,25,28,29,32,45]. For example, for some learners, negative feedback is more than discouraging: it is an explicit judgment of their abilities. Recent work in educational psychology has found that learners' sensitivity to critique have a strong relationship to self-reported motivation, self-reported performance levels in college courses, and avoidance of further opportunities to receive critical feedback [2,32]. Other work has found that females pay greater attention to the valence of critique (positive or negative) and that they are more likely to view negative critique as indicative of global ability on any task, rather than ability at a particular task [45]. Moreover, research on self-efficacy shows that building confidence at a skill requires not only success on tasks, but the sort of success learners believe is due to their own perseverance and creativity [3,4]. Dweck [14] has argued similarly that learners develop *self-theories* of themselves, appearing to have either a fixed mindset (where they believe intelligence is inborn) or a growth mindset (where they believe that intelligence can improve with hard work). All of these theories and findings appear to be at play in learners' first encounters with computer programming [29,39]. Our work builds on these ideas, investigating how redirecting negative feedback away from the learner and back to a personified computer entity affects learning.

Our research follows a long tradition of efforts to create programming environments for beginners [23]. Many of these technologies have focused on increasing learner motivation by incorporating new factors to entice learners to explore computational activities. For example, Logo [44] and more recently EToys [22] both created computational spaces for children to explore music, language, and mathematics; Light-bot [31] pushed players to take the robot's point-of-view of the environment to successfully navigate through levels; Playground [15] and LEGO Mindstorms [37] had similar goals, enticing children with the modeling and simulation of phenomena from the world or actually enabling them to write programs that sense the world. These approaches and others like them seek to entice learners with their intrinsic curiosity about the world and its processes.

Other approaches have motivated children with opportunities for self-expression. Play [48], My Make Believe Castle [34], Hands [42], ToonTalk [19], Klik & Play [33], Stagecast [47], Toque [49] and others all focus on enabling learners to create novel animations and games. Similar efforts have been made at the college level with projects such as Georgia Computes! [11] and Game2Learn [5], which encourages students to create and test their own games. Examples include Bug Bots [12] – a game where players attempt to repair robots by dropping tiles into a flowchart representing a computer program – and Virtual Bead Loom [8] – a game where students are encouraged to learn looping functions to create bead artwork instead of placing beads one at a time. Other systems that have added to these self-expression goals the ability to share the content one has created. For example, MOOSE Crossing invites learners to create characters and spaces in a virtual, multi-user text-based world [10]; more recently, Storytelling Alice [24] and Scratch [35] have focused on enabling learners to tell and share stories. Kelleher et al. [24] were one of the first to demonstrate that opportunities and affordances for storytelling can significantly improve learners' motivation to program. Our work follows these traditions, but provides learners with the story, allowing them to contribute to its progress by interacting with a character in a game.

While all of the systems discussed thus far aimed to increase motivation, several systems have aimed to lower demotivating factors in programming tools. Such approaches include simplifying the textual programming language syntax [10,43], designing languages that mimic how children describe program behavior [42], preventing syntax errors entirely by designing program construction interfaces that use drag and drop interactions (e.g., [7,22,35]) or form filling [33,34,47] rather than text. Others have attempted to simplify the debugging of programs by enabling learners to select "why" questions about program output [28,30]. Our research follows the same vein as these projects, aiming to mitigate factors inherent to programming that would diminish motivation by changing the programming environment. However, in contrast to prior work, our work will not add new capabilities to the programming environment, but rather changes how the existing capabilities of tools relate to the learner through the delivery and presentation of feedback and suggestions.

Given practice, novice programmers develop strategies to effectively understand unfamiliar code [16,18,21]. Working with a partner often affords the benefit of having working off each others' strengths and splitting up the work accordingly. Research exploring the effectiveness of pair-programming in introductory courses have shown that there are significant benefits for both teammates [9,36] and individuals [9]. This work has been extended to pair-debugging for novice programmers by Murphy et al., who report that interactive pairs often attempt more problems, and that critical pairs who reflected on their work often were more likely to successfully identify and resolve bugs [38]. Similarly, recent work has demonstrated that (cognitive) apprenticeship, where beginners are given regular feedback by experts, yields a higher retention rate of students in a beginner computer science course [50].

Our research builds on the ideas from these studies by having the learner and computer game character co-create the code that will accomplish the game goals. Previous studies have found that by simply telling participants that they were on the same team as a computer and representing this with armbands of the same color, participants showed greater affinity towards computers, being more willing to cooperate with it, conform to it suggestions, and assess the computer as more friendly and intelligent than computers on an opposing team [40]. Our work will shed new insight on how changing the role of the computer from an authoritative figure to a collaborator needing assistance will affect learner motivation.

3. METHOD

The goal of our study was to investigate the role of programming tool feedback on learners' motivation to program. To do this, we designed the programming game *Gidget*, shown in Figure 2, which asked learners to help a damaged robot fix its faulty programs, in order to accomplish its missions. Our study had two conditions – control and experimental – manipulating the *personification* of the robot protagonist, Gidget. By personifying Gidget, we aimed to increase the agency of the character, adding human-like qualities to an otherwise cold and emotionless entity. In the control condition, Gidget was represented as a faceless terminal screen that provided terse, impersonal feedback in response to commands and error messages (Figure 1). In contrast, the experimental condition

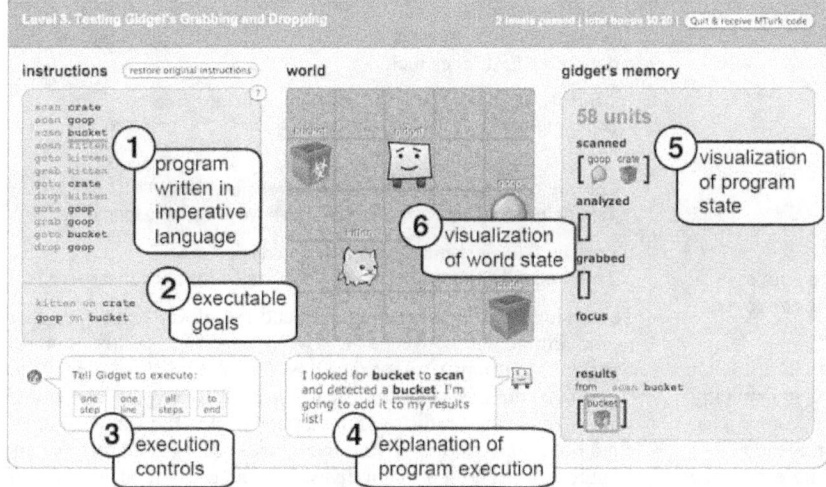

Figure 2. Gidget, shown here in its experimental condition, where learners help a damaged robot fix its programs.

represented Gidget as an emotive robot that included the use of personal pronouns such as "I" in the feedback, coupled with facial expressions corresponding to the runtime error state of the program. Participants were recruited on Amazon Mechanical Turk and offered 40¢ for completing the first level and 10¢ for each additional level completed. The total bonus and the levels completed were displayed in the upper right corner of the interface, along with a button giving the participants the option to quit at any time (Figure 2). The key dependent variable in our study was *levels completed* as a measure of learners' motivation to program.

Our null hypothesis was:

> H₀: There is no difference in *levels completed* between the control condition, using conventional, emotionless feedback and the experimental condition, using personified feedback.

In the rest of this section, we describe the game in more detail and discuss the experiment designed to test this hypothesis.

3.1 The Game

Our online game, called *Gidget* (shown in Figure 2), is an HTML5 and JavaScript application using jQuery. The game was tested for compatibility on MacOS X, Windows 7, and Ubuntu Linux 10 using Apple Safari 5, Mozilla Firefox 3.6 & 4.0, and Google Chrome 10 (we could not support Internet Explorer because it lacked the *contentEditable* attribute, which was used to implement the editor).

In the game, learners are guided through a sequence of levels that teach the design and analysis of basic algorithms in a simple imperative language designed specifically for the game. When players begin, they are told a story that motivates the game: there has been a chemical spill in a small town that has caused all the locals to evacuate and is threatening the local wildlife. The only thing that can safely protect the animals and clean the spill is a small robot capable of identifying and solving problems. Unfortunately, the robot was damaged during transportation, and now struggles to complete its missions, generating programs that *almost* solve the problems, but not quite. It is up to the learner to help the robot by figuring out and fixing the problematic code it generates. In this sense, the learner and the robot are a team, working together to save animals, clean up the spill, and ultimately shut down the hazardous chemical factory.

The primary activity in the game is to learn how to communicate with the robot via commands to help it accomplish a series of goals. The levels, goals, language, and user interface, however, were designed to teach specific aspects of algorithm design. The first 9 levels focus on teaching the 7 basic commands in the robot's syntax grammar and variations on how they can be written, each containing some invalid syntax that the learners must understand and correct. The subsequent 9 levels teach useful design patterns for composing these commands to achieve more powerful behaviors, each containing some semantic error in the ordering of the composite command sequences. In each level, one or more goals (Figure 2.2) are specified in terms of executable tests.

Table 1 explains Gidget's 7 commands. Learners were able to access a similar syntax reference as Table 1, but without the explanations, through the ? button at the top right of the editor. Each of the 7 commands could be followed by a ',' and subsequent command, allowing Gidget to iterate over a set of things with a given name. For example, if there were multiple kittens in Figure 2, the command "goto kitten, grab it" would iteratively go to each kitten, grab the kitten, and then go to the next kitten. The 'focus' stack in Figure 2.5 determines how the keyword 'it' is resolved; the 'results' stack in Figure 2.5 tracks matching names for each command.

In the game, Gidget programs are primarily capable of findings things in the 'world' (Figure 2.6), going to them, checking their properties, and moving them to other places on the grid. In some cases, objects have their own abilities, which Gidget can invoke like a function. After each execution step, the effect of these commands are shown in the 'memory' pane (Figure 2.5) and explained by Gidget (Figure 2.4) to reinforce the semantics of each command. Each step also costs Gidget 1 unit of '*energy*' (displayed at the top of Figure 2.5), forcing learners' to carefully consider how to write their code to complete each level within the allotted number of energy units.

In each condition, the robot is detailed in its interpretation of each command in its program. Not only does it explain what action it is taking in each step (Figure 3) and visualize these changes to the data structures it maintains in memory (Figure 2.5) to support its

Table 1. Gidget command syntax and semantics.

scan *thing*
  Enables Gidget to goto all things with name *thing*. Scanned things are added to the set named *scanned* in Gidget's memory.

goto *thing1* [avoid *thing2*]
  Moves Gidget to all of the things matching the name *thing1*, one square at a time If a thing to avoid is given, for each step that Gidget takes, he attempts to find a path that stays at least 1 square away from things with the name *thing2*.

analyze *thing*
  Enables Gidget to ask all things with name *thing* to perform an action. Analyzed things are added to the set named *analyzed* in Gidget's memory.

ask *thing* to *action thing* *
  Causes *thing* to perform *action*, if action is defined. Zero or more things are passed as arguments. Gidget's execution is suspended until the thing asked has completed requested action.

grab *thing*
  Adds all things with name *thing* to the set named *grabbed* in Gidget's memory, removing them from the grid and constraining their location to Gidget's location.

drop *thing*
  Removes all things with name *thing* in that were previously grabbed from the set *grabbed* set.

if *thing* is[n't] *aspect*, *command*
  For each thing with name *thing* that has been analyzed, execute the specified command if that thing contains an aspect of name *aspect*.

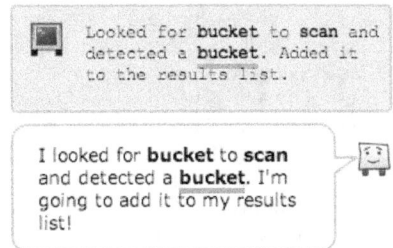

Figure 3. The two communication styles used to express either a positive or neutral affect. Positive affect is conveyed through the robot's facial expressions.

execution, but when it arrives at a command that it does not recognize or a command with missing information, it explicitly highlights this missing information and explains to the learner what interpretation it is going to make of the ambiguous command before proceeding (Figure 1). Moreover, in the case of parsing errors, the system opens up a syntax guide mentioned previously, highlighting the syntax rule that Gidget guessed was being used.

To aid the players with debugging, we implemented four execution controls for the code: *one step*, *one line*, *all steps*, and *to end* (Figure 5). The *one step* button evaluates one compiled instruction in the code, just like a breakpoint debugger does, but also displaying text describing the execution of the step (Figure 3). The *one line* button evaluates all steps contained on one line of the code, jumping the the final output of that line immediately. The *all steps* button evaluates the entire program and the goals in one button press, but animates each step. The *to end* button does the same as *all steps*, but does not animate anything.

3.1.2 Control vs. Experimental Condition

Personification of the robot's appearance was a key manipulation in our experiment. In the control condition, Gidget was designed to be a cold, emotionless computer terminal – something that the player would feel minimal emotional attachment towards. In contrast, in the experimental condition, Gidget was designed to be more human-like – a cute, unconfident robot with changing facial expressions based on the success of its execution. In the control condition, Gidget had two distinct states: an error/fail state that was shown during any syntax or runtime error, and a neutral state that was shown otherwise (Figure 4). The error state, with its large, jarring stop icon, attempts to capture the style common to compiler error messages. In contrast, the experimental condition had three distinct states for Gidget: an error/fail state that was shown during any kind of error, a success state that was displayed when a goal was completed, and a neutral state that was shown otherwise (Figure 4). These facial expressions were specifically designed to make Gidget more human-like and add affect to its messages throughout the game (Figure 3).

In both conditions, Gidget was designed to be verbose to help players know what was going on with the code during execution. The messages in the control condition were terse, actionable facts about the program state, presented in conventional fixed-width *Courier New* font. The text in the experimental condition contained the exact same information, using the softer, sans-serif *Verdana* font (Figure 3), but was personified in three specific ways. We started with the control text, then followed one or more of these rules: use a personal pronoun (e.g. "I," "you"), admit failure (e.g. "I don't know this command"), and express affect (via exclamation points and emoticons). Examples include:

Control: "Unknown command, so skipping to next step."
Experimental: "I don't know what this is, so I'll just go on to the next step."

Control: "Dropped cat. Removing from memory banks."
Experimental: "I dropped the cat. I'll remove it from my memory."

Control: "ERROR: Nothing to *ask* by that name."
Experimental: "Hmm... I couldn't find anything to *ask* by that name."

The dialogue pane between Gidget and the player exhibit another major difference between the two conditions. In the control condition, the player is portrayed as a satellite dish (Figure 5) to signify that there is a large physical distance between the learner and robot, requiring radio communication. In the experimental condition, players are given the choice between three avatars (Figure 5) to represent themselves. This image is used in place of the satellite dish from the control condition, signifying that there is closeness and teamwork between Gidget and the player.

Next, the shape of the communication text boxes are different between the two conditions (as seen in Figure 3). The control condition was designed to look visually cold and direct. In contrast, the experimental condition used comic speech-bubbles for both Gidget and the player with the intention of having the exchange look like a conversation (Figure 3). These themes were extended to other parts of the interface, where the control condition's interface boxes have shaper curves than their experimental condition counterparts, which have larger, rounded corners.

Furthermore, there were labeling differences between conditions. First, level titles in the experimental condition were composed of the control conditions' level name with the addition of "Gidget" to add agency. For example, level 1 was titled "Testing Scanner" or "Testing Gidget's Scanner," and level 5 was titled "Utilizing Special Items" or "Using Special Items with Gidget." In the same manner, the memory pane was labeled "Memory banks" in the control condition, and "Gidget's memory" in the experimental condition.

Finally, sound effects were played in both conditions when Gidget performed an action or when a major event, such as Gidget running out of energy or Gidget not completing his goals, occurred. They were designed to supplement the text and provide additional depth to the world as Gidget moved through it (Figure 2.6). All sound effects were identical between conditions, except the general error and parser error sounds, which were manipulated to evoke different feelings. Errors in the control condition used sounds similar to those heard in operating systems when a critical error occurs. In contrast, errors in the experimental condition used sounds to attract players' attention without making it seem like the computer was "yelling." These sounds were deliberately chosen to add or subtract from the personification between the two conditions.

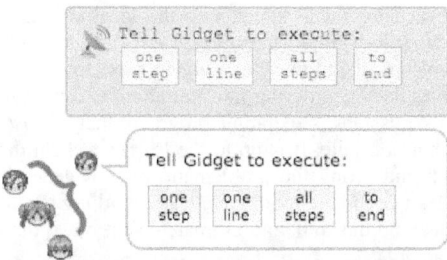

Error/Failure   Neutral   Success

Figure 4. Representations of Gidget based on its game condition - control (*left*), and experimental (*right*) - and state.

Figure 5. Communications pane representing the user in the control (*top*) and experimental (*bottom*) conditions. Players in the experimental condition are given the option to choose an avatar to represent themselves when they start the game.

3.2 Recruitment

Previous studies have shown effects due to giving computers personality traits in adult populations of varying ages [17,40,41]. We focused on replicating these studies in programming tools for adults of a similar age range. To recruit these individuals, we used Amazon.com's Mechanical Turk, an online marketplace where individuals can receive micro-payments for doing small tasks called Human Intelligence Tests (HITs). It is an attractive platform for researchers because it provides quick, easy access to a large workforce willing to receive a small monetary compensation for their time [46]. Since workers are sampled from all over the globe, Mechanical Turk studies have the benefit of generalizing to varied populations more than samples from limited geographic diversity that are more common in traditional recruiting methods [26]. However, due to the nature of the low monetary compensation and anonymity of the workers, careful consideration has to be taken to ensure that participants are not "gaming the system" [13,26]. To address this, we required that participants complete at least one level to receive credit for the HIT, ensuring that they actually had to interact with Gidget and the code before being allowed to quit.

3.3 Pricing & Validation

Since our game had a total of 18 levels, we decided that we would compensate our participants with a base rate and a nominal bonus payment for each level they completed. Previous studies have found that higher payment does not necessarily equate to better results [20], so we wanted to calibrate our payments to established market prices. To do this, we observed Mechanical Turk HITs tagged "game" for a period of 14 days. These HITs were further filtered to include only those that had an actual gameplay element as the main component as opposed to tasks such as writing reviews for third-party games. From these HIT descriptions, we constructed a list of 'reward' and 'time allotted' values, along with any explicit bonus payments mentioned. Our goal was to set a base reward that was high enough to attract participants, but also as low as possible to minimize participants' sense of obligation to spend time on our HIT. Likewise, we wanted our bonus payment per stage to have a minimal factor on participants' decision to continue the game.

Based on our data, we determined our optimal base reward as 30¢ for starting the HIT, and an additional 10¢ for each level completed. To ensure participants actually tried the game, we required that they complete at least one level to get paid. This meant the minimum compensation any participant received was 40¢. Participants were not informed of the total number of levels, eliminating this factor from their decisions to continue playing the game. Finally, we deliberately avoided mentioning anything about programming in the HIT description and tags to prevent people from self-selecting out of the HIT because of its association with programming. However, since the HIT description included the words "game" and "robot," we may have introduced some gender-biased self-selection effects.

To further validate our pricing model and detect defects and usability problems in the game, we conducted a pilot test on Mechanical Turk with 12 paid participants. In addition, an informal, 4-participant, lab study was conducted to gather information that we could not capture from Mechanical Turk. In this lab study, participants were asked to think-aloud while playing the game to test the clarity of the instructions and observe any problems they had with the interface. Observational study participants were volunteers and were not compensated for their time.

The pilot study results verified that participants were willing to complete levels and that the system functioned as-intended overall. Based on the data we received, we clarified some of the post-game survey questions and fixed several minor defects. We also set the ceiling for submission time to 3 hours to make the HIT less intimidating, as setting it too high could be misinterpreted by potential participants as the task being overly difficult. The observational study surfaced unclear instructions, confusing interface elements, defects, and usability problems in the game. Based on this information, we improved the text and interface elements, running another pilot to ensure that the usability and clarity of the game had improved.

Figure 6. Geographical distribution of the 116 novice programmers in our study, spanning 24 countries.

3.4 The Participants

On game load, each participant was randomly assigned one of two conditions: control or experimental. This information, along with their current state in the game were logged on the client-side to ensure participants would not be exposed to the other condition, even if they refreshed their browser. Once a participant chose to quit, they were given a post-survey and a unique code to receive payment for their submission. The survey was designed to get demographic information (e.g. gender, age, education, country), identify prior programming experience, and solicit feedback and attitudes about the game. In addition to the survey responses, we automatically collected the following information from each participant upon quitting: the number of levels completed; time stamps for level start, level complete, quit, and any execution button invocations;, all character-level edits to each level's program, execution button presses, game condition, choice of user avatar (if in the experimental group), and payment code.

We defined "novice programmers" as participants who reported in the survey that they have never had: 1) "taken a programming course," 2) "written a computer program," or 3) "contributed code towards the development of a computer program." This information was cross-validated with an additional question later in the survey that asked them to rate their agreement with the statement, "I identify myself as a beginner/novice programmer."

Because we deliberately chose not to mention anything about programming in our HIT description, we were not able to control for a specific target audience. Therefore, we recruited a large sample of 250 participants from Mechanical Turk, with 116 meeting our criteria as being novice programmers.

Since the scope of this paper is how personification of the computer and its feedback affects novice programmers, these 116 participants are the primary focus of our analysis. This was a balanced, between-subjects design with 58 participants in each condition. Demographic data revealed that there that participants from the control and experimental conditions were well proportioned, with no significant differences between groups by gender, age, or education. There were a total of 50 females and 66 males with a mean age of 27.5 (SD=8), ranging from 18 to 59 years old. As shown in Figure 6, participants were spread across 24 countries, with most participants coming from the USA (27.6%) followed closely by India (22.4%). About 13.8% of participants were the lone representatives of their respective countries. Many did not provide geographical data (24.1%). Consistent with other Mechanical Turk study demographics, our sample of novice programmers were well-educated [13,26], answering that their highest level of education achieved was: less than high school (<1%), high school (13%), some college (23%), an associates degree (3%), a bachelor's degree (38%), a masters degree (14%), or a doctoral degree (6%).

4. RESULTS

In this section, we provide quantitative evidence for a number of patterns based primarily on the 116 logs and survey responses collected from the participants identified as novice programmers. Our dependent measures were not normally distributed so non-parametric tests were used for analyses. Our level of confidence was set at α=0.05.

4.1 Difference in Levels Completed

The minimum and maximum number of levels completed for both conditions were the same, at 1 and 15, respectively. The median number of levels completed for the control and experimental conditions were 2 and 5, respectively. There was a significant difference in the number of levels participants completed between the two conditions (Wilcoxon rank sums: W=3803, Z=2.3, N=116, p<.05) – meaning that we reject our null hypothesis.

The distribution of 'levels completed' (Figure 7) shows that a large number of participants from both groups quit the game after completing the first level. This was particularly true for those in the control group, who lost 41.3% of their members in contrast to the 29.3% lost by the experimental group. The large drop off in the sixth level for both conditions will be addressed in the discussion section, below. Since all participants were classified as novice programmers and there was no statistical difference in demographics, this suggests that our personification of Gidget in the experimental condition had a positive effect on participants' motivation to play.

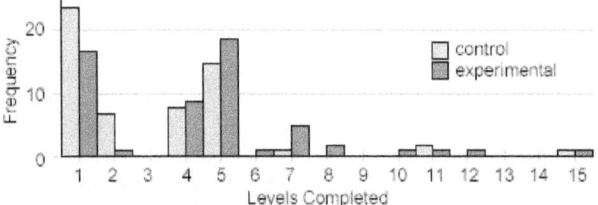

Figure 7. Histogram of *levels completed* for each condition.

4.2 No Difference in Play Time

The minimum time spent playing the game for the control and experimental condition was 5.4 minutes and 8.4 minutes, respectively. The maximum time spent playing the game was 2.81 hours and 2.97 hours respectively. The median overall play time for the control and experimental conditions were 27.1 minutes and 35 minutes, respectively. There was no significant difference in the length of time participants in either condition played the game overall (W=3689.5, Z=1.6, N=116, n.s.).

Since the previous result showed that the experimental group completed more levels than the control group, we checked to see if participants in either group were spending more time per individual level. To do this, we calculated the median time each participant took to complete the levels they attempted, and then compared the two resulting distributions of medians. We found that there was no significant difference in the median time to successfully *complete* levels between conditions (W=3407.5, Z=0.08, N=116, n.s.). Likewise, there was no significant difference in the time participants spent on the level they attempted, but did *not* complete (W=3387.5, Z=-0.03, N=116, n.s.).

The difference in levels completed, but the lack of significant difference in playing time suggests that those in the experimental condition learned commands (i.e., by completing more levels) more efficiently. This suggests that something in our manipulation caused the experimental condition participants to better understand and use the commands to fix Gidget's problematic code. We address possible explanations for this in our discussion.

4.3 No Difference in Execution

There were no significant differences in how frequently the participants used the four execution control buttons overall (*one step*: W=3693.5, Z=1.7, n.s., *one line*: W=3532, Z=0.8, n.s., *all steps*: W=3488, Z=0.5, n.s., *to end*: W=3740, Z=1.9, n.s.; N=116).

Since we found previously that the experimental group completed more levels than the control group, we checked to see if there was a difference between the conditions for the number of code executions used per individual level. To do this, we calculated the median number of code executions each participant used to complete the levels they attempted, and then compared the two resulting distributions of medians. This was repeated for each execution button. We found that there were no significant differences in the median number of code executions for *completed* levels by condition (*one step*: W=3293, Z=-0.5, n.s., *all steps*: W=3061.5, Z=-1.9, n.s., *to end*: W=3305.5, Z=-0.5, n.s.; N=116). However, we found that the use of *one line* was significantly different: W=2987.5, Z=-2.3, N=116, p<.05. On closer inspection of the data, we found that this difference was due to participants in the control condition using a higher (median) number of *one line* code executions. This means that participants in the control condition were running their code line-by-line, but skipping some of the finer details provided by the *one step* execution.

Finally, we checked both conditions to see if there was a difference in the raw number of code executions for levels the participants attempted but did not complete. We found that there were no significant differences between conditions in the number of code executions for levels that participants attempted but did *not* complete (*one step*: W=3339.5, Z=-0.3, n.s., *one line*: W=3310, Z=-0.5, n.s., *all steps*: W=3303.5, Z=-0.5, n.s., *to end*: W=3483, Z=0.5, n.s.; N=116). Since participants quit on different levels of varying difficulty, this suggests that those from both conditions put approximately the same amount of effort into testing and executing their code before deciding to give up, independent of the level they were playing.

4.4 Differences in Survey Feedback

There was no significant difference in participants' self-reported level of enjoyment playing the game between the two conditions (W=3117, Z=-1.1, N=116, n.s.). Likewise, there was no significant difference in participants' reporting whether they would recommend the game to a friend wanting to learn programming (W=3629.5, Z=1.4, N=116, n.s.). These results are consistent with reports by Nass et. al, who found that participants did not attribute success or enjoyment of an activity to changes in their performance [40].

There was, however, a significant difference in participants' reporting that they wanted to help Gidget succeed (W=3901, Z=3.1, N=116, p<.01). Participants in the experimental condition were significantly more likely than those in the control condition to agree to the statement, "I wanted to help Gidget succeed."

4.5 Comparison to Experienced Programmers

To contrast our reported findings, we briefly present data from participants who did not qualify as novice programmers. These were the participants who reported in the survey that they have: 1) taken a programming course, 2) written a computer program, or 3) contributed code towards the development of a computer program. After trimming data that was unusable due to data transmission errors, we had 120 participants with prior programming experience, 61 in the control condition, and 59 in the experimental condition.

This experienced group completed a wider range of levels in both conditions, with the median number of levels completed for the control and experimental conditions being 5 and 4, respectively. However, unlike our major finding from the novice group, there was not a significant difference in the number of levels completed between the two conditions in the experienced group (W=3392.5, Z=-0.9, N=120, n.s.). Likewise, there was no significant difference in the overall play time between conditions (W=3376, Z=-1.0, N=120, n.s.).

Like the novice programmers, there was no significant difference in experienced participants' self-reported level of enjoyment playing the game between the two conditions or whether they would recommend the game to a friend. In addition, unlike the novice programmers, the experienced participants did not show a significant difference in wanting to help Gidget succeed (W=3624, Z=0.3, N=120, n.s.).

Finally, there were no significant differences in how frequently the participants used three of the four execution control buttons overall (*one step*: W=3256.5, Z=-1.6, n.s., *one line*: W=3398.5, Z=-0.9, n.s., *all steps*: W=3751, Z=0.9, n.s.; N=120). However, there was a significant difference in the number of code executions for *to end*: W=3139, Z=-2.2, N=120, p<.05, where participants in the control condition used the button more frequently than those in the experimental condition. This suggests that the experienced programmers attempted to treat the game more as a traditional edit-compile-run cycle, rather than debugging the program step-by-step.

5. DISCUSSION

Our findings demonstrate that more personified programming tool feedback can increase novice programmers' motivation to program. More specifically, we have shown that casting the computer as a verbose but naïve and unconfident teammate that blames itself for errors has demonstrated to have a positive effect on novice learners' performance in learning a simple textual programming language. We also found that novice programmers exposed to this unconfident teammate were more likely to report that they wanted to help it.

These results, combined with the lack of a significant difference in median time spent on levels or execution of the program, suggests that the experimental group was likely making better use of the information provided by the robot than the control group. One possible explanation for this is that by personifying the feedback provided by the programming environment, experimental group participants were more likely to *attend* to the information content in the messages, and thus more likely to understand the program semantics. This is supported by our finding that the control group participants were significantly more likely to use the "one line" execution control, skipping over many (but not all) of the robot's messages. Another interpretation is that both groups attended to the messages similarly, but the phrasing led the experimental group participants to somehow process the information more deeply, by framing it as human rather than computer. Future studies should explore these possible interpretations, isolating the effect of personification on attention to feedback.

Although our results suggest that our manipulation increased success on learning, we did not find that participants were willing to spend more time playing the game. This may be due to the unconstrained nature of Mechanical Turk tasks, which provide no additional extrinsic incentives to continue; it may also be due to difficulties that learners encountered in particular levels of the game. This was particularly true of level 6, where there was a major drop off of participants in both conditions (Figure 7). This level introduced conditional statements, suggesting that it is an inherently difficult concept for novice programmers to comprehend. More work needs to be done to uncover how feedback tool personification affects other aspects of motivation such as wanting to continue to work on a problem after multiple failures on a single level.

Our analysis of the performance of experienced programmers also suggests that the motivation and learning effects due to personification may diminish with experience. It is likely that the experienced programmers playing the game quickly learned the semantics of the language and did not need to read the feedback provided by the programming tool in order to complete each level.

5.1 Threats to Validity

Our study has a number of limitations that limit its generalizability. First, Mechanical Turk allows participants to self-select into HITs given that they meet certain qualifications. Our HIT did not require any special qualifications and used the default setting from Amazon. Although we tried to account for factors that would affect the HITs listing on Amazon's HIT page, those who filtered for higher-paying HITs would be less likely to find our HIT, whereas those filtering for a tag labeled "game" would be more likely to find our HIT.

Also, the game was accessible by computer, connected to the Internet, listed on a website requiring login. Although not directly translatable to programming ability, gaining access to the game requires a fair amount of computer knowledge. As our demographic data indicated, our participants were well-educated, with 86% of them reporting that they had some college education or beyond.

Finally, though small, there was an economic incentive for participants to participate in the study. Moreover, they would receive a bonus payment for levels they completed. Since these economic incentives would not exist in a place like a classroom, it is unclear how or findings would generalize to other extrinsically motivated learning contexts. For instance, Mechanical Turk turk users have a choice of which tasks to engage in; students in a classroom often do not.

6. CONCLUSIONS & FUTURE WORK

We have presented Gidget, a game intended for novice programmers who are tasked with helping a damaged robot complete its missions by debugging its defective code. By personifying the robot – characterizing it as fallible, having it convey information about coding errors conversationally, and having it take the blame for mistakes – we have found that novice programmers complete more game levels than learners who received more conventional feedback, in a comparable amount of time. Given our results, we conclude that personifying the computer and making it less authoritative has many immediate motivational and learning benefits for novices wanting to learn how to program.

Our results also suggest several directions for future work. We want to further refine our gameplay elements to better understand exactly which specific manipulations accounted for the experimental group's players to complete more levels in the same amount of time. For example, were they were more attentive to Gidget's personified text, or was Gidget's face? Adding more instructional content or altering the economic incentive (from Mechanical Turk) may also yield additional insights. We also want to explore the effectiveness of Gidget in introductory programming courses to see if our results hold with students in a classroom setting. If these findings can be replicated in other learning contexts, they may have a significant effect on how feedback is provided to learners in a wide range of computing education contexts.

7. ACKNOWLEDGEMENTS

We would like to thank the second author's daughter, Ellen Ko, for her extensive input on game dynamics and level design. This material is based in part upon work supported by the National Science Foundation under Grant Number CCF-0952733.

8. REFERENCES

1. Amazon Mechanical Turk. http://www.mturk.com
2. Atlas, G.D., Taggart, T., & Goodell D.J. (2004). The effects of sensitivity to criticism on motivation and performance in music students, *British J. of Music Ed.*, 21(1), 81-87.
3. Bandura, A. (1977). Self-efficacy: Toward a unifying theory of behavioral change. *Psychological Review*, 84: 191-215.
4. Bandura, A. (1986). Social foundations of thought and action: A social cognitive theory, *Englewood Cliffs*, NJ: Prentice-Hall.
5. Barnes, T., Richter, H., Powell, E., Chaffin, A., & Godwin, A. (2007). Game2Learn: building CS1 learning games for retention. *ITiCSE*, 121-225.
6. Beckwith, L., Burnett, M., & Cook, C., (2002). Reasoning about Many-to-Many Requirement Relationships in Spreadsheet Grids, *IEEE VL/HCC*, 149.
7. Begel, A. (1996). LogoBlocks: A Graphical Programming Language for Interacting with the World. *EECS, MIT*.
8. Boyce, A., & Barnes, T. (2010). BeadLoom Game: Using Game Elements to Increase Motivation and Learning. *FDG*, 25-31.
9. Braught, G., Eby, L.M., & Wahls, T. (2008). The effects of pair-programming on individual programming skill. *SIGCSE*, 200-204.
10. Bruckman, A. (1997). MOOSE Crossing: Construction, Community, and Learning in a Networked Virtual World for Kids. *MIT Media Lab*. Boston, MA.
11. Bruckman, A., Biggers, M., Ericson, B., McKlin, T., Dimond, J., DiSalvo, B., Hewner, M., Ni, L., & Yardi, S. (2009). Georgia Computes!: Improving the Computing Education Pipeline. SIGCSE, 86-89.
12. Chaffin, A., & Barnes. T (2010). Lessons from a course on serious games research and prototyping. *FDG*, 32-39.
13. Downs, JS., Holbrook, MB, Sheng, S., & Cranor, L.F. (2010). Are your participants gaming the system?: screening mechanical turk workers. *ACM CHI*, 2399-2402.
14. Dweck, C. S. (1999). Self-Theories: Their role in motivation, personality, and development. *The Psychology Press*.
15. Fenton, J. and Beck, K. (1989). Playground: An Object Oriented Simulation System with Agent Rules for Children of All Ages. *ACM OOPSLA*, 123-137.
16. Fitzgerald, S., Lewandowski, G., McCauley, R., Murphy, L., Simon, B., Thomas, L. and Zander, C., (2008) Debugging: finding, fixing, and flailing, a multi-institutional study of novice debuggers. *Computer Science Education*. v18. 93-116
17. Fogg, B. J., & Nass, C. (1997). How users reciprocate to computers: an experiment that demonstrates behavior change. *ACM CHI*, 331-332.
18. Gross, P. and Kelleher, C., (2010). Non-programmers identifying functionality in unfamiliar code: strategies and barriers. *JVLC 21, 5*, 263-276.
19. Harel, I. Children Designers. (1991) *Ablex Publishing, N.J.*
20. Hsieh, G., Kraut, RE, & Hudson, SE. (2010). Why pay?: exploring how financial incentives are used for question & answer. *ACM CHI*, 305-314.
21. Jeffries, R. (1982). A comparison of the debugging behavior of expert and novice programmers. *AERA Annual Meeting*.
22. Kay, A., Etoys and Simstories. http://www.squeakland.org
23. Kelleher, C. and Pausch, R. (2005). Lowering the barriers to programming: A taxonomy of programming environments and languages for novice programmers. *ACM CSUR*, 37(2),83-137.
24. Kelleher, C., Pausch, R., & Kiesler, S. (2007). Storytelling Alice Motivates Middle School Girls to Learn Computer Programming. *ACM CHI*, 1455-1464.
25. Kinnunen, P., & Simon, B. (2010). Experiencing programming assignments in CS1: the emotional toll. *ICER*, 77-86.
26. Kittur, A., Chi, E.H., & Suh, BW. (2008). Crowdsourcing user studies with Mechanical Turk. *ACM CHI*, 453-456.
27. Klein, J., Moon, Y., Picard, R.W. (1999). This computer responds to user frustration. *ACM CHI*, 242–243.
28. Ko, A. J., Myers, B. A., & Aung, H. (2004). Six Learning Barriers in End-User Programming Systems. *IEEE VL/HCC*, 199-206.
29. Ko, A. J. & Myers B.A. (2009). Attitudes and Self-Efficacy in Young Adults' Computing Autobiographies. *IEEE VL/HCC*, 67-74.
30. Kulesza, A. (2009). Approximate learning for structured prediction problems. *UPenn WPE-II Report*.
31. Light-Bot. http://armorgames.com/play/2205/light-bot
32. Linderbaum, B. (2006) The Development and Validation of the Feedback Orientation Scale. *J. of Management*, 1372-1405.
33. Lionet, F., & Lamoureux, Y., *Klik and Play*, Maxis, 1994.
34. Logo Computer Systems, Inc., *My Make Believe Castle*, 1995.
35. Maloney, J., Resnick, M., Rusk, N., Silverman, B., Eastmond, E. (2010). The Scratch Programming Language and Environment. *ACM TOCE*.
36. McDowell, C., Werner, L., Bullock, H., & Fernald, J. (2002). The effects of pair-programming on performance in an introductory programming course. *SIGCSE*, 38–42.
37. MindStorms. http://www.mindstorms.lego.com
38. Murphy, L., Fitzgerald, S., Hanks, B., & McCauley, R. (2010) Pair debugging: a transactive discourse analysis. *ICER*, 51-58.
39. Murphy, L. and Thomas, L. (2008). Dangers of a fixed mindset: Implications of self-theories research for computer science education. *ITiCSE*, 271-275.
40. Nass, C., Fogg, B.J., & Moon, Y. (1996). Can computers be teammates? *International J. of Human-Computer Studies*, 45, 669-678.
41. Nass, C. (2000). Machines and Mindlessness: Social Responses to Computers. *J. of Social Issues*, 56, 81-103.
42. Pane, J. Myers, B.A., & Miller, L.B. (2002). Using HCI Techniques to Design a More Usable Programming System. *IEEE VL/HCC*, 198-206.
43. Papert, S. Mindstorms: Children, Computers, and Powerful Ideas. *Basic Books New York, NY*.
44. Resnick, M., Martin, F., Sargent, R., & Silverman, B. (1996). Programmable Bricks: Toys to Think With. *IBM Systems J.*, vol. 35, no. 3-4, 443-452.
45. Roberts, T.A. (1991). Gender and the influence of evaluations on self-assessments in achievement settings. *Psychological Bulletin*, vol. 109(2), 297-308.
46. Ross, J., Irani, I., Silberman, M. Six, Zaldivar, A., & Tomlinson, B. (2010). Who are the Crowdworkers?: Shifting Demographics in Amazon Mechanical Turk. *ACM CHI*, 2863-2872.
47. Smith, D., Cypher, A., & Tesler, L. (2002). Programming by example: novice programming comes of age. *CACM*, 75-81.
48. Tanimoto, S., & Runyan, M. (1986). Play: an iconic programming system for children. *Visual Programming Environments*, 367-377.
49. Tarkan, S., Sazawal, V., Druin, A., Golub, E., Bonsignore, E.M., Walsh, G., & Atrash, Z. (2010). Toque: designing a cooking-based programming language for and with children. *ACM CHI*, 2417-2426.
50. Vihavainen, A., Paksula, M., & Luukkainen, M. (2011). Extreme apprenticeship method in teaching programming for beginners. *SIGCSE*, 93-98.

The "Prototype Walkthrough": A Studio-Based Learning Activity for Human-Computer Interaction Courses

Christopher D. Hundhausen
School of Elec. Eng. and Comp. Sci.
Washington State University
Pullman, WA 99164
+1-509-335-4590
hundhaus@wsu.edu

Dana Fairbrother
College of Education
Washington State University
Pullman, WA 99164
+1-509-335-1738
danafairbrother@wsu.edu

Marian Petre
Faculty of Mathematics & Computing
The Open University
Walton Hall, Milton Keynes
+44-1908-65-33-73
m.petre@open.ac.uk

ABSTRACT

For over a century, *studio-based* instruction has served as an effective pedagogical model in architecture and fine arts education. Because of its design orientation, human-computer interaction (HCI) education is an excellent venue for studio-based instruction. In an HCI course, we have been exploring a studio-based learning activity called the *prototype walkthrough*, in which a student project team simulates its evolving user interface prototype while a student audience member acts as a test user. The audience is encouraged to ask questions and provide feedback. We have observed that prototype walkthroughs create excellent conditions for learning about user interface design. In order to better understand the educational value of the activity, we performed a content analysis of a video corpus of 16 prototype walkthroughs held in two undergraduate/graduate HCI courses. We found that the prototype walkthrough discussions were dominated by relevant design issues. Moreover, mirroring the justification behavior of the expert instructor, students justified over 80 percent of their design statements and critiques, with nearly one-quarter of those justifications having a theoretical or empirical basis. These results suggest that prototype walkthroughs can be useful not only in helping to teach HCI design, but also in helping to gauge students' evolving design knowledge.

Categories and Subject Descriptors
K.3.2 [**Computer and Information Science Education**]: *Computer science education, Curriculum.*

General Terms
Design, Experimentation, Human Factors.

Keywords
Studio-based learning and instruction, prototype walkthrough, design crit, HCI, user interface design

1. INTRODUCTION
For over a century, studio-based instruction has served as an effective pedagogical model in architecture and fine arts education. In this model, students iteratively develop solutions to a series of design problems. In periodic "design crits" (design critiques), students present their evolving solutions to their peers and instructors for feedback and discussion.

User interface design is a central skill taught in an upper-division computer science course on human-computer interaction (HCI). In such a course, students often undertake a capstone design project that takes them through all phases of the user-centered design process [15], including initial data gathering, user interface prototyping, and usability testing. Because of its focus on design, a human-computer interaction (HCI) course has been identified as an excellent candidate for studio-based instruction (e.g, [1, 11, 16]).

Within the context of a multi-institutional research project in which we are adapting and refining the studio-based instructional model for computing education [8], we have been exploring a new kind of studio-based learning activity—the *prototype walkthrough (PW)*—in our undergraduate/graduate HCI course at Washington State University. In preparation for PWs, student capstone project teams develop low fidelity user interface prototypes of their evolving project designs, and a set of five core tasks to be completed with their prototypes. In PW sessions lasting approximately 20 minutes each, project teams simulate their low fidelity prototypes in front of the class. A student from the audience serves as the test user by interacting with the prototype, and thinking aloud in the process. At any point, the audience can jump in with questions, comments, or feedback. After the five tasks have been completed, the instructor invites the class to engage in a reflective design discussion intended to help the project team improve its design.

Our exploration of the PW activity raises a pair of basic research questions regarding its educational value as part of an HCI course:

RQ1:	*To what degree does the PW promote discussions that are relevant to user interface design?*

RQ2:	*To what degree do students participate in those discussions?*

Resonant with situated learning theory [12], the PW activity is designed to provide opportunities for varying levels of participation in a community of practice. In particular, it provides experts (HCI instructors) with opportunities to model the application of the design knowledge explored in an HCI course, while providing learners (HCI students) with opportunities to practice applying their emerging design knowledge. In design discussions, such design knowledge manifests itself most readily in the ways in which, and extent to which, design critiques and suggestions are justified. This observation leads to an additional research question regarding the educational value of PWs:

> RQ3: *How are design critiques and suggestions justified?*

This paper addresses these questions by presenting a detailed content analysis of a video corpus of 16 PWs, which were run within successive offerings of the conjoint undergraduate/graduate human-computer interaction course at Washington State University. In furnishing the first-ever detailed video analysis of design discussions within an HCI course, our study makes three key contributions to the computing education literature:

1. It introduces the PW as a novel studio-based learning activity for HCI education.
2. It presents a rigorous content coding scheme that can be used to analyze critical discussions about user interface design.
3. It provides a rich descriptive account and analysis of the design discussions promoted by PWs, thus providing evidence of their educational value.

The remainder of this paper is organized as follows. In Section 2, we present the background and related work on which our study builds. Section 3 details the design of our study. Sections 4 and 5 present and discuss the study's key results. Section 6 presents conclusions and discusses future work.

2. BACKGROUND AND RELATED WORK

A form of "design crit" in the *studio-based* instructional model, the PW activity explored in our study engages students in discussions with experts about their user interface designs and how to improve them. A rich legacy of empirical work, nicely synthesized by Cross [3], has explored the behaviors, activities, and processes of both novice and expert designers. In a similar vein, the literature on computer-supported collaborative learning is replete with content analyses of discussions that take place during learning activities, with a focus on how representations serve to mediate those discussions (e.g., [19]).

Within computing education, we have previously performed such analyses of "design crits" anchored in visual representations of algorithms in both an upper-division algorithms course [5] and a CS 1 course [6]. The study presented here contributes to all of these lines of work by performing the first detailed content analysis of critical discussions about user interface design within a course on human-computer interaction design.

Kehoe [11] calls the kind of "design crit" on which our study focuses *critical design dialog*, and points out that it differs from other forms of learning discussions in that it is directed toward critiquing students' work in a public forum, with the dual-aim of (a) influencing the trajectory of the work, and (b) providing opportunities for students to learn from each other's design work and feedback. Kehoe [11] (see also [16]) makes a strong case for the educational value of critical design dialog as a means of learning about HCI design. In brief, she argues that the kinds of design problems that are common in HCI are fuzzy and have no clear-cut solutions. Design principles and heuristics that might guide one to solutions are necessarily vague; learners often find them to be unclear and overly ambiguous [18], leading to their getting stuck during the design process [17]. Learners, she argues, can therefore best develop design competence when they (a) receive feedback on their own designs that is also connected to more general design principles and heuristics, and (b) observe how experts think about design. Critical design dialog provides ideal conditions for both.

In addition to Kehoe's arguments in favor of critical design dialog as a valuable HCI learning activity, the activity has a strong foundation in situated learning theory [12]. According to this theory, one gains competence within a community of practice by having opportunities to participate, in increasingly central ways, in the practices of the community. Critical design dialog, as manifested in the PW, provides such multi-faceted opportunities for participation. In PWs, students can observe expert critiques of design, remaining on the periphery of the discussions as audience members. As they become more comfortable, they can gradually explore opportunities to offer their own critiques and suggestions. As design team members, students are placed in the position of presenting, justifying, and defending their own designs. This constitutes more central participation in design practice; it is akin to the situation of an expert designer at a real-world company.

Computing educators have explored the use of studio-based learning in individual computing courses (e.g., [10, 13]) and even in entire degree programs (e.g., [4]). In one of the few published studies of studio-based learning in HCI education, Reimer and Douglas [16] describe their implementation of an undergraduate HCI course based on the studio model. The course included weekly design crits that were similar in spirit to the PWs described here. The key difference was that, in the design crits, the design teams themselves simulated their user interfaces for demonstrational purposes, rather than enlisting a student audience member as a test user. While Reimer and Douglas did not present a video analysis of their design crits, their observation that the design crits "fostered a highly interactive and constructive learning atmosphere" ([16], p. 201) well resonates with the findings presented here.

In a similar vein, Cennamo et al. [2] performed a detailed qualitative comparison of design studios in both industrial design and human-computer interaction courses, gleaning insights into how these studios promoted the generation and analysis of design ideas. Likewise, Arvola and Artman [1] compared HCI students' studio work in a traditional space against that in a computer-augmented space. While their study focused on studio activities that were far less structured than the PWs we studied, it is similar to our study in that it extensively analyzed video footage.

3. EMPIRICAL STUDY

We conducted our empirical study in conjunction with the spring 2007 and spring 2008 offerings of CptS 443/543 ("Human-Computer Interaction"), the conjoint undergraduate/graduate HCI course at Washington State University taught by the first author. Using a mix of lecture and small group activities, and a pair of textbooks [14, 15], the course explored the application of relevant theories, principles, and processes to the design of interactive software. A focal point of the course was a capstone user interface design project, which students were required to complete in teams of two to three. Student teams could choose the focus of their projects, or they could take on a project suggested by the instructor. During the tenth week of the 15-week semester, project teams presented prototypes of their evolving designs to the class within PW sessions scheduled during regular course lecture periods. These were the focus of this study, which we describe in further detail below.

3.1 Participants and their Design Projects

The spring 2007 course offering enrolled 13 upper-division undergraduate students and two graduate students, while the spring 2008 course offering enrolled 13 upper-division undergraduate and ten graduate students. All but four of these students were computer science or computer engineering majors who had minimally completed a sequence of core courses in software design. The other four students came from a mix of majors, including geology and management information systems. None had taken a prior course in HCI.

Our study considered the PWs of all seven project teams in the 2007 course offering, and nine of the 11 project teams in the 2008 course offering (two were not recorded because of technical difficulties with the video equipment). Table 1 presents the key attributes of the 16 project teams whose PWs were considered in the study. As can be seen, the projects on which they focused were diverse. Moreover, whereas project teams constructed their prototypes mostly out of simple art supplies (pen, paper, transparencies) in the 2007 course offering, most project teams in the 2008 course offering constructed their prototypes using WOZ Pro [9], a computer-based low fidelity prototyping tool we have developed specifically for this purpose.

3.2 Prototype Walkthrough Procedure

Prior to participating in the PWs, project teams were required (a) to perform at least two early data gathering activities (e.g., interviews, questionnaires, field observation) in order to establish the functional, usability, and user experience requirements for their project, (b) to develop a low fidelity user interface prototype based on those requirements; and (c) to formulate a set of five core tasks that their prototype had to support. Project teams brought the prototype and set of tasks to the PW sessions, which took place in a small classroom during the two 75-minute lecture periods of the tenth week of the fifteenth week semester.

All students were required to attend and participate in the PWs. Each project team was assigned a 20-minute slot for their walkthrough; students whose team was not immediately presenting were required to observe the walkthroughs, and to fill out a structured evaluation form intended to provide feedback for the presenting project team. Each PW began with the instructor calling a project team to the front of the room. The project team randomly chose a member of the audience to serve as the "test user" for the PW. The team proceeded to provide a brief description of the prototype interface they had designed, along with a general task scenario. At this point, the project team handed the test user a written set of task instructions, and projected their prototype onto a large screen at the front of the room. Depending upon the prototyping technology used, either an overhead projector or LCD projector was used for this purpose.

The test user proceeded to complete the set of tasks as the project team simulated their prototype's user interface. The test user was instructed to read each task aloud prior to performing it, and to think aloud while performing each task. In order to perform tasks, the test user directly pointed at and manipulated elements of the image projected on the large screen, describing his or her actions along the way (see Figure 1). Audience members and the instructor were welcome to interrupt the walkthrough at any time with questions or comments. The walkthrough ended when the test user completed all five tasks, or the 20-minute time limit had been reached, at which point the instructor initiated a round of applause for the presenting project team and called on the next scheduled project team.

Table 1. Key Attributes of the project teams studied

Team	Size	Project Focus	Prototyping Technology Used
Sp07-1	3	Distributed team problem management	Art supplies
Sp07-2	2	Smart home event scheduler	Art supplies
Sp07-3	2	Campus map route finder	HTML/Javascript
Sp07-4	2	Personal travel blog site	Art supplies
Sp07-5	2	N-body simulator	Art supplies
Sp07-6	2	DVR Remote Control	Art supplies
Sp07-7	2	Power utility mapping software	Art supplies
Sp08-1	2	Smart home control system	WOZ
Sp08-2	2	Low Fidelity UI Prototyping Tool	WOZ
Sp08-3	2	Custom grid-based game builder	HTML
Sp08-4	2	Poker Game	Power Point
Sp08-5	3	Online code review environment	WOZ
Sp08-6	2	Campus map route finder	Power Point
Sp08-7	3	Recipe management software	WOZ
Sp08-8	2	Custom Game Builder	WOZ
Sp08-9	2	Group Collaboration Tool	HTML/Javascript

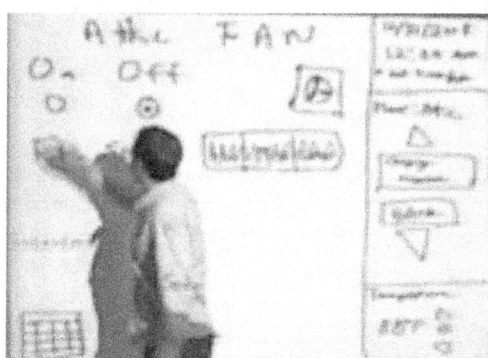

Figure 1. A test user interacting with a prototype within a prototype user interface within a PW

3.3 Data Collection and Analysis Method

Using a video camera positioned near the middle of the classroom and focused on the projected screen, we obtained 4.91 hours of high-quality video footage of the 16 PWs. In order to analyze the content of the talk that took place within our video corpus (RQ1), we began by partitioning the talk into *segments*, where a segment was defined as a single thought or idea uttered by a single participant. We then iteratively developed the coding schemes described below by watching a subset of the walkthrough sessions and adding and refining categories until no new ones emerged. As we did this, we composed a coding manual with detailed categorical descriptions, rich examples of how to distinguish among categories, and step-by-step instructions for coding. Those interested in using or adapting our coding schemes should consult this manual, which we have made available online [7].

Table 2 presents and briefly describes the nine top-level categories in our content coding scheme. Because of its perceived relevance to the HCI course, Design Talk was of particular interest in this study. Table 3 presents a more detailed look at Design Talk in terms of its six subcategories. While they are intended to provide an overall feel for the categories, we emphasize that the descriptions provided in these tables are necessarily terse, and lack sufficient detail and examples for one to make reliable distinctions. We refer interested readers to the coding manual cited earlier [7] for more detailed descriptions.

We also note that the categories in these tables are listed in order of decreasing priority. In cases in which, despite our detailed categorical definitions, we felt a given segment could be coded into multiple categories, we always coded the segment into the category with the *highest* priority.

In order to gauge the extent to which students and the instructor participated in PW discussions (RQ2), we additionally classified each segment according to role of the participant who uttered it:

- *instructor*—the first author of this paper, an HCI expert with two years of industrial experience who taught the course and moderated each PW;
- *design team member*—a member of the two or three-person student team whose prototype was being tested;
- *audience member*—a member of the student audience;
- *test user*—the student who acted as the test user; and
- *class*—at least two speakers in any of the previous speaker categories (reserved only for segments coded as *Laugh*).

Recall that RQ3 focuses on exploring justifications of design critiques and suggestions. To that end, we developed a scheme for classifying design justification statements according to the *basis* of the justification. Table 4 describes the twelve justification basis categories in this scheme. These categories are listed approximately from strongest to weakest, based upon our perception of what an HCI expert would take to be a good justification. The top four categories are rooted in either established principles (e.g., those described by Norman in [14]) or empirical evidence. Categories that appear further down the table have more to do with personal experience, intuition, or practical concerns. The last category in the table accounts for justifications with no apparent basis.

In order to verify the reliability of our coding schemes, the first and second authors independently coded a 20 percent sample of the video corpus with respect to both the content and the justification basis schemes. We attained a level of agreement of 84 percent (0.82 kappa). Having reached a high level of inter-rater reliability, we had the second author code the remainder of the video corpus.

4. Results

Table 5 presents key summary data on the 16 PWs in our corpus. On average, a PW session lasted 18.4 minutes (SD = 7.4), and contained 176.9 coded segments (SD = 61.1), including 54.2 design talk segments (SD = 36.8) and 16.5 justification segments (SD = 11.6). Not surprisingly, session length was strongly correlated with the number of segments in the session (r = 0.687, p = 0.003). Interestingly, session length was also strongly correlated with the number design talk segments in the session (r = 0.647, p = 0.007) and the number of justification statements in the session (r = 0.698, p = 0.003).

Table 2. Top-level content coding categories

Category	Description	Example
Design Talk	Talk focused on design, including justifications, critiques, suggestions, issues, and strategies	See Table 3.
User Interface Talk	Talk focused on the functionality and appearance of the user interface being tested.	"There's a button at the bottom of the screen." "Show me how this works."
Task Description Talk	Talk focused on the task being performed in the PW	"Was I supposed to do Task 1?"
Task Execution Talk	Talk focused on what the test user is doing or thinking as s/he performs tasks	"I'm clicking here, and I want to change the date."
Activity Talk	Talk directed toward running the PW activity	"It's your turn now." "Any questions?"
Project Talk	Talk focused on the scope or focus of the team's project	"Our project is building a smart home interface."
Took Talk	Talk focused on the prototyping technology being used in the PW	"These sticky notes are awkward." "Go to "Run" mode in WOZ Pro."
Laugh	Laughter uttered by at least two people	[Laughter]
Off Task Talk	Talk unrelated to the PW activity	"My job interview went well!"

Table 3. Design Talk subcategories

Category	Description	Example
Justification	Justifies statements about design (critiques and suggestions) or the design of the interface under test	See Table 4.
Critique	Makes a statement about the goodness of the design	"I don't think that design will work."
Suggestion	Suggests an alternative design	"I think you should re-label the button."
Issues and Strategies	Discusses design issues, assumptions, strategies for arriving at new designs, and tradeoffs among design alternatives	"You might need to iterate again on this."
Meta-talk	Design talk that transcends the specific design under consideration, including comparisons with other designs and general conceptual design issues	"It's a question of how to do good layout." "The issue really is, what is a screen link?"
Encouragement	Congratulates the designers or encourages them to continue their work	"You'll get there." "Keep at it."
Response	Responds to design talk or expresses understanding of design.	"Good point." "That's a tough call." "I see where you're coming from."

Table 4. Justification basis subcategories

Category	Description	Example
Design principle	Appeals to, or implicitly enlists, an established design principle.	"That's a poor natural mapping."
Test user behavior	Based on what the test user actually did, thought, or expected during the prototype walkthrough.	"The user stumbled when he saw it."
Past user behavior	Based on the behavior of a user in a past user study (out prior to the PW).	"Users had trouble with this in a previous study."
Other computer software	Appeals to the design of other similar computer software.	"I think the way Photoshop does it is better."
Limitations of prototyping technology	Based on perceived limitations of the prototyping software used for the walkthrough.	"Art supplies made it difficult to create polished buttons."
Implementation Difficulty	Based on the perceived difficulty of implementing the design in a given way.	"Ideally, you could freeform draw it, but that would be hard to implement."
Limitations of PW Activity	Based on limitations of the PW activity, including the tasks and their ordering.	"The fact that he did these tasks in a certain order gave him an advantage."
Personal Experience	Based on the speaker's personal experience.	"When I've done this in the past, I've always had trouble with making tables."
Hypothetical user	Appeals to what a hypothetical user might do or think in given set of circumstances	"A user wouldn't know how to interpret that."
Logic or common sense	Based on logic, reason, or common sense, or the need to accommodate "real world" scenarios.	"The label needs to be changed because the current label doesn't make sense."
No basis	Justification that has no apparent basis	"It's the best we could come up with."

Table 5. Summary data on PW sessions

Session	Dur. (Min)	Total Segments	Design Talk Segments	Justification Segments
Sp07-1	21.5	143	58	12
Sp07-2	24.0	160	34	5
Sp07-3	8.1	100	3	0
Sp07-4	15.6	101	32	12
Sp07-5	34.1	216	85	39
Sp07-6	24.1	195	77	36
Sp07-7	13.4	126	7	4
Sp08-1	8.8	100	24	13
Sp08-2	18.0	241	102	34
Sp08-3	19.1	190	44	20
Sp08-4	17.5	236	108	23
Sp08-5	27.5	259	75	23
Sp08-6	21.5	238	65	30
Sp08-7	22.4	270	116	32
Sp08-8	8.5	108	18	7
Sp08-9	11.0	148	19	8

In this section, we treat the *individual PW session* as the unit of analysis. Hence, the percentages we present and analyze reflect the *mean* percentages of categorized talk across the 16 PW sessions, not the *overall* percentages of categorized talk in the 16 PW sessions combined. Analyzing the data in this way gives equal weight to each PW session, rather than weighting each session by its length.

4.1 PW Content and Contributions

We first explore our data relevant to RQ1 and RQ2. Figure 2 presents the mean percentage of talk dedicated to each of the high-level content categories within a PW session. Within each category, the talk is broken down further by participant type. As Figure 2 indicates, three categories of talk dominated the PW discussions:

- Design Talk ($M = 27.8\%$, $SD = 13.5\%$), which focused on actual user interface design issues;
- User Interface Talk ($M = 24.7\%$, $SD = 11.6\%$), which focused on helping PW participants better understand the user interface being tested; and
- Task Execution Talk ($M = 23.0\%$, $SD = 10.1\%$)—the test user's think aloud protocol, which provided a basis for evaluating the strengths and weaknesses of the user interface being evaluated.

Inspection of Figure 2 suggests that each participant type contributed in different quantities to the PW discussions. Figure 3 brings this into sharper focus by presenting the mean percent contribution of each participant type. As Figure 3 illustrates, members of the design team who were simulating their interfaces contributed roughly one-third of the discussion content—the most of any participant type. Not far behind were the test user, who thought aloud while completing tasks with the design team's prototype interface, and the course instructor, who facilitated the PW sessions; both contributed roughly one-quarter of the discussion content on average. Audience members were not as extensively involved, contributing 10 percent of the talk. The

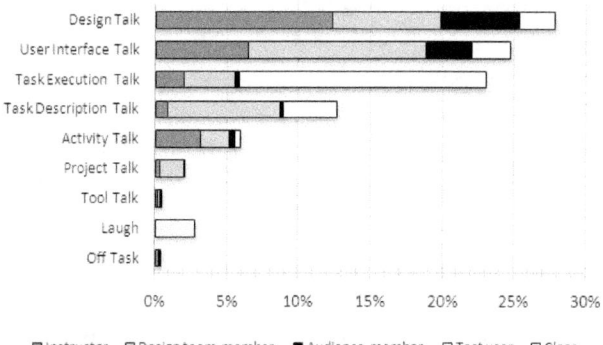

Figure 2. Mean PW session content classified by content category (see Table 2) and participant type. Note that the "Class" participant type applies only to "Laugh" content.

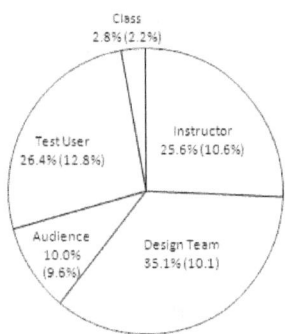

Figure 3. Mean contribution of participant types to all talk (standard deviations in parentheses)

"class" speaker type, used only in conjunction with Laugh segments, contributed just under three percent, reflecting the fact that, on average, roughly three percent of PW discussion content consisted of laughter.

In examining Figure 2, one also sees that each participant type contributed different types of talk to the PW sessions. According to a chi-squared test of homogeneity, the distribution of talk across our high-level content categories varied significantly by participant type, $\chi^2(18, N = 2741) = 1370.0$, $p = < 0.0001$.[1]

Figure 4 takes a closer look at Design Talk, breaking it down both by the subcategories described in Table 3, and by participant type. As can be seen, roughly one-third of Design Talk statements consisted of critiques of the user interfaces being presented in the PWs ($M = 12.7\%$, $SD = 23.8\%$), or suggestions for improvement ($M = 20.5\%$, $SD = 9.7\%$). Roughly another third of Design talk statements either justified those critiques and suggestions, or justified the design of the user interfaces being considered in the PWs ($M = 35.1\%$, $SD = 15.3\%$). The remaining third of Design Talk was dominated by discussion of issues and strategies, and direct responses to other Design Talk.

Figure 4 suggests that participant types contributed in different quantities to Design Talk. Figure 5 illuminates these differences by presenting the mean contribution of each participant type. As Figure 5 shows, over 40 percent of Design Talk statements came

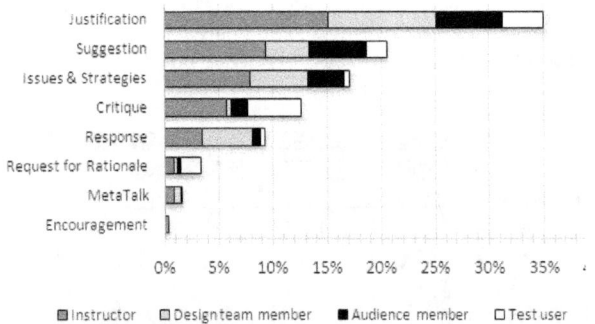

Figure 4. Design talk content classified by Design Talk subcategory (see Table 3) and participant type

---

[1] Because chi-squared tests of homogeneity test categorical frequencies, they cannot be applied to session means. Hence, this test was applied to the corpus as a whole. When we performed chi-squared tests on each of the 16 PW sessions individually, we obtained similar statistically significant results.

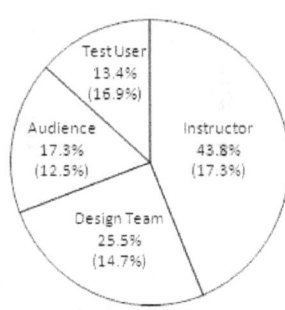

Figure 5. Mean contribution of participant types to Design Talk (standard deviations in parentheses)

from the instructor, with design team members contributing roughly one quarter of the statements, and test users and audience members each contributing less than one-fifth of the statements. Interestingly, the four participant types' contributions differ from their contributions to overall talk: Whereas the instructor and audience members contributed a *greater* percentage to Design Talk than to overall talk, design team members and the test user contributed a *smaller* percentage.

Figure 4 also indicates that participant types contributed different types of Design talk. A chi-squared test of homogeneity confirms that the distribution of talk across Design Talk subcategories differed significantly by participant type, $\chi^2(12, N = 871) = 68.3$, $p < 0.0001$. This is consistent with the findings for overall talk, and reflects the differing roles that participants played in the PW activity.

4.2 How Design Statements Were Justified

We now shift to an exploration of data relevant to RQ3. On average, 9.7% ($SD = 5.2\%$) of the segments of each PW session were coded into the Design Justification category. Figure 6 breaks these segments down according to the taxonomy of justification bases presented in Table 4, For each justification basis, a stacked bar additionally indicates the contribution of each participant type.

As the chart indicates, an average of 30.0% ($SD = 18.6\%$) of justifications were rooted in either empirical evidence (test user behavior, past user behavior), or the design principles taught in the course. Of the remaining justifications, appeals to common sense ($M = 22.9\%$, $SD = 12.5\%$), a hypothetical user ($M = 20.6\%$ $SD = 17.2\%$), other software ($M = 8.0\%$, $SD = 7.4\%$), and personal experience ($M = 5.2\%$, $SD = 7.0\%$) were most common. Practical concerns, including perceived difficulties in implementing a given design ($M = 3.59\%$, $SD = 4.1\%$), limitations of the prototyping technology 3.3%, $SD = 5.5\%$), and limitations of the PW activity itself ($M = 2.9\%$, $SD = 5.9\%$), were less common. Just 3.6% ($SD = 4.7\%$) of justifications had no basis whatsoever.

We believe empirical evidence and design principles form the strongest basis for critiques and suggestions regarding user interface design. These are the "good" kinds of justifications that HCI instructors would like to model, and that HCI students would ideally learn to enlist within an HCI course. Given this, we wondered whether the instructor (an HCI expert with two years of industrial experience) enlisted significantly more "good" justifications than the students. To explore this, we pooled (a) design principle, test user behavior, and past user behavior into one category ("good" justifications), and (b) the audience, test

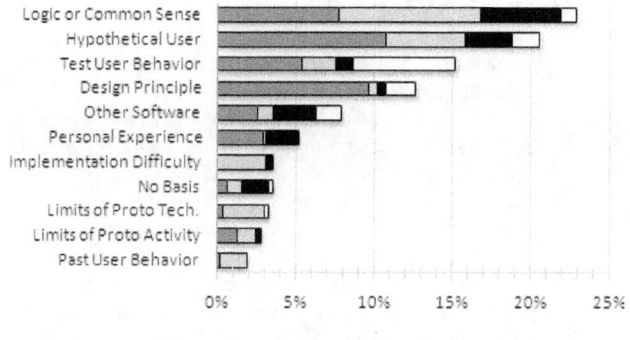

Figure 6. Justifications classified by basis (see Table 4) and participant type

user, and design team into one category ("all students"). After partitioning our data in this way, we found that, on average, 32.5% (*SD* = 30.0%) of the instructor's justifications, and 24.7% (*SD* = 26.8%) of all students' justifications were "good." According to a non-parametric Kruskal-Wallis test, the difference was not statistically significant, (df = 1, H = 0.25, p = 0.62). In other words, we could find no distinguishable difference between the instructor and students with respect to the goodness of their design justifications.

5. DISCUSSION

The results just presented provide a rich descriptive account of the PW activity, including the content of the discussions it promoted, the degree to which people participated in those discussions, and the strategies people used to justify design. In light of these results, we now reconsider the three research questions we posed for this study.

5.1 Relevance of PW Discussions

In order for the PW activity to be a valuable learning activity in an HCI course, it needs to promote discussions that are *relevant* to the course. Accordingly, our first research question focused on the degree to which the PW activity promoted discussions that are relevant to user interface design issues.

Our results provide strong evidence that the discussions were, in fact, dominated by relevant issues. Indeed, on average, Design Talk consumed nearly 28 percent of PW discussions. In addition, User Interface Talk, which is arguably also highly relevant to user interface design because it considers the functionality and presentation of the user interfaces under test, constituted nearly 25 percent of PW discussions. Taken together, Design Talk and User Interface Talk constituted over half of PW discussions on average. Nearly all of the other talk, while not directly related to user interface design, was at least related to the PW activity. Less than one percent of PW discussion talk was off-task.

5.2 Student Participation in PW Discussions

Given our theoretical framework (situated learning theory [12]), which holds that learning takes place through increasingly central participation in community practices, our second research question considered the degree to which students participated in the PW activity. Our results provide solid evidence not only that students participated extensively in the PW activity, but also that the activity promoted levels of participation that differed both quantitatively and qualitatively according to the role that students played in the activity.

At the periphery of the PW activity were student audience members, who contributed the least to the discussions (10 percent). In this role, students mainly observed the activity; however, when they did contribute, their contributions were most likely to be on the topics that were most relevant to the course: Design Talk and User Interface Talk. We speculate that, in their roles as somewhat detached observers, audience members were in a good position to focus and reflect intently on user interface and design issues, without being distracted by the procedural details of the activity.

More centrally involved in the PW activity were the test users, who completed tasks with the interface. One of the key skills to be developed in an HCI course, especially one that consists mainly of computer scientists (as was the case in the courses we studied), is the ability to step away from one's interest in technology development, and into the shoes of users of the technology [14]. The PW activity provided students with valuable opportunities to do just that. Test users were actively involved in the activity, contributing about one quarter of the overall talk task. Owing to the nature of the role, most of test users' contributions were Task Description and Task Execution segments, although they also contributed modestly to Design Talk and User Interface Talk.

Most centrally involved in the PW activity were design team members, who were charged with describing tasks, simulating their user interface, and ultimately explaining and defending their designs. In this role, students had valuable opportunities to engage in two authentic practices of the software industry. First, they got a taste of what it might be like to run a low fidelity prototype test—an important early evaluation activity. Second, they got a taste of what it might be like to present a preliminary design to a software team with an especially critical eye.

Because they were responsible both for describing the tasks to be performed, and for simulating their interface for those tasks, design team members contributed more Task Description Talk and User Interface Talk than any other participant role. They also contributed the most Project Talk, which focused on their overall interface design projects, including its background and history.

5.3 Approaches to Justifying Design

We believe a hallmark of HCI expertise is the ability to make statements about design that are firmly grounded in empirical evidence, established theories, and established design principles. Accordingly, our third research question focused on the ways in which design statements were justified. We found that, on average, just 3.6 percent of design statements had no justification, whereas 30 percent of design statements were rooted in empirical evidence or an established theory or principle. We might have hoped that more than 30 percent of design statements would be grounded in evidence or theory; however, there were no significant differences detected between students (M = 24.7%, SD = 26.8%) and the instructor, an HCI expert (M = 32.5%, SD = 30.0%). Moreover, without data from similar empirical studies of design discussions in the software industry, we have no way of knowing whether our results differ from those in the software industry.

6. CONCLUSIONS AND FUTURE WORK

In this paper, we have introduced the PW, a studio-based learning activity for HCI education. We have presented a detailed content analysis of 16 PWs that took place in a conjoint undergraduate/graduate HCI course. For HCI educators considering the use of the PW in their own courses, our study furnishes at least three key pieces of empirical evidence:

- PWs promote pedagogically-relevant discussions and active student participation.
- PWs provide students with opportunities to apply their emerging HCI design knowledge by grounding their design statements in empirical evidence and established theories and principles.
- PWs provide opportunities for increasingly central participation in a community of HCI practice [12].

Our findings must be interpreted with some caution. Although they are based on data from two different classes, the same instructor taught both classes at the same university. Hence, the impact of the instructor and the local university culture of the cannot be overlooked. Moreover, the instructor is also the first author of this paper. However, when he taught the course, he had no knowledge of the study's research questions and coding scheme, which were developed over a year later.

We believe that detailed analyses of in-class *processes* like the ones presented here are an important complement to traditional studies of student *outcomes* in computing education. Not only can they provide evidence of learning *in-context*; they can also give insight into how best to design activities in order to promote learning and engagement

The analyses we have presented represent a "quick tour" of our results. In ongoing work, we are preparing a longer article that presents our results in greater depth. The article will include (a) a more detailed analysis of justifications, with analyses of justification *strength* and a richer account of justification bases than could be provided here; (b) an exploration of session-to-session differences, in order to identify features that promoted productive design discussions; and (c) a qualitative analysis of discussions.

Given that computing instructors have limited class time to accommodate studio-based activities like the PW, we would like to explore, in future work, the possibility of conducting studio activities asynchronously online. To that end, we are developing the Online Studio-Based Learning Environment (OSBLE), a learning management system specifically tailored to support the collaborative critical review of student-constructed artifacts. We plan to use OSBLE as a basis for performing detailed empirical comparisons of face-to-face and asynchronous reviews of user interface designs, computer code, and other key disciplinary artifacts of the computing profession.

7. ACKNOWLEDGMENTS

This research is funded by the National Science Foundation under grant nos. CNS-0721927 and CNS-0939017. Contributions to this work by other members of the research team—Michael Trevisan, N. Hari Narayanan, Dean Hendrix, Martha Crosby, Margaret Ross, and Rita Vick—are gratefully acknowledged. Collaboration between C. Hundhausen and M. Petre was supported by M. Petre's Royal Society Wolfson Research Merit Award.

8. REFERENCES

[1] Arvola, M. and Artman, H. 2008. Studio life: The construction of digital design competence. *Digital Kompetanse*. 3, February (2008), 78-96.

[2] Cennamo, K. et al. 2011. Promoting creativity in the computer science design studio, *Proc. 42nd ACM SIGCSE Symposium*, ACM, New York, 649-654.

[3] Cross, N. 2001. Design cognition: results from protocol and other empirical studies of design activity, *Design Knowing and Learning: Cognition in Design Education*, C.M. Eastman et al., eds., Elsevier Sci., Oxford, 79- 103.

[4] Docherty, M. et al. 2001. An innovative design and studio-based CS degree, *Proc.32nd SIGCSE Symposium*, ACM, New York, 233-237.

[5] Hundhausen, C.D. 2002. Integrating algorithm visualization technology into an undergraduate algorithms course: Ethnographic studies of a social constructivist approach. *Computers & Education*. 39, 3 (2002), 237-260.

[6] Hundhausen, C.D. and Brown, J.L. 2008. Designing, visualizing, and discussing algorithms within a CS 1 studio experience: an empirical study. *Computers & Education*. 50, 1 (2008), 301-326.

[7] Hundhausen, C.D. et al. 2009. Studying Prototype Walkthroughs in an HCI Course: Video Analysis Manual (ver. 20), http://eecs.wsu.edu/~veupl/pub/PW-v20.doc.

[8] Hundhausen, C.D. et al. 2008. Exploring studio-based instructional models for computing education, *Proc. 39th SIGCSE Symposium*, ACM Press, New York, 392-396.

[9] Hundhausen, C.D. et al. 2008. The design and experimental evaluation of a tool to support the construction and wizard-of-oz testing of low fidelity prototypes, *Proc. 2008 IEEE VL/HCC Symposium*, IEEE, Piscataway, NJ, 86-90.

[10] Hundhausen, C. et al. 2010. Does studio-based instruction work in CS 1?: an empirical comparison with a traditional approach, *Proc.41st ACM SIGCSE Symposium* ACM, New York, 500-504.

[11] Kehoe, C.M. 2001. *Supporting critical design dialog*, Unpublished Unpublished Ph.D. Thesis, College of Computing, Georgia Institute of Technology.

[12] Lave, J. and Wenger, E. 1991. *Situated Learning: Legitimate Peripheral Participation*. New York. Cambridge University Press.

[13] Myneni, L. et al. 2008. Studio-based learning in CS2: An experience report, *Proc. 46th ACM Southeast Conference (ACM-SE 2008)*, ACM Press, New York, 253-255.

[14] Norman, D.A. 1990. *The Design of Everyday Things*. New York. Doubleday.

[15] Preece, J. et al. 2002. *Interaction Design: Beyond Human-Computer Interaction*. New York. John Wiley & Sons.

[16] Reimer, Y.J. and Douglas, S.A. 2003. Teaching HCI design with the studio approach. *Computer Science Education*. 13, 3 (2003), 191-205.

[17] Sachs, A. "Stuckness" in the design studio. *Design Studies*. 20, 2, 195-209.

[18] Schön, D. 1987. *Educating the reflective practitioner*. San Francisco. Jossey-Bass Publishers.

[19] Suthers, D. and Hundhausen, C. 2003. An experimental study of the effects of representational guidance on collaborative learning processes. *Journal of the Learning Sciences*. 12, 2 (2003), 183-219.

Learning Web Development: Challenges at an Earlier Stage of Computing Education

Thomas H. Park   Susan Wiedenbeck
College of Information Science and Technology
Drexel University
3141 Chestnut Street
Philadelphia, PA 19104 USA

{thomas.park, susan.wiedenbeck}@drexel.edu

ABSTRACT
Web development can provide a rich context for exploring computer science concepts and practicing computational creativity. However, little is known about the experiences that people have when first learning web development. In this paper, we investigate the help-seeking activity of forty-nine students in an introductory web development course. By applying content analysis to the help forums of the course, we characterize the challenges they encountered and sought help for, relating them to *development*, *instruction*, *technology*, *content*, and *design* issues. We apply a second level of content analysis to the development issues, identifying aspects of learning HTML, CSS, and JavaScript that challenged students most often. Finally, we identify several computational concepts that relate to these challenges, including *notation*, *hierarchies and paths*, *nesting*, *parameters and arguments*, and *decomposition and abstraction*. We conclude with a discussion on the implications of our findings for computing education.

Categories and Subject Descriptors
K.3.2 [**Computers and Education**]: Computer and Information Science Education – *computer science education, curriculum, literacy*; I.7.2 [**Document and Text Processing**]: Document Preparation – *hypertext/hypermedia, markup languages, scripting languages*.

General Terms
Design, Human Factors

Keywords
web development, computing education, help seeking

1. INTRODUCTION
Web development can benefit computing education by building two bridges: one that links programming courses to more elementary stages of computing education, and another that links new learning experiences to the extensive computing experiences that students already possess.

Permission to make digital or hard copies of all or part of this work for personal or classroom use is granted without fee provided that copies are not made or distributed for profit or commercial advantage and that copies bear this notice and the full citation on the first page. To copy otherwise, or republish, to post on servers or to redistribute to lists, requires prior specific permission and/or a fee.
ICER'11, August 8–9, 2011, Providence, Rhode Island, USA.
Copyright 2011 ACM 978-1-4503-0829-8/11/08...$10.00.

First, web development can serve as a context for an earlier stage of computing education. Here, we mean "earlier" in the sense that it precedes programming, independent of the age or education level of the learner. An introductory web development course can bridge computer literacy courses that teach the effective *use* of applications with programming courses that teach the effective *creation* of them. Through HTML and CSS, students have the opportunity to interact with computer science concepts and create computational artifacts even before taking their first programming course. Students can in turn appreciate and gain confidence in acting as designers of software rather than merely users [27]. Eventually, web development can provide a natural progression to programming through languages like JavaScript.

There is a growing emphasis on computing education that precedes the introduction of programming. Students entering post-secondary computer science (CS) programs have been noted to lack an effective model of computers, presenting "a serious obstacle" to learning [2]. Lu and Fletcher [18] put forth the analogy that programming is to CS as proof construction is to mathematics; while primary and secondary education builds a substantial foundation of mathematics prior to proof construction, such a foundation is largely absent for students learning to program. diSessa [5] calls for computation to be considered a basic literacy in its own right, on equal standing with reading, writing, and mathematics as subjects that all people should be taught. Wing [32] similarly asserts that computational thinking develops problem-solving skills that can benefit everyone, not just programmers-in-training. Resnick [24] stresses the importance today of possessing technological *fluency* – the ability to design and create "things of significance" using computing technology.

Though a number of case studies demonstrate the viability of web development in CS curricula [16, 19, 23, 30, 29], they are positioned mainly as *programming* courses. Interviews conducted by Dorn and Guzdial [7] similarly focus on the programming knowledge that professional web developers have acquired. Further research is needed to determine how web development can help build the *foundations* that benefit students later when learning to program.

Second, web development provides an opportunity to relate new concepts to contexts that are already personally and socially meaningful to students. Students are likely to enter a web development course possessing substantial experience with the web – as of September 2009, 93 percent of Americans aged 12 to 17 have been online [15]. The ideas that students have formed about computing based on these experiences are robust, and regardless of their correctness, they can act as building blocks for further learning [17].

This meaningful context can also bolster student enthusiasm toward computing. Through a series of interviews, Rosson, Ballin, and Nash [26] illustrate the diverse ways that web development can entice people to engage more deeply with computing. Guzdial [10] describes an introductory CS course for non-majors that adopts the theme of *computation for communication* – programming to manipulate audio, video, and other forms of media. Compared to traditional CS courses, this media computation course was effective in attracting students and keeping them engaged [9]. The authors recount, "…many reported that learning how the Web works and creating their own pages was the most enjoyable aspect of the course" [8]. These results are particularly encouraging given that many professional web designers express a desire to learn more advanced computing concepts, but believe CS programs to be too far removed from the creative design and real-world audience that motivate them [6].

Given the potential of web development for earlier stages of computing education, the goal of our study is to understand *how* it can effectively serve this purpose. Our approach is to identify the aspects of an introductory course for which students lacking a CS background and programming experience seek help. By characterizing these challenges, we aim to attain a better understanding of the experiences that students have learning web development.

First, we want to explore the full range of challenges faced when learning web development. Second, we are specifically interested in the challenges encountered when learning to manipulate HTML, CSS, and JavaScript code. Finally, we wish to identify computational concepts that underlie these challenges. We suspect that most of the challenges are not idiosyncratic, but relate to common computational concepts. By recognizing these concepts, students can establish a generative foundation to resolve future, unforeseen challenges, ensuring that their knowledge does not obsolesce as rapidly as the particular technologies used to gain it [12].

We recognize that these challenges have the potential to be both obstacles and opportunities for the classroom. Certainly, they can impede progress and induce frustration, anxiety, and attrition among students. Yet, challenges are also an important element of learning, contributing to student motivation and satisfaction [1]. They set the stage for "teachable moments" [11]; in other words, conceptual conflict induced by a challenge can lead to a restructuring of beliefs and the assimilation of new ideas [22]. They can spur help seeking, certain forms of which are a valuable skill for learning [20]. By resolving challenges with the aid of an instructor or classmate, the student can learn to resolve similar issues without assistance [31]. Lastly, help seeking can lead to collaborative problem solving, benefiting the helper and the observer as well as the help seeker.

In summary, our research questions are:

1. What are the challenges that students without programming experience encounter in an introductory web development course?

2. What are the challenges that students without programming experience encounter specific to HTML, CSS, and JavaScript?

3. How do the identified challenges relate to computational concepts?

In the rest of our paper, we describe our method, present our results, and discuss their implications for computing education.

2. METHOD

To uncover challenges that students face when learning web development, we examined help-seeking activity in an online course. We describe our methods in the following sections.

2.1 Data Collection

The introductory web development course was offered online to students pursuing Master's degrees in Library and Information Science. Students enter this course with extensive computing experience as end users, but negligible programming experience.

The course ran for ten weeks and introduced the topics shown in Table 1. During the first eight weeks of the course, each student developed a website incrementally as new topics were introduced, using a barebones text editor. During the final two weeks of the course, students developed a second website and were free to use any tools of their choice. Help forums were available where they could post questions to classmates and the instructor. Participation in the forums was voluntary.

Data was collected from two sections of the course taught in the fall terms of 2008 and 2009. A single instructor, who operated independently of the authors, taught both of these sections. From the forums, we collected each post's body, title, author, and timestamp. These sections comprised 49 students (39 females, 10 males). A total of 747 posts organized in 213 threads were collected. On average, students posted 15.24 times (SD=16.52). Figure 1 depicts the distribution of posts among the students.

Table 1. Overview of course topics

Week	Topics
1	Internet overview, FTP setup, copyright
2	HTML, XML, CSS, basic formatting, deprecated tags and attributes
3	Tables, lists, links, design concepts, hexadecimal color values
4	Visual design, graphic images, file types and formats, table layouts, web 2.0, navigation
5	Graphic image creation, background tiles and gradients, search engines, CSS
6	Framesets, inline frames, JavaScript
7	JavaScript, rollover buttons, style sheets
8	Image maps, layout with CSS, CGI
9	Forms, CGI, JavaScript form validator, accessibility
10	RSS, meta tags

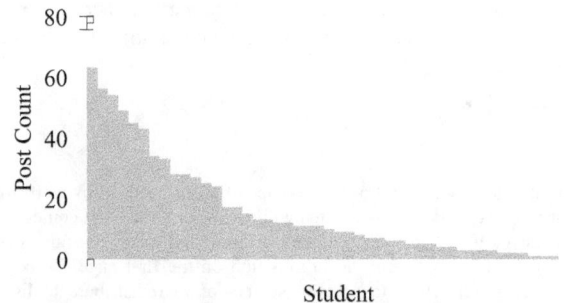

Figure 1. The post count for each student. The most active student made 63 posts, while three students did not post at all.

2.2 Data Analysis

To this data, we applied content analysis, a technique for making valid and reliable inferences "from texts (or other meaningful matter) to the contexts of their use" [14]. We selected the thematic unit of analysis, which can flexibly range from a single sentence to multiple paragraphs. Each post was initially classified as a single instance of help seeking, but was examined further to determine if it contained multiple, distinct codes. In such cases, we divided the post into the appropriate number of thematic units.

To address the first research question, codes were developed inductively from the data to categorize issues that students sought help for through the forums. These codes are summarized in Table 2. Two researchers independently coded a random sample using this code set, attaining over 90 percent agreement and Cohen's κ of 0.841. A κ value of 0.8 or greater generally indicates the reliable application of a code set. A single researcher coded the remainder of the dataset. Posts classified as containing no instances of help seeking were removed from subsequent analysis.

For the second research question, we took help-seeking instances pertaining to development and subdivided them into specific topics. This second level of codes is displayed in Table 3. A random sample was coded independently by two researchers using this code set, reaching nearly 90 percent agreement and Cohen's κ of 0.869. Again, a single researcher coded the rest of the data.

Table 2. Codes for categories of help seeking

Category	Description
Instruction	Asking questions about curriculum, instructions, and assessment
Content	Collecting, creating, and editing text, images, and multimedia
Design	Planning information architecture and visual design
Development	Creating and manipulating HTML, CSS, and JavaScript code
Technology	Selecting, installing, and configuring technology
None	Sharing general information and providing help

Table 3. Codes for topics in development help seeking

Topic	Description
Links	Creating links to other resources
Images	Embedding images
Image Maps	Creating image maps
Tables	Creating tables
Lists	Creating lists of items
Forms	Creating forms with input elements and actions
Frames	Creating framesets or inline frames
Backgrounds	Setting background colors, images, or tiling
Fonts	Setting font styles
Layout	Positioning and aligning elements
Functions	Modifying functions, attaching event handlers
Objects	Instantiating objects
Source Files	Managing source code at the file level

For the third research question, we followed the method described in [4] to derive relevant themes from patterns in the data. Our goal here was to provide an account of computational concepts underlying the help-seeking instances.

3. RESULTS

In this section, we present the results of our analysis, supplemented with illustrative excerpts from the data.

3.1 Categories of Help Seeking

The vast majority of issues students sought help for related to development, instruction, and technology. These three categories combined to make up nearly 90 percent of all help-seeking instances. Over half of all students sought help at least once for each of these categories. Table 4 provides a full breakdown of the help-seeking instances and Figure 2 shows how they occurred on a week-to-week basis spanning the ten weeks of the course.

Table 4. Help seeking by category

Category	Help-Seeking Instances		Students With At Least One Instance	
	Count	Percent	Count	Percent
Development	125	34.3%	25	51.0%
Instruction	109	29.9%	29	59.2%
Technology	89	24.5%	29	59.2%
Content	24	6.6%	16	32.7%
Design	17	4.7%	9	18.4%

3.1.1 Development

Over one-third (34.3 percent) of help-seeking instances related to developing HTML, CSS, and JavaScript code. As shown in Figure 2, students began seeking help of this type in week 2, coinciding with their first exposure to basic HTML and CSS. This activity peaked in week 7 with the introduction of JavaScript, which is not surprising given that it was the third distinct computing language introduced in the course and the first programming language most students had ever encountered. Development challenges remained substantial for the duration of the course and were precipitated by a range of topics. We provide a detailed rundown of these in Section 3.2.

3.1.2 Instruction

After development challenges, instructional issues (29.9 percent) were most prevalent among help-seeking instances. They remained remarkably consistent from week to week and were primarily requests to clarify an assignment's directions or requirements. We expect similar issues to arise in other courses, independent of the subject matter. Nevertheless, two instructional challenges were particularly relevant to our study.

First, one student expressed ongoing distress about the topics covered in the course, explaining that they did not follow modern web development conventions.

> P9: Why aren't we learning web standards? We shouldn't be using tables for website layout, or the font tag. This is no longer done. The only thing we should be using tables for is general information (small data stuff). I am ready to cry. I feel like to get an A in the class I have to do everything the wrong way.

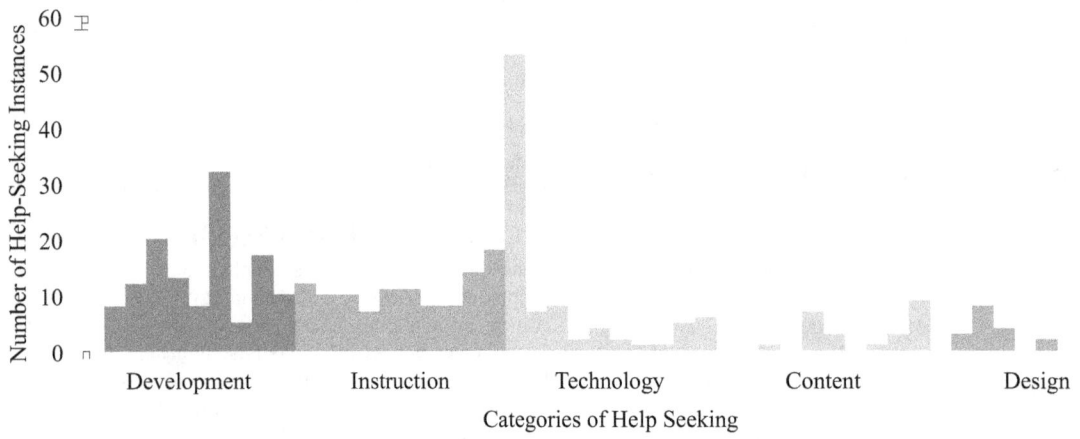

Figure 2. A week-by-week profile for each category of help seeking. Within each category (e.g., Development), the bars from left to right represent the number of help-seeking instances from week 1 to week 10 of the course.

Another student offered a counterpoint, stating that though established practitioners might not use these techniques, they were valuable for pedagogical reasons.

> P1: I know as a high school teacher if I started instruction where I wanted my students to end up, I would lose most of them. I often assign writing assignments that I am not going to correct for surface accuracy, in order to develop fluency. And what about reading? The point of reading instruction is not phonics or reading out loud, but one takes the students through those steps in order to develop silent reading comprehension. You are like the advanced student who needs enrichment activities... I know it must be frustrating, but I hope you can hang in there until the rest of us reach your level.

The first student responded by explaining that even as a beginner, she preferred to learn techniques that adhered to web standards from the start:

> P9: I am not super advanced or anything. I just know some of the web standards rules... I hope the professor gets into CSS soon. I really do not want to design my website in tables, and this global table layout makes me sick to my stomach.

A second instructional challenge faced by many students pertained to the online communication of code. Various forms of media were used to share code during the course, including videos, text documents, and forum posts. Students discovered that some of these media were not well suited for this purpose. A number of students reported difficulty reading code in videos due to their low resolution. In several other instances, students reused example code from Word documents where straight quotation marks (i.e., " ") had inadvertently been replaced with smart quotation marks (i.e., " "), causing errors that were difficult to diagnose. Finally, students often included snippets of their code in their help forums posts. On certain occasions, additional code was automatically affixed to these snippets as a security measure, which students found difficult to disentangle from the original code.

3.1.3 Technology

Technological issues were at the root of about one quarter of help-seeking instances (24.5 percent), creating a significant hurdle at the outset of the course. Web development depends on a wide range of technological concerns beyond the code, including activating shell accounts, configuring FTP programs, and managing web servers. Troubleshooting problems related to these tasks was hampered by the online nature of the course and the diversity of system configurations used by the students. Technological issues in particular sapped student motivation. While attempting to connect to an FTP server and grappling with authentication errors, one student remarked:

> P20: I followed the same exact path you did to try to solve this problem. I still cannot connect... This kind of stuff makes me want to just drop this class. Unfortunately, I need it to graduate this quarter.

Students considered these tasks distractions, diverting their attention from what they perceived as the main purpose of the course. In the first week of the course, a student reported:

> P24: I've dropped the class for now. There seems to be too many problems unrelated to what we are supposed to be learning.

After the initial technological challenges were resolved, other issues emerged on occasion in later weeks and created new impasses.

3.1.4 Content

At 6.6 percent, only a small share of help seeking related to content, revolving around questions about intellectual property. Students asked how copyright and fair use applied when appropriating logos, stock photography, and streaming video from other sources.

3.1.5 Design

Design issues constituted the smallest portion of help-seeking instances at 4.7 percent. These occurred mainly in the early stages of the course when design topics were introduced. Students sought advice on the visual design and information architecture of their sites, for instance figuring out which pages should be included in the main menu.

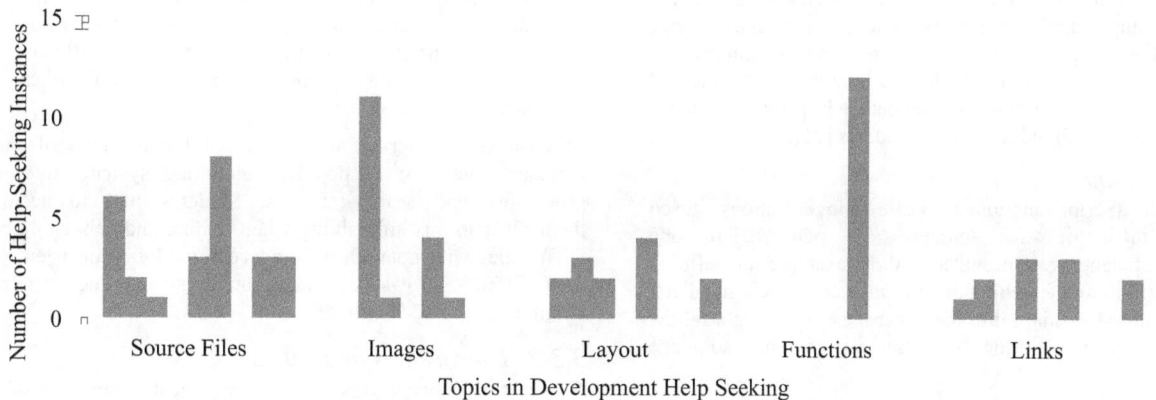

Figure 3. A week-by-week profile for select topics in development help seeking

3.2 Help Seeking for Development

Next, we take a more granular look at help-seeking instances pertaining specifically to the development of HTML, CSS, and JavaScript code. Table 5 shows the different topics that motivated development help seeking and Figure 3 provides a week-by-week profile. For each of these topics, students faced a variety of barriers, such as determining how to use code elements and understanding their outputs [13]. We discuss the most common of the issues in turn.

Table 5. Development help seeking by topic

Topic	Help-Seeking Instances		Students With At Least One Instance	
	Count	Percent	Count	Percent
Source Files	26	20.5%	12	24.5%
Images	17	13.4%	11	22.4%
Layout	13	10.2%	10	20.4%
Functions	12	9.4%	8	16.3%
Links	11	8.7%	7	14.3%
Background	11	8.7%	7	14.3%
Tables	8	6.3%	7	14.3%
Objects	7	5.5%	3	6.1%
Lists	6	4.7%	3	6.1%
Forms	5	3.9%	3	6.1%
Frames	5	3.9%	3	6.1%
Image Maps	4	3.1%	3	6.1%
Fonts	2	1.6%	2	4.1%

3.2.1 Source Files

Among development-related issues, students posted most often about organizing and accessing source code at the file level (20.5 percent). Examples of this included questions about declaring correct document types, assigning different applications to handle source files, and affixing appropriate file extensions. A number of students operated under the misconception that because source files were assigned to default applications based on their file extensions, they could not be accessed using other code editors or web browsers. In another case, a student weighed in on the appropriateness of using the .html file extension for XHTML code.

> P19: I too saved them as html. I believe from the reading that it is fine for xhtml to be saved as html. It doesn't have its own extension.

The frequency of source file issues provides evidence that beyond the manipulation of code at the text level, the management of code at the file level raises a number of challenges for novices.

3.2.2 Images

A significant proportion of development help seeking involved embedding images into web pages (13.4 percent). Students had encountered broken images as end users in the past, but were now in a position to diagnose and act on them.

> P20: I am not sure what I am doing wrong here. After I put the code in for my image upload the only thing I see on my web page is a white box with a red x in it. I have seen this so many times before on other web sites but never knew what it meant other than there should be a picture in its place.

Troubleshooting such a problem, one student remarked:

> P32: Try renaming homeUp.jpg to homeUP.jpg. I [think] this will fix your problem, darn case sensitive browsers! ;-) At least that is my theory at the moment.

Usually, broken images were a result of an incomplete or incorrect path to the image file. Though they were introduced in week 4, students reported difficulties as late as week 8 of the course.

3.2.3 Layout

Layout was another challenge faced by students, motivating 10.2 percent of development help-seeking instances. Students often had difficulty implementing the layouts they envisioned.

> P22: I just created the table containing my thumbnails (not clickable yet), but my tables seem to land wherever they feel like on the page... I can't figure out the rhyme or reason behind it...

Students discovered that they could not specify an element's position by simply applying a property to that element. Instead, layout involved a great deal more indirection and complexity, determined by an interaction of rules, surrounding elements, and the context in which the page was rendered. In prior interviews, layout was similarly found to mystify students [21].

3.2.4 Functions

The use of JavaScript functions to create rollover buttons caused substantial difficulties for students (9.4 percent). In one assignment, students were provided with an example for defining rollover functions and attaching them to images as event handlers, and were required to adapt it to their websites. Assisting a fellow student who was working on this assignment, someone commented:

> P45: I'm not sure if this is all of what's not working, but there are some places in the script definition where you need to replace text with the actual information about your buttons…

Students seeking help with JavaScript functions demonstrated a shallow understanding of the code, unclear on which parts to leave untouched to preserve behavior and which to modify to work with their own sites. As shown in Figure 3, students sought a great deal of help in week 7, during the rollover button assignment, but not in subsequent weeks. This is perhaps an indication of low engagement with this topic.

3.2.5 Links

Closely paralleling difficulties with images were ones creating links (8.7 percent). The most frequent case was a broken link that did not point to its intended destination. Just as with broken images, students would specify an incorrect path to the destination, most often when using relative paths. Another common error students made was forgetting to pair an opening anchor tag with a closing tag. One student confessed:

> P32: I try and create both my opening and closing tags at the same time and then add the content because I have a tendency to forget closing tags. Lets not talk about the time it took me 2 days to figure out why half my page had a link (forgot a </a> to close the link tag).

Even after learning the common culprits for broken images and links, students at times had trouble identifying these errors within their own code. Though relatively basic topics, students sought help for images and links into the later weeks of the course. These difficulties acted as hindrances when students dealt with more advanced topics.

3.3 Computational Concepts

We identified a number of computational concepts that tie together the challenges that students encountered in the course. These concepts include notation, hierarchies and paths, nesting, parameters and arguments, and decomposition and abstraction, which we discuss in the following sections.

3.3.1 Notation

Students grappled with the formal nature of HTML, CSS, and JavaScript notation when translating their intentions to instructions. For instance, when creating links and images, students made minute errors with case sensitivity, white space, and missing delimiters. In their study of problem types in an introductory programming course, Robins et al. [25] found these problems of "little mechanical details" to occur most frequently. A student sums up this challenge of formal notation:

> P14: If there is one thing to learn in this course, it's that the details matter when it comes to writing code… One error – one tiny typo, and sometimes your whole code ends up broken! So be careful when writing your code.

This formality contrasts with the flexibility not only of natural language, but also of popular computing systems like word processors and search engines. Students had to acclimate themselves to this inflexibility when writing and debugging code. Difficulties with notation were exacerbated by inconsistencies in how different browsers handled faulty syntax and barriers to communicating code online.

3.3.2 Hierarchies and Paths

A second concept underlying the most common of the development challenges were access paths, which are used to specify the location of a target within a hierarchy. Students used both absolute and relative paths when creating links, embedding images, and referencing external files. Here, a student diagnosed a problem that another student was having while attempting to reference a file:

> P27: Make sure you have a directory in your class folder on the server that is called "javascript_form folder". If you don't have that directory, your code is not finding your validation script. If you put the .js file in your root class directory with all of your other .html files, then just remove the part of your code that includes "javascript_form folder" in the path.

During the course, students also interacted extensively with hierarchies and paths when managing files on their local machines and using SSH and FTP programs to navigate a server.

3.3.3 Nesting

Nesting – embedding constructs within instances of themselves – is a central feature of markup languages like HTML. Content is enclosed in pairs of tags, and one set of tags is often contained within another. Students were prone to making errors due to the nested nature of markup, forgetting to close tags and instead treating them as sequential commands to be invoked one after another.

> P46: <font size="4">Here is an example of short refrigerator story using the word My<font size="3">

Nesting was most prominent when constructing tables and lists. One student attempted to build a list within a list and described her difficulty escaping the sub-list.

> P5: Okay, my nest is a mess. ha. i see numbers everywhere that i didn't even put in. :0(Also, my nest keeps stretching to the right, and I am not sure how I managed to do this!

Through HTML, students gained extensive experience navigating multiple levels of nested code.

3.3.4 Parameters and Arguments

HTML elements are comprised of tags, attributes, and values, which loosely serve as functions, parameters, and arguments respectively. For example, in `<img src="image.gif">`, `img` is the tag specifying the function, `src` is a parameter of that function, and `"image.gif"` is a particular argument for that parameter.

One student assigned an attribute to an element, and wondered if the attribute required a closing tag of its own.

> P14: Does the <body bgcolor="colorname"> need a closing </> somewhere, and if so where? Or is the </body> closing tag used to close this command?

Parameters and arguments also appeared in the course with the introduction of JavaScript functions and objects.

3.3.5 Decomposition and Abstraction

Students encountered several cases of decomposition and abstraction while learning web development. Decomposition, breaking a program down into subprograms in order to simplify development and maintenance, was practiced when students moved CSS code that was in-line with HTML code to external style sheets. Students were initially unclear on the process and purpose of these changes.

> P46: I don't understand step 7 and 8... It says to open the document from which you cut the styles. So from what I understand, after you cut and paste everything into a new document and name it whatever.css. You then re-open the old index.html document and delete the opening and closing style tags. What style tags are they referring to? Everything that we just added in chapters 7-10 we now have to delete?

After an exchange with classmates, the student began to realize the benefits of decomposition.

> P46: ...so we are creating only one css page that will work for ALL of our .html pages?

Abstraction, hiding the details irrelevant to the current task, was also an aspect of the course. External style sheets and JavaScript files enabled students to readily reuse CSS and JavaScript functionality in their websites without regard for how they were implemented. The use of CSS selectors such as IDs and classes was also a common case of abstraction, allowing students to apply a style to a set of elements with a single command.

4. DISCUSSION

We have characterized a broad range of challenges that students without programming experience encounter when learning web development, and specific difficulties related to HTML, CSS, and JavaScript code. We next discuss the implications of these findings on the role of web development in computing education.

Prior research has found that contextualizing a computing course can foster motivation and engagement among students. However, our study illustrates that this approach can also increase the complexity of the course. The breadth of challenges students sought help for underscore this tradeoff, particularly with technological issues when configuring a variety of software. Because their websites were live on the web, students also expressed concern regarding matters of privacy and intellectual property. Finally, the protests of the student who wished to follow web standards raise the issue of real-world authenticity [28]. Just as the promise of learning authentic practices can generate student motivation, compromising this authenticity on pedagogical grounds can have a strong negative effect.

Many web development courses [16, 19, 23, 30, 29] include a programming component, and the course in our study was no exception. In ten weeks, students were introduced to three distinct computing languages, had their first taste of procedural programming, and learned a wide array of topics beyond that. However, students experienced significant difficulties even with basic aspects of development, such as creating HTML links and lists. Indeed, Blackwell has noted that "as with the use of JavaScript, even the abstractions of HTML provide the opportunity for syntax errors, runtime errors, or bugs in the form of unintended or exceptional behaviors" [3]. Furthermore, students demonstrated a shallow engagement with JavaScript. Taken together, these findings suggest that instead of a web development course that "sprints" toward programming, a more elementary version that delves deeply into HTML and CSS, while reserving JavaScript for a later course, may better serve some learners. Particularly for students without prior experience, a few weeks of instruction may not be a sufficient introduction to JavaScript. Instead, it is likely to create confusion and instill a negative disposition toward learning to program.

Lastly, we have identified a set of computational concepts that permeate the challenges students encounter when learning web development. *Notation* puts students into the mindset of instructing computers using carefully specified language. *Hierarchies and paths* offer ways of thinking about familiar systems such as file systems and the web, while setting the stage for more advanced topics like traversing the JavaScript Document Object Model (DOM). *Nesting* makes frequent appearances in HTML, giving students practice with navigating multiple levels of nested code. Through HTML, students can become familiar with the notion of *parameters and arguments*. By separating content (HTML) from presentation (CSS) and behavior (JavaScript), students apply *decomposition and abstraction in order* to manage complexity. Through an elementary web development course, these computational concepts are introduced in simple, concrete forms and lay the groundwork for further learning.

It should be noted that for many web development courses, including the one in this study, the primary goal is not to teach computer science per se, but to arm students with practical skills for creating and maintaining websites. Even for these courses, the computational concepts we have discussed can serve as an organizing principle. By explicitly addressing such concepts in a web development course, educators can help students to form viable mental models. The end goal in these courses too is to attain generative knowledge that can be applied to web development beyond any particular technology or situation.

5. CONCLUSIONS

This paper reports our investigation of the challenges that students without programming experience encounter in an introductory web development course. We identified a variety of challenges, closely examining those that relate to the development of HTML, CSS, and JavaScript code. We also outlined a set of computational concepts that underlie these challenges and present an opportunity for computing education.

By applying content analysis to the help forums of the course, we were able to study the challenges that caused students to seek help. However, this approach provides only a partial picture. In cases where students read the forums without actively participating, sought help from alternative sources such as a friend or online reference, or simply floundered, difficulties have gone undetected. Furthermore, through our approach, only in some instances did we get a sense of the effect that these challenges had on student confidence and motivation for learning web development. As mentioned in the introduction, challenges can contribute positively to motivation, be dispassionately accepted as part of the course, or act as a source of frustration and discouragement. How different types of challenges impact students differently remains an open question.

Nevertheless, our study provides insight into the experiences that people have in the beginning stages of creative computation, and lends support for web development as a pedagogically rich context for an earlier stage of computing education.

6. REFERENCES

[1] Ames, C. and Archer, J. 1988. Achievement goals in the classroom: Students' learning strategies and motivation processes. *Journal of Educational Psychology*, 80, 3, 260-267.

[2] Ben-Ari, M. 1998. Constructivism in computer science education. In *Proceedings of the ACM Special Interest Group on Computer Science Education (SIGCSE)*, 257-261.

[3] Blackwell, A. 2002. First steps in programming: A rationale for attention investment models. In *Proceedings of the IEEE Symposia on Human-Centric Computing Languages and Environments (HCC)*, 2-10.

[4] Braun, V. and Clarke, V. 2006. Using thematic analysis in psychology. *Qualitative Research in Psychology*, 3, 2, 77-101.

[5] diSessa, A. 2001. *Changing Minds: Computers, Learning, and Literacy*. MIT Press, Cambridge, MA.

[6] Dorn, B. and Guzdial, M. 2010a. Discovering computing: Perspectives of web designers. In *Proceedings of the International Computing Education Research Workshop (ICER)*, 23-29.

[7] Dorn, B. and Guzdial, M. 2010b. Learning on the job: Characterizing the programming knowledge and learning strategies of web designers. In *Proceedings of the ACM SIGCHI Conference on Human Factors in Computing Systems (CHI)*, 703-712.

[8] Forte, A. and Guzdial, M. 2004. Computers for communication, not calculation: Media as a motivation and context for learning. In *Proceedings of the Hawaii International Conference on System Sciences (HICSS)*.

[9] Forte, A. and Guzdial, M. 2005. Motivation and non-majors in CS1: Identifying discrete audiences for introductory computer science. *Transactions on Education*, 48, 2, 248-253.

[10] Guzdial, M. 2003. A media computation course for non-majors. In *Proceedings of the Annual Conference on Innovation and Technology in Computer Science Education (ITiCSE)*, 104-108.

[11] Hansen, E. 1998. Creating teachable moments... and making them last. *Innovative Higher Education*, 23, 1, 7-26.

[12] Klassner, F. 2000. Can web development courses avoid obsolescence? In *Proceedings of the Annual Conference on Innovation and Technology in Computer Science Education (ITiCSE)*, 77-80.

[13] Ko, A., Myers, B., and Aung, H. 2004. Six learning barriers in end-user programming systems. In *Proceedings of the IEEE Symposium on Visual Languages and Human-Centric Computing (VL/HCC)*, 199-206.

[14] Krippendorff, K. 2004. *Content Analysis: An Introduction to Its Methodology*. Sage Publications, Thousand Oaks, CA.

[15] Lenhart, A., Purcell, K., Smith, A., and Zickuhr, K. 2010. Social media and young adults. *Pew Internet & American Life Project*, http://pewinternet.org/Reports/2010/Social-Media-and-Young-Adults.aspx.

[16] Lim, B. 1998. Teaching web development technologies in CI/IS curricula. In *Proceedings of the ACM Special Interest Group on Computer Science Education (SIGCSE)*, 107-111.

[17] Linn, M. 1995. Designing computer learning environments for engineering and computer science: The scaffolded knowledge integration framework. *Journal of Science Education and Technology*, 4, 2, 103-126.

[18] Lu, J. and Fletcher, G. 2009. Thinking about computational thinking. In *Proceedings of the ACM Special Interest Group on Computer Science Education (SIGCSE)*, 260-264.

[19] Mercuri, R., Herrmann, N., and Popyack, J. 1998. Using HTML and JavaScript in introductory programming courses. In *Proceedings of the ACM Special Interest Group on Computer Science Education (SIGCSE)*, 176-180.

[20] Nelson-Le Gall, S. 1985. Help-seeking behavior in learning. *Review of Research in Education*, 12, 1, 55-90.

[21] Park, T. and Wiedenbeck, S. 2010. First steps in coding by informal web developers. In *Proceedings of the IEEE Symposium on Visual Languages and Human-Centric Computing (VL/HCC)*, 79-82.

[22] Piaget, J. 1950. *The Psychology of Intelligence*. Routledge, London, UK.

[23] Reed, D. 2001. Rethinking CS0 with JavaScript. In *Proceedings of the ACM Special Interest Group on Computer Science Education (SIGCSE)*, 100-104.

[24] Resnick, M. 2001. Closing the fluency gap. *Communications of the ACM*, 44, 3, 144-145.

[25] Robins, A., Haden, P., and Garner, S. 2006. Problem distributions in a CS1 course. In *Proceedings of the Australasian Computing Education Conference (ACE)*, 165-173.

[26] Rosson, M., Ballin, J., and Nash, H. 2004. Everyday programming: Challenges and opportunities for informal web development. In *Proceedings of the IEEE Symposium on Visual Languages and Human-Centric Computing (VL/HCC)*, 123-130.

[27] Schulte, C. and Knobelsdorf, M. 2007. Attitudes towards computer science-computing experiences as a starting point and barrier to computer science. In *Proceedings of the International Computing Education Research Workshop (ICER)*, 38-49.

[28] Shaffer, D. and Resnick, M. 1999. "Thick" authenticity: New media and authentic learning. *Journal of Interactive Learning Research*, 10, 2, 195-215.

[29] Sridharan, K. 2004. A course on web languages and web-based applications. *Transactions on Education*, 47, 2, 254-260.

[30] Treu, K. 2002. To teach the unteachable class: An experimental course in web-based application design. In *Proceedings of the ACM Special Interest Group on Computer Science Education (SIGCSE)*, 201-205.

[31] Vygotsky, L., Cole, M., John-Steiner, V., Scribner, S., and Souberman, E. 1978. *Mind in Society: The Development of High Psychological Processes*. Harvard University Press, Cambridge, MA.

[32] Wing, J. 2006. Computational thinking. *Communications of the ACM*, 49, 3, 33-35.

Computing as the 4th "R":
A General Education Approach to Computing Education

Quintin Cutts
School of Computing Science
University of Glasgow
Glasgow, Scotland
+44 141 330 5619

quintin.cutts@glasgow.ac.uk

Sarah Esper   Beth Simon
Computer Science and Engineering Dept.
University of California, San Diego
La Jolla, CA USA
+1 858 534 5419

{sesper,bsimon}@cs.ucsd.edu

ABSTRACT
Computing and computation are increasingly pervading our lives, careers, and societies –a change driving interest in computing education at the secondary level. But what should define a "general education" computing course at this level? That is, what would you want every person to know, assuming they never take another computing course? We identify possible outcomes for such a course through the experience of designing and implementing a general education university course utilizing best-practice pedagogies. Though we nominally taught programming, the design of the course led students to report gaining core, transferable skills and the confidence to employ them in their future. We discuss how various aspects of the course likely contributed to these gains. Finally, we encourage the community to embrace the challenge of teaching general education computing in contrast to and in conjunction with existing curricula designed primarily to interest students in the field.

Categories and Subject Descriptors
K.3.2 [**Computer and Information Science Education**]: Literacy.

General Terms
Human Factors.

Keywords
general education, peer instruction, active learning, CS0.

1. INTRODUCTION
Computing education is seen as increasingly important, with Wing and others arguing for a grounding in fundamental computational principles for the entire population [24]. Actions are being taken to address this. For example, the UK Royal Society has been commissioned to report on the state of computing education in UK schools [19], and the US National Science Foundation and the College Board are supporting the development an Advanced Placement course, CS Principles, which aims to "broaden participation in computing and computer science."[8]

In Fall 2010, we ran a pilot of the CS Principles course at a US R1 institution. One of five pilots, ours was unique in that it served the needs of a university general education (GE) course for 570 students. This raised the question of how a GE computing course should be defined, or, put another way, what should every person know, assuming they never take another computing course? In this report, we tell the story of our experiences in putting together a GE course grounded in the CS Principles framework, and of how it impacted students and our views of GE computing.

As we taught the course we paid close attention to the student experience, with all authors attending all lectures and listening-in directly to students' discussions in the class. When prompted (in Week 8), *the vast majority of students self-reported a range of long-term gains* as a result of taking the course. Analysis of their open-ended responses shows students reporting increased confidence, changed views of technology in the world around them, increased technical problem solving skills, transfer of computing skills to other areas of their life and increased communication skills. Reports of "learning to program" were very rare (and mostly limited to computing majors). These results were very compelling to us as computing educators, with the following examples being representative:

> We learned in Alice that computers do exactly what you have them do.

> Programming allows a person to think more logically, thinking in order and debugging allows the user to gain valuable problem solving skills. Aspiring to go to law school, thinking logically is extremely important and I think this has helped.

> It has given me confidence that I'm able to figure things out on a computer that I never would have thought that I could do.

We will argue that *the gains reported by the students form an excellent definition of a general education course in computing*. Notably we believe that engaging students in "learning programming" is critical to the experience – as it provides students very direct control over the computer. Finally, we draw conclusions on the ordering of computing courses at the introductory level to maximize opportunity of access to computational thinking skills development for all students.

2. INSTANTIATING A CS GENERAL EDUCATION COURSE
Here, we briefly overview the instructional design of our course – though we refer the reader to full details in [20]. Our course was based around:

- existing university needs for an academically-rigorous digital literacy course involving logical thinking and the ability to create digital artifacts in subsequent courses,
- the CS Principles framework, particularly the six defined computational thinking practices of analyzing effects of computation, creating computational artifacts, using abstractions and models, analyzing problems and artifacts, communicating processes and results, and working effectively in teams, and
- published experiences in teaching CS0-type courses.

It included 7 weeks of Alice programming [5] and 2 weeks of Microsoft Excel. Alice is a beginners graphical programming environment: graphical both in the sense that programs create and manipulate 3D worlds, and that writing programs consists of snapping visual tiles together on screen. Most critically, we designed the course around a best-practice pedagogy, Peer Instruction (PI) [13], to engage students in deep learning of computing concepts. We made this decision a) based on the evidence from physics and other disciplines that its use dramatically increases learning [7] and b) because it had worked well in previous programming courses [21]. We were particularly interested in PI's ability to focus students on *understanding how programs work*, not just getting them to work.

In the standard PI model, before class, students gain preparatory knowledge typically by reading the textbook and then complete a pre-lecture quiz on the material. In this class, we leveraged the ability to have students work directly in the Alice programming language to assign, exploratory homeworks – which guided them in reading the textbooks for understanding [20]. During class, lecture was largely replaced by a series of multiple-choice questions (MCQs). These typically focused on deep conceptual issues, common student misconceptions or problems [20]. Students followed a process by which they answered a question individually (using a clicker), discussed in an assigned group of 3, and answered a second time. This was followed by a class-wide discussion led by both the students and the instructor. This is the core of the PI pedagogy. Additional course components included a weekly 2-hour closed-lab programming assignment, one midterm, one final, and a multi-week Alice programming project ("make a digital contribution to communicate your views on an issue facing society").

We hoped the PI methodology, with its focus on analysis and discussion, would influence the students' experience positively. Rather than simply "playing around" with Alice, we believed that the PI activities would engage them in the authentic practices [3] that underlie computing experts' thinking and activities; that by asking them to analyze code and discuss it with each other, they would experience via legitimate peripheral participation what actually happens in software developers' cubical walls, or in the IT support center of a major company.

3. STUDENT EXPERIENCE

We sought answers to questions like: "What if this is the last computing course these students ever take? What are they getting out of it? Does this satisfy us with regards to what an informed populace should know?" We were teaching "programming" but our lectures focused students on analyzing programs to illuminate core concepts. We personally don't believe "ability to write a program" should be a GE course goal. We asked students about their experience in lab during Week 8:

Learning computing concepts may have opened many doors for you in your future work. Although you may not ever use Alice again, some of the concepts you have learned may become useful to you. Some examples include:

- *Understanding that software applications sometimes don't do what you expect, and being able to figure out how to make it do what you want.*
- *Being able to simulate large data sets to gain a deeper understanding of the effects of the data.*
- *Understanding how software works and being able to learn any new software application with more ease, i.e. Photoshop, Office, MovieMaker, etc.*

Aside from the examples given, or enhancing the examples given, please describe a situation in which you think the computing concepts you have learned will help you in the future.

Though this question may seem leading, the topic had been discussed frequently in lecture, and the question needed to be explicit enough for 500+ students to clearly understand what "kind" of answer we sought. Students were informed that any thoughtful answer would receive full credit. A few responses did imply that students had already "been good" as using computers, and class hadn't changed that. Through analysis of this data, we consider students' perceptions of the "general education in computing" effect of the course.

3.1.1 Methodology

After preliminary, ad-hoc review of the responses (N=521) by two of the authors, one author developed a set of descriptive categories reflecting commonly observed themes. Next that author and one other separately coded a random 10% sampling of the dataset, discussed the results, and refined the categories and descriptions until reaching agreement on that sampling. Then both individually coded a new 10% sampling, reaching an 85% inter-rater reliability (counting matches for agreement on each code for each response). Then one of those authors and the third author coded the remaining data (with the third author reviewing the first 10% sample as a training set).

3.1.2 Results

The categories we identified are shown Table 1, along with prevalence (one response could be coded into more than one category, avg. 2.1), with an example illuminating the category.

4. DISCUSSION

Overall, we were satisfied at the ways in which the students felt the course experiences had impacted them. We patently did not want students to think they were "made to learn programming" and we specifically tried to differentiate the course from one seeking to attract students into the CS major or prepare them to take another programming course. Although the content of our syllabus doesn't differ much from such courses, we utilized the course design to engage students in a different experience - specifically through the in-class peer instruction discussions.

4.1 The Student Responses Define General Education Computing

We argue that the students' statements form a core understanding about what general education in computing should be.

We recognize the students' descriptions as a set of transferable skills and attitudes: confidence to have a go with technology; a new appreciation/awareness of that technology; problem solving skills to plan out solutions to problems and then to enact them, detecting and correcting bugs along the way; and communication skills appropriate for discussing issues about computing systems.

Table 1. How The Course Will Help in Your Future: Categories of Student Responses ordered by Prevalence.

Category	Example Response
Transfer, Near (64%): can apply new skills in software use	Using new machinery like sound editing equipment ... will require the ability to manipulate and design using the basic commands to form unique creation. Similar to Alice we will be restricted to the amount of actions we can perform sometimes but through our creativity we can manipulate the basic commands of the music program to create variations not standard to the system. Like how we mad[e] frogs appear to be hopping when in actuality the Alice program does not have a specific method that makes frogs hop.
Personal Problem Solving Ability: Debugging (39%): can logic it out, attempt to or deal with unexpected behavior	I have learned how to target problems when I am working on a computer and use the process of elimination to try to fix the problem instead of just restarting the computer like I used to. This skill partially developed from taking CSE3 and becoming more comfortable with working with new computer programs and dealing with bugs in Alice.
Personal Problem Solving Ability: Problem Design (29%): can develop plan to solve technical problem, can see what requirements exist	We learned in Alice that computers do exactly what you have them do. Using this knowledge, we can understand how programs like Excel and Numbers work and learn that when we are using these programs, we need to specify and be exact with what we are doing in order for the programs to meet our needs and plans.
View of Technology (25%): greater appreciation or understand of technology	Now, every time I find myself playing a video game, I actually understand what makes it work. That these games are not magically produced, that it takes time, skill, and sufficient funds to create these games. I appreciate these games more than before taking this class.
Transfer, Far (23%): can use problem solving skills in other areas of life	I feel that learning the language of computing definitely helps you understand dense reading a lot more efficiently. I personally have noticed that my in-depth understanding of Computer Science wording has helped me understand my mathematical theorems and proofs more regularly than before.
Confidence (21%): increased ability to do things on computer, a can-do attitude	The things I learned in Alice can help me not to be so frightened in general when dealing with technology. Although I am not certain I have absolutely mastered every concept in Alice, I am certain that I have learned enough to bring me confidence to apply these ideas in the technological world. This is a big deal for me, as I do consider myself quite technologically challenged. I think this class has given me tools for life, that can be applied to both my life at home, socially, and at work.
Communication (7%): communicate better about technology	In today's technologically-centered world, using a program like Alice gives us valuable exposure to discussing things technically with other people and explaining clearly what we are trying to do.

To rate the value of these skills, consider the typical knowledgeable IT person, the colleague any office worker calls over when they're having trouble with their PC. He or she is the confident problem solver who can talk to you about your problem. Even though they may not know directly about your software or your issue, they know they'll get there with some educated exploration. Their skills and attitudes bear a striking similarity to those described by our students.

As to whether such skills should form part of a general education requirement, there are two pertinent questions: do all citizens need this skill/attitude set; and is it necessary to formally teach it? The recent push for a broader computing education indicates that society is beginning to accept the importance of computing skills for all; and we use Turkle [23] to argue that a concerted effort is required. Turkle argues that the adoption of computing technology to support our thinking processes has in fact shaped the way we think. Specifically, the Apple Macintosh-style direct-manipulation interfaces introduced in the 1980s encourage us not to look under the surface and not to attempt to understand or appreciate systems deeply. She argues that we have been seduced into an expectation that systems will be easy to use and we are surprised and unprepared when they aren't.

As an example, consider a modern word processing package – a far cry from early, glorified text editors like MacWrite. The underlying document model of the modern version would have been the domain of a professional typesetter in years gone by, yet users expect to be able to intuit the model largely via direct manipulation with what they see on screen. The combination of increasing complexity with incorrect expectations only leads to frustration. When software does something unexpected, most users have no training in how to go about understanding what is going on, and few skills in identifying or correcting the problems they are experiencing. Consequently, to them, software has become something magical and beyond their control.

We can relate each of our students' response categories to the manner in which Turkle's argument suggests most computer users are likely to think.

- *Confidence*: Software systems are too complex for me to understand. When they don't do what I want, I don't know what to do. I can't have an effect.
- *Appreciation*: I don't have any insight into how the technology works and I've never been encouraged to look "under the hood".
- *Problem solving*: Software and computers are meant to be easy to use – I shouldn't need to plan ahead to complete my task; when something happens I don't expect, I haven't a clue where to start – I have to get someone to help me.
- *Transfer*: I've only just mastered Word. Now I've got to start all over again with Excel. Nightmare! It's a different world.
- *Communication*: I can't get the IT person to understand my problem at all. It's as if he's from a different planet.

We suggest that through our GE course, students gain the ability to balance the inherent complexity of software against the knowledge that, with effort and use of appropriate skills, they can understand the software or "figure it out". In particular, they can understand the complex models underlying software via a process of inductive reasoning based on experimenting with the software.

4.2 Comparison with Existing "First" Computing Courses

In schools, there exist current courses that could possibly be viewed as a GE in computing, varying from training in the use of IT, through programming courses, to the introduction of computer science concepts. We assess whether these styles of courses are likely to deliver experiences that our students described.

Before beginning, we acknowledge Papert's early radical general intellectual training based around programming in Logo [16]. There is much commonality between the skills he describes his students developing and those described by our students. A key difference is that of scale – our students are in a traditional mass education system whereas Papert describes a more personalized self-exploratory learning environment.

4.2.1 IT training courses.

IT training is typically centered on the direct use of typical office-oriented packages. For example, the Scottish education system features a 5-14 Information and Communication Technologies (ICT) strand in its national curriculum – traditionally involving follow-the-steps-style worksheets [11]. Assessment often features simple factual recall or production of artifacts – and transferability of skills is hard to assess. Crucially, such courses drive towards outcomes such as "I can create a PowerPoint presentation", rather than anything to do with the understanding of or communication about how to be an effective IT user. In a survey of over 2000 Scottish school pupils [14], it was clear that this curriculum was found to be both boring and a totally inappropriate forerunner to later computing courses. Worse, anecdotal evidence suggests that many incoming university students are barely-adequate IT users. Furthermore, contrary to popular opinion, Bennett [2] demonstrates that the evidence for Digital Natives [17] is far weaker than is widely reported.

4.2.2 Preparation for programming courses

These courses introduce the excitement of creating programmed artifacts without going into the traditional heavyweight detail of a standard CS1. Examples include courses that use robots or the Scratch[18], Alice, or Greenfoot [10] programming environments.

We are unable to ascertain whether students taking these classes have also experienced changes similar to those our students report – though published work does not report such findings. In [15], students' attitudes regarding interest in computing increases in an elective Alice-based CS0 course. Our students were given the same survey, but no statistically significant increase in attitudes occurred – perhaps because students' interpretation of the terms in the questions changed from pre-test to post-test; perhaps because they did not choose to take the course and were not as likely to be pre-disposed to come to like computing. In future work, we seek to better understand this result.

We speculate that the focus in these courses is typically on the excitement of getting programs working, rather than on the deep understanding and articulation of what the students did. For example, in [18], the digital fluency associated with Scratch involves "designing, creating and inventing". Teachers of course do want the deep understanding, but much of the student activity and assessment, where there is any, is most-likely focused on "can you do it?" As Section 4.3 shows, we view the core difference between our course and other programming-oriented courses is the emphasis on articulating deep understanding.

4.2.3 Non-programming introduction to computer science: Excite programs

There is a wide range of programs that aim to introduce computer science without involving programming at machines. The most well-known of these is CS Unplugged [1], and author Cutts has run a similar effort called CS Inside [9]. Both the US and the UK are considering adopting aspects of these programs into nascent school curricula. We refer to these as *excite* programs, because a key aim is to excite participants about core aspects of CS in order to increase enrollment in future computing courses. Indeed, the origins of both programs lie firmly in university outreach activities. The activities of the programs were originally designed for one-off, non-assessed sessions where excitement is the core goal, with learning as a secondary goal. They do use active and often kinaesthetic learning methods that undoubtedly are highly engaging for the participants.

We speculate that the learning activities of these programs will not form an effective general education, as our students' responses define it, for a number of reasons:

- Their main focus is to raise awareness of a broad range of computer science topics, (e.g., data representation, algorithms, cryptography, intractability, etc.) rather than on a narrower core set of transferable skills and attitudes.
- Whilst the active learning embedded in the activities does foster core skills such as problem solving and group work, or core attitudes such as the deterministic nature of algorithms (and hence programs and computers), the rather self-contained nature of each learning activity goes against on-going step-wise development of these skills.
- Their separation from the world of software and machines is likely to make transfer of core generic realizations about the structure and use of computer systems difficult.

4.2.4 A matter of speculation

Here, we have only been able to speculate that alternative course formats considered for introductory computing do not effectively fulfill a general education role. We urge those teaching any of the formats covered here to replicate our open-ended reflection question, presented in Section 3, with their students. Particularly interesting would be the effect on students taking such courses as a *requirement*, as ours did, and not by elective choice.

4.3 Key Effects of the Instructional Design

The Peer Instruction Effect. We believe our instructional design centered in analyzing code (in homeworks, discussion questions in class, and (naturally) programming labs) impacted students. Certainly, instructors hope students in programming courses with standard lecture develop code analysis skills, but it is rare that we focus class time engaging students in that practice for themselves. Even in lab-based lecture environments, students' work with live programming may not engage them in analysis. As Stephen Cooper advised us [4], some students may just play around randomly trying things until they get the desired result. From our classroom observations (two authors observed and engaged students in their group discussions during lectures), the use of PI gave students the opportunity to viscerally develop the understanding that computers are, likely contrary to their previous experiences, deterministic, precise, and comprehensible. Through vigorous, constant engagement in the struggle to not just *create* programs or *learn to use* computing concepts like looping and abstraction, but instead to *analyze, debug, and critique* Alice code, students seem to have internalized these three core attributes of computational systems. We see evidence of this in some students' responses regarding their experiences when something goes wrong on the computer. They now recognize the problem might be the fault of the computer or it might the fault of the user. This stands in contrast to their stated previous beliefs that it was always their fault (or in some cases always the computer's fault). This seems a critical first step in an increased sense of empowerment that should serve them positively in their futures.

Furthermore, the general education literature provides strong evidence in support of the PI process as a way of promoting deep learning. Teasley [22] demonstrates that speaking out one's understanding improves learning; articulating it to a peer even more so. Craig et al. [6] show that paired learners gain as much from watching a video of a tutor at work with another student as from one-to-one tutoring – interesting for the similarities to class-wide discussion (a form of dialogue between individuals seeking clarification and the instructor). Finally, Karpicke has shown in a number of studies, e.g. [12], that testing promotes more learning than studying. We are testing students in every class session, both with the quiz and discussion questions.

Programming with a Visual Execution Model. Could we provide students an equivalent experience by teaching a PI-based course using Excel or other computing applications? Our experience suggests the value of a visual, scaffolded novice programming environment like Alice is that it provides students the most direct form of interaction with the computer possible – programming-language-level control without the distraction of syntax errors and in a way such that every part of their program's execution is visible to them (we didn't cover the topic of variables). Crucially, the mapping from their program code to an observable execution model is very straightforward. To the extent that other existing or future environments meet these criteria, we believe they would work effectively, too. Key is that students engage with a basic programming interface that manages cognitive load, enabling them to focus on core computational concepts.

Instructor Recommendations. Specifically because the technical content of this course matches that of typical introductory programming courses, it is especially important for the instructor to stay focused on the GE goals of the course. It is challenging to change one's habits from rewarding and assessing success in *creating* programs to success in *analyzing and communicating about* programs. How does this challenge play out in class? While clicker questions in class may ask students to select a line of code to complete a program, or to read a program and select a description of what the code does – the manner in which the instructor must interpret students' clicker votes to the question must reflect the goal of analysis, not correctness. Even if more than 95% of the class gets a question correct, that doesn't mean that students have a thoroughly correct understanding of why the answer is right. Moreover, they must still be given the opportunity to practice discussion of the question, providing their explanations to each other, engaging in interactive questioning and justification, and modeling for each other methods of thinking about the problem. In class-wide discussions, as many students as possible should be asked to explain in their own words, both why the correct answer is correct, but also how they figured out the other answers were wrong.

Even more challenging for the instructor is to consider completely different kinds of questions than one traditionally asks on introductory programming exams; questions that ask what is the best explanation of why something is (e.g. why do we used a counted (for) loop instead of a while loop) and even questions (on exams) that ask students to not only give an answer, but to explain their analysis that led them to that answer. Testing whether students can merely "write code", with no other explanation or analysis required, seems to be of limited importance.

4.4 General Education First: An Issue of Equity?

From our experiences of deep reading of students' reports on the impact of the class, we propose that one feature underlies many of our coded categories: the experience of coming to a *new understanding of what a computer is and how one can interact with it*. Overall students seem to grasp that computers are:

1. Deterministic – they do what you tell them to do
2. Precise – they do exactly what you tell them to do, and
3. Comprehensible – the operation of computers can be analyzed and understood.

Is it possible that this visceral understanding (compared to acceptance of telling or quasi-belief) lies at the core of the development of computational thinking skills? Moreover, if one does not yet have this core understanding (as it seems many of our highly-selected college students did not), what is the impact of, for example, a CS Unplugged activity on cryptography, or a course on using Excel effectively for data analysis?

Author Cutts has extensive experience of working with Scottish school teachers and pupils to instill discipline-appreciation through CS Unplugged-style activities. From his experiences, students may overwhelmingly report increased excitement or interest from these experiences, but measurements of learning vary – with a large portion of students seeming having missed even the basic points of the session. This is reflective of learning reports in introductory computing courses. Even in those courses (perhaps CS0) targeted to work with students of any ability, the performance gap for some students seems unassailable. Every instructor has anecdotes of students trying earnestly to master programming, but still failing, if not the course, then failing to develop deep understanding of the core concepts. It is only natural, given repeated experiences, that this may lead instructors to adopt a fixed mindset regarding *some* students' abilities to program. The myth of the programming gene is not so easily dismissed by any experienced instructor.

We posit that lack of understanding that computers are deterministic, precise and comprehensible may be a key factor leading many to struggle, seemingly in vain. Certainly, many students might enter our courses lacking this belief. But some may come to develop it on their own and others may simply be willing to accept yet more incomprehensible magic in the process of programming. We suggest that only some students, with a possibly indefinable set of life experiences, enter our classrooms believing computers can make sense and be reasoned with. Reiterating Turkle's argument [23], as computing has embraced "more intuitive" human interfaces, we have likely actively discouraged attempts to reason about computer interactions.

Core Competencies Before Appreciation. We propose that the community further study the effect of combinations of general education and *excite* or discipline-appreciation courses. Based on our students' claims of the confidence and ability they will have in future engagement with computers and in their increased understanding of where computing concepts exist in their everyday technology use, we propose excite and discipline-appreciation courses will be much more effective when preceded by a GE computing course. As a comparison, multiplication (let alone any advanced mathematical concept) is likely a mystery when taught to students lacking understanding of addition.

It's true, as outreach instructors, we may not have as much fun or personal excitement in teaching a course with the design and goals as outlined here. Not surprisingly, English teachers usually prefer to teach specializations such as poetry or Shakespearean Literature over basic composition. This may be a combination of the fact that students have already moved a bit up the expertise ladder making them easier to communicate and work with. It may be because these courses allow an instructor to better share their passion for a deeper and more nuanced engagement with their subject. It may be that students are more likely to be in such courses based on their own choice, rather than as a requirement. But we suggest that instructors consider the deeply rewarding contribution that lies in opening the eyes of all to the skills and attitudes required to live in the computing age.

Where Have You Left Them? Is 7 weeks of Alice and 2 weeks of Excel, with a carefully supporting instructional design, sufficient to define the grounding in the fundamental principles of computation? Perhaps not. This course didn't even cover variables. Yet students seem to feel they have been given the keys to do something useful, something meaningful – with a minimum subset of computational elements. Given more time, one can prioritize more experiences or understandings we want all citizens to have. However, unless *starting* with programming, these efforts will be hamstrung. We look with interest to see how others adopt and expand this curriculum. Interestingly, by the end of this course, students not only change their views on computing, but they get a significant springboard into traditional introductory programming education. In the short term, this seems a valuable component of any computing course taken by many.

5. Conclusions

We encourage the community to consider the needs of a GE curriculum in computing – in contrast to and in conjunction with courses designed to interest students in the field. We provide an example of engaging best-practice pedagogy in teaching a supportive programming language (e.g. Alice) and see that students report gaining long-term skills and confidence as a result of the course, outcomes that we view as core for a GE in computing. Based on our experiences, we hypothesize that GE computing courses should be taken before other computing courses: including application skills courses, excite courses, or more mainstream programming courses. Moreover, we posit that doing so is a key matter of improving the equity of access to learning in those courses. We encourage the computing education community to engage with GE courses that lift the veil of secrecy and elitism from the field and use of computing.

6. ACKNOWLEDGMENTS

This work was supported by the NSF CNS-0938336 and UK's HEA–ICS. The authors thank Sally Fincher and Steve Draper.

7. REFERENCES

[1] Bell, T., Alexander, J., Freeman, I. and Grimley, M. 2009. Computer Science Unplugged: School Students Doing Real Computing Without Computers. *New Zealand J of Applied Computing and Information Technology*, 13(1), 20-29.

[2] Bennett, S., Maton, K. and Kervin, L. 2008. The 'Digital Natives' Debate: A Critical Review of the Evidence. *British J. Educational Technology*, 39(5), 775-786.

[3] Brown, J.S., Collins, A. and Duguid, P. 1989. Situated Cognition and the Culture of Learning. *Educational Researcher*, 18(1) 32-42.

[4] Cooper, S. 2010. Personal communication.

[5] Cooper, S., Dann, W. and Pausch, R. 2000. Alice: a 3-D tool for introductory programming concepts. *J. Computing Sciences in Colleges*. 15(5) 107-116.

[6] Craig, S., Chi, M. and VanLehn, K. 2009. *J. Educational Psychology*, 101(4), 779-789.

[7] Crouch, C. and Mazur, E. 2001. Peer Instruction: Ten years of experience and results. *Am. J. Physics*. 69 (9) 970-977.

[8] CS Principles website: http://csprinciples.org

[9] Cutts, Q., Brown, M., Kemp, L. and Matheson, C. 2007. Enthusing and informing potential computer science students and their teachers. *SIGCSE Bulletin* 39(3),196-200.

[10] Henriksen, P. and Kolling, M. 2004. Greenfoot: Combining Object Visualisation with Interaction. *Companion to 19th annual ACM SIGPLAN conference on Object-oriented programming systems, languages and applications*, 73-82.

[11] Information and Communications Technology: 5-14 National Guidelines. 2000. Learning and Teaching Scotland.

[12] Karpicke, J. and Blunt, J. 2011. Retrieval Practice Produces More Learning than Elaborative Studying with Concept Mapping. *Science* Vol 331, no. 6018, 772-775.

[13] Mazur, E. 1997. *Peer Instruction: A User's Manual.* Prentice Hall, Saddle River, NJ.

[14] Mitchell, A, Purchase, H.C. and Hamer, J. 2009. Computing Science: What do Pupils Think? *14th ITiCSE*, 353.

[15] Moskal, B., Lurie, D. and Cooper, S. 2004. Evaluating the Effectiveness of a New Instructional Approach. *35th SIGCSE*, 75-79.

[16] Papert, S. 1980. *Mindstorms: Children, Computers and Powerful Ideas*. Basic Books, New York.

[17] Prenksy, M. 2001. Digital natives, digital immigrants. *On the Horizon*, 9(5), 1–6.

[18] Resnick, M., Maloney, J., Monroy-Hernandez, A., Rusk, N., Eastmond, E., Brennan, K., Millner, A., Rosenbaum, E. Silver, J., Silverman, B. and Kafai, Y. 2009. Scratch: Programming for All. *Comm. ACM* 52(11), 60-67.

[19] Royal Society. 2010. *Current ICT and Computer Science in Schools – Damaging to UK's Future Economic Prospects?* Press release.

[20] Simon, B., Esper, S. and Cutts, Q. 2011. *Experience Report: an AP CS Principles University Pilot*. Technical Report CS2011-0965. University of California at San Diego.

[21] Simon, B., Kohanfars, M., Lee, J, Tamayo, K., Cutts, Q. 2009. Experience report: Peer instruction in introductory computing. *41st SIGCSE*, 341-345.

[22] Teasley, S. 1997. Talking About Reasoning: How Important is the Peer in Peer Collaboration? In *Discourse, Tools, and Reasoning: Essays on Situated Cognition*. Springer-Verlag, Berlin, 361-384.

[23] Turkle, S. 2003. From Powerful Ideas to PowerPoint. *J. Research into New Media Technologies*, 9(2), 19-28.

[24] Wing, J. 2006. Computational Thinking. *Comm. ACM* 49(3), 33-35.

Integrating Students' Prior Knowledge into Pedagogy

Colleen M. Lewis
Graduate School of Education
University of California, Berkeley
Berkeley, CA 94720, USA
ColleenL@berkeley.edu

ABSTRACT
A dissertation overview addressing what resources students bring to learning to program, which may provide explanations for why some students are more or less successful learning to program.

Categories and Subject Descriptors
K.3.2 [**Computers and Education**]: Computer and Information Science Education

General Terms
Human Factors

Keywords
Qualitative methods, prior knowledge

1. INTRODUCTION
There is a sense in the field of computer science that students can be separated "into those who can do well and those who can't" [2]. No known factors predict success (see [9] for a review) and researchers argue that differences in "innate talent for programming" [5] or differences in "a fundamental ability" [7] cause the observed bimodal distribution of grades (reported by [2] [6] [7] and [8]). While many initiatives seek to provide more students access to computer science, particularly women and minorities, even prominent members in this equity focused community claim that "Introductory classes should weed students out based on ability and potential" [1]. The focus on static features of intelligence [4], such as "innate talent"[5], "fundamental ability" [7], and "ability and potential" [1], obscures opportunities to develop pedagogy that will help all students be more successful and in the worst case a focus on static features can be used to justify and perpetuate low representation of women and minorities in computer science.

In response to the lack of factors that can predict success learning to program, I hypothesize that student success is shaped not simply by having a particular non-programming competence, such as a skill or set of skills from math, but the degree to which students make productive use of their non-programming competence when learning to program. Emphasizing qualitative methods [3], I address the questions of what productive non-programming knowledge students bring to the computer science classroom, how this knowledge can contribute to success, and how computer science pedagogy can take advantage of it.

Copyright is held by the author/owner(s).
ICER'11, August 8–9, 2011, Providence, Rhode Island, USA.
ACM 978-1-4503-0829-8/11/08.

Identify productive prior knowledge: In Phase 1, I will investigate non-programming resources and non-programming strategies that support students' success. To do this, I will analyze what elements of students' problem solving actions plausibly build from prior non-programming knowledge.

Explore a subset of hypothesized prior knowledge: In Phase 2, I will conduct clinical interviews focused on exploring students' non-programming knowledge that was identified in Phase 1. These interviews will focus on exploring students' resources and ability to adapt these resources to programming contexts.

Develop pedagogy to build upon prior knowledge: In Phase 3, I will embed within an existing online curriculum metacognitive prompts and methods to encourage students to apply non-programming techniques that were productive for participants in Phase 2. Using a design experiment methodology, I will iteratively refine curriculum based upon qualitative analyses of the effectiveness in individual teaching experiments.

2. REFERENCES
[1] Barker, L. J., McDowell, C., & Kalahar, K. (2009). Exploring factors that influence computer science introductory course students to persist in the major. *ACM SIGCSE*, 40, 282-286.

[2] Bornat, R., Dehnadi, S. & Simon (2008). Mental models, consistency and programing aptitude. *Proc Tenth Australasian Computing Education Conference*, Wollongong, Australia, Jan 2008.

[3] diSessa, A. A. (1993). Toward an epistemology of physics. *Cognition and Instruction*. 10 (2 & 3) 105-225.

[4] Dweck (2007). Mindset: The new psychology of success. New York, NY: Random House, Inc.

[5] Lister, R. et al. (2004). A multi-national study of reading and tracing skills in novice programmers. *Working group reports from ITiCSE*,119-150.

[6] McCracken, W.M. et al. (2001). A multi-national, multi-institutional study of assessment of programming skills of first-year CS students. *ACM SIGCSE* 33(4), 125-140.

[7] Reges, S. (2008) They mystery of b := (b = false). *ACM SIGCSE*, 39, 21-25.

[8] Robins, A. (2010). Learning edge momentum: a new account of outcomes in CS1. *Computer Science Education*, 20(1), 37-71.

[9] Simon et al. (2006). The ability to articulate strategy as a predictor of programming skill. *Proc Eighth Australasian Computing Education Conference*, Hobart, Australia, Jan 2006.

Student Views on Learning Concurrency

Jan Erik Moström
Department of Computing Science
Umeå University
Umeå, Sweden
jem@cs.umu.se

ABSTRACT

We interviewed eight students to better understand what kind of difficulties students have when learning concurrent programming. According to these interviews students does not consider concurrency to be radically more difficult than other Computer Science subjects – something that is in contrast to many research papers. Instead the students found concurrency to be an interesting and fun subject that they considered to be approximately equal in difficulty to other subjects. For some, the added complexity only acted as inspiring challenge.

Categories and Subject Descriptors

K.3.2 [**Computers and Education**]: Computers and Information Science Education—*Computer Science Education*

General Terms

Theory

Keywords

Concurrency, Student experience

1. INTRODUCTION

There are many paper available where the authors discusses the problems students have when learning concurrency. In these papers it is not uncommon to find statements that claim that students have problem with X and that the use of tool/language Y will help them. However, some authors do not give any empirical evidence or other references that support their claims of what causes student problems. And it is not uncommon to find a description of a tool/language with no actual evaluation of its usefulness.

When we did a survey of the problems these research papers [1] we were able to categorize the problems into nine groups: concurrency in general, previous experiences, nondeterminism, tools and programming languages, synchronization, creating a mental model, limited by examples, debugging and testing, and finally, problem solving.

2. INTERVIEWS

We did a series of interviews to investigate if the students experienced the same problems that teachers and researchers think they have. The students were asked about their experiences of learning concurrency, during the interviews they were asked to expand on any difficulties they had experienced.

The general impression from these interviews is that the students were *very* positive towards concurrency, much more positive than the author had expected. The students said that it was both an important and a fun subject but not radically more difficult than other subjects. Their answers to the interview questions can be summarized as follows: *It is fun/interesting* – the students seem to be interested in the subject. *Difficulties of concurrency* – most of students said the they had no serious problem with concurrency. *Difficulties with tools and languages* – students at one university had experienced serious problems with the environment, others made no specific comments. *Testing and debugging* – three students explicitly mentioned the complexity of debugging concurrent systems. *Visualization* – only one student mentioned something that could be interpreted as a wish for a visualization tool.

Notable is the lack of mentions of visualization, the one student who - indirectly - mentioned this, only did so in passing. We think this is quite interesting since to many of the surveyed papers emphasize the importance of visualization. We can not explain this difference based on the available data.

3. CONCLUSION

This study only scratches the surface on an interesting subject. The study has a number of limitations that make it impossible to make any far-reaching conclusions. However, it indicates that the students might not experience the same problems that teachers and researchers think they have. Further research is needed to investigate in more detail what problems students experience.

However, we found it very encouraging to see that students had such a positive view on concurrency.

4. REFERENCES

[1] J. E. Moström. Learning concurrency – what's the problem? In *preparation*, 2011.
[2] J. E. Moström. Students experience of learning concurrency. In *preparation*, 2011.

Building Professional Identity as Computer Science Teachers: Supporting Secondary Computer Science Teachers through Reflection and Community Building

Lijun Ni
School of Interactive Computing
Georgia Institute of Technology
Atlanta, GA, USA
lijun@cc.gatech.edu

ABSTRACT
This is a summary of my thesis work, which examines the sense of identity HS CS teachers hold and explores ways of supporting their identity development through a professional development program focusing on community building and teacher reflection.

Categories and Subject Descriptors
K.3.2 [**Computers and Education**]: Computer and Information Science Education–*computer science education.*

General Terms
Design, Experimentation, Theory

Keywords
CS Teacher Identity, Community, Reflection, Professional Development

Introduction
Quality computing education requires quality computing teachers. Teacher education literature, especially teacher identity theory, suggests that a strong sense of teacher identity is a major indicator or feature of committed quality teachers. However, it could be a big issue to establish teacher identity for high school (HS) CS teachers under the current educational system in the U.S., without consistent certificate standards for CS teachers and with computing usually excluded from the core curriculum. The current system does not provide a *typical* context for teachers in the U.S. to build a sense of identity as a CS teacher.

This thesis work centers upon understanding the sense of identity HS CS teachers hold and exploring ways of supporting their identity development through a professional development (PD) program: the Disciplinary Commons for Computing Educators (DCCE). DCCE is an effort dedicated to supporting local computing educators, with a main focus on promoting reflection on teaching practice and community building. With scaffolded activities such as course portfolio creation, peer review and peer observation among a group of HS CS teachers, it offers opportunities for CS teachers to explicitly reflect on and narrate their teaching, which is a central process of identity building through their participation within the community.

In this work, I first conducted an empirical study exploring the teacher identities CS teachers held and factors that contributed to those perceived identities. I then designed and implemented the intervention program (DCCE) to explore how we can support their identity development as a CS teacher, through facilitating reflection on their teaching practices within a community of CS teachers. I used narrative inquiry as a methodological approach to investigating CS teachers' sense of identity through analyzing teachers' narrations on their teaching.

Current findings offer examples of different self-identification and identity features from those who saw themselves as CS teachers, Business teachers, or teachers in both CS and another subject (Math or Business). Overall, these results indicate that a sense of identity as CS teachers was not guaranteed among those who were currently teaching HS CS. These teachers felt isolated and felt the lack of peers and community. Some teachers were not committed to or confident in their CS teaching. Also, four factors were identified that contributed to these perceptions: their educational background and certification, perceptions about the CS field, curriculum and department hierarchy, and the availability of CS teacher communities.

The four cases in study 2 present different examples of participating teachers' identity statuses and changes that happened through their participation in DCCE. Current results indicate that these participants were able to develop a sense of affinity identity with a group of CS teachers, while they failed to build the institutional identity as a CS teacher under the current educational system. These teachers also experienced different self-identity statues and change trajectories along with their participation in DCCE. Results from this study also indicate a potential model of supporting CS teacher identity development through facilitating community building and promoting reflection and learning among those teachers. DCCE provided an inviting context for teachers to explore their identity and achieve a sense of identity as a CS teacher. Participants were able to affirm good practices, see similarities among their teaching, identify ways of improving and get inspired to grow CS programs. These affordances supported their CS teacher identity development by helping them become more confident and committed to CS teaching, get inspired to learn, and build a sense of belonging to a group of CS teachers.

Findings from this research suggest guidelines for designing teacher education and PD programs for building committed, quality CS teachers.

Pedagogical Content Knowledge in Programming Education for Secondary School

Mara Saeli
Eindhoven University of Technology
Eindhoven School of Education
Eindhoven, the Netherlands
m.saeli@tue.nl

ABSTRACT
Dissertation overview, addressing the concept of Pedadogical Content Knowledge for the teaching and learning of programming for secondary education.

Categories and Subject Descriptors
K.3.2 [**Computer Science Education**]: Computer and Information Science Education.

General Terms
Human Factors.

Keywords
Pedagogical Content Knowledge, Programming, Secondary School, Teaching, Learning.

1. INTRODUCTION
The Netherlands is a country where Computer Science (CS) education for secondary school is in its infancy and already facing a crossroad about its future [1]. At the moment it is an elective course, introduced in the school year 1999/2000 [2] and examined only at school level. As for teachers, the official Master programs of Computer Science Education started only in 2006; until than, teachers of other subjects could attend the so called CODI-traject (Consortium for Retraining Teachers towards Computer Science Education; in Dutch: Consortium Omscholing Docenten Informatica) in order to obtain a degree in Computer Science Education. Currently there are about 350 CS teachers [3], most of whom did not receive a formal teacher training in CS, but attended the CODI course. The common scenario is that there is only one CS teacher per school. Considering that in the Netherlands there are around 650 secondary schools, it means that only around the 50% of schools provide a CS curriculum. Also, the majority (67%) of these teachers in 2007 were 50 years old, or more, and therefore coming towards the end of their career.

Summarizing, it is not clear whether CS education in Dutch secondary school will have a future. A research project has been therefore designed to investigate the status of CS education in the Netherlands. To do so, it has been chosen to examine the Pedagogical Content Knowledge (PCK) of this subject, with special focus on Programming. PCK is that expertise that allows teachers to represent, in an effective way, the subject to their students [4]. Therefore, by examining Dutch teachers' PCK it is possible to understand the quality of teaching that is being offered in the country.

Although PCK has been already considered in the CS education research community [6][7], it was soon realized that a knowledge about the PCK was not available yet [5]. It was therefore decided to first conduct an exploratory research with the aim of portraying such knowledge.

The research question leading the exploratory study was: "What is the PCK of Programming in the context of Secondary School education?" The data have been collected in four countries: Italy, Belgium, Lithuania and the Netherlands, using semi-structured group interviews. The results of this study have then been used to examine Dutch textbooks with the twofold goals of devising a research instrument for content analysis and to understand the quality of textbooks available in the Netherlands. In a last study Dutch teachers' PCK has been analyzed by mean of an online questionnaire, comparing their answers to the standard defined in the exploratory study. Also, using the results of the study aimed at examining textbooks, possible relationships between the textbooks used by teachers and their PCK are investigated.

The results of this PhD project (supervised by Prof. Wim Jochems, Prof. Bert Zwaneveld and Dr. Jacob Perrenet) will enable the Dutch government to ponder about the future of this very important discipline in the context of secondary education.

REFERENCES
[1] Van Diepen, N., Perrenet, J. & Zwaneveld, B. (2011). Which Way with Informatics in High Schools in the Netherlands? The Dutch Dilemma. *Informatics in Education*, 10(1), 123-148.

[2] Grgurina, N. (2008). The first decade of Informatics in Dutch High Schools. *Informatics in Education*, vol. 7, no. 1, 55-74.

[3] Schmidt, V (2007). Vakdossier Informatica 2007. SLO – Nationaal expertisecentrum voor leerplan-ontwikkeling. DOI=:www.slo.nl/downloads/archief/341330003_Vakdossier_2007_informatica.pdf/

[4] Shulman, L. S. (1986). Those Who Understand: Knowledge Growth in Teaching. *Educational Researcher*, 15, 4-14.

[5] Saeli, M., Perrenet, J., Jochems, W.M.G.m Zwaneveld, B. (2011c). Teaching Programming in Secondary School: a Pedagogical Content Knowledge Perspective. *Informatics in Education*, vol. 10, no 1, 73-88.

[6] Ragonis, N., & Hazzan, O.: Disciplinary-Pedagogical Teacher Preparation for Pre-service Computer Science Teachers: Rational and Implementation. *LNCS*, vol. 5090, pp. 253-264.

[7] Woollard, J. (2005). The Implications of the Pedagogic Metaphor for Teacher Education in Computing. *Technology, Pedagogy and Education*, 14 (2): 189-204

Copyright is held by the author/owner(s).
ICER'11, August 8–9, 2011, Providence, Rhode Island, USA.
ACM 978-1-4503-0829-8/11/08.

Encouraging Students to Think of Code as an Algorithmic Symphony: The Effect of Feedback Regarding Algorithmic Abstraction During Code Production

Leigh Ann Sudol-DeLyser
Carnegie Mellon University
Pittsburgh, PA
leighann@cmu.edu

ABSTRACT

Students' ability to reason and abstract about code is an important factor in the development of their expertise in producing code. The literature has primary focused on the correlation between measures of students' ability to abstract about code and other skills. The studies and proposed work in my thesis take a mixed methods approach to understanding the impact of feedback regarding algorithmic abstraction and application of contextual scaffolding to problems on the learner.

Categories and Subject Descriptors

K.3.2 [**Computers & Education**]: Computer and Information Sciences Education

General Terms

Human Factors

Keywords

Programming, Pedagogical IDE, Abstraction

1. RESEARCH QUESTIONS

Novices learning CS often struggle with the translational aspect of generating correct syntactical statements as they attempt to write their solutions. The studies proposed in my thesis focus on the problem-solving process where students are formulating a solution and then translating the solution into a language appropriate for the computational device (code production). In code production current systems provide mostly syntactic or results-based feedback to students. In addition to feedback, contextual scaffolding also has the potential to assist students by providing cues to apply during the translation process. There is a debate in the cognitive science literature about the impact of contextual scaffolding on student learning. The hypothesis examined by the thesis are:

(a) Feedback regarding the abstract nature of algorithms will produce better performance in writing of code by novices;

(b) Contextual scaffolding impacts performance in the writing of code by novices;

2. RESEARCH PLANS

The thesis statements will be investigated and tested using a combination of quantitative and qualitative methods focusing on students' performance during and immediately after code writing tasks.. A pedagogical IDE will be constructed to implement the feedback to students.

2.1 Study 1: Refining the Model

This study involves a qualitative analysis of student think-aloud protocols during code production. The students will write code to solve simple array algorithms and either receive feedback from a standard java compiler and JUnit tests, or feedback regarding the algorithmic errors they make. Results of this study will be used to refine the feedback and model of student production for the task domain.

2.2 Study 2: Learning Gains

Study 2 involves a tutoring system which uses a pedagogical IDE to provide students with feedback regarding the algorithmic components of their code. This feedback is compared to feedback focused on the resulting values of a code execution. An experimental design is used to assign condition and a pre and post test will evaluate the learning gains.

3. CONTRIBUTIONS

This work moves beyond the correlational work to inferring causality of algorithmic abstraction and problem contextualization on student learning. The technical contributions of the thesis is a novel approach to generating appropriate pedagogical feedback for novices engaged in a code production task as a part of their learning.

Copyright is held by the author/owner(s).
ICER'11, August 8–9, 2011, Providence, Rhode Island, USA.
ACM 978-1-4503-0829-8/11/08.

Author Index

Anderson, Ruth E. 3
Bagley, Spencer 53
Bailey Lee, Cynthia 45
Boustedt, Jonas 61
Carbone, Angela 33
Chinn, Donald 33
Clear, Tony 33
Corbett, Albert 101
Cutts, Quintin 133
de Raadt, Michael 33
Denny, Paul 53
Dorn, Brian 69
D'Souza, Daryl 33
Eckerdal, Anna 61
Esper, Sarah 133
Fairbrother, Dana 117
Fincher, Sally 27
Fisler, Kathi 39
Guzdial, Mark 11
Hanks, Brian 53
Harland, James 33
Hewner, Michael 11
Hubwieser, Peter 77
Hundhausen, Christopher D. 117
Jadud, Matthew C. 85
Jin, Wei 101
Kinnunen, Päivi 19
Ko, Andrew J. 109
Krishnamurthi, Shriram 39
Laakso, Mikko-Jussi 33
Lee, Michael J. 109
Lewis, Colleen M. 3, 139
Lister, Raymond 33
Marceau, Guillaume 39
Mazur, Eric 1
McCartney, Robert 61
Moström, Jan Erik Erik 141
Mühling, Andreas 77
Ni, Lijun 143
Park, Thomas H. 125
Petre, Marian 117
Philpott, Anne 33
Porter, Leo 45
Robins, Anthony 27
Rodrigo, Ma. Mercedes T. 85
Saeli, Mara 145
Sanders, Kate 61
Sheard, Judy 33
Simon, ... 33, 93
Simon, Beth 19, 45, 53, 133
Snowdon, Susan 93
Sudol-DeLyser, Leigh Ann 147
Tabanao, Emily S. 85
Tenenberg, Josh 27
Thomas, Lynda 61
Warburton, Geoff 33
Wiedenbeck, Susan 125
Yasuhara, Ken 3
Zander, Carol 61
Zingaro, Daniel 45

www.ingramcontent.com/pod-product-compliance
Lightning Source LLC
Chambersburg PA
CBHW081421230426
43668CB00016B/2312